Paull F. Baum.

AAA — I
AEE — II, IV
AII — I, III
AOO — II
EAE — I, II
IAI — III, IV

LOGIC
DEDUCTIVE AND INDUCTIVE

BOOKS BY JOHN GRIER HIBBEN, Ph.D.

PUBLISHED BY CHARLES SCRIBNER'S SONS

LOGIC, DEDUCTIVE AND INDUCTIVE,
  net $1.40
THE PROBLEMS OF PHILOSOPHY . *net* 1.00
HEGEL'S LOGIC . . . . . *net* 1.25
INDUCTIVE LOGIC 1.50

LOGIC

DEDUCTIVE AND INDUCTIVE

BY

JOHN GRIER HIBBEN, Ph.D.

STUART PROFESSOR OF LOGIC IN PRINCETON UNIVERSITY

NEW YORK
CHARLES SCRIBNER'S SONS
1906

To

JOHN DAVIDSON

IN APPRECIATION OF THE VALUABLE SUGGESTIONS
RECEIVED IN THE PREPARATION OF THIS BOOK,
AND OF THE KINDLY INTEREST EXPRESSED
IN MANY WAYS THROUGH YEARS OF
AN INTIMATE FRIENDSHIP

Ὁ μὲν γὰρ συνοπτικὸς διαλεκτικός, ὁ δὲ μὴ οὔ.
—Plato: Republic VII, 537 C.

PREFACE

This book consists of two parts, — the Deductive and the Inductive Logic. The former treats of the general nature of our thought processes as well as the fundamental principles and practice of deduction, and is now published for the first time. The latter is my Inductive Logic which was published in 1896, now revised and incorporated in this volume. It has been my endeavor to present in connection with the more formal and traditional treatment of the deductive logic also some considerations which have been contributed by the discussions of the modern logic and which find expression in such works as those of Sigwart, Lotze, Erdmann, Green, Bosanquet, Venn, and others.

The illustrations and examples contained in the text are taken as far as possible from the sphere of everyday experiences, in order that they may represent modes of actual reasoning pursued by the common run of mankind. With this end in view, all the stock examples which have grown old and infirm in the service of many generations of students in logic have been omitted. Moreover, the material as well as the formal significance of the judgments employed in reasoning has been emphasized in order that the student may come to regard logic as a living process of thought functioning in a normal and natural manner, and not as an artificial manipulation of certain dead elements mechanically adjusted one to another.

The illustrations which appear in the Inductive Logic, and which are taken from the experiments of Faraday, Tyndall, Darwin, Pasteur, Lubbock, and others, are quoted for the most part at considerable length, not merely because in the concrete case the universal principles of reasoning and of method are often most forcibly discovered, but also because the experiments of such pioneers in research actually create these methods of investigation, or at least serve to render them exact and definite.

In Chapter XIV, Part I, "A Generalization of Immediate Inferences," I have presented some original material, — this being an attempt on my part to summarize all the possible transformations of any given proposition according to a scheme suggested by the Aristotelian square of opposition, and developed along similar lines. In addition to the general field usually covered by writers on deductive logic, there is appended a discussion on "Extra-syllogistic Reasoning," being Chapter XVIII, Part I.

I wish to avail myself of this opportunity to express my appreciation of the suggestions and help which I received from my colleagues, Dean Andrew F. West and Professor Winthrop M. Daniels, in the preparation of the Logical Exercises which appear at the end of Part II.

J. G. H.

PRINCETON, N.J.,
December 23, 1904.

CONTENTS

PART I

DEDUCTIVE LOGIC

CHAPTER I

THE NATURE OF THOUGHT 3

Definition and nature of Logic, 3. Thought as reflection, 4. The four functions of thought, 4. Concept, judgment, inference, 10. Logic as a normative science, 11.

CHAPTER II

THE CONCEPT 13

Relation of identity to diversity in concepts, 13. The natural history of the concept, 15. Logical and empirical concepts, 16. Genetic concepts, 22. Thought and language, 23.

CHAPTER III

THE JUDGMENT 25

The essential nature of judgment, 25. Universal and singular judgments, 26. Relation of judgment to reality, 27. The element of necessity in judgment, 30. The universal element in judgment, 31. Judgment and language, 33. Subject, predicate, and copula, 33.

CHAPTER IV

THE UNIVERSAL JUDGMENT 36

The categories of Aristotle, 37. Heads of Predicables, 38. Various types of judgment, 40. Extension and intension, denotation and connotation, 42.

CHAPTER V

DEFINITION 44
    Nature of definition, 44. Real and nominal definition, 44. Rules of definition, 45. Definition by description, 47. Definition for purpose of identification, 48. Genetic definition, 48.

CHAPTER VI

DIVISION AND CLASSIFICATION 50
    Nature of division, 50. Rules of division, 51. Dichotomy, 51. Contrary and contradictory, 52. Trichotomy, 53. Empirical and logical divisions, 54. Nature of classification, 55. Artificial and natural classification, 56. Serial classification, 58. Effect of the doctrine of evolution on theory of classification, 59. Classification of the sciences, 61. Classifications of Bacon, Comte, and Spencer, 62.

CHAPTER VII

THE SINGULAR JUDGMENT 67
    Its relation to the universal judgment, 67. Impersonal, perceptive, and demonstrative judgments, 67. Determinate reference, 68. Indeterminate reference, 69. Judgment concerning a proper name, 69.

CHAPTER VIII

THE NEGATIVE JUDGMENT 73
    Nature of the negative judgment, 73. Its function of exact determination, 74. Its positive ground, 75. Significant negation, 75. Implication in negation, 76. Infinite negation, 77.

CHAPTER IX

THE CATEGORICAL, HYPOTHETICAL, AND DISJUNCTIVE JUDGMENTS 78
    The nature of each, 78. Their relation to universal and singular judgments, 79. Their relation to the progressive stages of knowledge, 81. Modality of judgments, 83.

CHAPTER X

THE NATURE OF INFERENCE 85
    Logical and psychological elements in inference, 85. Objective and subjective necessity, 87. Data of perception, 88. System as ground of inference, 89. The implicit and explicit, 92. Inference mediated through the universal, 93. Conceptual processes, 94. Explanation, 94. Relation of inference to judgment, 95.

CHAPTER XI

THE LAWS OF THOUGHT 98
    The law of identity, 98. The law of contradiction, 100. The law of excluded middle, 101. The law of sufficient reason, 102.

CHAPTER XII

IMMEDIATE INFERENCE 103
    Immediate inference, a misnomer, 103. The processes of implication and transformation, 103. The square of opposition, 104. Practical suggestions based on opposition, 108.

CHAPTER XIII

ON TRANSFORMATIONS OF JUDGMENT FORMS . . . 110
    Conversion, 110. Content and form in conversion, 113. Obversion, 114. Contraposition, 114.

CHAPTER XIV

A GENERALIZATION OF IMMEDIATE INFERENCES . . 117
    Summary of possible transformations, 117. The A square, 118. The E square, 119. The I square, 120. The O square, 120.

CHAPTER XV

MEDIATE INFERENCE — THE SYLLOGISM 122
    Structure and functions of the syllogism, 122. Distribution of terms, 125. Rules for criticism of validity of syllo-

gisms, 126. Modification of these rules in special cases, 129. Enthymeme, 130. Prosyllogism, episyllogism, and the sorites, 132.

CHAPTER XVI

MOOD AND FIGURE 134
    The valid moods, 134. Figure, 137. Mnemonic lines, 139. Reduction, 140.

CHAPTER XVII

THE HYPOTHETICAL AND DISJUNCTIVE SYLLOGISMS . . 142
    Hypothetical syllogism, 142. Disjunctive syllogism, 145. Dilemma, 145. Trilemma, 148.

CHAPTER XVIII

EXTRA-SYLLOGISTIC REASONING 149
    Reasoning from particulars to particulars, 149. The typical case a disguised universal, 151. Inference based upon given relations, 152. Its relation to the underlying system, 154. The logic of relatives, 156.

CHAPTER XIX

FALLACIES 157
    Formal fallacies, 157. Material fallacies, 158. Equivocation, 158. Amphiboly, 159. Composition, 159. Division, 160. Accent, 160. Figure of speech, 160. Accident, 161. Converse accident, 161. *Ignoratio Elenchi*, 162. *Non sequitur*, 164. *Petitio Principii*, 164. *Non causa pro causa*, 165. Many questions, 165.

PART II

INDUCTIVE LOGIC

CHAPTER I

INDUCTION AND DEDUCTION 169
    Various opinions concerning their relative importance, 169. Regarded as different phases of one and same process, 170. Their relation to the ground of inference as system, 170. Their relation to the universal, 171. Truth and fact, 171. Mutual dependence of deduction and induction, 172.

CHAPTER II

THE ESSENTIALS OF INDUCTION 175
    The inductive hazard, 175. Basal postulate of induction, 176. Its epistemological nature, 177. Reduction, 177. Law and rule, 180. Law as a hypothetical universal, 181. Induction in practical affairs of life, 181. Scientific spirit, 182.

CHAPTER III

TYPES OF INDUCTIVE INFERENCE. 183
    Method of enunciation, 183. (*a*) Perfect induction, 184. (*b*) Incomplete induction, 186. (*c*) Probability, 186. Method of Analogy, 187. Method of Scientific Analysis, 188. The causal element in these various methods, 189.

CHAPTER IV

CAUSATION 195
    Phenomenal significance of causal concept, 196. Philosophical significance, 197. Logical significance, 198. Origin of belief in uniformity of nature, 199. Popular and scientific idea of cause, 201. Causal analysis, 202. Limitations of knowledge, 203.

CHAPTER V

THE METHOD OF CAUSAL ANALYSIS AND DETERMINATION . 206

Sequence, 206. Concurrence, 207. Coexistence, 208. Collocations, 209. Transfer of energy, 211. Quantitative determination, 211. Observation and experiment, 213. Negative determination, 217. Pseudo-causal connections, 219.

CHAPTER VI

MILL'S INDUCTIVE METHODS — THE METHOD OF AGREEMENT 222

The five methods, 222. Agreement, 224. Symbolical representation, 225. Variation of instances, 227. Observation, 228. Simple enumeration, 228. Sequence and coexistence, 229. Criticism of this method, 229. Agreement as a method of suggestion, 232. Illustrations, 232.

CHAPTER VII

THE METHOD OF DIFFERENCE 236

Its relation to agreement, 236. Its characteristic features, 236. Symbolical representation, 238. Relation to negative determination, 239. Difference and combinations, 239. Criticism of the method, 240. Practical difficulties, 242. Illustrations, 245. Blind experiments, 247.

CHAPTER VIII

THE JOINT METHOD OF AGREEMENT AND DIFFERENCE . 248

Relation to method of difference, 248. Its characteristics and symbolical representation, 249. Illustrations, 250. Advantages of this method, 257.

CHAPTER IX

THE METHOD OF CONCOMITANT VARIATIONS . . . 258

Characteristics and symbolical representation, 258. Quantitative determination, 259. Graphical representation, 260. Advantages in its psychological impressions, 261. Illustrations, 262. Comprehension of unknown forces by this method, 266. Precautions in using this method, 267.

CONTENTS xv

CHAPTER X

THE METHOD OF RESIDUES 271
    Characteristics and symbolical representation, 271. A deductive method, 272. Its function suggestive, 273. Illustrations, 273. Its practical value, 277.

CHAPTER XI

PREDICTION AND VERIFICATION 278
    The inducto-deductive method, 278. Illustrations, 279. Bacon's anticipations of nature, 283. Scientific thought, 284. Indirect method of prediction, 286. Exceptional phenomena, 288. Generalization, 289. Mathematical method, 290.

CHAPTER XII

HYPOTHESIS 291
    Its relation to induction, 291. Illustrations, 292. Function of the imagination in hypothesis, 299. Analysis and synthesis, 300. Requirements of a logical hypothesis, 301. Consilience of inductions, 309. *Experimentum Crucis*, 310. Mill and Whewell controversy, 312.

CHAPTER XIII

ANALOGY 314
    Analogy and induction, 314. Natural kinds, 314. Analogy and classification, 315. Teleological analogy, 317. Suggestion the chief function of analogy, 323. Requirements of true analogy, 325. Analogy and probability, 329.

CHAPTER XIV

PROBABILITY 330
    Probability and causal determination, 330. Relation to enumerative induction, 332. Various kinds of inference in sphere of probability, 333. Coincidence and cause, 345. Circumstantial evidence, 346. Probability and method of residues, 350.

CHAPTER XV

PAGE

EMPIRICAL LAWS 351
    Various degrees of probability in inference, 351. Various kinds of empirical laws, 352. Empirical uniformity resulting from the method of agreement, 357. Empirical laws and laws of an ultimate nature, 357.

CHAPTER XVI

INDUCTIVE FALLACIES 359
    Errors of perception, 360. Errors of judgment, 362. Errors of imagination, 366. Errors of the conceptual processes, 369. The psychological nature of these fallacies, 372.

CHAPTER XVII

THE INDUCTIVE METHODS AS APPLIED TO THE VARIOUS SCIENCES 374
    Method varies with different kinds of phenomena, 374. Difficulties in method due to complexity of phenomena, 378. Phenomena of one science interpreted in the light of others, 380. Deductive method of some sciences replaced by the inductive, 381.

CHAPTER XVIII

HISTORICAL SKETCH OF INDUCTION 385
    Socrates, 385. Plato, 385. Aristotle, 386. Roger Bacon, 387. Leonardo da Vinci, 388. Telesius, 389. Campanella, 389. The experimental investigators, 390. Francis Bacon, 390. Locke, 392. Newton, 393. Herschel, 394. Whewell, 395. Mill, 396.

LOGICAL EXERCISES 399

INDEX 435

PART I

DEDUCTIVE LOGIC

CHAPTER I

THE NATURE OF THOUGHT

Logic is a word derived from the Greek λόγος, which means thought or reason; and in this origin may be found the essential significance of logic, — that it treats of the nature and of the laws of thought. Before it is possible to appreciate the characteristic features of the laws of thought, it is necessary to understand the general nature of the processes of thought themselves. While the process of thought is various, its most common and conspicuous manifestation may be described as that phase of the mind's activity which regards any specific object which may be presented to it in the light of the general body of knowledge. For example, a person may chance to pick up a stone, which he holds in his hand for a moment and immediately throws away. It has been in the focus of his attention for a fleeting moment only, and has excited no activity of thought whatsoever. He has observed but has not thought about it. Suppose, however, it does arrest his attention and he begins to think about it, what is the nature of this thinking which goes on in his mind? If his knowledge of geology is meagre, the result of the application of it to the special object of inquiry may be merely the assertion that the stone which he holds in his hand is some kind of a fossil. If, however, his knowledge is more extensive and has grown out of a wide experience, he will be able no doubt to refer the fossil in question to its proper geological age, and to give some satisfactory description of the general nature and habits of that species of animals to which it belongs, thus, in a measure more or less explicit, reconstructing its probable life history. Thinking, therefore, may be defined in one of its aspects at least as the process of interpreting the special by the general, or the new experience by the old.

This definition of thought may be further illustrated by the word reflection, which is often used as synonymous with thought. Thus we say that we will reflect about a certain proposition, which is equivalent to saying we will think about it. The process of reflection is essentially one of illumination. The very word reflection suggests the light ray which flashes from one object of vision to another; so, also, in a figurative sense, it signifies the illumination which one object of knowledge sheds upon another. In the reflecting mind, the new element of experience, whatever it may be, is held in the focus of the light rays which converge to that point from all the surrounding parts of the general body of knowledge until its essential nature is fully revealed.

In this process which we call thinking, or reflecting, there are in all four functions involved.

1. The first function of thought consists in the transformation of the crude data of knowledge furnished by the senses into forms of such a nature that they can be readily used in the various operations of our thinking processes. The form which thought necessarily assumes for the prosecution of its own activity is always that of a universal idea; that is, an idea which possesses a oneness of meaning but admits of an indefinite variety of application. The universal is sometimes called a group idea, or a class idea, by which a number of individuals are embraced under some one general designation. If our body of knowledge consisted merely in the total number of particular experiences arranged in the form of a series wherein each separate term remained distinct and completely unconnected with any other term, then obviously new experiences could be added to, but never could be assimilated with,

such a body of knowledge. Indeed, a disconnected array of isolated experiences would hardly merit the name of knowledge at all. On the contrary, the elements constituting the body of our knowledge must be so related and coördinated that similar elements fall together in such a manner that a single thought form shall be able to express them all. Thus, when a geologist says that a certain stone is a fossil, he means that in his general body of knowledge he has framed an idea known by the word symbol "fossil," which embraces under it innumerable special cases, and that one of these is the stone in question. Thus objects of perception can be grasped by the mind and become definite objects of thought. This grasp of the mind by which a number of special cases are held together by a single idea of a nature so universal as to comprehend them all is known as the process of conception, and the universal idea itself which is the result of that process is known as the concept. This word is from the Latin *concapio*, to take together. The corresponding German word is *Begriff*, which has the same root as our English word "grip." In the concept the mind grasps all the essential features which characterize a given group or class of objects, and holds them together in such a manner as to constitute an elemental thought form. The process of thinking, therefore, is fundamentally a conceptual process, and this primary function of thought consists in constructing whatever is given through the processes of perception into the forms of concepts.

2. The second function of thought consists in the reduction of the total mass of concepts to some kind of systematic order. Every concept as it is formed must be received into the general body of knowledge and assigned to its proper place and position. The concepts must be arranged in their due rank and order according to their natural relations of coördination or subordination. In order that our concepts may be used as instruments of knowledge, they must admit of a constant and consistent reference to the general system

of which they form constituent parts. These elemental forms of thought must have their origin in order and not in chaos. They must be subject to underlying laws of relation, and not to accident or caprice. Thus the botanist not only possesses an idea of the general nature of a certain species of plant, that is, a concept of it, but he knows also definitely its particular relation to the classified system of plants as a whole. He is able therefore to describe the species in question by the relative position which it occupies in the system itself. Knowledge of the species is obtained not merely through an understanding of what it is, but also of what its proper setting may be.

3. The third function of thought consists in referring whatever may be before the consciousness as the object of thought to its appropriate concept. Such a reference is a process of interpretation, and represents the central and most essential feature of all thinking. This mode of interpretation may be brought about in several ways.

(a) In the first place, any one portion of our general body of knowledge may be interpreted in the light of some other. Thus by way of interpretation or explanation I may refer one concept to another concept which embraces it as a smaller class or group within a larger one; *e.g.* the Trappists are a Roman Catholic brotherhood.

(b) Again, the concept lends itself to a further use as an instrument of knowledge, by revealing the various characteristics which constitute its nature according as the trend of thought at the moment may happen to emphasize one or another of them. In the ordinary processes of thought we never use a concept in the totality of its significance. We attend only to a single phase of the concept's meaning at a time; and our thought selects always that particular phase of the meaning which is pertinent to the special object of thought under consideration. Thus the concept, government, is an exceedingly complex idea, and may be considered from various points of view, — as to its general nature, whether democratic, monarchial, despotic, etc.; or as to its special functions, whether that of the judicial, legislative, or executive. The concept as a complex idea may always be subjected to a more precise determination by the concentration of thought upon one or more of its special attributes or relations.

(c) In the third place, a particular experience in the field of sense perception may be interpreted by referring it to the appropriate concept of which it may be regarded as a special case. The knowledge given through the senses is rendered more definite by this reference of it to a concept which serves to illumine it.

This process of thought which renders the elements of consciousness more definite by a reference in any one of the three ways mentioned above to some interpreting concept is known as the judgment. There is a universal tendency of thought to transform every concept into the form of a judgment, because the very presence of a concept in consciousness challenges our thought to express some definite assertion concerning it, and such an assertion is itself a judgment. As long as there is sustained interest in any concept which occupies the focus of attention, there is a constant play of thought about it; we turn it over in our minds; we examine it on all sides; we put questions to ourselves about it; and the result is a series of judgments as regards its nature and the several relations which it sustains to cognate concepts. Thus our general knowledge serves to illumine the specific portion of it which is the special object under contemplation. So also when the object of consciousness is a particular object of sense perception, we form a judgment by referring it to its appropriate concept. Thus in the judgment, Arsenic is a poison, we have as it were a cross-section of our knowledge in general; but in the judgment, this substance which is in the test-tube before me contains arsenic, the reference is to a special object in the field of vision which is interpreted by means of its appropriate concept.

Every new experience which is more than a fleeting impression, and which is drawn into the field of our attention, gives rise to one or more judgments of this latter kind. As I am writing, I look out from a hillside which commands a wide prospect; and as I observe the various objects in the field of vision, my thought immediately refers them to their appropriate concepts by way of more definite characterization. There is the winding road through the valley, separating the green meadow from the wood beyond; in the meadow cows are grazing; by the side of the road flows a stream, rushing over its rocky bed and losing itself in the dark shadows of the wood; in the distance are the uplands again bounded by the horizon line, above which the clouds are hanging low and threatening. Such a description of the various objects of perception within a field of vision forms a series of particular instances referred to their corresponding concepts. They are simple judgments of identification,— a reference of an object immediately before us to a familiar idea which through its word symbols satisfactorily describes it. Such a scene however naturally gives rise to more complex ideas, which represent the fourth function of thought.

4. This fourth function of thought consists in the process of unfolding whatever may be necessarily implied in our judgments, but is not explicitly asserted. Thus in the scene described above, I am able to make certain statements which are warranted by the facts, but which are not the result of simple observation. I am led to venture the assertion that there are trout in the stream before me; that by reasonable skill and perseverance a fisherman may hope to fill his creel there in a few hours; that the threatening clouds, the east wind, and sultry atmosphere will bring rain; and that it would be wise under such conditions to fish worm rather than fly. Judgments such as these are far more complex than the simple judgments of identification or recognition. We may call them judgments of elaboration. What is actually given is combined with our general knowledge in such

a manner as to render explicit the full measure of all which is necessarily implied. Thus the assertion that the stream contains trout is based upon an experience of many years, and in this way the past is used as a means of interpreting the present. In like manner my past experience of atmospheric conditions enables me to interpret the present conditions as indicating the approach of rain. Moreover, the dark and stormy day is judged to be more suitable for worm than fly fishing, because on account of the coming rain the natural flies will not be on the wing, and the rain itself will wash from the hillsides and banks into the stream grubs and worms, which the expectant trout will be in readiness to take. My general knowledge has enabled me in this particular case to make statements which go beyond that which is actually perceived, but which nevertheless I am constrained to believe true, because necessitated by what is known. And this is the essential feature of all inference.

But inference is not confined to the interpretation of that which is given in perception. It may serve also to interpret any part of our general body of knowledge by any other part, or by the whole. Thus two judgments of a universal nature may be brought together in such a manner that their combination furnishes elements of knowledge which are not given by either judgment separately. We know, for instance, that the sum of the angles formed on the same side of a straight line at a given point equals two right angles; also, that the exterior angle formed by extending a side of a triangle equals the two opposite and interior angles. These two judgments, when put together, necessitate the inference that the sum of the angles of a triangle equals two right angles. Inference therefore is essentially a process by which our thought combines given elements of knowledge in such a way that the result contains something which the given elements in their isolation fail to disclose.

There are some general considerations in reference to these four functions of thought which should be presented. In the first place, the word function itself is significant. It indicates an activity which is dependent upon other activities correlated with it.. Each of the four functions of thought is closely connected and coördinated with the other functions, and no one is complete in itself. The concept is an essential element of the judgment, for the judgment is merely the concept rendered definite through assertion. Moreover, inference is a process which consists essentially in the expansion and elaboration of our judgments. Inference is itself a judgment, only it is a judgment which is reached indirectly. And in the formation of any judgment it is exceedingly difficult to eliminate altogether the inferential elements, inasmuch as every judgment contains more than is actually given in perception, or in a series of perceptions. The result rests largely upon that which is necessitated by our general knowledge, and this is essentially inference.

In these coördinated relations which unite concept, judgment, and inference, it is natural to regard judgment as the central function of thought. From this point of view the concept may then be defined as the judgment in its potential form; that is, the concept contains in an indefinite way all the possible elements of knowledge which it is the function of the judgment to make explicit. The inference is the judgment, as we have seen, exhibited in its relation to other judgments upon which it depends as the warrant of its validity. The concept is an abridged form of judgment, while the inference is an expanded form; and the unit of thought, therefore, which lies at the basis of all thought processes is the judgment. It is to thought what the element is to chemistry.

Again it is to be observed that in the process of interpreting a given object of knowledge by means of its corresponding thought form, it happens that the object in question, say a given object in the field of vision, will in some measure at least modify the thought form to which it is referred. Thus every new experience is both interpreted by our general body of knowledge, and also in turn widens the range of that knowledge and changes its nature to a greater or less extent. Especially is this true concerning any object of knowledge which is so new as to be wholly unfamiliar. There is then no appropriate thought form to which we can refer it. We must so analyze the properties of the object in question and compare it with other instances of the same general kind, as to construct a basis for the formation of a concept which shall embrace the new order of phenomena under consideration. Such a new concept has to be fitted into the main body of concepts, and the process of readjustment among the old concepts is sometimes a most complex and difficult one. This is illustrated in a striking manner by the newly formed concept of radium and the various properties of radio-activity. To receive this new concept into the main body of concepts requires a readjustment of our former ideas of matter, conservation of energy, etc., which is almost revolutionary.

Again, among the philosophical sciences, logic is usually grouped with ethics and æsthetics under the general class of the so-called normative sciences. A normative science is one which refers all its phenomena to some standard, or norm of value to which they are required to conform. The standard in ethics is that of the right or the good; in æsthetics, of beauty; and in logic, of truth. Truth may be defined as correspondence with reality. The real is the world as it is constructed by us in consciousness. It is coextensive with the whole received body of knowledge. It is the world which is revealed to us through the senses, it is true; but at the last analysis it is that world as we interpret and understand it.

To say therefore that the logical demand of our concepts is that they must be true signifies that every concept must clearly and adequately embody the essential features of all the particular instances in experience which have formed the basis of its derivation; the concept moreover must be capable of a constant reference, that is, it must not contain any element of variability which prejudices its integrity as a concept. To say that a judgment must be true signifies that when the judgment expresses the general relation of any concepts to each other within the same system, it must conserve the general order which characterizes the system as a whole, and all interrelated parts of it; and when the judgment is of the form of a particular experience referred to its appropriate concept, then all such references must be exact. To say that an inference must be true signifies that the conclusion reached through the process of inference must be of such a nature that every element of it will find complete warrant in that which is adduced as its ground. The logical standard, therefore, which must be realized in all cases demands clear and adequate concepts of a constant meaning arranged in an orderly system, so that every reference to it of any particular object of thought must be exact, and every inference based upon it must be valid. While truth may manifest itself in many ways as clearness, adequacy, constancy, consistency, exactness, or validity, nevertheless these are all but various instances of a single elemental principle which underlies the ultimate standard of logical thinking.

CHAPTER II

THE CONCEPT

THE concept as a form of thought embraces a number of phenomena which, however much they may differ, have nevertheless an underlying unity. The ratio of the elements of similarity to those of diversity in our concepts is by no means a constant one, but admits of considerable variation.

1. In the first place, the diversity may be reduced substantially to zero, as for instance in such a concept as that of a silver dollar. The differences which exist between the several particular cases of this general concept are so minute as to be overlooked; the similarity alone attracts the attention. Each one is an exact copy of every other, and the idea of any diversity is here practically eliminated.

In reality, however, no two phenomena are precisely alike. As Leibniz once remarked, " No two leaves on the same tree are alike." And Plato in the same vein has said that "If two things were exactly alike, there would not be two but one." Therefore, while the element of diversity may be reduced to zero as regards its practical relevancy and as regards the essential significance of the concept in question, nevertheless it is always present in some appreciable degree and may be discovered to a discriminating observer.

2. There is a second class of concepts wherein the diversity is more apparent, and yet the likeness is quite as obvious. Thus the concept, dog, embodies all the characteristic features of the dog race, and yet is so elastic and ample an idea as to hold in one and the same mental grasp such diverse breeds as the mastiff, the bull-dog,

the French poodle, the greyhound and dachshund. A concept such as this is typical of the general run of concepts which require no unusual penetration to disclose the fundamental elements of similarity in spite of the wide range of differences.

3. There is, however, a third class of concepts which require more than ordinary insight, it may be the insight of genius, in order to discover the unity which lies hidden beneath an obscuring mass of manifold differences. It required the analytic mind of a Newton to grasp under one concept such diverse phenomena as the fall of a body to the earth and the moon's revolution about its orbit. In the one case there is motion in a straight line, in the other the motion is in the path of an ellipse; in the one the body actually falls to the earth, in the other it is forever falling but never falls. Nevertheless, the two are similar. The course of the moon may be resolved into two distinct motions; the one centripetal, which is a direct falling toward the earth, the other the centrifugal, which holds the former in check and modifies the direct fall toward the earth so that the result is the present elliptical orbit of the moon. Therefore it may be truly said that the moon is always falling toward the earth in a manner precisely similar to that of the ordinary falling body upon the earth's surface. The only difference is the counter force which is operative in the one case and not in the other. Such a difference however so obscures the general features of resemblance in the resulting phenomena that a surface observation devoid of any deeper reflection may pronounce them so different as to possess no point in common. It is characteristic of the trained mind that it is able to penetrate beneath the surface and discover points of similarity which escape the notice of unreflecting observation. Fortunately for the generality of intelligence, the phenomena of human experience for the most part fall together into natural groups whose underlying bond of unity is perfectly obvious. Nature is so prodigal of her creations

that innumerable individuals of the same species are forced upon our attention. The common events of life repeat themselves with a regularity which compels the recognition of a constant and common principle as their basis. Therefore it becomes a natural habit of mind to see things together by reason of their common features. The most primitive of all our judgments, and that which lies at the foundation of all other judgments, is that which is based upon the recognition of similarity among phenomena. The concept has its origin in the recognition of similarity among several percepts.[1] As Schopenhauer has remarked, "We get the stuff and content of our concepts from observation." In our observation, the various instances of some one general kind of phenomena fall together in our minds on account of their similarity. They form a series of similar percepts, each term of which differs from every other term, and yet all in a certain sense are alike. The mind grasps the essential features of similarity, fusing them together according to an underlying unity which persists in spite of the differences. The result is the concept. In such a process, the mind has subjected the various percepts to an analysis which separates whatever is peculiarly individual in each instance from the elements which are characteristic of the series as a whole. This is essentially a process of abstraction; it is what Aristotle calls ἀφαίρεσις. There is also a complementary process of synthesis, πρόσθεσις according to Aristotle, which consists in building up the common elements obtained by the analysis into a complete whole. The resulting product is in no sense merely an image in the mind of the blended percepts, but is essentially an ideal construction of thought which is sufficiently comprehensive and elastic to admit of application to all particular cases of it. These processes of separating and uniting, of tearing down and building up, of analysis and synthesis, have become so con-

[1] In the terminology of psychology, the process of perceiving is called perception; the resulting product, however, is known as the percept.

firmed a mental habit that we are not conscious of them, but come to regard our concepts in the light of original mental possessions rather than thought forms which we ourselves have fashioned out of the various phenomena in experience.

The unconscious blending together of the essential characteristics of a group of phenomena forms a concept which is at first barely more than a general impression, a vague mental grasp of the kind of objects represented by it. The mind has not yet worked over its first impressions and has not formed the crude data of its perception into clear and adequate concepts. The concept at this preliminary stage of its evolution is called empirical, signifying that it is the result of a superficial experience which has been subjected to no critical analysis whatsoever. The word empirical in philosophy signifies whatever is the result of experience; it has, however, a secondary meaning which implies that the experience in question is a limited one. It is in this secondary sense that the phrase empirical concept is used. On the other hand, the logical or scientific concept, as it is often called, is one which has been formed as the result of some conscious effort to analyze the various phenomena which form the basis of the concept in question so as to obtain a clear and adequate idea of their essential characteristics. The logical concept differs from the empirical in the following particulars : —

1. The logical concept is always characterized by a growing loss of particularity. The preliminary rough draft of our concepts always shows the coloring of the particular instances whence they have arisen. Our first experiences are necessarily few in number, and they are not sufficiently numerous to afford a basis for the elimination of all characteristics which are not essential. Certain features which may be common to a limited number of instances will often disappear when that number is increased. The disappearance of such characteristics or their appearance in a sporadic manner merely proves that they do not belong to the essence

of the concept. It is an evidence of an ignorant or untrained mind that it associates its concepts with particular experiences. Such an intellect we are pleased to call provincial or insular. The nature of the logical concept is always indicated by its independence of the special case. Thus the concept of gravitation is not confined to the earth's attraction of bodies upon its surface. It rises above such a particular instance, and presents the idea of universal attraction, of which the force of gravitation upon the earth is but a small and insignificant instance.

The objection has been urged by Berkeley for instance that this growing loss of particularity in the concept indicates an increasing indefiniteness, inasmuch as the elimination of one particular attribute after another tends to reduce the concept itself to a bare form stript of all definite features. Consequently, it is insisted, our concept of a rose must be one devoid of any specific color, form, or fragrance, and our concept of a dog must be one of no particular breed, habit, or disposition; concepts, therefore, are but the spectral forms of real objects. This view, however, is based upon a radical misunderstanding of the essential nature of a concept. For the concept is freed from the particular attributes which characterize the various percepts only in a certain sense. While these attributes are not preserved as such in the concept, they are nevertheless conserved. The particular attribute of color, or of form, or of habit is indeed dropped out of mind in framing the concept, but there is always a compensation for the loss of the particular by substituting in its place the possibility, not only of the attribute in question, but of all others of the same general kind. Instead of the particular we have the potential which admits of an indefinite degree of variation. Thus the concept of a rose admits of any shade of color whatsoever which is compatible with the whole range of experience regarding roses. In this adaptability to all possible varieties of color, the potential color of the concept is vastly richer in content, and far more comprehensive, than the single color of any particular rose could possibly be. So, also, the concept of a dog is not confined to a particular breed; it embraces the potential of all the possible breeds of dogs. Indeed, the mental process of constructing a concept may be regarded as that of transforming the various observed attributes of the same general order into a potential attribute which is lodged in our minds as a comprehensive symbol embracing every possible variety of detail.

This potential variation in any concept should not remain indefinite and vague, but should have definitely prescribed limits. Thus the color possibility of the concept of a rose possesses a very wide range of variation; that of the violet, however, is narrowly circumscribed. The leaf of a beech tree shows a definite pattern, which is preserved in the midst of a variation which is essentially one of size alone, and that within known and easily recognized limits. In the leaf of the sassafras tree there is a far wider possibility of variation. On one and the same tree of this species there are leaves of three distinct patterns. Whatever may be our concept of the sassafras leaf, it must certainly provide for this characteristic variation of form. Moreover, the range of variation may itself be subject to a variation under changing circumstances. The leaf of the maple is in its normal appearance green. It admits of a wide variation of shade but always within the limits of the one color. In the autumn tints, however, there is a remarkable expansion of the range of variation, the green turning into the various shades of brown, yellow, red, gold, and crimson. The possibility of a wide range of variation in the attributes of our concepts render them as thought forms exceedingly elastic in the processes of thinking, while, on the other hand, the definite limitation of their possible variation renders them quite as serviceable for exact reference and determination. There is thus a double gain both of precision and facility in the exercise of our thought activity.

2. There is a second characteristic of the logical concept in distinction from the roughly generalized empirical concept; namely, that it is freed from all dependence upon any mental picture in order to render it clear and intelligible. This feature of the logical concept grows out of the former given above,—the growing loss of particularity; for the particular can be represented to thought in the form of a memory image of the original experience. Not so, however, with the universal idea which lies at the basis of the concept. The concept is not a composite picture in the mind of a series of percepts. As far as a mental picture might suggest resemblances, we would naturally classify together the whale and the fish, or the bat and the bird. Dissociated however from the representations of the outer appearance of these animals, the bat, as regards the essential elements which go to make up the concept, is far more closely allied to the whale than to the bird. The mental picture is indeed a help to our thinking, but strong minds must learn to forego such adventitious aid. The undeveloped mind — that of the savage, or the child — is dependent upon pictures, symbols, or figurative representations. In the process of education, as the mental activity becomes trained and disciplined, the need of colored chalk, of illustrative diagrams, and of picture-books, becomes less and less in evidence. In the evolution of the religious sentiment, this is noticeable in a marked degree. The early religions, notably that of Judaism, endeavored to convey spiritual truth through an appeal to the senses mediated by a brilliant symbolism. This, however, was superceded by that religion which laid stress upon a worship in spirit and in truth, with no indirect appeal to the thought through the senses, but by means of ideas which directly enlightened the eyes of the understanding. An appreciation of the truth in this wise is essentially logical inasmuch as the truth appears in a form which appeals immediately to the reason.

3. A third characteristic of the logical concept is its

tendency to progressive differentiation; that is, a breaking up into smaller concepts which are more precisely determined, and more distinctly separated in thought one from the other. The first rough concepts which are formed embrace without discrimination all sorts of individual instances which may happen to present any surface resemblances whatsoever. The child may have at first but one vague concept which applies equally well to a cow, a horse, and a mule. Later in the growth of knowledge, this indefinite concept breaks up into more definite ones, and the child learns to discriminate between the cow and the horse, and between the horse and the mule. Wherever there is knowledge which is comprehensive and exact, the corresponding concepts are nicely differentiated and precisely determined. For most persons, it is a sufficient identification of a bird to recognize it as a hawk. But for the ornithologist such a reference is altogether too general and indefinite. He wishes to know which one of the several different species of hawk the particular bird may happen to be. Nothing is gained however by the mere multiplication of the number of concepts, unless at the same time we are able to discriminate between them. The discriminating mind is essentially the logical mind. The means by which our concepts may receive more precise determination will be discussed later in the chapter on the negative judgment.

There are two ways by which our concepts may be broken up so as to give rise to new concepts. The one has already been mentioned,—the analysis of the concept into smaller and smaller groups, each group, however small, representing a complete whole, or complex of attributes. The other does not regard a complex of attributes which together constitute the characteristic features of a distinct species of plant or animal; it regards the rather some single attribute and concentrates the attention upon that. This attribute is first viewed in all the particular instances where it occurs, and then fashioned into the form of a concept by considering it, in and by itself, quite apart from any of the instances which illustrate it. Such a concept is known as an abstract concept. It is our idea of a particular quality or attribute of a thing apart from the thing itself. The concrete concept, on the other hand, is our idea of a thing as composed of a complex of attributes, and none of them separated in thought from the thing in which they all inhere. Thus we have the abstract concept of motion as distinct from the concrete concept of a moving body; the abstract concept of a sweet or sour flavor as distinct from the concrete concept of sugar, or of a lemon, in which the attributes sweet and sour may find expression. So also we have the abstract concepts of activities apart from any actors, such as speaking, swimming, fighting, etc. There may be abstract concepts not merely of attributes and activities, but also of relations which may exist between different objects of perception, or between concepts as the case may be, quite apart from the objects or concepts thus related, such as the concept of cause and effect, of organization, of sequence, or of coexistence. There may be also abstract concepts involving a combination of several attributes, and yet held apart from any definite thing or object of knowledge in which they inhere, such as the complex concepts of freedom, of philanthropy, of the good, the true, the beautiful. The possibility of the various forms of abstract concepts and of the resulting combinations which may be made out of the separated elements is indeed without limit. Our logical faculty is thus given an indefinite scope. The ability to combine the given elements of knowledge into new forms gives to our thought a mighty instrument of discovery and of progress.

4. There is still another characteristic of the logical in distinction from the merely empirical concept, a characteristic, however, which is realized only in that higher order of concepts which merit the designation of scientific. The nature of these concepts is radically distinct from that of

the most accurately formulated concepts of the kind which has so far been described. Instead of representing a correlated nexus of common characteristics which discover themselves to observation in the several special cases, this new order of concepts represent rather the fundamental constructive principle, which both underlies the actual production of every particular instance, and also serves to preserve the integrity and constancy of its being as well. Such a principle may assume various forms. It may express simply the method of producing the different instances which fall under a single concept. Thus the concept of a <u>conic section</u> represents the several sections which may be made of a cone, according as the angle of the cutting plane is varied. There will result consequently either a point, straight line, circle, ellipse, parabola, or hyperbola. A mere observation of the general features of these lines would never disclose their common nature. They fall together in one and the same group on account of their common origin, while a simple variation in the manner of their production gives rise to a pronounced differentiation in the results.

Again the constructive principle may represent a summation of all the component elements of the object in question, with possibly the formula of their relative proportions added. Thus the concept of sulphuric acid can be represented by the symbol, H_2SO_4, an exact statement of the chemical elements in the proper proportions which constitute the essential nature of the compound. A concept of this kind is very different from that concept of sulphuric acid which represents its several properties and affinities.

Again, this constructive principle may appear in the form of a law which is operative in producing and sustaining the various organisms which may be referred to it. Thus the concept of <u>natural selection</u> represents a most comprehensive law, which explains the origin of new species in the evolution of natural organisms. Every species has its own constructive principle, which, if discovered, would form the truest and most satisfactory concept of that species. These various forms of the concept representing a constructive principle rather than a mere complex of common attributes are known by the one name of <u>genetic</u> concepts; that is, concepts which refer to the common origin of a class of particular instances, rather than to the characteristic features of their common nature.

There now remains to be considered a topic of considerable interest and importance, namely, the relation of the concept to the word which serves as its symbol. As a symbol the word does not exist for itself, but only for the meaning which it represents. A symbol always refers to something which lies outside of itself, and language is a system of symbols by means of which thought finds significant expression. The word λόγος has a twofold meaning in Greek — (a) the thought itself and (b) the word or words which stand for the thought. Aristotle calls the one ὁ ἔσω or ὁ ἐν τῇ ψυχῇ λόγος, and the other ὁ ἔξω λόγος, — that is, the one, the inner logic; the other, the outer logic. Language, therefore, is the external symbol of the inner thought. We have seen that the logical concept is characterized by a freedom from all entanglements with any particular percepts, or anything like a picture representation of the same. In this respect, the word as a symbol forms a most excellent vehicle for the expression of concepts in their pure thought significance. For the word is perfectly colorless and is freed from all local or temporal associations. The growth of language has paralleled in this respect the growth of thought, inasmuch as there has been a constant tendency for words to lose whatever original associations of a particular or pictorial nature they may have had. The Hebrew word for anger was derived from a root which signified the boiling over of a pot of water, a suggestive picture of the heat and energy of passion. This primitive picture, however, has passed away and only the significant thought remains. So, also, the word green meant, according to its derivation, the color of growing things, the green natural objects; but now its meaning has burst these limitations and possesses a far wider scope.

There is also a parallel differentiation of words accompanying the progressive differentiation of thought. Professor Max Müller refers to the fact that the Hawaiians have only one word to express the various ideas of love, friendship, gratitude, kindness, and respect. To discriminate between the different shades of meaning which these several ideas signify, a corresponding variety of verbal symbols has been found necessary. Thus the inner and the outer thought have progressed together, and the line of progress is always toward a more complete definiteness of meaning, in which the finer distinctions of thought may be felt and expressed.

There is no doubt that clearness of thought is often greatly obscured by the medium of language. Words come to acquire strange twists and turns which are productive of much misunderstanding and error. It is the office of the logical mind to determine the meaning of words, and to use the word which most precisely and adequately expresses the thought. Obscurity in the use of language, however, may usually be traced to obscurity in thought. Clear thinking will always find a medium of clear expression.

CHAPTER III

THE JUDGMENT

THE essential function of the judgment is to give definiteness to the concept. When the concept appears in thought, it is never as a complete element in itself, but it is always as a constitutive element of a judgment. The concept exercises no more independent a function apart from the judgment than does the sap separated from the tree whose entire structure it permeates. If we attempt to hold the concept in the focus of thought, it will always appear elusive and indefinite. It becomes definite only as it suggests some judgment, or it may be a series of judgments of which it serves to form the basal element. We may seem at times to hold the concept before the mind as a naked, unattached idea; but it is a barely momentary result which is reached. The concept maintains such a shadowy form, only so long as we do not concentrate our thought upon it. As soon as it becomes in any sense an object of thought, it challenges some assertion either concerning its nature, or its relations to other concepts in our general body of knowledge. If we make a list of various concepts, such as iron, education, freedom, army, horse, bird, fern, and so on, the eye rapidly traverses such a list, instantly recognizing the meaning of each word, as it occurs, and immediately passing on to the next. But in such a process we have not really taken these various concepts into our thought. There has been merely a series of mental reactions in the recognition of the meaning of word symbols. Such a recognition is nothing more than the vague sense of familiarity which the several words are capable of arousing. If, however, an unfamiliar word should appear in such a list, it would immediately give us pause; we would begin to think about it, to turn it over in our minds, endeavoring to discover its general nature and the relations which it sustains to our other concepts. This would at once give us a series of judgments. Or if any one of the suggested words should elicit any special interest on our part, the various processes of thought would be found to react upon it in such a manner as again to yield a number of judgments. Thus if we allow our thought to dwell upon such an idea as that of education with something more than a mere passing recognition of a familiar word, then we at once find ourselves constructing some definite assertions concerning this idea, as to its general nature, its various forms, its methods and scope, and the fundamental principles which underlie its essential significance. Whenever a concept swings into the focus of thought, it at once forms a centre whence radiates a series of judgments. The judgment may be defined, therefore, as a concept which is rendered definite through some assertion concerning it. The concept is a potential judgment, or rather it is the potential of many judgments which are implicitly contained in it. The judgment is the concept in its unfolded form. The concept, moreover, may be regarded as an unstable compound which through the barest contact of thought separates into its elemental parts and relations expressed in the form of judgments.

There are two ways by which we may render any concept definite through assertion, thus producing two general types of judgment.

1. The concept may be referred to another concept which forms an essential element in its constitution, or else to one which sustains some essential relation to it. Thus we may have the judgment as follows: The constitution of a nation embodies the fundamental principles underlying the judicial, legislative, and executive functions of government. In such a judgment we have the interpretation of one

concept by others which enter into its composition as constitutive elements of it.

We may have also a judgment which expresses relations between concepts as the following: Liberty is not possible in a country where there is no respect for law.

In both of these illustrations the judgments relate to our knowledge in general.

2. A concept, however, may be made definite by a reference to some particular instance which illustrates it, or a particular instance in turn may be referred to a concept which interprets it. Thus the concept of philanthropy may be made clearer and more definite by a reference to certain specific persons and their deeds; and on the other hand a special case, as a peculiar light in the northern sky, may be explained by a reference to a familiar concept which serves to interpret it, such as the aurora borealis. Under this head of a reference of the particular experience to its corresponding universal, we have the great body of our judgments of identification or recognition, — such as, This plant is a fringed orchis, or That is a red-winged blackbird, or That substance is combustible. In these cases, the particular instance is referred to the appropriate class or group within which it naturally falls, or to a general attribute which characterizes it.

Of the two forms of judgment, thus outlined, the former represents some phase of our knowledge in general; the latter, the application of some phase of our general knowledge to some special case.

Whether the judgment consists of the characterization of our knowledge in general, or the interpretation of a particular experience by means of our general knowledge, it remains true that in either case the judgment itself must rest upon a sound basis of reality. A judgment which cannot show some basis of reality upon which it rests is a judgment in name only. It may be a fancy, a dream, a query, a hope, but it is not a judgment. In this particular respect, the judgment may be defined as the reference of a concept to reality.

This is more obvious in the second form of judgment, where there is a reference of a particular experience to a concept, for in this case the reality which underlies the particular experience in question furnishes the evident basis of reality to the judgment itself. Thus if one should say, That is the wreck of a sailing vessel, then the actual object of perception evidencing its own reality to the senses is to be regarded as referred to the general concept, a wreck of a sailing vessel, which thus identifies and explains it.

It is well to remark in this connection that every object of perception evidences its own reality to the senses, and this sense of reality attaching to an object is as definite and as clear a quality of the object as its form, size, color, or any of its various properties and activities.

This attribute of reality must be regarded as a simple, unanalyzable element of consciousness which is immediately given and attested in the very process of perception itself.

The reference to reality in the first kind of judgment — that is, a judgment which relates to our knowledge in general — is not so patent; but nevertheless the reality is present as an unseen but secure foundation for the truth of the judgment. In this first form of judgment wherein one universal idea is related to another universal idea, where do we find any basis of reality? If one idea can be explained by another idea, in that very process it would seem that we had swung clear of reality altogether. This is not so, however. Take the judgment, The collie is an excellent sheep-dog; here the reference to reality is not direct, it is true, but it is indirect. These concepts, collie and sheep-dog, have their origin in a series of perceptual experiences, and whatever reality may lie at the basis of the percepts is conserved in the concepts which emerge from them.

Conceptual reality is based upon perceptual reality. The concept is real in the sense that it traces its origin to the several concrete instances whose reality basis is disclosed in perception. When the latter is wanting, the possibility of the reference of the concept to reality is at once removed. Thus we may have an assertion which has the form but lacks the substance of a genuine judgment, such as the following: The Centaur is an animal which has the body of a horse with the head and shoulders of a man. . Here is a concept, standing as the subject of a judgment, which can lay claim to no perceptual ancestry in our experience. We can form a clear mental picture of it; it can even be rendered intelligible to the understanding of a child; but there is no real experience at the root of the idea, and therefore it is nothing but a spectral form of a judgment. Every true concept in distinction from a pseudo-concept, such as that of a Centaur, or a Jabberwock, and the like, is referable to some real experience in much the same way as the genuine dollar note may be referred to the gold coin which it represents and by which it is redeemable. The counterfeit note presents the same general appearance as the genuine, but it has a different history, and must be traced to another origin which is of such a nature as to render it base and valueless.

There is, however, a certain phase of reality which characterizes many of our judgments, and which underlies the very processes of judgment themselves, but has no origin in perception. This is the reality which is discovered in the very nature of thought itself. It is essentially a thought reality, and as such we become aware of it quite independently of any particular experience, and only by it indeed is our experience rendered intelligible. This kind of reality is illustrated in those self-evident truths which are the common possession of all rational beings, such as the axioms of geometry, the principle of universal causation, the appreciative judgments of moral worth or æsthetic value. Such judgments are given as examples of a large group of judgments which evidently imply as their basis a form of reality which cannot be traced to an origin in mere perception.

There is, of course, that school in philosophy which denies the possibility of any reality of this kind, but insists that all forms of reality whatsoever, when completely analyzed, will reveal an ultimate origin in experience, and that the so-called intuitive truths have had their beginnings in consciousness at the earliest stages in human development, and have been transmitted through many generations, attaining in each generation more complete expression, and more exact formulation; consequently for us they appear in thought as judgments which seem to be self-attested and to have no origin in our particular experiences. In the present discussion as to the nature of the reality which underlies our judgments, this question has no direct bearing. We find in our consciousness certain judgments which, for us, at least, whatever their remote origin may be, appear as intuitive truths evidencing their own reality with a compulsion of thought quite as irresistible as that which attests the reality of any object which we may see, or hear, or touch.

These forms of reality whether attested by perception or by the necessity of thought itself have this in common, — they present themselves to consciousness in such a manner that we are constrained to yield them a permanent and constant recognition. To refuse a place to them in thought would mean the denial of our intellectual integrity. Reality, as regards its significance for logic, may be defined as that which we are constrained to think. The real compels our thought. The dream or fancy can be dispelled by the waking consciousness or the commanding will. Not so, however, with the real object of perception, or the necessary implications of thought. The ghost is laid by the reassuring judgments of common sense, but not the lightning, the thunder, the storm which have overtaken us. The child's world is one in which there is no sharp distinction between fact and fancy; especially is this true with the child's world of play. But contact with the world of growing knowledge brings many disillusions and the reduction of many cherished fancies to the impossible and absurd.

It is not strictly a question of logic,—this question concerning the ultimate nature of reality. It is essentially a question of metaphysics, for metaphysics has primarily to do with the ultimate nature of things,—of time, of space, of causation, of God, man, and the world, and therefore of the ultimate nature of the reality itself which underlies these various manifestations of it. The special question which metaphysics puts is this: Does our knowledge of the world represent it really as it is? May not reality be very different from that which it appears to be in my perceptions? Are the sea, the sky, the wood, portrayed in my thought with an exact correspondence to the reality which constitutes them what they are? It is evident that there is here room for much discussion, for much difference of opinion, and for much confusion of thought as well. But logic is satisfied from its point of view, if there is assurance that in the body of knowledge which represents our world as we conceive it there are elements which maintain a constant character, and that whatever we come to think about them is due to a necessity which underlies their essential nature. Logic therefore is not concerned with the ultimate nature of reality, but it does demand as the basis of all knowledge certain elements which are grounded in necessity and admit of a constant reference in thought.

Moreover, that which appears to the individual as a necessary experience, a necessary truth, or a necessary demonstration receives constantly through intercourse with one's fellow-men a social confirmation and verification. We find for the most part that our judgments run parallel to those of the generality of mankind. What we think, other men think. What is true for me, I believe is true for you also. The debatable area of conflicting opinion is to be regarded as knowledge in the making. Questions which divided men's minds a generation or two ago are many of them now settled, and the results formulated in universally accepted judgments. Even where there may remain an outstanding difference of opinion, there is always some common ground of necessity which is recognized; and the lack of agreement is due to the fact, not that the basis of our knowledge is uncertain and shifting, but that human judgment is fallible, owing to the limitations of experience, the want of insight, the presence of prejudice, or the undue submission to authority. All these disturbing elements enter into the processes of thought and cause perturbations of judgment. In spite however of such disagreements, the presence of an underlying necessity as the basis of knowledge is attested and sealed by the general agreement of our judgments with those of our fellows. The communication of thought, the communal interests and activities, the industrial and social faith which is preserved between man and man, the laws both written and unwritten which command respect and obedience, the universally recognized standards of civilized life, all attest a common recognition of one and the same element of necessity, and a common interpretation of the many phases of its manifestation.

The difference between the man who is sane and one who is not lies in the absence of this social factor of agreeing judgments. With the insane mind there is a feeling of necessity which, however, is without foundation. The world in which he lives and moves and has his being is for him a necessary world. But in it he dwells alone. No one else can enter it, or understand his view of it. He believes that he is Julius Cæsar, or Napoleon, and it may be consistently thinks and acts in that character. But for him there is no fellowship in thought, for his experiences are not believed and his judgments stand in conflict with those of all the rest of mankind.

It is incumbent upon us, therefore, as logical beings, to make sure of the basis of reality which we believe underlies our judgments. In the investigation of any subject concerning which we regard ourselves entitled to a judgment, not only should we seek as wide a range of observation as is possible concerning the facts upon which we found the judgment, but we should acquaint ourselves also with what other men have thought and have written upon the subject. This is to be done, not that we may slavishly acquiesce in their judgments, but that by a critical examination of all that is known and reported we may be the better able to defend our own position, or the more reasonably to modify or to abandon it as the case may be.

We come now to discuss the relation of the judgment as a form of thought to its corresponding expression by means of language. The judgment expressed in language is known as a proposition. The grammatical form of a proposition consists of subject, predicate, and copula. The copula is some form of the verb "to be" either expressed or implied. It is always implied in any verb which may appear in a proposition. Thus the proposition, He rows a boat, is equivalent to the proposition, He is rowing a boat; wherein the verb "to row" breaks up into the participle of the verb combined with the auxiliary verb "to be." This can occur with any verb whatsoever, and therefore in any verb there is implied some form of the verb "to be"; consequently every proposition may be regarded as composed of subject, predicate, and copula.

The logical function of these three parts of speech needs some further exposition. In the first place, there is a distinction between logical subject and predicate on the one hand, and grammatical subject and predicate on the other. The logical subject of every proposition is some phase of reality; the logical predicate is always the significant idea which the judgment contains applied to this phase of reality in order to characterize or interpret it. The judgment in this connection may be defined as the interpretation of some phase of reality by means of some universal idea. The reality is the logical subject; the universal idea interpreting it is the logical predicate. This statement may be illustrated as follows: Let us take a judgment of the type in which a particular experience is interpreted by means of a concept,—This is an excellent essay on the labor question. Here the subject, denoted by the demonstrative adjective "this," refers directly to a point of the world of reality, evident to the senses, something visible and tangible; the predicate is the complex concept, "an excellent essay on the labor question," which is asserted of the subject in question. The thought form interprets the perceived reality simply. In this type of judgments, the logical subject and predicate coincide with the grammatical subject and predicate.

In the other form of judgment which is a characterization of some phase of our knowledge in general, the logical subject and predicate do not coincide with the grammatical subject and predicate. For instance, let us consider the proposition, — All permanent reforms emanate from the people. Here the grammatical subject is "all permanent reforms"; the grammatical predicate is that they "emanate from the people."

Now it is the function of the copula to fuse together the grammatical subject and predicate into one idea which forms the heart of the judgment and its real logical predicate. For while language separates the grammatical subject and predicate, the two must be conceived as merely parts of one and the same idea in thought. The grammatical predicate, in this case the phrase "emanate from the people," is an essential characteristic of the grammatical subject, "permanent reform"; together they form but a single idea, namely, a permanent reform emanating from the people. This is the logical predicate which is affirmed of this particular phase of that reality which lies at the basis of every true judgment, and though not expressed in the grammatical form of the proposition nevertheless constitutes its logical subject. The logical significance of this judgment, if explicitly expressed, would be somewhat as follows: The

THE JUDGMENT

world of reality as I am constrained to regard it is such as to necessitate that all permanent reforms should emanate from the people. And this may serve as a type of all our universal judgments; they affirm of some phase of reality the central idea which constitutes the heart of the judgment itself. A false judgment contains at its heart a central idea to which there is no corresponding subject in the real world of knowledge.

When we come to put into words the single idea which always lies at the root of the essential unity of the judgment, why do we separate this unitary idea into two, the grammatical subject and the grammatical predicate? The reason is that while the idea in question represents a single unified thought, it is nevertheless complex and capable of an analysis into two component elements, one the grammatical subject and the other the grammatical predicate. Judgment is a process which consists in relating one phase of an idea to another phase of the same idea, and in rendering evident the unity which underlies them. The grammatical subject forms one of these phases; the grammatical predicate forms the other. The copula serves to bring them together and to affirm their unity. Thus every proposition is the expression of the complementary processes of analysis and synthesis; the analysis is expressed by the grammatical subject and predicate, the synthesis by the force of the copula whose function it is to blend the two into one logical idea which forms the very essence of the judgment itself.

In connection with this discussion of the relation of language to thought, it would be well to call attention to the meaning of the word term in logic. A term is any word or combination of words considered as a part of a proposition, that is, as subject or predicate. The term, therefore, is the expression in language of the concept as an integral part of the judgment.

CHAPTER IV

THE UNIVERSAL JUDGMENT

JUDGMENTS, as we have seen, are of two kinds. The first represents some one or other of the many phases of our general knowledge. The second serves to interpret the special case in the light of general knowledge. The first type is known as the universal judgment. Our general body of knowledge is composed of judgments of this kind, and if they are to prove serviceable in the interpretation of special cases as they arise, they must together form an orderly system. The concepts which form the constitutive elements of these judgments are all interrelated. Every concept represents a point whence radiate lines of connection with many other concepts. It is impossible to frame a judgment which shall contain a concept out of all relation to other concepts.

If, for instance, we analyze the full significance of the abstract concept of redness, we at once relate it in our thought to the general color system, which in turn we refer to light as its source. The idea of light at once suggests the ether vibrations which affect the retina of the eye, and this, in turn, the transmission of the physiological disturbance which occurs in the retina to the optic lobes of the brain, and then the resultant reaction which is attended by the consciousness of a color sensation. Thus the examination of any concept will reveal an indefinite number of relations extending into the general body of our knowledge. Their formulation gives rise to a series of descriptive judgments. Our knowledge therefore so far as it is worthy the name

THE UNIVERSAL JUDGMENT 37

of knowledge, represents an organized system of relations. Moreover, there are certain general principles which underlie the process of organizing the various elements of knowledge. These principles pertain to the very nature of thought itself, and man has universally employed them in constructing his world of knowledge. These fundamental principles are called the categories of thought. They indicate the various possible ways by which conceptual elements are related so as to form the unitary idea which lies at the basis of the judgment.

As given by Aristotle, the categories, ten in number, are as follows: —

1. οὐσία   substance   6. πότε   time
2. ποσόν   quantity   7. κεῖσθαι posture or attitude
3. ποιόν   quality   8. ἔχειν   having
4. πρός τι relation   9. ποιεῖν acting
5. ποῦ   place   10. πάσχειν being acted upon

Thus any concept whatever may be regarded from one or more of these points of view, — as to its substance, what it is; as to its various attributes, its dimensions and weight; the relations which it sustains; its space and time conditions; its relative position as regards its surroundings; as to what it may possess; as to how it acts; and how it is acted upon. The list exhausts the possibilities of description. The word κατηγορία, as used by Aristotle, means assertion or predication. The table of the categories presents the possibilities of the various kinds of assertion. We have seen, moreover, that a judgment is a process essentially of assertion. The categories therefore give us the possible varieties of judgment. These categories suggest a corresponding division of words into the various parts of speech. The substance corresponds to the noun; quantity, quality, and relation to the adjective; place, time, and posture to the adverb; having, acting, and being acted upon to the verb. Thus we have outlined the possibilities, not only of thought relations, but of the expression of the same in language.

There are, moreover, certain considerations in reference to these categories which enable us to coördinate the various portions of our knowledge so as to form out of them a system which shall show unity and order. These considerations are as follows:—

The first category is substance; the other nine categories give the various kinds of possible attributes which together serve to determine the essential nature of any concept, that is, its substance, this first of the categories. Of these various attributes, some will be common to a number of concepts. This will enable us to group similar concepts together. Other attributes will be unique as regards some particular concept. They will serve as a distinguishing mark of the concept in question. Others again appear in certain special instances of a concept, but not in all. This serves to mark the distinction between constant and variable attributes, a distinction which is exceedingly valuable from the standpoint of logic; for it draws the line between attributes and relations which have a universal validity and those which are shifting and uncertain.

The above considerations are formulated under five technical terms, known in logic as the Heads of Predicables; that is, the various ways in which a predicate given by any one of the categories may be affirmed of a subject, or of the concept regarded in the light of the first category, substance. These terms are as follows:—

1. Genus.
2. Species.
3. Property.
4. Differentia, or Specific Difference.
5. Accident.[1]

[1] Aristotle gives but four forms, including "species" under "genus," and instead of "differentia," giving "definition."

They are the Heads of Predicables, as given by Porphyry (230–300 A.D.) in his *Introduction to Aristotle's Treatise on the Categories.*

Genus and species are relative terms and can best be defined together. The genus is always a larger class which embraces two or more smaller classes under it by reason of their common attributes.

The species is any one of the smaller classes which is embraced under the genus.

The property is an attribute which pertains to the very nature of the concept itself.

The differentia is that particular property which serves to distinguish a given species from all others belonging to the same genus.

The accident is an attribute which does not pertain to the essential nature of the concept, and therefore may be present or absent without affecting the integrity of the concept in question.

These distinctions may be illustrated in the following proposition: —

Democracy (*species*) is a form of government (*genus*) in which the supreme power is vested in the people (*differentia*); it is attended by certain dangers due to the dissipation of responsibility (*property*); it is regarded in the United States by some as a proved success, by others as still in the experimental stage (*accident*).

The several species under one genus are called cognate species.

A generic property is one which grows out of the idea represented by the genus, and which therefore all cognate species have in common.

A specific property is one which grows out of the idea represented by the differentia, and belongs therefore only to one of a number of cognate species.

Genus and species, being relative terms, a concept may be regarded as a species relative to a genus which embraces it, but a genus relative to the various species which it embraces.

There is however the summum genus, which can be referred to no larger class, and also the infima species, which cannot be broken up into any smaller classes.

In the light of these various distinctions, we may group our judgments in several classes, according to the different ways by which the concepts in these judgments are related.

1. The possibility of referring a species as a subject to its corresponding genus as a predicate; *e.g.* The purple martin is a swallow.

2. The possibility of referring a genus as a subject to the various species under it which together form the predicate; *e.g.* The swallow may be a purple martin, a barn swallow, a cliff swallow, etc.

3. The possibility of describing any species as a subject by one or more of its properties as a predicate; *e.g.* Cast iron has a specific gravity of 7.20.

The special case of this group is where the property chosen is the differentia of the species; *e.g.* Capital is wealth which is actually used for producing more wealth.

4. The possibility of describing a concept by its accident; *e.g.* Some animals can swim.

A judgment in this latter form is known as a particular judgment. It is not a statement in terms of a universal; neither indeed can it be as long as the predicate is an accident of the concept which appears as subject.

It must not be overlooked, however, that any predicate which is an accident may be raised to the higher level of a property in reference to any concept, provided that concept is only more specifically limited. Thus if we change the above proposition by inserting the limiting adjective "web-footed," the predicate at once becomes the property of the subject thus limited, and instead of a particular judgment, as in the former case, we now have the universal judgment,

— All web-footed animals can swim. In general it may be said that an accident of any species always becomes the property of that same species under certain definite restrictions. Every accident, therefore, is a potential property. To call any attribute of a species an accident is a confession of ignorance, for if we only know the corresponding limitation of the species in question, the accident at once is transformed into a property.

If our knowledge were perfect, we should be able to explain all accidental variations, even the most minute and seemingly insignificant. Each so-called accident could then be regarded as a property and be referred to some constant element within the nature of the concept itself as its cause. Every variation in nature, whether of color, or form, or peculiarities of habit and disposition, has a good and sufficient reason why it is what it is and not anything else. To call such variations mere accidents of a species is of course a confession of ignorance. This leads us to the fifth possibility of reference.

5. The possibility of referring properties of concepts to definite conditions as their cause. The causal relation when expressed or implied in a judgment not only renders that judgment more definite and consequently serves to perfect the order of the general body of knowledge, but it also furnishes the ground for the judgment itself and consequently serves to justify it. Take for instance the proposition, A conic section formed by a cutting plane parallel to the base of a cone is always a circle. Here the circle, as regards a conic section in general, is an accident, but as regards a conic section under the condition that the cutting plane is parallel to the base, it is an essential property. The condition determines the property, and the two are related as cause and effect. So, also, to further illustrate this relation, the freezing or boiling of water may be regarded as accidents, so far as the concept of water in general is concerned. They are, however, properties of water when

specifically determined by the freezing and boiling conditions.

Knowledge, therefore, which is vague and indefinite, gives rise to judgments whose predicates are accidents of the subject concept. Definite knowledge, on the other hand, always gives rise to judgments whose predicates are properties of the subject concept. The bond of connection or inherence between any species and its property forms the ground of the universal judgment.

In the various relations which concepts may sustain to one another in the general scheme which has been given, there are, in the main, two points of view from which a concept may be regarded, giving rise to two different kinds of judgment. The one point of view is known as that of extension and the other that of intension. The extension of a concept refers to the range of its application. The intension refers to the various properties which constitute its meaning. The term denotation is used as equivalent to extension; and connotation as equivalent to intension. The term content is also used in much the same sense as connotation or intension. By some writers the terms extension and intension are applied to concepts, while denotation and connotation are applied to terms, the language symbols of concepts. In ordinary usage, however, extension and denotation are used interchangeably; so also intension and connotation. Two questions naturally arise in reference to any concept: the first, what is its meaning? and the second, to what extent within the range of our knowledge may it be applied? It is obvious that these two questions are mutually dependent. It is impossible of course, to know the number of special cases to which the concept may be applied if we know nothing of its distinctive properties; and, on the other hand, we can know nothing of the distinctive properties unless we possess some knowledge of the special cases illustrating them.

The distinction between intension and extension gives

rise to two topics known as definition and division. Definition is the process of unfolding the connotation of any term, and division is the process of unfolding the denotation of a term; that is, the former tells what it is, the latter to what instances it may be applied. These two processes we will now consider more in detail.

CHAPTER V

DEFINITION

DEFINITION is the process of unfolding the connotation of a concept. A statement giving the complete connotation, however, would be overloaded and would weigh down our thought and its expression with a superfluous burden. If a definition serves to locate a concept in its proper region within the general body of knowledge, and in addition distinguishes it from all other cognate concepts which may fall within the same general area of thought, then it may be said to perform its function satisfactorily. The function of definition is expressed by the following rule: Definition consists in referring any concept to its proximate genus, *i.e.* the genus immediately above it, and also in giving its appropriate differentia.

To define means to set limits or bounds. This rule indicates two defining circles: the first, the genus, marks the larger area within whose range the concept belongs; the second, the differentia, draws a narrower circle which separates the concept within it from all others which lie within the outer circle, and yet outside this inner circle of more exact specification. This method of defining is a procedure which should always be followed when it is possible. There are other modes of definition which are less complete, but which it is sometimes necessary to employ, as will be shown later. The above method, however, is preferable, as it alone can give what is known as the essential definition.

A distinction is drawn by some logicians between a real and a nominal definition. The real definition is regarded as one which gives the meaning of the concept; the nominal, as giving the meaning of the term which is the language symbol of the concept. Some writers, as Sigwart and Mill, declare that there can be no such thing as a real definition, inasmuch as the process of defining consists in unfolding the meaning of words. Definition, from this point of view, is merely the art of fitting the word to the idea which it represents. It seems to me, however, that the process of definition must primarily refer to the meaning of the thought, and only in a secondary sense to the meaning of the word which is the symbol of the thought. For the symbol can have no meaning, except as it represents some thought behind it. And, in the second place, to define means to render definite. Consequently, a definition of terms presupposes always a preliminary transformation of our ideas from an indefinite to a definite state of determination. It is thought determination alone which can afford a basis for exact verbal definition. To draw a line of distinction between a real and a nominal definition is to misunderstand the relation which obtains between a symbol and that which it symbolizes.

There are certain rules which should be observed in definition: —

1. The term defined should be coextensive with the definition, neither greater nor less. The following is an example of the violation of this rule: Logic is a normative science. Here the term "normative science" is not coextensive with "logic," for it includes ethics and æsthetics as well as logic.

2. The definition should not contain any superfluous material. Take the following definition: — An hallucination is a fancied perception (genus) without basis of fact (differentia), and which indicates an abnormal state of consciousness. The latter clause, while quite true, is altogether superfluous. The definition should be always in as concise a form as possible.

3. The definition should not repeat the term to be defined either explicitly or implicitly. The violation of this rule is

known as defining in a circle (*circulus in definiendo*). In an examination recently given the terms "percept" and "concept" were defined as follows: — A percept is that which is perceived. A concept is that which is conceived. These definitions are incorrect also for another reason, because they contain no proper genus. Instead of a true genus to which the term defined is referred there is substituted the indefinite and unsatisfactory phrase "that which."

Under this head of explicit or implicit repetition of the term to be defined may be included all synonyms of the term in question. There is the following remark of Hume which illustrates this. Speaking of the definition of the term "efficacy," he says: "I begin with observing that the terms of *efficacy, agency, power, force, energy, necessity, connexion,* and *productive quality* are all nearly synonymous; and therefore it is an absurdity to employ any one of them in defining the rest. By this observation we reject at once all the vulgar definitions which philosophers have given of *power* and *efficacy;* and instead of searching for the idea in these definitions, must look for it in the impressions from which it is originally derived."[1]

It sometimes happens that in a compound term the incidence of the definition falls only upon one of the elements which compose the compound. In such a case, the other element of the compound term may be repeated in the definition. Thus the terms, "vesper-sparrow," "gun-metal," "armored cruiser," may be defined by referring each to its appropriate genus, "sparrow," "metal," "cruiser," and then giving its corresponding differentia.

4 A definition should never be in obscurer language than the term to be defined. The violation of this rule is called "*ignotum per ignotius.*"

An example of this is the following: A state is an ethnic unit which lies within a geographical unit.

[1] Hume, *A Treatise of Human Nature.* Edited by Green and Grose, p. 451.

Sometimes, however, in defining technical terms it is necessary to use technical words, and an impression is given to the uninitiated at least of an obscure definition. Such a definition is Herbert Spencer's of evolution. "Evolution is a continuous change from an indefinite incoherent homogeneity to a definite coherent heterogeneity through successive differentiations and integrations." In this definition every term used has a definite connotation with which every student of the subject has become familiar, and therefore to such an one this definition is exceedingly luminous.

5. A definition should never contain negative expressions when it is possible to state it by means of the proper positive terms.

The following is a violation of the rule: —

A utilitarian is one who does not believe in an intuitional basis of morals.

It is always desirable to define any term by what it is rather than by what it is not.

There are certain terms, however, which by their very nature admit of a negative definition only. Such terms are the following, — anarchist, blindness, unarmored cruiser, supernatural, and the like.

There are other forms of definition which are substituted for the ideal form *per genus et differentiam.* Sometimes they are mere makeshifts at definition, when one is ignorant of the true genus or differentia; and often for some special reason they better serve the purpose of a satisfactory definition.

They are as follows: —

1. Definition by description. When the genus or the differentia is unknown, then the concept may be described by its various properties. A person thinks that he has discovered a new species of plant. He is in doubt as to its precise differentia. An exact definition is impossible. He wishes, however, to publish some account of it. The only course which is possible under the circumstances is to give

a complete description of it, especially as regards those properties in which it deviates in any marked degree from the type. The description may serve as a basis for the discovery of the real differentia.

It often happens when one begins a new study, and the material he has to deal with is unfamiliar, that precise definitions are impossible. At this preliminary period description must take the place of definition. Later with the mastery of the subject comes the possibility of framing satisfactory definitions.

2. Definition for the purpose of identification. Instead of the differentia which may be a property that is not evident to a surface observation, there may be substituted in the definition another property which is readily observable and which serves as a mark of identification. Thus we may define an acid as a chemical compound which turns blue litmus red. It is not a definition of an acid, but it is a most convenient formula of identification. Or we may define sassafras as a tree of the laurel family whose bark has an aromatic odor or taste. Such formulæ are most valuable as working definitions. Sometimes the property which best serves as a basis for identification is a very insignificant one. Thus the color markings of birds, such as the white tail-feather of the vesper-sparrow, may furnish a convenient and perfectly satisfactory basis for identification. It may be that the peculiar mode of flight may serve a similar purpose. In all such instances a superficial property is substituted for the differentia.

3. The genetic definition, which refers the concept to be defined to its origin. The genetic definition, in giving the origin of the concept, furnishes at the same time a method by which special instances of the concept may be produced, and made available for observation and experiment. Thus the genetic definition of sulphuric acid is given by the formula H_2SO_4. Here the compound is defined by the component elements of which its essential nature consists. The

genetic definition of a certain dye would be in terms of the formula by means of which the dye may be produced. So also all recipes, prescriptions, and methods of construction may be regarded as definitions of this class. Any concrete instance may be produced at will by following the suggestions contained in the definitions. Thus it is a genetic definition of a right cylinder that it is a solid body conceived as generated by the rotation of a rectangle about one of its sides as an axis. So also the various colors of the spectrum may be defined in terms of the number of vibrations corresponding to each color.

The genetic definition is one which has always a practical significance inasmuch as it furnishes knowledge in such a form as to subserve the ends of utility. It not only tells us the meaning of certain ideas, but it also indicates how we may apply them in the arts, the sciences, and the practical needs of our lives.

CHAPTER VI

DIVISION AND CLASSIFICATION

DIVISION is a process by which the denotation of a concept is exhibited. The result is that form of judgment in which the subject term represents the concept regarded as a genus, and the predicate term contains the several species which fall under it. The process of definition always underlies that of division, for we must know the differentia of each species before it is possible to consider it as a distinct group under a given genus. In dividing a concept into its appropriate species, one may proceed in a number of different ways according to the point of view he may choose to take. The point of view determines in every case the so-called principle of division (*fundamentum divisionis*).

Thus we may divide the general concept, education, according to the principle of the progressive stages of education regarded as a process, as primary, secondary, collegiate, university, and professional; or the principle chosen may be that of the general nature of the course of studies pursued, such as the common school, academic, scientific, technical, etc.; or again, the principle of division may be an historical one, giving the periods of ancient, mediæval, and modern education. It is obvious that the principle of division will vary according to one's special interest or purpose. There is thus a wide range of possibility as regards the analysis of our various concepts. There is no beaten road for thought to travel, but each one may cut out his own path. In the midst of this variety of choice, however, there are certain rules which logic imposes upon the free play of thought. Within the bounds of these restrictions the inventive spirit

DIVISION AND CLASSIFICATION

may range at will; but the violation of them brings confusion and inconsistency of thought. The rules are:—

1. There must be but one principle of division. A violation of this rule, for instance, would be such a division as that of the concept "education" into primary, secondary, collegiate, technical, scientific, and professional.

2. The members of a division should be mutually exclusive; no two members of a division should overlap. The above example illustrates the violation of this rule also. The following furnishes another illustration: The division of the discontented classes in society into socialists, anarchists, nihilists, and populists.

While the violation of the first rule produces overlapping divisions, nevertheless the same error may be due to other causes even when the requirements of the first rule are realized.

3. The division must be exhaustive. No possibility should be overlooked and omitted from the division. Thus if we divide conduct into two classes, the moral and immoral, the division is at fault because of its incompleteness. There is still a third class which is omitted, namely, that of conduct which is morally indifferent, and concerning which it is not possible to affirm that it is either moral or immoral.

There is a particular method of division known as Dichotomy which provides for an exhaustive division under all circumstances. It consists in dividing a concept into two parts, according to the presence or the absence of a differentiating attribute which is chosen as the principle of division. This may be illustrated by the so-called "Tree of Porphyry," which exhibits a continued division of that most general and all-comprehensive concept, being.

DEDUCTIVE LOGIC

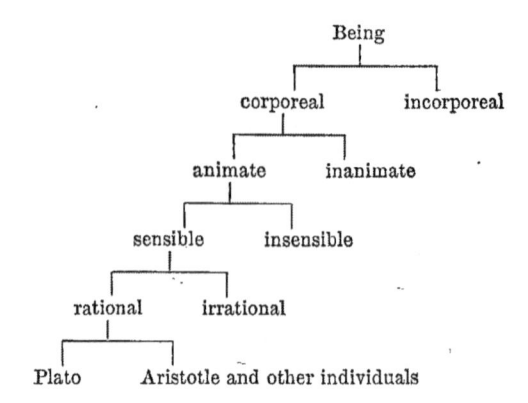

```
                        Being
                    ┌─────┴─────┐
                corporeal    incorporeal
              ┌─────┴─────┐
          animate      inanimate
        ┌─────┴─────┐
     sensible    insensible
   ┌─────┴─────┐
rational    irrational
┌─────┴─────┐
Plato    Aristotle and other individuals
```

Such a division is more curious than satisfactory, for one of the members in each successive division is left indefinite, being designated by what it is not, rather than by what it is. Moreover, if a positive term is substituted for the negative, and its precise connotation is attempted, it will in all probability not be a complete opposite of the first term of the dichotomy. If this is the case, the division itself is not complete, for the dividing of a concept into two members which are not exact opposites renders it possible to interpolate between them one or more possibilities which do not belong to the one or the other of the extremes. In this connection it is necessary to distinguish between contradictory and contrary or opposite terms.

Contradictory terms are such that they divide the whole universe of thought between them and admit of no middle ground.

Contrary terms stand opposite to each other as extremes, but there is a possibility of middle ground between them.

Animate and inanimate are contradictory, bitter and sweet are contrary terms.

A dichotomous division requires its terms to be related as contradictories. There is perhaps no error in division which is more frequent or more insidious than this, of dividing a concept into members which sustain contrary rather than contradictory relations to each other. This is seen particularly in debate where an opponent will often confront one with a choice of alternatives, either this course or that, when, however, there is a third possibility unnoticed, or purposely ignored. It is the third possibility which we should always have in mind, and endeavor to discover whenever the necessities of a dichotomous division are forced upon us. There can be no free choice of the mind unless all possibilities are presented.

On this very account division very often takes a threefold form, that of Trichotomy; because when a concept is divided into two members exhibiting some one or more opposed characteristics, a third member representing a mediating position between the two naturally suggests itself. This form of division which expresses extreme terms in relation to the middle ground between them has played an important rôle in the history of philosophical thought. For instance Aristotle's theory of morals was based upon the principle that right conduct always lies between two extremes, neither of which commends itself to the reason. Thus courage, which is the mean between cowardice on the one hand and rashness on the other, takes rank as a virtue and is freed from all criticism which is called forth naturally by the extremes. So, also, according to Aristotle, temperance is the virtue which avoids the extremes of ascetic abstinence and unbridled desire.

The trichotomous division is further illustrated in the dialectical method which grew out of the teaching of Kant, and which was developed by Fichte and brought to its complete expression by Hegel. The meaning of "dialectic" may be gathered from Plato's usage of the term, which with him signified the process of argument between two disputants, who in their controversy for and against a given proposition render this exceedingly valuable service, namely, that the course of debate brings to light whatever fundamental elements of truth the opposed positions may have in common. This idea Hegel has applied to the evolution of all truth which he declares develops progressively through three stages. The first is the thesis, the primary proposition as originally affirmed; the second is the antithesis, the opposed proposition; the third is the synthesis, the reconstruction of these two from a higher point of view which discloses the unity underlying the two extreme positions. Hegel insists that a scheme such as this forms a universal programme according to which the evolution of all thought must proceed.

A distinction is drawn in logic between the so-called empirical and logical divisions. A logical division is one which applies the principle of division to any given concept, and notes all the possible members of the division which result from such a process. The empirical division is the result of a critical examination of the logical division to the end that all members of such a division which cannot be realized actually in experience may be eliminated. A strictly logical division may give certain ideal groups which are rendered impossible actually because of certain necessities of the concrete situation, or because of the general economy of nature.

As an illustration of the former, the genus, regular polyhedron, may be divided according to the number of the bounding planes. Now applying to the genus the principle of division which is the number series, and without taking into consideration any other limiting conditions whatsoever, we get regular polyhedrons according as their faces are: —

4, 5, 6, 7, 8, 9, 10, 11, 12, 13, 14, 15, 16, 17, 18, 19, 20, etc.

However, a second question forces itself upon our consideration. Are the space conditions such that all of these supposed regular polyhedrons can be actually constructed?

The answer is that only the following are possible, those having sides as follows: —

$$4, 6, 8, 12, 20.$$

Thus the formal division has been corrected through an appeal to the actual conditions which are imposed by the existent space relations.

Again to illustrate what may be called the limitations due to the economy of nature, we have the following division of mankind, according to differences of color: White men, black, red, yellow, orange, green, etc.

Such a division is the result of applying a color principle of division in its full rigor and extent to the concept in question. When, however, we ask in addition the question as to the prodigality of nature in this respect, we find that the actual colors found among the various races of man are limited, and therefore our division must be corrected by striking out such colors as green, orange, etc., which have no empirical confirmation in fact.

There is a difference as regards order of procedure between dividing a concept simply according to the possible variations of some selected property irrespective of any consideration of the actual limitations which may occur in experience, and starting with actual classes as they have been observed in experience, and grouping them together in a system as related members of one and the same genus. This latter process is that of classification which will be considered next.

Classification is a term which is used for the most part interchangeably with division, but, as regards strictly logical usage, classification is a process which is the inverse of division proper. The problem of classification, therefore, is that of arranging given classes into a system whose unity is such that it can be regarded as forming the underlying ground of the several classes in question. Moreover, classification proper represents usually a more elaborate scheme than simple division. In classification the process of division is many times repeated, so that the original genus not only has its species grouped under it, but each species in turn may be regarded as a new genus, and its corresponding species indicated, and so on until a series of *infimæ species* is reached.

A classification may be of two kinds, either artificial or natural. In an artificial classification, the principle of classification selected is some characteristic which is external to the essential nature of the elements to be classified. In a natural classification, the principle of classification selected is a property which forms a constituent part of the essential nature of the elements to be classified.

1. In an artificial classification the characteristic which is selected as the basis of the classification is either an accident, or at least an unimportant property of the elements to be classified. The consequence is that the various members of the classification which fall together in the same group possess in common only this arbitrary or artificial mark selected as the basis of classification, and are dissimilar in all other respects.

This kind of a classification is best illustrated by the alphabetical catalogue of books in a library. The initial letter of the author is regarded as a differentiating mark. It brings together in one group an indiscriminate variety of books which have in common merely the one artificial mark. Such a classification, however, serves its purpose most satisfactorily in furnishing a convenient key for reference.

An artificial classification generally may be said to perform some such function as this, namely, of realizing some definite and specific purpose, and is therefore essentially a working classification. It must not be thought that an artificial classification is necessarily an imperfect or unsatisfactory classification. On the contrary, for the end to which it is designed, it serves a most useful purpose.

2. A natural classification is based upon one or more

properties directly connected with the essential nature of the elements to be classified. In a natural classification the members which fall together in the same group should not only agree as regards the common property which is selected as the basis of the classification, but also as regards a large number of cognate properties. A property therefore should be selected as the basis of classification which has the largest number of correlated properties inseparably connected with it, so that whenever the given property is present, the correlated properties will always accompany it. Such a property is known as a diagnostic property. It is like the significant symptom which indicates to the physician the nature of a disease, because the symptom in question always has a number of other symptoms correlated with it and which forms therefore a basis of exact diagnosis. A diagnostic attribute, therefore, will bring together in one and the same group members of the classification which have in common not merely a large number of properties, but these properties form a system of correlated and interconnected elements which together constitute what is known as a natural kind. In a natural classification, the various members therefore form these groups of natural kinds, or, as they are sometimes called, real kinds. In a zoölogical classification we would have such natural kinds as vertebrates, mammals, reptiles, etc. The mammals, for instance, have not merely the differentiating mark in common, but also a complex system of correlated properties which are built about the central and distinguishing property of the kind.

Natural classifications obtain in all the sciences, wherein the subject-matter is arranged in groups according to a natural determination of kind. The classifications of animal and plant life are the best illustrations which we have of natural classification. A natural classification furnishes an excellent basis for comparative study, for, in the method of grouping according to kind, resemblances are most easily observed and significant relations suggested, while at the same time characteristic differences are rendered most prominent. It often happens in a natural classification that the fundamental property chosen as the basis of the classification, and which is of such a nature as to determine the essential structure or function of a definite kind, is necessarily of such a nature that it is not disclosed to a surface observation. Thus the classification of birds, for instance, is based largely upon fundamental differences in anatomical structure. Birds, not as we see them, but as they are when stripped of plumage and in their nakedness, are the real objects of consideration in such a system of classification. The result is that in the same group there will appear side by side a number of birds whose surface markings are exceedingly disparate, such as the blue jay and the crow, or the English sparrow and the cardinal. It is always a broadening experience, as regards our habits of thinking, when we are able to discover some essential similarity at the basis of a marked surface dissimilarity.

In arranging the various cognate species in any scheme of classification, they should be arranged in some kind of order so that the more closely allied species are placed side by side. It is not only necessary to exhibit the unity underlying each distinct species, but also the connection which exists between several species closely related to each other. This is especially to be desired when several cognate species together form a series of progressive development. In such a series, every term representing a distinct species should occupy a place in the classification which will at once show its dependence upon the terms preceding it, and its influence in turn upon the terms which follow it. Every term thus looks before and after, and the series as a whole is characterized by an ever increasing complexity of attributes and functions. This principle of an ordered series in classification, which the doctrine of evolution has emphasized, is applicable not merely to the classification of animal and plant life, but has a far wider sphere of application. Herbert Spencer has taken the theory of biological evolution, and has applied it with skill and insight to the various branches of knowledge, as politics, sociology, history, psychology, ethics, etc., so that as a result the classification of the subject-matter in these disciplines shows a graded series of progressive development.

The doctrine of evolution, moreover, has affected the general theory of classification in the further demand that the progressive series should exhibit as far as possible the transition cases between the most closely allied of cognate species. In the traditional view of classification according to natural kinds, it was held most stoutly that each member of a series of cognate species — that is, each natural kind — must be regarded as cut off wholly from every other, even from that with which it is most of kin. It is the ancient doctrine of the immutability of species. The theory of evolution, however, insists that the seemingly distinct species shade off by inappreciable degrees of difference, so that the gap between any two may be filled up by transition cases showing the possibility of a continuous transformation from one to the other. These transition cases, or missing links, cannot always be supplied in experience; but the contention of the evolutionist is that in many cases they have been supplied, and that if our experience were not so limited, they could be supplied in many more. There is an illustration, however, which does show a classification in which the transition cases between groups may be shown perfectly without any defects due to the limitations of experience. This illustration is from the sphere of mathematics, and therefore is relieved of the complexities and consequent difficulties which obtain in reference to natural phenomena. We know that the various conic sections may be divided into the following groups, — the point, straight line, circle, ellipse, parabola, and hyperbola. These are not to be regarded as distinct classes, each one lying wholly outside of all the others, but as so related that the circle for instance may be exhibited as the special case of the ellipse, and that it may be shown how through a continuous transformation the ellipse may become a circle. In like manner, the parabola may pass over into the ellipse on the one hand, or into the hyperbola on the other.

When also limiting cases between species are forthcoming in biological classification, they serve to form a graduated series in which the presence of transition cases between allied groups discloses their underlying unity. The traditional doctrine of the immutability of species breaks down in the face of such instances. The distinct groups of fishes and amphibians are differentiated by the presence of gills in the one and of lungs in the other. In the case of the so-called group of Dipnoi, the African mud-fish, there were discovered in one and the same animal both lungs and gills. It forms, therefore, an intermediate transition type between the fishes and the amphibians. Moreover, the links which the existing forms of animal life have not been able to supply have been found in many cases in the record of extinct forms preserved in the various geological strata of the earth's surface.

The unity of widely divergent species is illustrated by Von Baer's law, that the history of evolution of species in the race is repeated in miniature in the development observed in the embryo of each individual. Thus the egg of a bird in the various stages of transformation passes through a series of forms, resembling in a rough way it is true, but still resembling successively a worm, then a fish, then an amphibian, then a reptile, and finally the full-formed bird. That all these variations in form are due to variations in the one constructive basal principle is clearly seen, inasmuch as the different transformations occur within the one organism, bounded by the enveloping wall of the egg. It is the function of classification, therefore, to show whenever it is possible the unity which underlies its various groups, and holds them together in a single system through bonds not of external relation merely, but of an inner kinship.

Every science naturally seeks to arrange its material in an orderly manner which results in some scheme of classification. In the sciences such as zoölogy and botany, the systems of classification are developed to such an extent of detail that the intermediate genera and species between the summum genus and the infima species are specified by a series of terms which serve to indicate a more and more elaborate degree of specification. These terms in their order of specification are as follows: kingdom, group, sphere, class, order, family, tribe, genus, subdivision, species, variety, and finally, the separate individuals. These terms may not all be used in any one system, but they form a kind of skeleton scheme, any parts of which are available for the general purposes of classification. It should be remembered in this connection that the terms genus and species, according to logical usage, are to be regarded always as relative terms applicable to any classes whatever, which are subordinated one to the other. Thus the term order is a genus as regards the family, but species as regards the class.

In a system of classification, the names assigned to various species are often compound terms made up of the genus and differentia of the species, *e.g.* fringed gentian, red-winged blackbird, smooth-coated collie, etc. The name not only indicates its place in the general system of classification, but is at the same time a shorthand expression of its definition.

Not only has each science a classification of its own material, but attempts have been made also from time to time to classify the various sciences in some one general system which shall show their essential relations and dependencies. This has proved to be a most engaging problem to philosophical minds, a problem, however, as perplexing as it is absorbing. There have been three attempts in modern times which are of special interest,—

the classification of the general branches of knowledge by Bacon, and the classifications of the sciences by Comte and Spencer.

Bacon's classification of all learning, his so-called "Intellectual Globe," is based upon the threefold division of the mind, — memory, imagination, and reason, to which correspond the three general divisions of learning, history, poetry, and philosophy. The classification in its main lines and without going into all its minute ramifications is shown on facing page.[1]

This classification affords abundant scope for the exercise of one's critical faculty as regards the validity of the various divisions which Bacon makes in the course of his analysis of human learning.

Bacon insisted that every classification of human knowledge should exhibit its various members as branches connected with a common trunk; the classification of Comte is based upon a principle radically different. His purpose is to show the various sciences in their order of progressive development. He insists that together they form a series of increasing complexity in which each science is dependent upon those before it, and is itself a natural propædeutic to those which follow it.

Comte's classification of the sciences proceeds in the following order: Mathematics, Astronomy, Physics, Chemistry, Biology, Sociology, the Science of Morals. In order that the significance of this series may be fully appreciated, the following passage from Comte is appended: —

"In morals we study human nature for the government of human life. All our real speculations, the most abstract and the most simple not excepted, necessarily converge toward this human domain, for indirectly they help us to the knowledge of man under his lower aspects, on which the nobler are dependent. . . . Paramount as the theory of our emotional nature, studied in itself, must ultimately be, without this

[1] Bacon, *The Dignity and Advancement of Learning*, Book II, etc.

DIVISION AND CLASSIFICATION 63

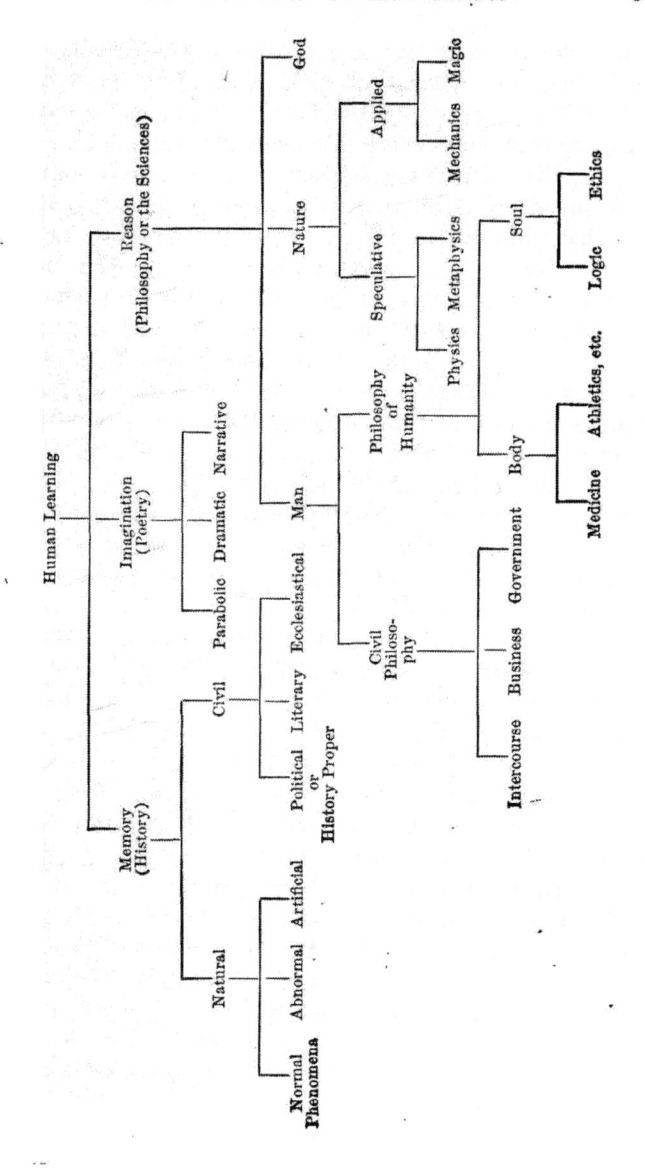

Human Learning
- Memory (History)
  - Natural
    - Normal Phenomena
    - Abnormal
    - Artificial
  - Civil
    - Political
    - Literary or History Proper
    - Ecclesiastical
- Imagination (Poetry)
  - Parabolic
  - Dramatic
  - Narrative
- Reason (Philosophy or the Sciences)
  - God
  - Nature
    - Applied
      - Mechanics
      - Magic
    - Speculative
      - Physics
      - Metaphysics
  - Man
    - Philosophy of Humanity
      - Soul
        - Logic
        - Ethics
      - Body
        - Medicine
        - Athletics, etc.
    - Civil Philosophy
      - Intercourse
      - Business
      - Government

preliminary step it would have no consistence. Morals thus objectively made dependent on Sociology, the next step is easy and similiar; objectively Sociology becomes dependent on Biology, as our cerebral existence evidently rests on our purely bodily life. These two steps carry us on to the conception of Chemistry as the normal basis of Biology, since we allow that vitality depends on the general law of the combination of water. Chemistry again in its turn is objectively subordinate to Physics, by virtue of the influence which the universal properties of matter must always exercise on the specific qualities of the different substances. Similarly Physics become subordinate to Astronomy when we recognize the fact that the existence of our terrestrial environment is carried on in perpetual subjection to the conditions of our planet as one of the heavenly bodies. Lastly, Astronomy is subordinated to Mathematics by virtue of the evident dependence of the geometrical and mechanical phenomena of the heavens on the universal laws of number, extension, and motion."[1]

Mr. Spencer takes exception to Comte's arrangement of the sciences in serial order, insisting that such a grouping of the sciences represents neither their logical dependence or their historical dependence. In this connection he gives his definition of a true classification which may be of interest to quote here as we have already emphasized the fundamental principle which lies at its basis. "A true classification," says Mr. Spencer, "includes in each class those objects which have more characteristics in common with one another, than any of them have in common with any objects excluded from the class. Further, the characteristics possessed in common by the colligated objects, and not possessed by other objects, involve more numerous dependent characteristics. There are two sides of the same definition. For things possessing the greatest number of attributes in common are things that possess in common those essential at-

[1] Comte, *System of Positive Polity*, Vol. IV, pp. 161-162.

tributes on which the rest depend; and, conversely, the possession in common of the essential attributes implies the possession in common of the greatest number of attributes."[1]

The classification of Mr. Spencer proceeds upon this principle with the following result: —

Science is
- that which treats of the *forms* in which phenomena are known to us — Abstract Science { Logic, Mathematics }
- or
- that which treats of the phenomena themselves
  - in their elements
    - Abstract-concrete Science { Mechanics, Physics, Chemistry, etc. }
  - in their totalities
    - Concrete Science { Astronomy, Geology, Biology, Psychology, Sociology, etc. }[2]

In the above the terms abstract, abstract-concrete, concrete, need some further explanation in order that one may understand the sense in which Mr. Spencer uses them. By abstract sciences he would designate those sciences which deal with fundamental principles detached from any particular incidents which may illustrate them; as, for instance, the necessary relations which obtain in logic and mathematics and which may be proved and formulated quite apart from any concrete demonstration. By the compound term abstract-concrete he means those sciences which are partly concrete inasmuch as they investigate actual phenomena themselves, but abstract inasmuch as the phenomena investigated are only detached portions of more complete

[1] Spencer, *Essays, Scientific, Political, and Speculative*, Vol. II, p. 76.
[2] *Ibid.*, Vol. II, p. 78.

wholes, as, for instance, the examination in chemistry of the special properties of oxygen by themselves and apart from the whole body of chemical phenomena. By the purely concrete sciences, Mr. Spencer refers to those sciences which investigate phenomena pertaining to complete aggregates, and the relation of all separate parts to one combined whole. Thus, as Mr. Spencer says: "The geologist does not take for his problem only those irregularities of the earth's crust that are worked by denudation; or only those which igneous action causes. He does not seek simply to understand how sedimentary strata were formed; or how faults were produced; or how moraines originated; or how the beds of Alpine lakes were scooped out. But taking into account all agencies coöperating in endless and ever varying combinations, he aims to interpret the entire structure of the earth's crust. If he studies separately the actions of rain, rivers, glaciers, icebergs, tides, waves, volcanoes, earthquakes, etc., he does so that he may be better able to comprehend their joint actions as factors in geological phenomena, the object of his science being to generalize these phenomena in all their intricate connexions as parts of one whole."[1]

These classifications of Bacon, Comte, and Spencer have been given here somewhat at length inasmuch as they present an excellent idea of the difficulties attending the classification of such complex phenomena, as well as to furnish suitable material for the exercise of one's critical faculty in respect to the measure in which these systems have realized the rigorous requirements of the laws of classification.

[1] Spencer, *Essays, Scientific, Political, and Speculative*, Vol. II, p. 89.

CHAPTER VII

THE SINGULAR JUDGMENT

THIS type of judgment differs from the universal judgment in the essential feature that it refers a single object of thought to our general body of knowledge which serves to interpret it, while the universal judgment is concerned solely with the universal characteristics and relations which obtain within the general body of knowledge itself. The singular judgment deals with special cases in the light of our general knowledge. The universal judgment deals only with the various phases of general knowledge in the light which is reflected from one part to another. The single instance which forms the subject of the singular judgment may be actually present in the field of perception, or it may be reinstated in consciousness through the processes of memory. The change in tense may be regarded as unessential, and the term perceptive judgment is often used as synonymous with singular judgment, whether the given perception is in the past or present time. The so-called narrative judgment is only the perceptive judgment referred to past time, and therefore does not constitute a distinct type of judgment.

If the whole field of perception is taken in an indefinite manner as the object of thought, and no particular part of it specified for special consideration, then the judgment which results is known as the impersonal judgment, *e.g.* It is raining, it is hot, it is a charming day, etc. The impersonal pronoun in such judgments refers to reality which is present in consciousness in a wholly undifferentiated manner. If, however, this indefinite range of reality is more precisely determined by focussing the consciousness at any one particular point in the field of perception, we have as a result the so-called demonstrative judgments, introduced by the demonstrative pronoun or adjective, *e.g.* This is magnetic ore; this black sand is magnetic ore. The latter is really a combination of two judgments, This is black sand, and it is magnetic. The perceptive judgment always originates at the focal point of the perceptual processes, just as the universal judgment originates at the focal point of the conceptual processes. A similar variety of assertion is also possible in reference to the perceptive or singular judgment as was found to obtain in reference to the universal judgment. Thus the single subject in perception, or in memory, may be rendered definite by referring it to its appropriate genus or species, or by describing it by its properties, differentia, or accidents.

There are two functions of the perceptive judgment which correspond in a general way to the two functions of definition and division. Corresponding to definition there is the function of determinate reference. And corresponding to division there is the function of indeterminate reference.

1. By determinate reference is meant the identification of the single object of perception in question with its appropriate genus or species, *e.g.* That is a fossil of the carboniferous age. In such a judgment we have satisfactorily disposed of the single object of perception by referring it to the general class to which it belongs. It is a process similar to that of definition. Indeed, this judgment may lead naturally to a definition of the general class to which we refer the specific object before us; for the question may be put, What is a fossil of the carboniferous age? The answer would be its definition. In every process of referring a single object of perception to the concept which explains it, the knowledge of the definition of the concept employed is always implicit in such a judgment. It is not explicitly stated, however, unless the terms used need to be further explained or illustrated. It should be remembered that a

CHAPTER VIII

THE NEGATIVE JUDGMENT

So far in this discussion, judgments of assertion only, or affirmative judgments, have been under consideration. We come now to the examination of the negative judgment. We have seen that the function of the copula in the affirmative judgment is to fuse into one the subject and predicate terms of the universal judgment, and in the singular judgment to assert that the given object in the field of perception or in memory is one with the concept to which it is referred. The process in either case is essentially constructive.

The negative judgment, on the other hand, holds apart the subject and predicate terms. It denies the possibility of explaining the one concept by the other, or of interpreting the single case by the universal in question. The negative judgment stands guard over our general body of knowledge, excluding whatever is altogether false, and also whatever may be false under certain conditions but may be true under others. It is thus through the process of the negative judgment that thought becomes discriminating. Our first judgments upon any unfamiliar subject are most naturally vague and indefinite. The truth which they contain is mingled with much that is erroneous. It may be, as is often the case, that a given object of perception is recognized as belonging to a certain genus, but we do not know to which one of several species under this genus it should be assigned. But as our knowledge grows, the various special cases become distinct through well-recognized differences, which, when stated, constitute a series of negative judgments. This process of differentiation serves to render knowledge more exact. This is essentially the method which Socrates pursued with his pupils, asking of them the meaning of some idea, such as virtue, or justice, and then examining the conventional definition given in the light of certain concrete instances of virtue or of justice which differed radically from the definition. Accordingly the definition had to be changed so as to adapt itself to these negative cases. In this manner vague and general notions upon which little thought had been bestowed were transformed into clear and precise ideas. The old dictum, *Omnis determinatio est negatio*, expresses the essential function of the negative judgment as that of exact determination through the process of negation. This process of negation sets a limit beyond which a given concept cannot be applied. A limit thus set serves as a boundary of exact determination. It marks always a line of distinction between what is and what is not as regards the essential nature of any concept. The process of exact determination by means of negation may be analyzed into its three component stages which form the programme of all exact thinking: —

1. The first rough draft of knowledge, which is necessarily vague and indefinite.

2. The critical limitation of this primary assertion by a number of negative judgments, which show where it breaks down, where it does not apply, and wherein the unessential may be eliminated.

3. The reconstruction of the original statement modified by the necessary restrictions, which the process of negative criticism has disclosed as essential. The result is knowledge in exact and definite form.

Thus the beginner in the study of chemistry has a vague idea of chemical affinity, — that certain elements enter into a number of various combinations to form compounds. But as his knowledge grows, he finds himself face to face with a series of negative facts, which must be reckoned with, —

namely, that all elements indiscriminately do not combine together; that they which are capable of combining do not do so in any proportions whatsoever; that combinations which are possible under certain temperature conditions are not in others; that elements which unite under ordinary circumstances will not unite in the presence of certain other elements. Consequently, when the idea of chemical affinity comes to be restated in the thought of the advanced student of the subject, it must be necessarily more definite and exact by reason of these very negative instances which have emerged in the course of his investigations.

Moreover, every negative judgment which possesses any value as knowledge must rest upon some positive ground. Mere denial of itself means nothing. For when pushed for a reason of our denial, we must be prepared to give some positive ground for the conviction that is in us. When we say, It will not rain to-night, our judgment rests upon our interpretation of the actual weather conditions. We venture the negative statement because we are positive concerning the significance of the present atmospheric conditions. And also, if we should say of a certain friend, He did not do the mean act of which he is accused, we rest such a denial upon our knowledge of his character, abundantly tested and proved by years of close companionship. If a person should affirm that he does not expect to be conditioned in a certain examination, and the only ground he could allege for his belief were merely the indefinite feeling that he would not fail, such an uncertain foundation would be absolutely worthless. A definite negation must have the ground of definite knowledge, or otherwise it has no force.

A distinction moreover is often drawn between significant and non-significant denial. Significant denial occurs within the region which lies near the line of differentiation between affirmation and negation. The non-significant denial occurs in the region remotely separated from this line of differentiation. Thus, to say that a chrysanthemum is not an animal would be a non-significant denial. But to say that one of the lower orders of animal such as that of the sea-anemone is not a chrysanthemum would be a significant denial, because it resembles the chrysanthemum in external appearance. There are so many marks in common that one may fail to recognize at the first glance the differentiating mark which separates the two cases.

Significant denial often carries with it also the implication that under certain changed conditions the relation or reference which is denied would become true. Thus the statement that water does not boil on the top of a mountain at 212°, implies that it would boil however at some other temperature. If we say that the elements, oxygen and hydrogen, will not unite in a one-to-one proportion, there is the implication that they will unite in some other proportion. Again the statement, that a certain man having made such a political blunder could not be nominated for governor, implies that had it not been for the political blunder in question, he might have been nominated for governor. A distinction however should be drawn between limiting conditions and conditions whose removal do not alter the force of the original denial. Thus in the statement, Do not trust the Greeks bearing gifts, the phrase "bearing gifts" is not a limiting condition, the removal of which would alter the statement at all. The meaning is, Do not trust the Greeks even though they bear gifts; that is, do not trust them at all. Likewise the statement, There are no ghosts in modern times, should not be interpreted as meaning that there were ghosts in ancient times. The nearer incompatible concepts approach a limit beyond which denial passes over into assertion the more significant does the denial become, and the greater the possible difference of opinion which may arise in reference to it. It is in the field immediately adjacent to the limiting cases that dispute arises. When I say that the American Beauty rose is not yellow, no one disputes such an assertion; and, moreover, there is no suggestion in this statement as to the real color of the American Beauty. But if I say that a certain shade of red does not match a given sample, the denial on my part may provoke a difference of opinion; and because the range of variation is so narrow, the implication is that the true color must be very near the one mentioned and within the region of the various shades of red.

If denial asserts an incompatibility between concepts which is absolute, — that is, if there is no common point of similarity at all between them, — the judgment is called an infinite negation. Such judgments being completely without significance are always nonsensical; *e.g.* A stone has no conscience. A triangle has no lungs. Between the limit on the one hand of the infinite negation, and on the other of the limiting case which separates denial from assertion, there are all grades of denial possible according to the order of their growing significance. Near the limit of assertion denial becomes the subject of dispute and controversy. Further removed the denial is unquestioned. Further still, it becomes a truism, a commonplace of knowledge, soon passing into the region of the grotesquely absurd and meaningless. To know just where assertion ends and where denial begins is characteristic of the exact mind; to know just where denial ceases to be significant is characteristic of the relevant mind.

CHAPTER IX

THE CATEGORICAL, HYPOTHETICAL, AND DISJUNCTIVE JUDGMENTS

THERE are three forms which our judgments may take, — the categorical, hypothetical, and disjunctive.

The categorical judgment is assertion in its simplest form, unconditioned, unanalyzed, and unexplained; *e.g.* That man is a half-breed; whales are mammals. It expresses either a fact, or else a generalization based upon a number of facts.

The hypothetical judgment is an assertion subject to a given limitation, or regarded under certain specified conditions. It does not refer to a concrete special case, but rather to the abstract universal relations which form the ground of all the possible special cases which may be conditioned by the relations; *e.g.* If in an isosceles triangle a line is drawn from the apex perpendicular to the base, it will bisect it; if hydrogen, oxygen, and sulphur unite in the proportions H_2SO_4, they will form sulphuric acid.

Our knowledge, it must be remembered, forms a system of interrelated parts. The hypothetical judgment is concerned essentially with the necessary connections which obtain between these various elements. It asserts the fundamental relations which exist between any ground and its consequence. In our body of knowledge regarded as a system, the hypothetical judgments constitute the basal lines of construction; by them part is related to part, and part to the whole.

The disjunctive judgment is an indeterminate assertion concerning various possibilities which may exist in reference to a given subject, and which are of such a nature that the establishment of the truth of any one necessarily excludes the others; *e.g.* The invading fleet may attack Newport, Cape Cod, or Gloucester. One may travel from New York to Philadelphia by the Reading, or the Pennsylvania railroads.

We have divided all judgments into two general types, — the singular judgment and the universal. Of these, the singular judgment is naturally categorical, for it is an assertion concerning a fact or a group of facts. If the categorical is changed in form so as to make it a hypothetical, this is done by reason of a universal hypothetical judgment of which the singular hypothetical judgment in question is merely a special case, and therefore the hypothetical nature is due to the universal relation which is assumed as underlying it. Thus in the judgment, If this substance is an acid, it will turn blue litmus paper red, we see that the hypothetical relation expressed concerning the special case is merely a single instance of a relation which holds universally. It is only in this indirect manner that a hypothetical judgment can apply to a special case. The hypothetical is essentially a mode of expressing universal relations. There are two cases in which the hypothetical form of judgment is naturally used.

1. When we wish to express the necessary connection of cause and effect between any given elements in a system of related parts, *e.g.* If you double the pressure, you halve the volume of gases.

2. When we wish to express a more exact differentiation of our concepts by means of a reference to their specific differences, *e.g.* If a triangle has two of its sides equal, it is an isosceles triangle. The hypothetical form is used also when the differentiating mark cannot be regarded as of the essence of the concept in question, and even when it is absolutely arbitrary, provided only it serves to point out unmistakably the concept in question. Thus the signal of Paul

Revere was in this form, If the enemy come by land, there will be a single light in the belfry; if by sea, two lights.

The essential function of the hypothetical is to show this relation of dependence of any one element upon another in a system of interrelated and coördinated parts. The system itself may be one of nature, or one arbitrarily assumed or agreed upon by mutual consent, or of common convention. The main thing is that the system should be of such a nature as to render the connection which constitutes the hypothetical relation absolutely uniform and necessary.

It is of course possible to change any categorical judgment of the universal form into a hypothetical. Thus, All crows are black, may be put into the form, If there is a crow, it is black. The hypothetical in this case is however not the natural form of expression, and the reason is that in such a judgment the necessary connection of ground and consequent is not brought to the fore. There must be in the very constitution of the crow a sufficient ground for its customary color; nevertheless its precise nature is unknown and lies in the background of the simple assertion itself. It can be said therefore in general that when a universal judgment presents an unanalyzed content, it takes the categorical form; when however the content is analyzed so as to exhibit within it the connection of ground and consequent, then it takes the hypothetical form.

Again, the disjunctive judgment naturally expresses a universal relation. When it refers, as it often does, to a special case, the disjunction is really based upon our knowledge of general conditions. When we say, for instance, that a certain line must be equal to, greater than, or less than some other given line, we do so because we know that any line whatsoever must be equal to, greater than, or less than any other given line. So also a physician may pronounce a suspicious case of sore throat to be either scarlet fever or diphtheria. His judgment in this case is grounded wholly upon his knowledge of such cases in general. Therefore, although the disjunctive judgment may in form deal with a single instance, it always contains by implication a reference to the universal conditions which are illustrated in the special case.

The disjunctive judgment, moreover, contains both a categorical and a hypothetical element. It is categorical inasmuch as it asserts a definite area of possibility. It is hypothetical inasmuch as the possibilities are related in such a manner that if any one is true, the others are false, and if any one is false, one of the others must be true. Such a hypothetical implication renders the disjunctive judgment significant; otherwise it would be without meaning. To illustrate this, let us examine the following disjunctive judgment, A certain murder was committed by an enemy or by a burglar. The categorical element in this assertion limits the possibilities to the two alternatives mentioned, and excludes suicide or any other possibility. The hypothetical element lies in the implication that if either one of the possibilities is proved, it negatives the other.

Moreover, the categorical, disjunctive, and hypothetical judgments may be regarded as various stages in the progress of knowledge from that which is indefinite and indeterminate to that which is definite and determinate.

The categorical judgment represents the primary stage of vague assertion, wherein the conditions upon which the asserted fact depends have not been fully analyzed.

The disjunctive is a statement of the various antecedents which may have given rise to the given fact.

The hypothetical is the critical analysis of these various antecedents, and the determination of that particular one which bears an essential and necessary relation to the fact in question.

All knowledge necessarily begins with a vague assertion. The very fact that it is a beginning renders the assertion vague. We hear, for instance, that a man has died suddenly under suspicious circumstances. Our first statement is merely that a murder has been committed. A closer examination of the surroundings will suggest various possibilities by way of explanation. We settle finally upon the definite conviction that the murder was committed by an enemy; because we know that the dead man had an enemy who had repeatedly threatened to take his life, and we have therefore the general hypothetical principle to guide us, that if a man has an enemy who has repeatedly threatened to take his life, that man's murder may be presumably traced to this as its explanation, provided there are no other guiding indications. Or if the question should be raised as to which one of several possible species is referred to in any given instance, then we have a series of significant hypotheticals to assist us in the exact determination. We may have the disjunctive statement that whales are either sperm whales or right whales. This is more precisely determined in our body of general knowledge by means of the two hypotheticals: if the whale does not have in its mouth baleen or whalebone, it is a sperm whale; but if it has baleen in its mouth, it is a right whale.

The process of the exact determination of a disjunctive judgment may be effected through a series of negative judgments as well as positive. Instead of determining any one member of a disjunction positively, by discovering its differentia or necessary condition, we may reach a like result by a process of elimination. If we have given several possible explanations of a certain situation we may examine each in turn and prove it to be impossible, and so narrow the range by successive elimination until one only is left. Negation becomes especially significant when there are but two possibilities in reference to any given situation. The elimination of either one leaves the other in full possession of the field. Thus, if in the case of a murdered man it can be proved negatively that he never had an enemy, and that there was no one who would have sought his life through hatred or because of an injury received, we are then forced to the explanation that the man was murdered by a burglar or some one other than an enemy. This process of elimination by negation is trustworthy so far as we are sure that the negative judgment is true, and that also we have completely embraced all possibilities in our disjunction.

We have seen that every process of judgment consists in establishing a unity of some kind among the elements of our thought. Now this unifying bond in judgment admits of a certain degree of variability, being more or less definite in nature. Its degree of variability determines what is known as the modality of judgments.

If this unifying bond is actual, the judgment is known as an assertorical judgment. If the judgment expresses a possible relation only, it is a problematical judgment. If the judgment expresses a necessary relation, — that is, where the unifying bond expresses not merely that which is but that which must be, — the judgment is known as apodeictic.

The categorical judgment naturally takes the assertorical form, e.g. x is y.

The disjunctive judgment naturally takes the problematical form; e.g. x may be y, or z, or w.

The hypothetical judgment naturally take the apodeictic form, e.g. If x is y, then z must be w.

There may, however, be a change of modality as regards any one of the forms of judgment, — categorical, disjunctive, or hypothetical. Thus the categorical judgment will be found in the various forms as follows: x is y, x may be y, x must be y. The first of these is the natural way of expressing the categorical; for the form, x may be y, implies other possibilities, and at least the negative possibility that x may not be y. Therefore the problematical mode of the judgment is to be regarded as implying a disjunctive. Moreover, the categorical form, x must be y, implies a hypothetical judgment as its basis, for the assertion of necessity naturally implies some knowledge of the fundamental relation of ground and consequent which underlies such necessity. Thus each phase of modality has its own natural form of expression; the assertorical expressing itself in the categorical judgment, the problematical in the disjunctive, and the apodeictic in the hypothetical.

CHAPTER X

THE NATURE OF INFERENCE

The nature of inference may be unfolded in two ways. We may consider what it is in its outward aspect; that is, through its phenomenal manifestation in what it effects; or it may be more strictly defined in terms of its warrant or ground. From the first point of view we examine inference as regards its psychological significance; that is, what is inference considered as a psychical experience, its nature, and characteristics? But we must consider also the second question, — whether there is any necessity limiting and determining the subjective experience, which presents the character of a law having universal validity. What goes on in the mind during the process of inference? Also, what is the rationale of such a process? These questions we will examine more closely, in order to show the nature of inference under the two aspects, the one psychological and the other logical.

It is a well-recognized fact in psychology that, in our simplest as well as the more complex perceptions, the interpretation of the data of perception always goes beyond the strict content of the data themselves. We see more than is given in the field of vision immediately before us. The mind supplies here and there the necessary parts that are lacking in the actual elements of perception, and yet which are necessitated by the known nature of that which is actually given. We form our judgment of distance indirectly, and not through direct observation. So, also, our idea of a third dimension is acquired by a process, marvellously complex, in which the data both indicate and yet are transcended by the results. Whether the nativist or empiricist holds the true position concerning original psychical experience, it still must be conceded according to either theory that the development of our perceptions corresponds to a law of growth based upon accumulated inferences. Inference has been defined as the indirect reference of a content to reality, and as such we see the beginnings of inference in the most simple of our perceptions. Every perception contains a direct reference to reality, but also something which in a greater or less degree is referred indirectly to reality. The fact that our knowledge as given in the complete perception contains more than is actually mediated through the avenues of the senses is due to the apperceptive processes of consciousness. Mind is active in perception, and not a mere passive receptacle. That which is given, the raw material of the senses, is elaborated and extended, as it is combined with the wealth of representative and conceptual material, which the mind brings to every new perception. To this extent, at least, the mind possesses a creative function. A certain appearance of sky, combined with peculiar conditions of wind and temperature, leads one to assert, with some degree of certitude, that it will rain before morning. The prediction is an inference based upon and growing out of the actual data of perception, and yet far outrunning them. We recognize a friend from his step or voice. The mere perception is only a sound. That it is associated with a person, and not an animal, or a thing, is an inference; that it is the particular person whom we recognize as a friend and can call by name, even before we turn around to confirm the opinion by direct testimony of vision, this is a still further inference. And even when we open our eyes in simple vision itself, we fill up many a gap in our minds, and give depth and distance, and interpret the contrasts of light and shade, and the play of colors, through the process of inference, although we may not be aware of the process itself, which is automatically operative through long-continued habit. When we thus regard inference as a psychological phenomenon, it may be readily explained by the laws of comparison, association, recognition, generalization, etc. And, as such, inference has a subjective force, at least, and leads to the habit of prediction and expectation. The will, influenced by the resulting belief, leads to activities consistent with such expectation.

Here, however, the question arises which is urged with such force by Hume, Is there objective validity as well as subjective necessity? This leads to a consideration of inference, from the second point of view, above mentioned. We may be constrained to believe certain things concerning the great world lying beyond the sphere of immediate consciousness; but what warrant have we in so doing, or what assurance that our conclusions are correct? May we not be deceived, after all, and by some psychological trick be led to regard the phenomena of consciousness as quite otherwise than that which obtains in reality? We may have a strong aversion to sitting down at a table where the number of persons will be thirteen. But has the subjective conviction, that one of the thirteen will die in the course of the year, any value when we come to refer it to reality, and ask ourselves the nature of the ground upon which the conviction is based?

On the other hand however it is quite a different kind of necessity which constrains us to judge that if a person jumps off of the roof of a house, he must surely fall to the ground below. Some grossly superstitious and ignorant people may believe the former with as obstinate a conviction as the latter, so that a purely psychological criterion of the strength of conviction is not at all adequate or satisfactory. Is there any other criterion? In what instances does this subjective constraint proceed from the necessities of reality? or, in other words, in what cases are we able to discover a logically grounded warrant which compels the inference, in distinction from the mere psychological compulsion which is occasioned by the psychical tendencies of association and generalization?

This leads us to consider the logical, in distinction from the psychological nature of inference. Inasmuch as the characteristic feature of inference consists in this, that while depending upon certain data of perception, it nevertheless wholly transcends them, the question naturally suggests itself, whether it is something within the data themselves, or without, by virtue of which the mind thus goes beyond them in the process of inference. If it lies wholly without the data, it must be something imposed upon them by the mind, and as such can have only a psychological force and value. For instance, the belief that if thirteen sit down together at a table, one will die in the course of the year, can have only a subjective value and significance. This is true in all cases where the necessity of conviction finds its origin in prejudice or in superstition, or it may be in the force of authority. In all such instances we feel the lack of a satisfactory logical ground. However, on the other hand, if the data of consciousness contain within themselves that which enables us to transcend them at the same time that we interpret them, there is external validity for our inference that has a logical worth. This seems at the first glance to be a paradox. How can any content enable us to state concerning it more than is contained within it? The answer to the seeming paradox is that every concept, and every perception as well, have both an explicit and implicit content. We never attain complete vision or perfect apprehension.

There are, moreover, many points of view, each giving additional knowledge concerning any phenomenon present in consciousness. We see, therefore, only in part, and yet that which is seen contains certain necessary implications concerning that which is not seen. In the progress of knowledge, subsequent observations, different points of view, are ever confirming and amplifying our inferences, enabling us to perceive immediately what formerly was only inferred. The process by which the implicit is becoming explicit indicates a necessary relation existing between that which is known mediately and that which is known immediately. Moreover, consciousness has been represented as a stream, or an intricately interwoven web,— something extremely complex. Every part is related both proximately and remotely. There is no such thing as an isolated perception; every perception has its complex relations and connections. So also every concept which is formed by generalization through comparison and abstraction of our perceptions as interpreted by us, possesses this characteristic of greater or less complexity. In this manner the world of consciousness is constructed, that is, the world as it is for us. This forms a complex whole made up of parts, which in themselves may be regarded as wholes, and yet which may be still further divided and subdivided.

Such an interrelated whole we may style a system, or, in other words, a complex whole whose parts are congruently arranged. The idea of system finds expression in the "Law of Totality,"— that our knowledge is capable of arrangement in a self-consistent and harmonious system, and which moreover in its content and form faithfully represents objective reality.[1] We find, therefore, that in the focus of consciousness at any one time, whether in the sphere of perception or in the region of representative or the conceptual processes, whatever is given carries with it always certain implications, and therefore certain necessary relations. This is specially emphasized in Bosanquet's definition of system: "System is a group of relations, or properties, or things, so held together by a common nature that you can judge from some of them what the others must be."[2] Two facts regarded as independent and considered separately may give no information beyond their explicit contents; but when conjoined, they imply more than the sum of their parts.

[1] Ueberweg, *A System of Logic and History of Logical Doctrine*, pp. 540 f.
[2] Bosanquet, *The Essentials of Logic*, p. 140.

How often two ideas in separate minds yield no result; but brought together, they give light. Isolation negatives inference. To unfold whatever is given in all its manifold implications is the process of inference. Its warrant lies in the fundamental postulate of knowledge which we are constrained to assume; namely, that our consciousness must be self-consistent throughout. Whatever is admitted as true must find a congruent place in the system to which it is possible to refer it. The necessity of fitting it in its proper place gives rise to certain implications which necessitate corresponding relations and attributes. And if it could not be put into such a place, we would feel that we should have to surrender the idea of self-consistency in the variously related elements of our consciousness. The very integrity of our mental life necessitates this conviction.

Therefore a part being given, we supply in our minds other parts, or the whole to which the given part must necessarily belong. To achieve this, with logical warrant, our knowledge of the part must be adequate to the extent that we know that the element under consideration cannot be complete in itself, but must be supplemented by its appropriately related elements which with it go to make up the complete system. We infer the nature of the flower not yet in bud by the sprouting leaf. The one necessitates the other by virtue of their common inherence in the same plant system. We know that figs do not come from thorns nor grapes from thistles. Columbus, noting the seaweed, and birds, and the drift of the sea, inferred a shore beyond, to which he was constrained by the necessities of thought to refer them. It is said of Cuvier that he was able to reconstruct part for part the entire frame and organism of an animal whose fossil tooth alone formed the original datum. He knew the system to which it must have belonged and to which it alone could possibly be referred. An interesting quotation from Cuvier himself illustrates most appropriately this function of inference. He says, in his *Ossemens Fossiles:*

"I doubt if any one would have divined, if untaught by observation, that all ruminants have the foot cleft, and that they alone have it. I doubt if any one would have divined that there are frontal horns only in this class; that those among them which have sharp canines for the most part lack horns. However, since these relations are constant, they must have some sufficient cause; but since we are ignorant of it, we must make good the defect of the theory by means of observation: it enables us to establish empirical laws which become almost as certain as rational laws when they rest on sufficiently repeated observations; so that now whoso sees merely the print of a cleft foot may conclude that the animal that left this impression ruminated, and this conclusion is as certain as any other in physics or morals. This footprint alone, then, yields to him who observes it the form of the teeth, the form of the jaws, the form of the vertebræ, the form of all the bones of the legs, of the thighs, of the shoulders, and of the pelvis of the animal which has passed by."[1]

In the common conduct of everyday life we infer beyond the immediate present experience to future happenings and in a similar manner. My train is half an hour late. I know I must miss my connections at the station ahead; for the train I am hoping to catch at that place is scheduled to leave five minutes after the time of arrival of the train I am now on. The time relations here necessitate my missing my connections. This is rendered still more certain if they are rival roads; on no account will one wait for the other. Moreover, the train I hope to make is made up and leaves the station in question, and so I cannot fall back upon the favoring chance that it also may be detained en route, and so enable me, after all, to reach it in time. Thus, with every additional knowledge of the system which forms the ground of my inference, and the various conditions which affect it, the validity of my inference is thereby increased.

[1] Quoted by Jevons, *Principles of Science*, 2d ed., p. 683.

Inference regarded as the analysis of a system of interrelated parts is illustrated in the following paragraph of Professor James: "The result of reasoning may be hit upon by accident. Cats have been known to open doors by pulling latches, etc. But no cat, if the latch got out of order, could open the door again, unless some new accident at random fumbling taught her to associate some new total movement with the total phenomenon of the closed door. A reasoning man, however, would open the door by first analyzing the hindrance. He would ascertain what particular feature of the door is wrong. The lever, *e.g.*, does not raise the latch sufficiently from its slot — case of insufficient elevation — raise door bodily on hinges! Or door sticks at top by friction against lintel — press it bodily down! I have a student's lamp of which the flame vibrates most unpleasantly unless the collar which bears the chimney be raised about a sixteenth of an inch. I learned the remedy after much torment, by accident, and now always keep the collar up with a small wedge. But my procedure is a mere association of two totals, diseased object and remedy. One learned in pneumatics could have named the *cause* of the disease and then inferred the remedy immediately."[1]

Inference, therefore, may be regarded as a deep penetrating insight. The explicit is that which lies upon the surface, which the mind immediately grasps, for it lies directly in the focus of consciousness. Whereas the implicit is beneath the surface, and is revealed only through a searching analysis. This difference may be exhibited through the distinction between the actual and the potential. A child regards gunpowder merely as a pile of coarse-grained sand. The man sees what the child sees, but also the existing possibilities under certain conditions of explosive force. He apprehends the potential as well as the actual; and his inference as to the possible results is based upon his superior insight. It is therefore the well-furnished mind which sees things

[1] James, *Psychology*, Vol. II, pp. 339, 340.

as most widely related, and discerns the potential as well as the actual manifestation, which will prove the most fertile in accurate inference, in prophetic suggestion, and in inventive resource.

The whole world of reality, as well as that of knowledge, may be considered as one system, embracing within the unity of its totality all the various systems with their complicated parts. From this point of view everything sustains relations to everything else in the universe. The original signification of the term universe is thus emphasized. This thought, no doubt, Tennyson had in mind in the following verse: —

> Flower in the crannied wall,
> I pluck you out of the crannies,
> I hold you here, root and all, in my hand,
> Little flower — but *if* I could understand
> What you are, root and all, and all in all,
> I should know what God and man is.

We can, in this connection, best exhibit the precise nature and function of the universal in inference. The possibility of unfolding the properties or relations of anything in all its implications depends upon our knowledge of the universal concept to which the properties or relations in question are naturally referred. While a singular proposition is the statement of the mere occurrence of a phenomenon, the universal always implies a knowledge of the conditions and relations of the phenomenon.[1] Insight is only possible where there is a wealth of universal concepts. We see an animal which we observe to be cloven-footed. We infer that it also chews its cud. We do not observe this. The assertion does not arise directly from observed reality, but indirectly through the generic concept that has grasped together the two attributes, of chewing the cud and cloven feet as always and necessarily coexisting in one and the same animal. Inference, in this sense, may be regarded

[1] See Green, *Philosophical Works*, Vol. II, pp. 284, 285.

as the indirect reference of knowledge to reality, and this is always mediated through the universal. The universal has this characteristic feature, that it preserves an identity in the midst of manifold differences. The same thought may be expressed by saying that the universal manifests a unity in the midst of diversity. However widely different, in many respects, the animals may appear that chew the cud, — as the cow, deer, sheep, etc., — there is always the constant characteristic that they are cloven-footed.

Such a point of identity furnishes the constant factor which determines the nature and the validity of the inference. Were it not for this conceptual power of the mind, this ability to grasp phenomena in their universal essence, and consider them as interrelated and connected, we could never pass beyond individual and particular experiences which would form a series of wholly disconnected events. Knowledge could not then form a self-consistent system, or inference possess any higher worth than a haphazard guess. As Green says, "A 'mere fact,' a fact apart from relations which are not sensible, would be no fact, would have no nature, would not admit of anything being known or said about it."[1]

Moreover, inference is not merely employed to extend the field of consciousness in unfolding supplementary elements lying beyond the sphere of direct cognition; the elements may all be given immediately, and inference employed to discover their connection and interrelations, and by virtue of what bond they belong in one or the same system. Inference here functions as explanation. A man is found dead; there are many wounds upon his person, and evidences of a struggle in an out-of-the-way place upon a lonely road. Such a combination of facts calls for an explanation which shall be consistent with them. The facts must all be correlated in a system whose related facts and the unity of the whole will completely satisfy the mind. The mind

[1] Green, *Philosophical Works*, Vol. II, p. 301.

is satisfied only when all hang together in what seems the only possible self-consistent coördinated system. The facts being given, they must be read backward to their origin. The other aspect of inference is the reading of facts forwards, or unfolding them in their necessary consequences. Inference is the reply to the natural questions of the mind, — whence and whither? And the process is essentially the same, whether its peculiar mode consists in the evolution or the involution of that which is given in consciousness.

Moreover, the mere psychological inference, the subjective extension of the data of consciousness without any objective ground or warrant, should ever be corrected, or even at times wholly set aside by means of the truly logical inference. Where the psychological experience, in transcending simple presentation, proceeds upon strictly logical grounds, and has objective validity as well as subjective necessity, we possess a warrant of the highest possible worth.

The relation of the process of inference to that of judgment may be expressed in the following definition that inference is a judgment plus the reason for it. Whenever the reason for a judgment is obvious, the inferential element falls into the background. The judgment then appears merely as a restatement of a well-known truth which no one would think of gainsaying, or as the result of referring a familiar object of perception to its generally recognized concept. But if the averred truth is challenged, or if the reference of the perceived object is not clear, then in order to make good the judgment, recourse must be had to some phase of the inferential process. We have the accepted judgment that lightning is a form of electrical discharge. Such a statement commands assent without question. But when Franklin proved the identity of these two phenomena, it was by a process of inference in which it was necessary to establish the common ground of these two phenomena. If one should point to a bird circling above a field in majestic lines of flight, and say, "That is an eagle," the observation would probably receive immediate assent. It would pass then as an obvious judgment of perception.

If, however, the statement should meet with dissent, or an opposed judgment should be urged that it is a crow, then the inferential element revealing the necessary ground of the judgment would at once come to the fore. It would be possible to point out that the flight of the bird is so characteristically the flight of an eagle that it could not be mistaken or confused with that of a crow. It will be readily seen that the inferential element is contained potentially in every judgment. A direct assertion, received without question, is the judgment in its simplest form. An indirect statement, showing that it must be true because of its necessary connection with some other judgment, is an inferred judgment. In the light of this distinction the difference between judgment and inference may be defined as follows:—

The judgment is a direct reference of a concept to reality.

The inference is an indirect reference of a concept to reality.

The differentiating line is evidently a variable one. Its variability depends upon the presence or absence of any occasion which demands a fuller explication of the ground of a judgment. As long as the ground is obvious and the judgment unchallenged, it is not necessary to offer any proof of it. If however it is necessary for any reason to give an explicit statement of the ground underlying a judgment, then at once the inferential element passes from its potential stage into its developed form as actually expressed. It is often the opposition of a negative judgment which provokes the inferential process underlying some positive assertion.

Inference may be deductive or inductive. It is deductive when the process shows that from a universal principle or law there must follow some special case, or some more special phase of that principle or law. It is inductive when the process shows that a general principle or law must result from the investigation of special cases.

When we reason that a man's conduct under certain given circumstances will be honorable or dishonorable, as the case may be, our inference is based upon our general knowledge of the man's character, and the inferential process is one of deduction. When however we reason that a man must have a certain kind of character in the light of a number of particular instances which we have observed, our inference is based upon our interpretation of these special cases as revealing an underlying universal nature which we call the man's character. Such a process is one of induction.[1]

[1] See Part II, Chapter I, on "Deduction and Induction."

CHAPTER XI

THE LAWS OF THOUGHT

In order that we may be able to justify our judgments and relate them to each other and to the main body of our knowledge, we must recognize certain fundamental and universal principles known in logic as the laws of thought. These laws are as follows: —

1. The Law of Identity.
2. The Law of Contradiction.
3. The Law of Excluded Middle.
4. The Law of Sufficient Reason.

1. The law of identity requires every concept to represent some phase of reality which remains essentially the same. This does not mean an identity which admits of no variety; for we have seen that it is of the very nature of the concept to manifest many shades of difference within the variety of special cases which illustrate it. It does mean however that in spite of manifold differences, there is a central core of essential identity which remains constant and unaffected by the various unessential changes. This law has been formulated in the simple expression $A = A$. Such an expression is true but meaningless, and were the law of identity restricted to such an expression of it, there could be no progress in thought, for every judgment would be a mere tautology lacking any significance whatever. The law would be more exactly formulated by the expressions $A = A' = A'' = A'''$, etc.; that is, every variety of A is nevertheless A, or every special case of A is the same as every other special case of A in spite of all differ-

ences. This law therefore is merely the expression of the unity which is the ground of all our judgments. Inasmuch as inference has been defined as the reference of a judgment to its proper ground, then this law, regarded as a law of inference, demands that such ground must be something abiding, no matter what variety of form it may assume. If the ground to which we refer a judgment in the process of inference is uncertain and shifting, then the inference itself is invalidated. Every inference therefore requires as its ground a relation which is constant, that is, identical with itself.

This abiding ground which gives validity to our inference may be either (1) a single thing or person whose self-identity is obviously preserved, or (2) it may be a universal whose very nature is such that it preserves a unity in spite of the manifold differences in the various instances which illustrate it. As an example of inference wherein the identity is that of a single person there is the story of Thackeray's of the old Abbé, who, one day conversing with a party of intimate friends, chanced to say, "A priest has strange experiences; why, my first penitent was a murderer." At this moment, the principal nobleman of the neighborhood enters the room. "Ah, Abbé! here you are; do you know, ladies, I was the Abbé's first penitent, and I promise you my confession astonished him!" The two statements of the Abbé and the nobleman become significant solely because of their identity of reference to one and the same individual.[1] Again in the case wherein the identical ground is not an individual but is a universal, a statement might be made that a certain cloth will fade. When asked for a reason, the reply might be, because that cloth contains a dye which always does fade. It is evident that the validity of such an inference depends upon the constant nature of the peculiar kind of dye in question. The showing of a universal property of the dye, such as that of fading,

[1] This illustration is taken from Bosanquet's *Essentials of Logic*, p. 140.

forms in this case the justifying ground of the inference that the cloth containing the dye will fade. A true universal assures an identical ground, and therefore the possibility of a constant reference as completely as does a single individual.

2. The law of contradiction is that judgments which are opposed to each other (as this is a, and this is not a; or a is b, a is not b) cannot both be true. The truth of either one renders the other false. This is essentially the axiom of consistency. It serves to buttress the law of identity. The latter demands the preservation of a unity in spite of differences. The law of contradiction draws a line of limitation as a boundary to these differences. Beyond such a line, the differences contradict the underlying unity which must be preserved in accordance with the law of identity. It prevents the reference of incompatible properties to one and the same subject at the same time and in the same sense.

The law of contradiction applies to judgments which are opposed in a contrary as well as a contradictory manner. The contradictory, it will be remembered, is the general term for the total area of negation lying outside the defining boundary of the positive term to which it is opposed. The contrary is any special case of the contradictory which may be designated by a part of the area of total negation. The judgments a is b, a is not b, are contradictorily opposed. The judgments a is b, a is c, are contrarily opposed whenever c is any property incompatible with b. To such judgments the law of contradiction also applies; if it is true that a is b, then the statement that a is c must be false.

We have seen that a bare denial as in contradictory opposition is not significant, and that significant denial rests upon the knowledge of some property or relation which is contrary to the alleged assertion which it opposes. Most of our denials, therefore, are contrary rather than contradictory. Inconsistencies arise in thought more often by the endeavor to unite properties slightly contrary than those wholly contradictory. Controversies which take the form, It is, It isn't, and are conducted by continued reiteration of bare assertion and denial, are always meaningless and futile. If a statement is made that a certain ore is gold, we may deny it merely by saying it is not. This is contradictory opposition. We may say also, It is iron pyrites, *i.e.* a special case of that which is not gold. The denial is significant and represents contrary opposition. The law of contradiction applies equally to the two cases. If the statement, It is gold, is true, then both of the following statements are negatived: It is not gold; also it is iron pyrites.

3. The law of excluded middle is, that between two judgments contradictorily opposed there is no middle or third judgment which is true. One or the other of the two given judgments must be true. This law, however, does not apply to judgments which express contrary opposition, for it is of the very nature of contraries that there is middle ground between the extremes which they represent. Both statements, x is greater than y, x is less than y, may be false, because of the middle possibility $x=y$. However, contrary statements in the light of special circumstances which render them an exhaustive disjunction come under the law of excluded middle, *e.g.* He had either to jump from the window, or perish in the flames. The circumstances were such as to leave no other course open. A contrary relation within a limited universe of discourse thus ranks as a contradictory relation because the limitation of the area of relevant subject-matter cuts out a middle ground which in an unlimited universe of thought might otherwise appear. Much of the loose thinking, especially in untrained and unreflecting minds, arises from the careless assumption of contradictory alternatives, when in reality they are merely contrary. The middle ground is overlooked, and logical confusion inevitably results. The law of excluded middle always secures an exhaustive

disjunction, and therefore renders a negative statement significant inasmuch as the other and opposed alternative is then necessarily true.

4. The law of sufficient reason is that every judgment must be based upon some satisfactory ground which fully justifies it. This law was first formulated by Leibniz (1646), and placed by him side by side with the law of contradiction. It is so intimately associated with the great philosopher that it would be worth while to have his own statement of it. "Our intellectual inferences rest on two great principles: the principle of contradiction, and the principle of sufficient reason, in virtue of which we know that no fact can be found real, no proposition true, without a sufficient reason why it is in this way rather than in another." This law is essentially the statement of the fundamental logical basis upon which all inference rests, namely, that our knowledge forms a system of inter-related and coördinated parts, and that any single element can be determined only when its relation is known to some other element or elements upon which it depends. It is a law which recognizes a reciprocal dependence of part to part throughout the entire body of knowledge. It is a corollary of this law that every judgment contains a potential inference; for every judgment is true in so far as it is based upon a sufficient ground, and to render explicit the ground upon which it rests is itself the process of inference.

In these four laws we find that certain logical demands are made to which all processes of thought must adhere. The law of identity demands a basis of constant reference; the law of contradiction, that of consistent treatment; the law of excluded middle, that of an exhaustive survey of possibilities; and the law of sufficient reason, that of adequate explanation. There are many rules which are given for guidance in the various processes of inference, which, however, are merely adaptations of some one or other of the several phases of these four fundamental principles.

CHAPTER XII

IMMEDIATE INFERENCE

In the traditional logic the distinction is drawn between immediate and mediate inference, the former being the direct reference of a judgment to its ground, the latter the indirect reference of a judgment to its ground through the medium of one or more intervening judgments. Such a distinction, however, will not hold. All inference is indirect. Indeed inference is defined as the *indirect* reference of a concept to reality. The difference between the so-called immediate and mediate inference is rather one of degree.

In the immediate inference from a given proposition in the form, All x is y, to the derived proposition, Some x is y, the process is not as direct as it seems. It assumes, tacitly at least, another mediating judgment that whatever is true of a class generically is true of every member of the class,— the old Aristotelian *dictum*. Such a judgment as this, however, is so obvious that it falls into the background, and the inference seems to be immediate. Immediate inference, therefore, may be regarded as an abbreviated form of inference in general. The term "immediate reference," however, in the history of logic, is not applied to any inference whatever which employs an obvious mediating judgment, but it is restricted to certain definite aspects of inference dependent upon general considerations of a self-evident character. These considerations give rise to two well-defined types of immediate inference according as the process is one of implication or transformation.

1. The process of implication depends upon the fundamental relations which exist between "all" and "some" and

between "yes" and "no"; that is, if we have a judgment, for instance, in the form of a universal affirmation, all are, what is implied in reference to the particular affirmation, some are, or the universal negative, none are, or the particular negative, some are not? The possible combinations which we are able to make with the terms, "all," "some," "none," "some not," give us four distinct types of judgment which for convenience of reference are designated by the four vowels A, E, I, and O as follows:—

$A =$ The Universal Affirmative; All x is y.
$E =$ The Universal Negative; No x is y.
$I =$ The Particular Affirmative; Some x is y.
$O =$ The Particular Negative; Some x is not y.

Judgments which differ as universal and particular are said to differ in quantity; those which differ as affirmative and negative are said to differ in quality. It will be seen that the question of the various implications involved in the relations which these several kinds of judgment sustain to one another, is a general question which has to do with the significance of the forms which all our judgments assume, whatever may be their content; for any judgment concerning any object of knowledge must be put in one or another of these four forms.

Now if a judgment in any one of these four forms is given as true, certain necessary implications will follow in reference to the other three. Likewise, if any judgment is given as false, certain necessary implications will follow.

In order to exhibit these relations in as clear a manner as possible, Aristotle devised the scheme of placing the four kinds of judgment each at a corner of a square, known as the Aristotelian square, or the square of opposition. The latter term is misleading, however, as all the relations are not opposed, but only those obtaining between affirmation and negation. A better term, which covers all the possible relations, is implication. The judgments are arranged about the square so that the universals are above, the particulars beneath, the affirmatives at the left, and the negatives at the right. This arrangement will give us the following: —

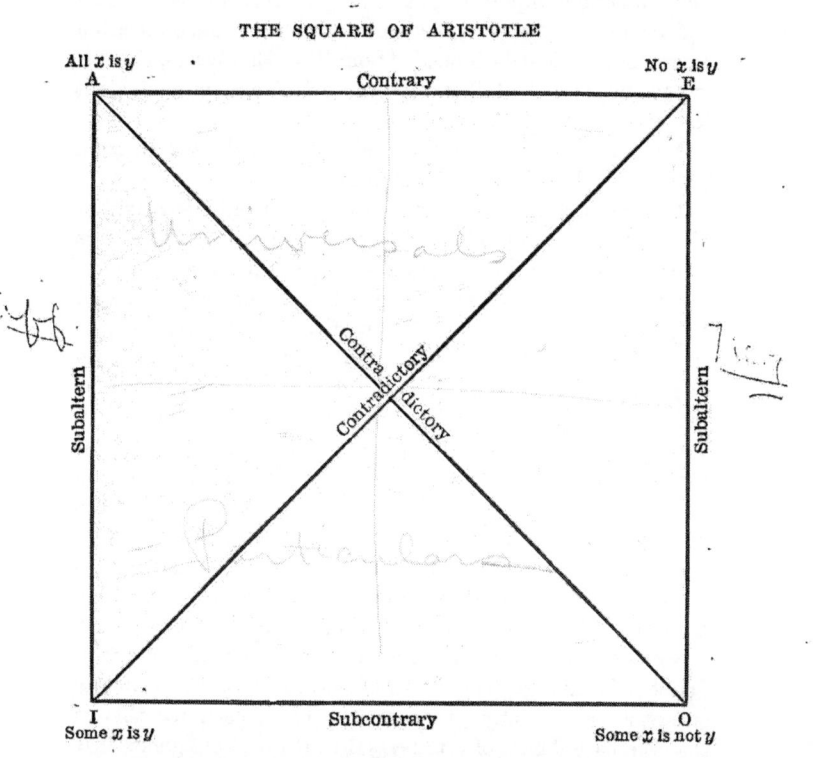

THE SQUARE OF ARISTOTLE

```
All x is y                  Contrary                   No x is y
    A                                                      E



       Subaltern                              Subaltern

                         Contradictory
                         Contradictory




    I                     Subcontrary                      O
Some x is y                                        Some x is not y
```

In the above, the word "some" is to be regarded as equivalent to "some at least." In the proposition, Some x is y, there is no indication, as far as the bare form is concerned, whether it may not also be true that All x is y, or, on the other hand, that Some x is not y. "Some," used in this sense, is the "some" of preliminary investigation, wherein a connection has been established between x and y, but the investigation is not fully complete. Upon further research, it may be that exceptions will be found which might render a generalization impossible, or it may be that the connection can be so firmly established as to admit of a generalization as regards its logical force. "Some," in this sense, lies between the terms "all" and "some only," and is equivalent to "some at least."

Now, as regards the various relations which this diagram illustrates, there are the following: —

1. The subaltern relation between the universal (either affirmative or negative) and its corresponding particular is so called because the particular is regarded as being subordinated to the universal. The relation between universal and particular is such that if the universal is true, the particular is true also; but if the particular is true, the truth of the universal is left in doubt. The truth of a particular judgment, as based upon the truth of the corresponding universal, follows from our fundamental law of identity, that the universal preserves its essential unity in all the particular forms of its manifestation. The indeterminateness of the universal, when the particular is given as true, is due to the possibility that the connection expressed by the particular judgment in question may be accidental, and therefore not a part of the essential content of the species as a whole.

Moreover, if the universal is false, the particular is left in doubt. It may be true or false, according to the concrete circumstances in any given case. The reason for this is that the bare denial of a universal is always ambiguous. It may be a total denial by confronting it with the opposite universal, or it may be a partial denial by pointing out exceptions to it; which, of course, render the affirmed universality false. But the falsity of a particular renders its corresponding universal false; for, if the particular statement is not true, much less will be the universal, which embraces the particular under it.

2. The contrary relation between A and E propositions is such that if either of the related judgments is true, the other

must be false, but if either is false, the other is indeterminate. For it is obvious that between "all" and "none" there is middle ground, and therefore they are related as contraries; and it is the nature of the contrary relation that, according to the law of contradiction, the truth of one renders the other false; and, as there is middle ground between them, the law of excluded middle does not apply, and therefore the fact that one is false merely leaves the other indeterminate.

3. The subcontrary relation between I and O is the inverse of the contrary. Here the falsity of either renders the other true, but the truth of either leaves the other indeterminate. This is perhaps more difficult to see. It should be remembered that "some" = "some at least." Now, if it is false that Some x is y, it must be true that Some x (at least) is not y, which latter statement is not incompatible with the fuller statement that No x is y, for it is merely a special case under it. But if it is true that Some x (at least) is y, we have seen that by the very significance of "some" thus interpreted, the question as to whether there may be exceptions expressed in the form Some x is not y is left in doubt.

4. The contradictory relations between A and O and between E and I are such that if either is true, the other is false, and if either is false, the other is true. This follows directly from the law of excluded middle. That the propositions, All x is y, and Some x is not y, have no middle ground between them is evident. It may be put in this way: if a judgment is always true, it admits of no exceptions, and if it has exceptions, it is not always true; if a judgment is not always true, it must have exceptions, and if it does not have exceptions, it must be always true.

These relations may be summarized as follows:—

1. Given A true, then I is true, the others false.
2. Given E true, then O is true, the others false.
3. Given A false, then O is true, the others unknown.

4. Given *E* false, then *I* is true, the others unknown.
5. Given *I* true, then *E* is false, the others unknown.
6. Given *O* true, then *A* is false, the others unknown.
7. Given *I* false, then *A* is false, the others true.
8. Given *O* false, then *E* is false, the others true.

These eight statements may be still further condensed as follows:—

I. Given *A* or *E* true, *I* or *O* false, the corresponding subaltern is the same, the others opposite.

II. Given *A* or *E* false, *I* or *O* true, the corresponding contradictory is opposite, the others unknown.

There are two practical suggestions which emerge from these dry symbols, which may prove not only interesting but also of some value. (1) The one is that the trend of logical thought is always from the universal to the particular, from "all" to "some," and that procedure in the opposite direction is one of the most fertile sources of error in thinking. It is the well-known fallacy of hasty generalization, namely, the collecting of a few instances of experience and immediately raising them to the rank of a universal. There is no procedure of thought which needs to be so carefully safeguarded as that from "some" to "all." (2) Again there is the principle which I would call, the economy of refutation. It is this: Whenever in discussion or debate a universal judgment is advanced, do not attempt to controvert it by the opposite universal, but rather by the opposite particular. There will be less difficulty in proving a particular, and thus a strategic point of advantage will be gained. If a proposition is advanced in the form All *x* is *y*, to refute it, it is only necessary to prove essential exceptions in the form of Some *x* is not *y*. Thus in the Harvard-Princeton debate in 1896, the question was, Resolved that Congress should take measures to retire all the legal tender notes. Princeton maintained the affirmative. Harvard's attack upon this position was not, as might have been expected, a universal negative, — namely, that no legal tender notes should be retired by Congress, — but a particular negative, that not all but only some should be retired. It is a useful rule to remember in debate, — never attempt to prove more than is necessary to overthrow your opponent's main contention.

CHAPTER XIII

ON TRANSFORMATIONS OF JUDGMENT FORMS

THE different forms of judgment may be subjected to various changes, some of which give slightly new shades of meaning, without however altering the logical force of the judgment itself. The original judgment and its transformation must be logically compatible. This is the criterion by which all transformations are to be tested. These transformations may be produced in various ways: by an interchange of subject and predicate; by a change in the quantity or quality[1] of the judgment; by the change of a term to its contradictory; or by certain complex changes involving all of these.

The interchange of subject and predicate is called the Conversion of a proposition.

If it is a proposition of the A form, All x is y, its simple conversion will give All y is x. This, however, alters the logical force of the original proposition; for, if we have given the form All x is y, it may be that the predicate y is the common mark of a number of species besides x, such as x, z, w, etc. Therefore, y is not a distinctive mark of x at all, and it does not follow that because All x is y, therefore All y is x. In the conversion of an A proposition the universal force is lost, and only a particular is possible. Thus All x is y becomes Some y is x. This is called conversion by limitation, or *conversio per accidens*.

With the universal negative, however, No x is y, a simple conversion is possible, because the negative asserts a complete incompatibility of x and y, and such being the case, it is a matter of indifference whether we say that x cannot be

[1] See page 104.

fused into any unity with y, or that y cannot be fused into any unity with x. Thus No x is y becomes by conversion No y is x.

With the particular affirmative form, Some x is y, a simple conversion into Some y is x is also possible, because if some x forms a unity with y, some y at least must be present with x to constitute that unity. Thus Some x is y becomes, by conversion, Some y is x.

But with the particular negative, Some x is not y, the simple conversion Some y is not x does not necessarily follow; for the subject y may represent a species and the predicate x its corresponding genus. Obviously, Some y is not x will be false, for the species must fall wholly within its corresponding genus. Thus if we have a judgment of this kind such as, Some reptiles are not snakes, and convert it, we get Some snakes are not reptiles, which is obviously false. Thus a particular negative cannot be converted.

The possibilities of conversion may be summarized as follows: —

			Converted
Given	A	All x is y	I Some y is x
	E	No x is y	E No y is x
	I	Some x is y	I Some y is x
	O	Some x is not y	No result

The above are the only transformations which are possible when we regard the form of the propositions merely. If, however, in addition to their mere formal structure, we take into consideration their content, — that is, the meaning of the subject and predicate terms and their relation to each other in any judgment, — then a greater range in conversion is possible.

Thus, in the universal affirmative, if the subject and predicate are coextensive terms, or if they are coördinate properties of the one and the same concept, then a simple conversion without change is possible. Given, All equiangular triangles are equilateral. By conversion we have All equilateral triangles are equiangular.

Or if the universal proposition is in the form of a definition, — *i.e.* a concept referred to its genus and differentia, — then simple conversion is possible. Democracy is government by the people. A government by the people is a democracy. It is evident that an indefinite reference of a concept to a class genus merely, or a description of a concept by one or more of its attributes, will give a proposition which admits of conversion only by limitation, *i.e.* change of "all" to "some"; but, on the other hand, a definite reference which serves to differentiate the concept in question admits of simple conversion.

The same observation applies to the conversion of a hypothetical judgment. Given a judgment of the form, If x is y, z is w, it does not follow that if z is w, x is y; for there may be other antecedents which will give us z is w, as well as the given one x is y. Thus, given the judgment, If the democrats win, they must carry New York State, it does not follow that if they carry New York State, they will win.

It is the aim of all exact thinking, of all scientific formulation especially, to render thought so definite that a simple conversion is possible. It is not sufficient to refer a species to a genus, which is a class embracing also many other species, but to so refer the species in question by means of its differentiating properties, that the reference will become distinctive. Moreover, while a given consequent may follow from many antecedents, it is the aim of exact thinking to connect certain specific marks which accompany that consequent with certain causal conditions present in some one of the many possible antecedents and not present in the others. Simple conversion is then of course possible.

Logical error arises when judgments expressing inexact references are converted simply by unreflecting persons. As, for instance, when an ignorant foreigner reasons that because all travellers who give unusually large tips are Americans, that therefore all Americans will give unusually large tips. The error is more apt to arise when subject and predicate, or antecedent and consequent, approach very near the boundary of simple conversion, but have not quite reached it. The margin is so narrow however that it is overlooked, and error naturally results. Thus, no one would think of converting the proposition, All United States Senators are members of Congress, into All members of Congress are United States Senators, but many might fall into the fallacy of converting the proposition, All the democrats in the Senate voted against the bill, into All Senators who voted against the bill were democrats.

The wider range of conversion which is rendered possible by the consideration of content in addition to that of form merely, may also be illustrated in the particular affirmative, Given, Some x is y; then, if it is known in addition that y is a species of x, we may convert the particular into a universal, and get All y is x as the result. Thus, if we have given the judgment that Some birds of prey are vultures, we can convert it so as to obtain All vultures are birds of prey.

Again, in the particular negative, conversion, which is not possible by consideration of form alone, becomes possible if, on examination of content, we know that the predicate is not a species of the subject. Thus, if we have given Some birds of prey are not hawks, we can convert it into Some hawks at least are not birds of prey. But if the predicate is a species of the subject, conversion is impossible, *e.g.* Some governments are not republics. The relation of form to content is such in general that not merely is it impossible to interpret the full significance of a proposition without knowing its content, but also it is impossible to assent to any formal statement whatsoever unless we know in addition the significance of the terms used. The proposition, All x is y, is a mere skeleton form, but in the actual judgments of our thinking x and y are replaced by definite concepts with a real significance. Our first thought, therefore, is whether the real concepts which we substitute for x and y in our symbolic form will admit of a universal affirmative assertion, or of a universal negative, etc. Form without content is meaningless; content without form is confusion. The one is always a function of the other.

We come now to a second kind of transformation, known as Obversion. It consists in a change in the quality of a proposition from affirmative to negative, or from negative to affirmative, and at the same time a compensating change of the original predicate to its corresponding contradictory. If the original proposition is true, a single change of quality would render the transformed proposition false, therefore the predicate term is changed by way of compensation, because the reference of any predicate to a subject has the same logical force as that of excluding the contradictory of that predicate from the same subject. Given, All such conditions are impossible, by obversion we have No conditions of such a nature are possible. The same process holds in the obversion of the other forms of judgment, and we have the following tabulated summary:—

	Given	Obverted
	All x is y A	No x is not-y E
	No x is y E	All x is not-y A
	Some x is y I	Some x is not-y O
	Some x is not y O	Some x is not-y I

The term "not-y" is usually expressed by some form of a negative affix such as *im*possible, *un*controllable, etc.

There are several complex transformations formed by the combined processes of conversion and obversion. Of these the so-called Contrapositive is formed by subjecting the given proposition to three transformations, as follows:—

1. Obversion.
2. Conversion.
3. Obversion.

Given the proposition: All scholarly work is logical,

1. By obversion, No scholarly work is illogical.
2. By conversion, No illogical work is scholarly.
3. By obversion, All illogical work is unscholarly.

In the final proposition, which is the contrapositive, it will be seen that the subject and predicate of the original proposition have been interchanged and each replaced by its corresponding contradictory. The contrapositive may be defined, therefore, as a transformation which substitutes for the given terms their corresponding contradictories, and at the same time interchanges the subject and predicate positions. The three processes by which the contrapositive is formed may be omitted, and the contrapositive formed directly according to the above definition. The processes, however, form the proof that this direct transformation is admissible.[1]

There is another proof for the contrapositive of a universal affirmative which is as follows: Given, All x is y; then All not-y is not-x. For what is not-y must be either x or not-x. But if it is x, it is also y, according to the given proposition. This, however, is impossible, for the same concept cannot be both not-y and y. Therefore, the other alternative must be true, namely, that not-y must be not-x, which was to be proved.

When an A proposition is given, its contrapositive is also an A proposition. When, however, the given proposition is of the E form, there is a loss of logical force, and the result of the three processes is an O proposition.

[1] Some logicians regard the contrapositive as the result merely of the two processes, obversion and conversion. This, however, is merely a matter of definition, and no confusion can result, because the additional process of obversion simply carries the operation one step farther.

Given, No insane persons are responsible, *E*.

(1) By obversion, All insane persons are irresponsible, *A*.

(2) By conversion, Some irresponsible persons are insane, *I*.

(3) By obversion, Some irresponsible persons are not sane, *O*.

In a similar manner it will be readily seen that the contrapositive of an *O* proposition is also an *O* proposition. The *I* proposition yields no contrapositive, because the first step of obversion gives an *O* proposition; the second step of conversion cannot be applied to an *O* proposition, and consequently the process is blocked at this point.

It is well to remember that the contrapositive is formed by taking contradictories of the original subject and predicate; for, if contraries are taken, the process is rendered invalid. For instance, if we have given the proposition, All honest acts are moral, the contrapositive, according to rule, would seem to be, All immoral acts are dishonest. This, however, is not true, and the reason is that the terms "honest" and "dishonest" are not contradictory but contrary, for between honest and dishonest acts there is the middle ground corresponding to acts concerning which the question of honesty is not raised at all.

CHAPTER XIV

A GENERALIZATION OF IMMEDIATE INFERENCES

As the various immediate inferences by opposition have been generalized in the ancient logical square, the question suggests itself, cannot a similar method be applied to the other forms of immediate inference? And the following is the result of the problem thus proposed.

The possible transformations of a simple proposition may occur in any of the following ways: by a change of the quality of a proposition, *i.e.* change from affirmative to negative and *vice versa;* or, by a change of quantity, *i.e.* from universal to particular and *vice versa;* or by a change of either subject or predicate terms by substituting for them their respective contradictory terms; or, by an interchange of subject and predicate in the proposition. Of these processes or combinations of them, the ones which are legitimate inferences are as follows:—

Having given, for example, an A proposition, All x is y, it is possible to infer:—

(1) The converse, Some y is x.
(2) The obverse, No x is not-y.
(3) Converted obverse, No not-y is x.
(4) Contrapositive, All not-y is not-x.
(5) Obverted converse, Some y is not not-x.
(6) Inverse, Some not-x is not y.[1]
(7) Obverted inverse, Some not-x is not-y.

---

[1] The inverse of a proposition has the same predicate, but for its subject the contradictory of the original subject.

These transformations may be comprehended in the following logical square: —

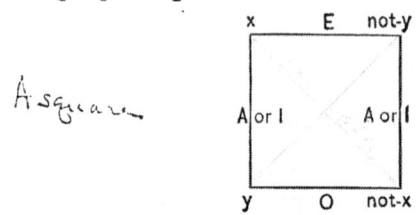

```
         x      E    not-y
          ┌───────────────┐
          │               │
       A or I           A or I
          │               │
          └───────────────┘
         y      O    not-x
```

A square (margin note)

Here I have placed the terms *x*, *y*, and their contradictions, not-*x*, not-*y*, in the corners of the square so that any term and its contradiction will be situated diagonally opposite. The letter *A*, *E*, *I*, or *O*, indicates that the two terms between which the letter is situated may be formed into a proposition of the character represented by that letter, and in every case such a proposition is a legitimate inference from the original proposition, All *x* is *y*. Thus, between the two upper terms, *x* and not-*y*, there are possible two universal negative propositions, one the converse of the other: —

    No *x* is not-*y*, *E*.
    No not-*y* is *x*, *E*.

Between the two lower terms, two particular negative propositions: —

    Some *y* is not not-*x*, *O*.
    Some not-*x* is not *y*, *O*.

Between either upper one as subject and corresponding lower one as predicate there is possible a universal affirmative. This gives: —

    All *x* is *y*, A.
    All not-*y* is not-*x*, A.

Between either lower term and corresponding upper one there is possible a particular affirmative. This gives: —

A GENERALIZATION OF IMMEDIATE INFERENCES 119

Some y is x, *I.*
Some not-x is not-y, *I.*

By comparison of these results with the legitimate inferences given at the beginning of this discussion, there will be seen an exact correspondence. This square, therefore, summarizes exhaustively all possible legitimate inferences.

I would note in passing that of the two inferences of the *O* form, while one is the converse of the other, still it is not derived from the other by conversion, which process is logically inadmissible, but is derived independently: Some y is not not-x, being the obverted converse, and Some not-x is not y being the inverse.

Again, when *E* is the original proposition, the possible inferences are:—

(1) No y is x.
(2) All x is not-y.
(3) All y is not-x.
(4) Some not-y is x.
(5) Some not-y is not not-x.
(6) Some not-x is y.
(7) Some not-x is not not-y.

All of these are comprehended in the same square as that indicating the inferences from an *A* proposition, provided the positions of y and not-y are interchanged. This gives the following square for inferences from an *E* proposition:—

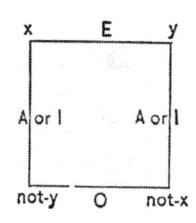

	x	E	y	
	A or I		A or I	
	not-y	O	not-x	

This agrees with the fact that an A proposition, All x is y, becomes by obversion an E proposition, No x is not-y; in this transformation it is observed that not-y has displaced y. Such a substitution will affect all inferences from the original proposition uniformly. With this one change, therefore, the inferences exhibited by the A square and the E square coincide throughout.

The I square is the same as the A square, with the exceptions that the E and A inferences become O and I, respectively, and that the propositions indicated by the two horizontal lines of the square are to be formed by reading from left to right *only*; also that no inference is possible between not-x and not-y, *i.e.* no contrapositive of an I proposition is possible. The I square is as follows:—

I square

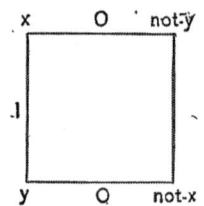

```
        x       O    not-y
       ┌─────────────────┐
       │                 │
     I │                 │
       │                 │
       │                 │
       └─────────────────┘
        y       O    not-x
```

The possible inferences based upon an I proposition are indicated in this square, and are as follows:—

(1) Some y is x.
(2) Some x is not not-y.
(3) Some y is not not-x.

The O square is the same as the I square, provided y and not-y are interchanged as above in the case of the E and A diagrams. The following is the O square:—

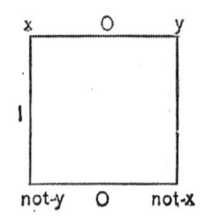

```
        x       O       y
       ┌─────────────────┐
       │                 │
     I │                 │
       │                 │
       │                 │
       └─────────────────┘
       not-y    O    not-x
```

The possible inferences based upon an *O* proposition are indicated in this square, and are as follows:—

       (1) Some x is not-y.
       (2) Some not-y is x.
       (3) Some not-y is not not-x.

There is no relation between y and not-x as a possible form of inference, inasmuch as the inverse of an *O* proposition is impossible.

CHAPTER XV

MEDIATE INFERENCE — THE SYLLOGISM

TRUE inference always contains an element of mediation. It is the process of grounding a judgment upon some other judgment essentially related to it, and which stands as the warrant of its truth. The reference of a judgment to another judgment as its ground implies a knowledge of a third judgment which expresses a universal and necessary connection between the two. The complete process of mediate inference, therefore, consists in exhibiting a judgment as the necessary result of the combination of two other judgments. Thus, the judgment that a certain heap of black sand is magnetic is justified when referred to its ground, namely, that it attracts iron filings. To complete the process, however, a third judgment is necessary, which shall express the constant bond of connection between the given judgment and its alleged ground, such as the judgment that whatever attracts iron is magnetic.

This form which mediate inference naturally takes is the syllogism, which is a process of combining two judgments so as to produce a third. The above judgments expressed in syllogistic form would be: —

> Whatever attracts iron is a magnet.
> This black sand attracts iron.
> ∴ This black sand is a magnet.

It will be observed that the two judgments which combine to produce the third have a term in common. This is the middle term of the syllogism. Moreover, the third judgment is formed by eliminating the middle term and taking as its subject and predicate respectively the remaining term in each of the two given judgments. The subject of the judgment thus formed is called the minor term of the syllogism, and the predicate the major term. Minor and major are applied to these terms because in any judgment the predicate generally refers to a larger class than the subject.

Of the two given judgments, the one containing the major term is called the major premise; and the one containing the minor term, the minor premise. The premises take their names from the major and minor terms, and not the terms from the premises. In most syllogisms, the major premise is placed before the minor; but this order is not essential to the structure of the syllogism, or is it by any means an invariable practice. The judgment which is derived from the combination of the two premises is called the conclusion.

It is the peculiar function of the major premise to exhibit some phase of our general knowledge; and of the minor premise, to exhibit some more particular phase of our general knowledge, or, as it more frequently occurs, some special case embodied in a concrete experience. It is the function, therefore, of the two combined, — that is, of the syllogism itself, — to apply universal knowledge to a special case so as to yield its true interpretation. The process is one which consists essentially in eliminating the middle or common term. It is the same process which we find in algebra. Equations are merely a special case of judgment. The following is in every respect a true syllogism: —

$$x = y.$$
$$y = z.$$
$$\therefore x = z.$$

There is, however, a difference between the algebraical equation and the ordinary logical proposition in this respect that in the equation it is a matter of indifference

124   DEDUCTIVE LOGIC

whether we say $x = y$ or $y = x$; but the proposition cannot be converted in this manner without impairing its logical significance.

Compare the following syllogisms:—

(1) All x is y. (2) All y is x. (3) Some x is y.
 All z is x.   All z is x.   All z is x.
∴ All z is y.   ∴ All z is y.   ∴ All z is y.

It is obvious that the first of these syllogisms is valid, the other two invalid. Moreover, it is evident that the position of the terms in the syllogism, as well as the kind of propositions employed in its structure, whether A, E, I, or O, have an essential bearing upon its validity. How this comes to pass and what criteria may be formulated for testing the validity of syllogisms will appear in the following exposition concerning the so-called distribution of terms.

A term is said to be distributed when it is used in a universal sense, and undistributed when it is used in a limited or partial sense. The word distributed is regarded as synonymous with universal, because it is of the nature of a universal to distribute or apply the full force of its significance to every individual case which is subsumed under it. In the proposition, All the schoolmen were logicians, the subject is distributed in the connection in which it is used, so that what is affirmed of the class that they were logicians can be affirmed of every individual of the class. The term logicians in this connection is undistributed, because it is only a part of the class of logicians that can be identified with the schoolmen.

In respect to the four propositions, A, E, I, O, the following are the possibilities as regards distributed and undistributed terms.

1. The universal affirmative distributes the subject but not the predicate. This will be evident, if the given propo-

sition be converted, for while *All x is y*, by conversion *Some y is x*.

∴ *x* is seen to be distributed, and *y* undistributed.

2. The universal negative distributes both subject and predicate. It is a matter of indifference whether we say No *x* is *y*, or by conversion No *y* is *x*. In the one case *x* is *wholly* excluded from *y*, but that is the same as excluding *y wholly* from *x*.

∴ *x* is distributed, and *y* is distributed.

3. The particular affirmative does not distribute either term. For Some *x* is *y* gives by conversion Some *y* is *x*.

∴ *x* is undistributed and *y* is undistributed.

4. The particular negative does not distribute the subject but does distribute the predicate. This cannot be shown by converting the given proposition, for the particular negative does not admit of simple conversion. However, given the proposition Some *x* is not *y*, it is evident that the subject, some *x*, is excluded wholly from *y*, therefore such exclusion must cut off all of *y* from that special some *x*, which is its subject.

∴ *x* is undistributed but *y* is distributed.

The above results may be tabulated as follows, the distributed terms being marked with a √ and the undistributed with a °.

All $\overset{\checkmark}{x}$ is $\overset{\circ}{y}$ *A*.

No $\overset{\checkmark}{x}$ is $\overset{\checkmark}{y}$ *E*.

Some $\overset{\circ}{x}$ is $\overset{\circ}{y}$ *I*.

Some $\overset{\circ}{x}$ is not $\overset{\checkmark}{y}$ *O*.

In determining whether a term is distributed in any given proposition, the distribution of the subjects will be readily recognized because indicated by the qualifying terms, "all," "some," "none," or "some not." The distribution of the predicates may be recalled by the following generalization which is obvious upon inspection of the above table.

Affirmative propositions do not distribute their predicates.

Negative propositions do distribute their predicates.

In reference to the criticism of any syllogism, there are two fundamental rules of distribution which must be observed: —

1. The middle term must be distributed at least once.
2. If a term is distributed in the conclusion, it must also be distributed in its premise.

The middle term must be distributed at least once in order to provide a common point of connection between the two premises. For if the middle term is undistributed in both premises, then the major term is related to a *part* of the middle term in the major premise, and the minor term is related to a *part* of the middle term in the minor premise, and there is no assurance whatever that these two parts have anything in common.

Given the premises (1) All x is y,
(2) All z is y,

the following diagrams will represent these relations respectively.

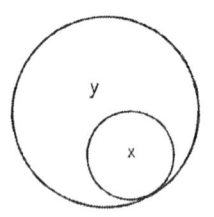

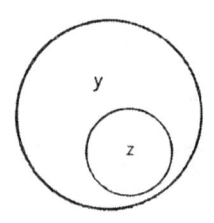

There is nothing in the above relations, however, to indicate whether within the common circle y, x and z be wholly apart as in the following diagram

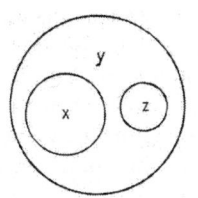

or whether they have some common ground as

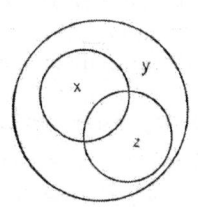

or whether x falls within z as

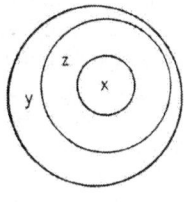

or whether z falls within x as

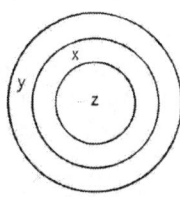

The relation between x and z is left wholly indeterminate by the given premises. If, however, the middle term is distributed at least once, it serves to bring the two premises into a logically significant relation freed from all ambiguity. It is not necessary, however, that it should be distributed twice; for the object of its distribution is to connect the two premises. This connection once effected, it is not necessary to secure it again; if the middle term should happen to be distributed in both premises, the existing connection is merely confirmed and in no sense invalidated by such twofold distribution.

The following syllogism will serve as a concrete illustration of the fallacy of an undistributed middle: —

    All agnostics repudiate the methods of metaphysical inquiry.
    All materialists repudiate the methods of metaphysical inquiry.
∴ All agnostics are materialists.

This conclusion does not necessarily follow. The middle term, being in the predicate of an affirmative proposition in each case, is undistributed.

The second rule that a term distributed in the conclusion must also be distributed in its premise, is directed against that illogical procedure from a term used in a partial sense to the same term used in the universal sense. In the discussion concerning the opposition of propositions, it was seen that the truth of the particular does not imply the truth of the universal. It is the same principle which emerges here. The truth of the universal carries with it, however, the truth of the particular; therefore, it is permissible to have a term distributed in the premise and undistributed in the conclusion. The beginner in logic is liable to confuse these two modes of procedure; therefore it should be especially held in mind that the invalid procedure is only from a term undistributed in the premise to the same term distributed in the conclusion, or from the particular to the universal. As a concrete illustration, take the following syllogism in which the distribution of terms is marked:—

All foreigners who are naturalized may vote.
No native-born citizens are foreigners who are naturalized.
∴ No native-born citizens may vote.

This conclusion is obviously incorrect; the major term is distributed in the conclusion and undistributed in the premise. When such invalid procedure is concerned with the major term, it is called the illicit process of the major term, or simply illicit major; when it is concerned with the minor term, it is the illicit process of the minor term, or illicit minor.

There are several special cases in which the general rules for distribution must be somewhat modified:—

1. The predicate of some affirmative propositions is distributed because of a special significance which it may possess. While according to form alone it would be undistributed, the sense may afford additional information which justifies its distribution. This is the same principle which was seen to operate in reference to the conversion of a universal affirmative proposition, All x is y to All y is x when x and y are coextensive terms.

Thus the following syllogism is invalid because of an undistributed middle:—

$$\text{All } x \text{ is } y.$$
$$\text{All } z \text{ is } y.$$
$$\therefore \text{All } z \text{ is } x.$$

Here the form alone serves as the test of its validity. But in the filling up of such a form with significant terms, the meaning may possibly render such a syllogism valid. Thus,

Every government by the people is a democracy.
The United States is a democracy.
∴ The United States is a government by the people.

The middle term in this syllogism is undistributed as regards its bare form. As regards the meaning of the terms the major premise may be converted simply, every democracy is a government by the people. The term democracy is in reality therefore distributed, the subject and predicate terms of the major premise being coextensive.

2. There are certain qualifying words which, while restricting the subject at the same time, distribute the predicate. In all propositions of this kind the subject is undistributed, and the predicate is distributed. The qualifying words are "only," "none but," "alone," and the like. In the proposition, None but members of the union will be employed, the subject is undistributed, and the predicate distributed; the logical force of this proposition will be the more readily seen if we convert it. It then becomes, All who are employed must be members of the union; in this form, the subject is distributed, the predicate undistributed, as it is a universal affirmative.

In the two syllogisms following, the first is valid, the second is invalid, being a case of undistributed middle:—

(1) None but members of the union will be employed.
A certain man was employed.
∴ He must have been a member of the union.

(2) None but members of the union will be employed.
A certain man is a member of the union.
∴ He must be employed.

In the criticism of the various modes of reasoning attention should be drawn to the fact that we seldom find our thought expressed in the form of a complete syllogism. Usually one of the parts of the syllogism is omitted, not, however, because its force is unessential to the reasoning process, but because it is so obvious that it is unnecessary to state it explicitly. This condensed form of the syllogism is known as the Enthymeme, so called, as its name indicates, because a part of the syllogism is not expressed but in the reasoning process is carried along *in the mind*. The omitted portion is usually the major premise; that is, the general principle of which the course of the reasoning in question forms the special case. Both the minor premise, or the conclusion, may also be omitted in the construction of an enthymeme. There are three kinds of enthymeme:—

1. With the major premise omitted.

This enterprise will tend to increase the public wealth, because it will promote the general happiness of the people.

2. With minor premise omitted.

That expedition is doomed to failure, because no small body of men insufficiently equipped and cut off from their base of supplies can ever reduce so strongly fortified a garrison.

3. With conclusion omitted.

All members of that conference were traitors to their party. And you were a member of that conference. Nothing more need be said.

The enthymeme may be tested as regards its validity by supplying the omitted part, and then applying the usual rules of the syllogism. But, inasmuch as the enthymeme expresses the immediate connection between two judgments, it may be subjected to direct criticism according to the following criteria: —

If the major premise is omitted, the enthymeme consists of a special case referred to its ground, This is x because it is y. The enthymeme is valid, provided the ground assigned for the special case applies as well to all other cases of the same kind; that is, according to the symbols used, if All y is x.

In the enthymeme, He is a free-trader because he is a democrat, the connection is a valid one provided all democrats are free-traders.

Again, if the enthymeme has the minor premise omitted, it may be expressed in symbols, as follows: —

A certain thing is x, because All z is x. In such a relation, the special case must be recognized as a special case of the universal; that is, we must know that the thing in question is z.

For instance, given the enthymeme as follows: That man is a German, for all the crew are Germans. The inference based upon the assigned ground is valid, provided we know that the man in question is a member of the crew; that is, if the single case falls with the area of the universal which is stated as its ground.

Syllogisms may be combined in various ways into chains of reasoning. When the conclusion of one syllogism becomes the premise of a second syllogism, the former is called the prosyllogism and the latter the episyllogism. When we combine a number of prosyllogisms and episyllogisms so that all the conclusions except the last are omitted, the chain of reasoning is called the Sorites. There are two forms of the Sorites, known as the Aristotelian and the Goclenian.[1]

These forms may be expressed symbolically as follows: —

I	II
Aristotelian Sorites	Goclenian Sorites
A is B.	D is E.
B is C.	C is D.
C is D.	B is C.
D is E.	A is B.
∴ A is E.	∴ A is E.

It will be seen that the middle terms cancel throughout, and the conclusion is formed from the remaining terms in the first and last premises. Thus, it may be reasoned that a certain political boss has caused his chosen man to be made governor of New York; for he controls the machine, and the machine controls the party, and the party controls the state vote, and the state vote creates the governor. The Sorites is commonly used to indicate the various links of cause and effect which may be interpolated between an effect and a remote cause.

The Sorites often appears in hypothetical form, for the reason that the causal relation is best expressed by a hypothetical. In the life of Sir James Fitzjames Stephen,

[1] Named from Goclenius, a German logician of the sixteenth century.

the following remark of his tutor appears, which illustrates the hypothetical form of the Sorites, and at the same time will serve to show how plausibly a Sorites may express a subtle fallacy: "If you do not take more pains, how can you ever expect to write good longs and shorts? If you do not write good longs and shorts, how can you ever be a man of taste? If you are not a man of taste, how can you ever hope to be of use in the world?"

CHAPTER XVI

MOOD AND FIGURE

A SYLLOGISM may be constructed by combining in various ways the four propositions, *A, E, I,* and *O*. The particular combination employed in any one syllogism constitutes the mood of that syllogism. Thus, to refer to a syllogism as having the mood *AAA,* means that the premises and conclusion are all universal affirmative propositions; the mood *EAE* means that the major premise is a universal negative, the minor premise a universal affirmative, and the conclusion a universal negative. The three letters designating the mood are to be interpreted in the order of major premise, minor premise, and conclusion.

The problem which the subject of mood presents is to find which moods are valid; for there are sixty-four possible permutations of three propositions out of four, repetitions such as *AAA* being allowed. In order to discriminate between the valid and invalid moods, the following rules must be taken to guide us: —

1. A particular premise gives a particular conclusion.
2. Two particular premises give no conclusion.
3. A negative premise gives a negative conclusion, and conversely if the conclusion is negative, one of the premises must be negative.
4. Two negative premises give no conclusion.

The first and second rules follow from the rules relating to distribution of terms; this is obvious upon simple inspection. The third rule as to a negative premise giving a negative conclusion and its converse is based upon the necessary

134

relation that if one of the two terms major or minor agrees with the middle term and the other disagrees, then they must necessarily disagree with each other; that is, the conclusion expressing this disagreement must be in the negative form. As to the rule that two negatives give no conclusion, it is evident that when the major and minor terms both are excluded from all relation to the middle term, no indication whatever is given as to their relation to each other. Accepting these rules therefore as binding, let us examine their effect upon the sixty-four possible permutations. This problem we will divide into two parts: —

(1) What pairs of premises are valid?
(2) What valid conclusions follow from them?

First, the major premise may be either *A, E, I,* or *O,* and the minor premise may be either *A, E, I,* or *O.* The permutations resulting from combining these letters to form possible pairs of premises are as follows: —

AA, AE, AI, AO.
EA, EE, EI, EO.
IA, IE, II, IO.
OA, OE, OI, OO.

Of these the following cannot stand as pairs of premises: —

EE, because there are two negatives.
EO, because there are two negatives.
II, because there are two particulars.
IO, because there are two particulars.
OI, because there are two particulars.
OE, because there are two negatives.
OO, because there are two negatives, and also two particulars.

Eliminating these tentative forms, there remain the following: —

AA, AE, AI, AO.
EA, EI.
IA, IE.
OA.

The second question is, given the above premises, what conclusions are possible?

AA will give as a conclusion either *A* or *I*; but will not give *E* or *O*, for a negative conclusion requires one of the premises to be negative. By inspection, after the same manner, it will be found that *AE* will give two conclusions, *E* and *O*; so also *EA*. The remaining, with the exception of *IE*, have each one conclusion, — *AII, AOO, EIO, IAI, OAO*.

The premises *IE* would seem to require the conclusion *O* and so form a valid mood *IEO*. This mood, in fact, squares with all the special rules which we have formed above to guide us in discussing this present problem. However, it is impossible to construct a syllogism in this form which does not contain an illicit major, for the conclusion, being negative, distributes the major term, and the major premise, being *I*, cannot distribute either subject or predicate term. For example, take the following syllogism: —

Some *x* is *y* *I.*
No *z* is *x* *E.*
Some *z* is not *y* *O.*

Y is here distributed in the conclusion, but not in the premise. The syllogism, therefore, in this form is impossible.

The valid moods which remain after this process of elimination which we have now completed are as follows:—

AAA	*AEE*	*EAE*	*AII*	*EIO*	*OAO*
(*AAI*)	(*AEO*)	(*EAO*)	*AOO*	*IAI*	

The three in parentheses are called the weak moods of the syllogism, because the conclusion in each case is really implied in the stronger conclusion immediately above it, and therefore they do not constitute distinct types. The truth of A always necessitates the truth of I, and the truth of E always necessitates the truth of O.

There remain all together only eight distinct types out of the sixty-four which are valid forms of the syllogism.

There is still a further problem which remains to be considered, whether all of these moods are valid irrespective of the relative positions of the major, minor, and middle terms in the syllogism. The position of the middle term in reference to the major and minor term constitutes what is known as the figure of the syllogism. If we represent the middle term by M, the minor term by S, and the major term by P, the four possible figures are as follows:—

I	II	III	IV
$M. P.$	$P. M.$	$M. P.$	$P. M.$
$S. M.$	$S. M.$	$M. S.$	$M. S.$
$\therefore S. P.$	$\therefore S. P.$	$\therefore S. P.$	$\therefore S. P.$

A change in the relative position of the terms will of course affect the matter of their distribution, and therefore the validity of the various moods in the different figures will turn upon the question of the distribution of terms. The two rules for distribution, it will be remembered, are as follows:—

(1) The middle term must be distributed at least once.

(2) If a term is distributed in the conclusion, it must be distributed also in the premise.

The following are the valid moods in the several figures, the invalid moods being stricken out, and the number appended being the number of the rule violated in each case:—

Figure I	Figure II	Figure III	Figure IV
AAA	~~AAA¹~~	~~AAA²~~ (AAI)	~~AAA²~~ (AAI)
~~AEE²~~	AEE	~~AEE²~~	AEE
EAE	EAE	~~EAE²~~ (EAO)	~~EAE²~~ (EAO)
AII	~~AII¹~~	AII	~~AII¹~~
~~AOO²~~	AOO	~~AOO²~~	~~AOO¹~~
EIO	EIO	EIO	EIO
~~IAI¹~~	~~IAI¹~~	IAI	IAI
OAO	~~OAO²~~	OAO	~~OAO²~~

The first figure is called by Aristotle the perfect figure, for it alone, he averred, conforms to the fundamental canon of all reasoning. This canon of Aristotle is called the *Dictum de omni et nullo*. It has come down to us from the mediæval logicians and is formulated as follows:—

Whatever is predicated affirmatively or negatively of a whole class must be predicated affirmatively or negatively of everything contained under that class. The affirmative predication is expressed by the phrase *de omni*, and the negative by *de nullo*.[1]

Thus the perfect syllogism is a process of applying our general knowledge (the major premise) to a special case (minor premise), the conclusion being the special case interpreted in the light of our general knowledge.

It will be readily seen, also, upon inspection, that the first figure is the only one of the four which proves any one of the four propositions, A, E, I, or O, as its conclusion.

The second figure proves only negative conclusions. It is used in proving distinctions between things.

The third figure proves only particular conclusions. The moods with an I conclusion are useful in proving a rule by positive instances; the moods with an O conclusion in proving exceptions to a rule. It will be noticed that in the third figure the strong moods AAA and EAE are

[1] Aristotle stated it, Whatever is said of the predicate is said of the subject.

invalid, but the weakened mood *AAI* and *EAO* are valid.

The fourth figure was regarded by Aristotle as merely an awkward variety of the figure, and therefore he ignored it altogether. His pupils, Theophrastus and Eudemus, however, added its five moods to Figure I, calling them indirect moods. The fourth figure is called the Galenian figure from Claudus Galenus (died about 200 A.D.), who insisted upon ranking it upon the same footing as the other three figures. In the fourth figure, also, the weakened moods take the place of their corresponding stronger moods, the latter being invalid.

The Latin schoolmen in the thirteenth century invented a system of mnemonic verses for the purpose of assisting the memory as regards the valid moods in each figure. While such a mechanical device is not needed by the student of logic, it is given a place in the text as a curious bit of logical history. It furnishes also an excellent illustration of the scholastic type of mind. The lines are: —

>*Barbara, Celarent, Darii, Ferioque* prioris;
>*Cesare, Camestres, Festino, Baroko,* secundae,
>Tertia, *Darapti, Disamis, Datisi, Felapton,*
>*Bokardo, Ferison,* habet; quarta insuper addit
>*Bramantip, Camenes, Dimaris, Fesapo, Fresison.*

The words printed in italics are artificial words having no significance whatsoever. Each word represents a mood, its three vowels indicating the propositions which it contains. The words "prioris," "secundae," etc., refer, of course, to the figure in each case. Thus *Barbara* signifies *AAA* of the first figure; *Disamis*, *IAI* of the third figure. Some of the consonants in these words are also significant, indicating the method by which the moods in any of the three figures may be reduced to the form of the first figure. Aristotle insisted that a mood in any other figure could be tested as regards its validity only after it had been changed so as to conform to the "perfect figure." This process is called reduction. The significance of the consonants in reference to this process is as follows: —

In the several words, *s* indicates that the proposition represented by the preceding vowel is to be converted simply; *p* indicates that the proposition represented by the preceding vowel is to be converted *per accidens*, or by limitation, that is, changing all to some; *m (mutare)* indicates that the propositions which stand as the premises are to be transposed; *k* means that an indirect proof is necessary in order to reduce the mood to the first figure. Moreover, the initial consonants of the so-called imperfect figures correspond with those of the moods in the first figure to which they can be reduced.

Thus *Darapti* reduces to *Darii:* —

The mood expressed by *Darapti* is *AAI* as in the following: —

$$\text{All } B \text{ is } A.$$
$$\text{All } B \text{ is } C.$$
$$\therefore \text{Some } C \text{ is } A.$$

The *p* in *Darapti* indicates conversion of minor premise *per accidens*; this gives the mood *A I I* which is the *Darii* of the first figure: —

$$\text{All } B \text{ is } A.$$
$$\text{Some } C \text{ is } B.$$
$$\therefore \text{Some } C \text{ is } A.$$

So also *Disamis* becomes *Darii:* —

Given the syllogism in the form of *Disamis:* —

$$\text{Some } B \text{ is } A.$$
$$\text{All } B \text{ is } C.$$
$$\therefore \text{Some } C \text{ is } A.$$

Here the first *s* indicates a simple conversion of the major premises, the *m* a transposition of premises, and the final *s* a simple conversion of the conclusion, all of which will result as follows: —

All *B* is *C*.
Some *A* is *B*.
∴ Some *A* is *C*.
or Some *C* is *A*.

The process of reduction has no practical value whatsoever; as a device to arrange the syllogism in proper form for the testing of its validity, it is wholly unnecessary. Every syllogism, whether of the first or of the other figures, may be tested quietly by the application of the rules concerning the distribution of terms. If the middle term is distributed, and no illicit process either of the major or the minor term is involved, the syllogism needs no further justification.

CHAPTER XVII

THE HYPOTHETICAL AND DISJUNCTIVE SYLLOGISMS

THE hypothetical syllogism is a syllogism in which the major premise is a hypothetical proposition, the minor premise a categorical, and the conclusion a categorical proposition also. The hypothetical proposition is of the general form, — If x is y, then z is w. The conditional clause is known as the antecedent, the following clause the consequent.

Let us examine some hypothetical proposition regarding it as a major premise, and putting the question as to how many syllogisms may be constructed by means of introducing various minor premises in connection with it. Let us take the proposition, If the Japanese are to be victorious in the war with Russia, they must take Port Arthur. With this proposition as a major premise, there are four minor premises possible according as we affirm or deny the antecedent, or affirm or deny the consequent, as follows: —

(1) They are victorious.
(2) They are not victorious.
(3) They have taken Port Arthur.
(4) They have not taken Port Arthur.

It will be observed that the first and fourth statements when taken in connection with the major premise give definite conclusions.

When we affirm the antecedent, They are victorious, the conclusion follows necessarily, They must have taken Port Arthur.

THE HYPOTHETICAL SYLLOGISM 143

Similiarly, when we deny the antecedent, They have not taken Port Arthur, the conclusion follows, They are not victorious.

Granting the truth of the major premise, these two conclusions must necessarily follow from the respective minor premises as above stated.

But when we come to the other two cases, the denial of the antecedent, or the affirmation of the consequent, the case is very different. If it is stated that they are not victorious, it does not follow that they did not take Port Arthur, for they might take Port Arthur and yet fail of victory for some other reason. And so also, if it is stated that they have taken Port Arthur, it cannot be inferred that they are victorious, for here again some other cause may have operated to prevent victory.

In general therefore the denial of the antecedent or the affirmation of the consequent leaves the conclusion indeterminate; for, as in the special case cited above, there may be some other antecedent which may give rise to the consequent as well as the particular antecedent connected with it in the given hypothetical proposition which forms the major premise. This possibility will always render the inference indeterminate. If however it is known that the given antecedent is the sole antecedent of the given consequent, and therefore every other possibility is eliminated, then the denial of the antecedent, or the affirmation of the consequent, will also give a determinate conclusion. This special case of the hypothetical syllogism may be recognized by the simple test of conversion. Thus if the hypothetical major premise can be converted simply, then any one of the four possible minor premises will yield a definite conclusion. Thus we have the proposition, If any substance turns blue litmus paper red, it is an acid. Here antecedent and consequent are reciprocally related, so that we can also state the proposition conversely, If the substance is an acid, it will turn blue litmus paper red.

With such a major premise, any one of four conclusions may be possible according as the antecedent is affirmed or denied, or as the consequent is affirmed or denied.

It is possible, moreover, to transform any hypothetical proposition into a categorical form. Let us take the hypothetical, If the patient takes this medicine, he will get well. The two minor premises which give indeterminate conclusions are as follows: —

(1) He does not take the medicine.
∴ Conclusion is left in doubt.

(2) He gets well.
∴ Conclusion is left in doubt.

Forming these into categorical syllogisms, we have: —

(1) The taking of this medicine will restore health.
The patient does not take the medicine.
∴ He will not be restored.

(2) The taking of this medicine will restore health.
The patient's health is restored.
∴ He has taken the medicine.

By examining these two conclusions, obviously invalid, it will be seen that the denial of the antecedent in a hypothetical syllogism is equivalent to the illicit process of the major term in the categorical syllogism, and the affirmation of the consequent is equivalent to the undistributed middle in the same. The inferences which are always possible in the hypothetical syllogism, the affirmation of the antecedent, or the denial of the consequent, are designated by the Latin phrases, *modus ponens* and *modus tollens* respectively.

The Disjunctive Syllogism. — In this syllogism we have as major premise a disjunctive proposition of the form, A is either B or C. There are four possible minor premises, — being the affirmation or the denial of either one of the alternatives. The conclusions which are possible depend upon the nature of the disjunctive major premise. There are the following cases: —

(1) If the disjunction is a strictly logical one,—that is, the terms mutually exclusive and the disjunction complete,[1] — then the affirmation of either alternative necessitates as a conclusion the denial of the other, while the denial of either one necessitates the affirmation of the other. The former is called the *modus ponendo tollens*, *i.e.* the mood which denies by affirming; the latter is called *modus tollendo ponens*, *i.e.* the mood which affirms by denying.

(2) If the disjunctive members are not mutually exclusive, the affirmation of the one does not necessarily deny the other. Thus we might have the disjunctive proposition, The disease is either pneumonia or typhoid fever. The assertion that it is pneumonia does not necessarily render the typhoid fever an impossibility; for a patient may have both diseases at the same time.

(3) If the disjunction is not complete, then the denial of one member of the disjunction does not necessitate the affirmation of the other, for one or more possibilities not expressed in the original disjunctive statement must be reckoned with. For instance, let us take the disjunctive syllogism, The prices of commodities will be either increased or lowered by this law.

              They cannot be increased.
             ∴ They must be lowered.

It may be shown that there is a third possibility, namely, the law does not affect the prices one way or the other.

The Dilemma. — This is a complex syllogism in which both hypothetical and disjunctive propositions are combined. The dilemma in its most complete form is constructed as follows: the major premise consists of two hypothetical propositions, — the minor premise, of a disjunctive; and the conclusion, of a disjunctive.

---
[1] See p. 51.

The minor premise may take either one of two forms. It may affirm disjunctively the two antecedents contained in the double hypothetical of the major premise; or it may deny disjunctively the two consequents contained in the same. If the former, the dilemma is called constructive; if the latter, destructive. The symbolic representation of these two forms may be expressed as follows: —

(1) The constructive dilemma.

If A is B, C is D; if E is F, G is H.
Either A is B, or E is F.
∴ C is D, or G is H.

(2) The destructive dilemma.

If A is B, C is D; if E is F, G is H.
Either C is not D, or G is not H.
∴ Either A is not B, or E is not F.

The above being the complete form of the dilemma, there may be certain variations introduced, as, for instance, instead of two consequents there may be only one, or instead of two antecedents there may be only one. The principle of the dilemma is, however, not affected by these changes. This principle is essentially that of presenting two possibilities with definitely determined consequences, so that a choice must be made between them which in either case results in embarrassment, confusion, or contradiction. The following dilemma, which will serve as a type of dilemmas in general, illustrates these various features: —

If the charges of the Senator from South Carolina are true, I am unfit to remain a member of the Senate; and if they are untrue, the man who made them is unfit to remain a member of this honorable body.

But they must be true or untrue.

∴ Either the Senator from South Carolina **is unfit or I am unfit** to remain a member of this body.[1]

[1] Extract from a speech of Senator McLaurin in answer to Senator Tillman's charges.

It will be observed that the minor premise of a dilemma states the possibilities to which a given situation gives rise, and the major premise states the necessary relations which these possibilities respectively sustain.

There are two parts of a dilemma where a structural weakness is apt to occur, which of course affects seriously the validity of the conclusion. The one weakness is an absence of necessary sequence between antecedent and consequent in either one or both of the hypothetical propositions which form the major premise. The other is the incompleteness of the disjunctive proposition which forms the minor premise. If the alternatives are not mutually exclusive, or if they are not exhaustive, error of course must result. Sometimes a specious argument in the form of a dilemma may be suddenly presented by an opponent in controversy or in debate, and produce a temporary confusion of mind because it is not known just where the fallacy of the dilemma is concealed. It is well to know therefore the exact sources whence errors in the dilemma are apt to proceed.

When, in the major premise of a dilemma, the consequents do not invariably follow from the given antecedents, or when other consequents also may follow which are not mentioned in the premise, then it is possible to form a counter dilemma which, starting from the same premises, reaches an opposite conclusion. Both the original dilemma and the counter dilemma in such cases are at fault, because they both start from an inadequately expressed hypothetical relation. An illustration of this is found in the classical incident of the Athenian mother who advised her son not to enter public life; "for," said she, "if you act justly, men will hate you, and if you act unjustly, the gods will hate you; but you must act either justly or unjustly; therefore public life will result in your being hated." The son, however, brought in rebuttal an equally plausible statement: "If I act justly, the gods will love me; and if I act unjustly, men will love me; therefore, entering public life will make me beloved."

Trilemma. — There is a still more complex form of the combined hypothetical and disjunctive propositions which is known as the trilemma. As the name indicates, the disjunction in the minor premise consists of three members. This is illustrated in the following statement regarding the Louisiana Purchase. It is averred that the sale of Louisiana to the United States was invalid; because, if it were French property, Buonaparte could not constitutionally alienate it without the consent of the Chambers; if it were Spanish property, he could not alienate it at all; if Spain had the right of reclamation, the sale was worthless.

CHAPTER XVIII

EXTRA-SYLLOGISTIC REASONING

The syllogism, as we have seen, is a form of inference which is essentially the interpretation of a special case in the light of a universal concept to which it can be referred. The function of the major premise is the statement of the universal principle or relation which forms the basis of the inference; that of the minor, the statement of the connection of the special case under consideration to this universal; that of the conclusion the investiture of the special case with the essential properties which belong to the universal. Now there are certain forms of reasoning which do not explicitly at least conform to this programme of the syllogism, and which judged by the formal rules of the syllogism must be regarded as invalid, but which nevertheless are commonly employed in our everyday inferences and whose validity is indisputable.

There is in the first place the so-called reasoning from "particulars to particulars." John Stuart Mill, as is well known, attacks the accepted view of the syllogism insisting that the reasoning process is never based upon a complete universal, but always starts with particulars and concludes with particulars.[1]

In this connection, he gives the following illustrations: —
"It is not only the village matron who, when called to a consultation upon the case of a neighbour's child, pronounces on the evil and its remedy, simply on the recollection and authority of what she accounts the similar case of her Lucy.

[1] Mill's *Logic*, Book II, Chap. III, § 3.

We all, when we have no definite maxims to steer by, guide ourselves in the same way; and if we have an extensive experience and retain its impressions strongly, we may acquire in this manner a very considerable power of accurate judgment, which we may be utterly incapable of justifying or of communicating to others. Among the higher order of practical intellects, there have been many of whom it was remarked how admirably they suited their means to their ends without being able to give any sufficient reasons for what they did; and applied, or seemed to apply, recondite principles which they were wholly unable to state. This is a natural consequence of having a mind stored with appropriate particulars, and having been long accustomed to reason at once from these to fresh particulars, without practising the habit of stating to oneself or to others the corresponding general propositions. An old warrior, on a rapid glance at the outlines of the ground, is able at once to give the necessary orders for a skilful arrangement of his troops; though if he has received little theoretical instruction, and has seldom been called upon to answer to other people for his conduct, he may never have had in his mind a single general theorem respecting the relation between ground and array. But his experience of encampments, under circumstances more or less similar, has left a number of vivid, unexpressed, ungeneralized analogies in his mind, the most appropriate of which, instantly suggesting itself, determines him to a judicious arrangement."

Mr. Mill is no doubt quite correct in this outline which he sketches of common procedure in inference. However, it cannot be claimed, and Mr. Mill is the last one to claim it, that every particular instance furnishes sufficient ground for an inference concerning a similar particular instance. On the contrary, it is only the particular instance of a certain well-defined kind which can give to such an inference the proper logical warrant and validity. And this special kind is one in which the particular instance ranks as a typical case. It stands in one's thought as the representative of the universal of which it is a special case. In our reasoning we speak of it in terms of its particularity, but the corresponding universal is always in the background of thought, and it invests the particular case with its essential significance. The particular is merely a disguised universal. The particular as mere particular is barren of any inferential result. When however it stands as representative of the universal of which it is a special case, then it serves as a valid ground of inference. When the village matron argues from her own child's case to that of some other child, she has in mind, dimly it may be, but nevertheless truly, some idea which embraces her child's case and her neighbor's in one and the same class. She knows, although it may not be explicit in her thought, that the cure of the child did not depend upon any circumstance peculiar to her constitution or nature, but that the treatment employed possessed some essentially efficacious tendency of a universal nature.

When the argument is, however, narrowed down to a single special case, and this is made the basis of an inference to another case which closely resembles it, then we have inference by analogy.[1] There is a marked difference between the special case which furnishes ground for inference, because it stands in our minds as a typical case representative of its appropriate universal, and on the other hand that special case which does not imply a universal at all, but immediately suggests some resemblance to a similar case and thus opens the way for reasoning by analogy. Analogy, as a form of inference, has attached to it an element of uncertainty so long as its basis is merely a particular instance. When that particular instance begins, however, to assume the characteristics of a typical case, and to direct the thought to its corresponding universal, then inference by analogy passes over by insensible degrees to the ordinary syllogistic inference, or inference by subsumption.

[1] See p. 186.

There is, again, another form of inference, which departs from the syllogistic type but which nevertheless possesses undoubted logical validity, such as the following: —

>   A is to the right of B.
>   B is to the right of C.
>   ∴ A is to the right of C.

Judged strictly by the logical rules of the syllogism, the above conclusion is invalid, because the given syllogism has four terms, A, B, the right of B, and the right of C. There is, therefore, no proper middle term; for B and *to the right of B* are different and can give no identical point of reference for the two premises. Nevertheless this syllogism holds. No one would think of denying its validity. However, its form alone does not warrant the conclusion; for we may construct a syllogism of the same form whose conclusion is invalid. For example, in the following syllogism: —

>   A is a friend of B.
>   B is a friend of C.
>   ∴ A is a friend of C.

it is obvious that the conclusion does not follow necessarily from the premises. Again, let us take a concrete example of a line of argument which appeals to many as quite cogent, but is nevertheless evidently fallacious, such as the following: —

>   Princeton has defeated Yale in base-ball.
>   Yale has defeated Harvard.
>   ∴ Princeton will defeat Harvard.

We are confronted therefore by this problem: —
Given the following syllogism,

>   A sustains certain relations to B.
>   B sustains similar relations to C.
>   ∴ A must sustain these same relations to C.

What kind of relations are they which necessitate such a conclusion, and what kind are they which leave the conclusion indeterminate; or, in other words, what are the precise criteria which will differentiate the truly logical ground from the illogical as regards the nature of the relations upon which the inference is based? The answer is not far to seek. It lies in the very nature of the syllogistic inference itself. We have seen that every valid inference must proceed from premises which have as common ground some identical point of reference.[1] If the premises are not joined at a common point of articulation, their logical force cannot be combined, and without the premises in combination, no conclusion follows.

Now, in the syllogism expressing relations of a perfectly general character as given above, the form alone does not give this necessary point of common reference. We must look, therefore, for some direct test as regards the nature of the relations as there expressed. If the relation which obtains in the major premise is the same as that which obtains in the minor premise, then evidently this identity of relation secures the desired identical point of reference, and therefore furnishes logical warrant for the derived conclusion. This identity of the relations obtaining in the major and minor premises can be established indisputably, however, only when these relations appear in a system of coördinated parts, wherein there is such simplicity that the relations of part to part, throughout the whole extent of the system, can be definitely and exhaustively comprehended. It is only simplicity of system that gives necessity of inference. Otherwise in relations which seem to be identical, there may lurk some unknown and essential differences. From the premises that A is a friend of B, and that B is a friend of C, the conclusion that A is a friend of C does not follow because the system in which these relations obtain is so exceedingly complex as to allow the possibility of a

[1] Bosanquet, *Essentials of Logic*, p. 74 f.

very wide divergence between phenomena, which upon the surface seem quite similar. Not so, however, with the premises, *A* is to the right of *B* and *B* to the right of *C*. The conclusion is left in no doubt, for the very reason that the given relations emerge in a system so simple that no new or unknown elements can be conceived as disturbing factors. Think however of introducing a change into this simple system. Regard it no longer as a plane surface, but as the surface of a sphere. The conclusion from the given premises does not follow necessarily.

Any system, therefore, which is of such simplicity as to assure the identity of given relations, will always furnish a logical ground for inferences of the kind we have been discussing. Such inference is called inference by construction rather than inference by subsumption. It is inference by construction because the mind takes the material furnished by the premises, and places it where it belongs in an underlying system which is explicitly or implicitly assumed. The conclusion follows because the construction has been made within that system and according to the possibilities which the nature of that system imposes. With any other system such a construction would not have necessitated the same conclusion. The conclusion that the square on the hypothenuse is equal to the sum of the squares on the other two sides follows only when we conceive our right-angled triangle as constructed upon a plane surface and not upon a sphere. If you say to me, "You must be a friend to my friend because you are a friend to me," my reply would be: "Not necessarily; for in the vast system of social relations exposed to the many perturbations arising from the qualities and the frailties of human nature alike, the relation of friend to friend is too complex, too subtle, too profound, to furnish any simple and constant basis of inference. There is here something more than a matter of mere magnitude and position."

In addition to the examples already given there are many

other simple systems, which for the most part grow out of the fundamental categories of thought, and which provide a logical ground upon which one may construct these inferences of relation.

There is the system which expresses solely the relations of degree, in which it is possible to construct inferences such as the following: —

A is taller than B.
B is taller than C.
∴ A is taller than C.

There is also the simple time system, giving the inference: —

A is older than B.
B is older than C.
∴ A is older than C.

We may have also somewhat more complicated relations within, however, an exceedingly simple system, as the following will show: —

A and B, two angles of a plane triangle, equal together 95°.
∴ C, the third angle, must equal 85°.

These illustrations might be multiplied. They are, however, sufficient to render clear the criteria regarding all inference concerning related elements of one and the same system. Whenever identity of relationship can be established, a valid inference is possible; and identity of relationship can be established only in systems of such simplicity that no unknown elements which might disturb the given relations can be conceived. Our thought must command the system; otherwise we are never justified in using that system as a basis of reasoning. It should be added, however, that the relations given in the premises may be exceedingly complex, provided only the system in which they inhere remains so simple that our knowledge commands it fully. Thus, in geometry, there is the possibility of indefinitely complex constructions; there are many steps in the reasoning process from the statement of the theorem to the joyful stage of the Q. E. D.; nevertheless, there must remain the constant simple system of space and magnitude relations which constitutes the ground of it all.

There is no limit to the length of a series which may express continued relations. We may have a related to b, b to c, c to d, d to e, and so on. The relations between proximate terms will not insure like relations between more remote terms necessarily. Here again our test comes to the fore. If in such a series the underlying system is so simple as to render the various relations identical in kind, then all terms of the series are brought within a closed circuit, as it were, and we can then pass in thought from the first to the last term as well as from the first to the second.

There is still another kind of inference which is based upon the nature of certain given relations and partakes of the general characteristics of immediate inference. It is this, that whenever we have given a judgment of the form, a is related to b, the given relation necessitates a converse relation, b is related to a. The converse relation is not identical, however, with the given relation, but has an essentially distinct significance, usually of an opposite nature. For example, we have given A is the father of B, therefore B is the son of A; New York is east of Chicago, therefore Chicago is west of New York. The following may be urged as an exception to the statement that the converse relation differs essentially from the given one: A is a friend of B, therefore B is a friend of A. However, this is only a seeming exception, for even in the relation of the most intimate friendship conceivable, the attitude, feeling, or disposition of one party in the friendship is never the same as that of the other. The precise nature of the converse relation will always depend upon the nature of the system in which the given relation obtains.[1]

[1] See Russell, *The Principles of Mathematics*, Chap. IX, on "Relations."

CHAPTER XIX

FALLACIES

FALLACIES or errors in reasoning may be formal or material. The formal fallacy is one which is due to the structure of the reasoning process itself; the material fallacy is due to the thought which underlies the structure. The formal fallacies have been treated indirectly at least in reference to the various rules of the syllogism, the violation of which of course results in a fallacy of this kind. It will be sufficient at this juncture merely to summarize these fallacies, the most important of which are as follows: —

1. Undistributed middle.
2. Illicit process of the major or minor term.
3. Denying the antecedent, or affirming the consequent of the hypothetical syllogism.
4. Inadequate disjunction of the several members of the major premise in the disjunctive syllogism; that is, when these members are not exclusive and therefore overlap.
5. The incomplete enumeration of possibilities in the major premise of the disjunctive syllogism.

The material fallacies may be divided, as did Aristotle, into two classes, — those fallacies which are due to language ($\pi\alpha\rho\grave{\alpha}$ $\tau\grave{\eta}\nu$ $\lambda\acute{\epsilon}\xi\iota\nu$, or *in dictione*); and those which are due to certain errors in the content of thought itself ($\check{\epsilon}\xi\omega$ $\tau\hat{\eta}s$ $\lambda\acute{\epsilon}\xi\epsilon\omega s$, or *extra dictionem*).

The fallacies which are due to language arise from the fact that both in single words and in syntactical forms there may lurk ambiguities of meaning. Any ambiguity of meaning in the course of reasoning violates the fundamental law of identity, which demands that a single and constant significance should attach to all the thought elements which go to make up the data and the processes of our reasoning.

The fallacies due to language are often referred to as <u>fallacies of ambiguity</u>. Their violation of the law of identity will be seen in the several instances which will be given. These fallacies are as follows: —

    1. Equivocation.   4. Division.
    2. Amphiboly.   5. Accent.
    3. Composition.   6. Figure of Speech.

1. *Equivocation.* — This fallacy consists in using a word or a phrase which is capable of a double meaning, as, for example: —

I have the right to publish my opinions concerning the present administration.

What is right for me to do, I ought to do.

∴ I ought to publish my opinions concerning the present administration.

The ambiguity here, of course, lies in the meaning of the word right, which in the one premise is to be taken in a legal sense, and in the other in a moral sense.

This fallacy is in reality a fallacy of four terms; that is, in every syllogism there should be only three terms, each term however being repeated. The law of identity demands that in this repetition the integrity of significance, as regards the repeated term, must be preserved. To introduce a term, therefore, which is ambiguous violates this fundamental principle of thought. The law of identity, however, it must be remembered, allows a certain margin of variation in meaning, provided only that the essential significance of the thought is not impaired. There is often a difference of opinion as to whether a change in meaning affects the essential significance of a concept or not. For instance, let us consider the following syllogism: —

Whatever menaces the public interests should be prevented by law.

The Great Northern Securities Merger menaces the public interests.

∴ It should be prevented by law.

Here the question is raised, Does this merger menace the public interests in the sense that it should be punished by law? And that, of course, is the point upon which the argument turns.

2. *Amphiboly.* — This is a fallacy in which the ambiguity lies in the syntax of the proposition rather than in the terms of which it is composed. The following, taken from a notice in the *New York Tribune*, will illustrate this: —

"To-morrow afternoon, at four o'clock, the Rev. J. A. Francis will deliver the third and last address of a series of plain talks to young men about their perils at the East 86th St. branch of the Y. M. C. A." The conclusion is obvious.

The following epitaph, also illustrating this same fallacy, I discovered several years ago on a tombstone in the old burying-ground at Concord, Massachusetts: —

"Sacred to the memory
of
——— ———
After living with her husband for fifty-five years, she departed in the hope of a better life."

3. *Composition.* — This is the fallacy due to the supposition that what may be affirmed of individuals separately may also be affirmed of them when taken together. It does not follow, for instance, that because the members of a football team are all individually excellent players, therefore the team play will show a similar order of excellence. This fallacy is also illustrated in the following quotation from John Stuart Mill: —

"No reason can be given why the general happiness is desirable except that each person, as far as he believes it to be attainable, desires his own happiness. . . . Each person's happiness is a good to that person, and the general happiness therefore a good to the aggregate of persons." It does not follow, however, that because each desires his own happiness, therefore all desire the happiness of the whole. The root of this fallacy is to be found in the neglect of the distinction between the distributive and the collective use of a term. A term is used distributively when it is applicable to each individual of the class separately; but collectively when it is applicable only to all the individuals which compose the class when taken together. It is the difference between "all" meaning each one, and "all" meaning all together.

4. *Division.* — This is the converse of composition, and consists in affirming of individuals separately what is true only when they are taken together. It does not follow, for instance, that because a certain board of directors has the reputation of being exceedingly conservative, therefore any individual member of that board is necessarily conservative also.

5. *Accent.* — This is a fallacy due to the undue accentuation of a word or clause in any statement so as to create an implication which the bare words themselves do not indicate, and which, moreover, was not intended by the author of the words. To quote from the text of an author and to italicize certain words will often necessitate an interpretation quite foreign to the author's mind. This is often done with malice aforethought, and is an eminently unfair and indefensible liberty to take with the thought of others.

6. *Figure of Speech.* — This is a fallacy of using different parts of speech having a common root as though they had precisely the same meaning. The fact is, however, that a noun may have a certain meaning, while an adjective derived from the same root will have acquired a twist of meaning or a subsidiary significance which will prevent their being regarded in the light of interchangeable terms. The following, also from John Stuart Mill, will illustrate this: —

"The only proof capable of being given that an object is

visible is that people actually see it. The only proof that a sound is audible is that people hear it. . . . In like manner, I apprehend, the sole evidence it is possible to produce that anything is desirable is that people do actually desire it." In this quotation, the relation of the word desirable to desire is not the same as the other two cited, namely, the relation of the word visible to the word see, and of audible to the word hear. Visible means that which can be seen; audible means that which can be heard; but desirable does not mean that which can be desired, — rather, that which ought to be desired.

We come now to the second division of the material fallacies, those which are due to inconsistencies of thought rather than to ambiguities in the expression of the thought. These fallacies are as follows: —

1. Accident.
2. Converse Accident.
3. *Ignoratio Elenchi.*
4. *Non Sequitur.*
5. *Petitio Principii.*
6. *Non Causa pro Causa.*
7. Many questions.

1. *Accident.* — This is expressed in the Latin phrase, *a dicto simpliciter ad dictum secundum quid.*

This is the fallacy of reasoning from what is true as a general statement (*simpliciter*) to the same statement which is restricted or conditioned in some manner (*secundum quid*).

The following is this fallacy of accident: —

Strychnine is a deadly poison, and therefore it can never be used as a medicine.

2. *Converse Accident.* — This is expressed in the Latin phrase, *a dicto secundum quid, ad dictum simpliciter.* This is the fallacy of reasoning from that which may be true under certain conditions or limitations, to that which however is not true when these conditions or limitations are removed. This is illustrated in the following argument which is very often heard: —

Certain men have risen to prominent positions who never

had a college education; therefore a college education is unnecessary to equip a man for his life's work.

In reference to these two fallacies, there is a passage in Lotze which is of interest, and which is well worth quoting here.

"Two general modes of fallacious thought are developed by the habitual commission of these fallacies, and illustrate them on a grand scale. The first is *doctrinairism*, the second *narrow-mindedness*. The doctrinaire is an idealist who refuses to see that though ideas may be right in the abstract, yet the nature of the circumstances under which and of the objects to which they are to be applied must limit not only their practicability but even their binding force. The narrow-minded, on the other hand, can recognize and esteem no truth and no ideal, even the most universally valid, except in that special form to which they have become accustomed within a limited circle of thought and personal observation. Life is a school which corrects these habits of mind. The parochially minded man sees things persist in spite of himself in taking shapes which he considers unprecedented, but he finds the world somehow survives it, and learns at last that a system of life may be excellent and precious, but that it is rash from that to argue that it is the only proper mode of orderly existence. And the enthusiast for ideals, when he sees the curtailment which every attempt at realization inflicts on them, learns the lesson which the disjunctive theorem might have taught him. Every universal P changes in the act of being applied from something that held *simpliciter* into something that holds *secundum quid*, — changes from P to $p,^1 p,^2$ or p^3; to refuse to accept it in any one of these, which are its only possible shapes, is to ask that it be realized under a condition which even logic pronounces impossible."[1]

3. *Ignoratio Elenchi.* — This is a fallacy which consists primarily in an ignorance of the nature of refutation. To

[1] Lotze's *Logic*, Vol. II, p. 5, Eng. trans.

refute an argument, its logical contradiction must be established. Any proof which falls short of this fails in its end. The nature of this fallacy has been enlarged in scope, so as to comprise any argument whatever which does not squarely meet the point at issue. It is, in many cases, not so much the ignorance of the point at issue, as purposely ignoring the point at issue. It is a natural method of argument when one has a weak case. Any subterfuge which withdraws attention from the point at issue tends, of course, to strengthen the weaker side, at least as regards the plausibility of its position. Suppose a student should be urged to spend more time upon his Latin or Greek, and he should excuse his negligence by insisting that in after life he would never find any practical use for his classics, — this would be the fallacy of *ignoratio elenchi*.

There are various ways in which this fallacy may be illustrated, as follows: —

(*a*) *Argumentum ad hominem.* — This is the fallacy wherein the argument is diverted from the merits of the case to the character or the position of one's opponent.

(*b*) *Argumentum ad populum.* — This is the fallacy of appealing to the passion or prejudice of an audience, rather than to their reason. It is essentially the argument of the demagogue.

(*c*) *Argumentum ad ignorantiam.* — This fallacy consists in taking advantage of the ignorance of the person or persons addressed who, consequently, lack the power of discrimination between the true and the false, the relevant and the irrelevant.

(*d*) *Argumentum ad verecundiam.* — This is an appeal to the sentiment of veneration for authority, instead of an appeal directly to the reason. The weight of great names is with some persons the most convincing of all arguments. Logically it is not an argument at all. It may serve to confirm truth, but it does not establish it.

(*e*) *Argumentum ad baculum.* — This repudiates all argument and resorts to force in order to establish one's point.

In distinction from these various kinds of subterfuges to avoid a direct facing of the question, there is the *argumentum ad rem*, or the *argumentum ad judicum*, *i.e.* arguing directly to the point at issue. All lines of argument should converge to this central point.

4. *The Fallacy of the Consequent, or Non Sequitur.* — This fallacy was defined primarily by Aristotle as the formal error of affirming the consequent. It has received, however, in the course of time, a far wider application, and has come to be applied to any loose argument whatever, in which the conclusion does not seem to follow from the premises. It is very convenient to have the phrase *non sequitur* wherewith to characterize such arguments.

5. *Petitio Principii.* — This is the fallacy of begging the question. This is an attempt to assume the conclusion without any attempt whatever to prove it. According to Aristotle this may take place in five ways: —

(1) To assume the point at issue directly. This, however, cannot be done without resort to some rhetorical device to conceal the absence of any real proof.

(2) To assume some more general truth which involves the point at issue.

(3) To assume particular truths which it involves.

(4) To assume the component parts in detail.

(5) To assume some necessary consequence of the point in question.

As an illustration of begging the question, take the following extract from a speech of a member of the House of Commons: "The bill before the House is well calculated to elevate the character of education in this country, for the general standard of instruction in all our schools will be raised by it."

Galileo accuses Aristotle of having committed this fallacy in his argument that "the nature of heavy things is to tend toward the centre of the universe, and of light things to fly from it; therefore, the centre of the earth is the centre of the universe."

There is a special form of this fallacy known as arguing in a circle, *circulus in probando*. This is an attempt to prove a conclusion to follow from a premise, when in truth the premise itself depends upon the truth of the conclusion as its ground. This is illustrated in the following statement taken from a letter written to one of our daily journals quite recently: "The left-handed man lacks will power, for, if not, he wouldn't be left handed."

6. *Non Causa pro Causa.* — This is the fallacy of regarding as a cause that which is not a cause. It is due to the lack of discrimination between a mere coincidence and a veritable cause. There is no fallacy, perhaps, which is so subtle as this one, and none which is more common. As an example of this fallacy, we may cite the exploded hypothesis of a mesmeric fluid to account for the various well-known phenomena of hypnotism; also the statement that nature abhors a vacuum to account for the rise of water in a pump; or the belief that any unusual appearance among the heavenly bodies, as that of a comet, is to be interpreted as a portent of disaster. Many of our common superstitions may be traced to this fallacy. Moreover, inasmuch as the causal relation naturally manifests itself in the form of a sequence, there is a special case of this fallacy which consists in the confusion of mere sequence with a causal connection; this is called the fallacy of *post hoc ergo propter hoc*. This is illustrated in the belief which many entertain, that when thirteen sit down together at a common board, one of the number will surely die within the year; or in the tendency so often observable to attribute the financial prosperity or distress of the country to some legislative measure recently enacted.

7. *The Fallacy of Many Questions.* — A better name for this would be the Fallacy of a Double Question, for it con-

sists in asking a question which is in the form of a single question, but which should have been put in the form of two separate questions. The question which is asked assumes that another question has been already asked and answered. This fallacy usually takes the form of asking a question about an assumed fact whereas the fact is itself in dispute. Thus the question, How much do you pay a certain member of your athletic team for his services, presupposes of course that some amount is certainly paid.

The following anecdote which appeared recently in one of our daily papers also illustrates this fallacy : —

"Charles Bradlaugh, the English free-thinker, once engaged in a discussion with a dissenting minister. He insisted that the minister should answer a question by a simple 'Yes' or 'No,' without any circumlocution, asserting that every question could be replied to in that manner.

"The reverend gentleman rose, and said, 'Mr. Bradlaugh, will you allow me to ask you a question on those terms?'

"'Certainly,' said Bradlaugh.

"'Then, may I ask, have you given up beating your wife?'"

This completes the table of fallacies usually given in treatises on logic. All the general types of fallacies are comprehended in it. There are fallacies, however, which do not distinctively fall under any one type, but are so subtly complex as to involve the errors of many. There are, again, others which arise out of special circumstances, and cannot be classified under any of the types mentioned. They, however, readily disclose themselves to the open mind which is freed from sophistry and prejudice.

PART II

INDUCTIVE LOGIC

CHAPTER I

INDUCTION AND DEDUCTION

THERE have been divergent tendencies in the history of logic, to make either deduction or induction alone the whole of logical procedure in the process of inference. The fact that the Aristotelian logic, which is essentially deductive, has been for centuries exclusively associated with logic as a whole, has left the impression upon many minds that it is the beginning and end of the logical encyclopædia. On the other hand, John Stuart Mill and his followers have attempted to analyze the syllogism so as to prove its essentially inductive character; and they maintain that all reasoning is inductive. This is the position in the main of Bacon, Locke, and Bain. Locke, for instance, insists that the syllogism is of less value than external and internal experience, induction, and common sense.[1]

So also, in a similar vein, Schleiermacher says: "The syllogistic procedure is of no value for the real construction of judgments, for the substituted judgments can only be higher and lower; nothing is expressed in the conclusion but the relation of two terms to each other, which have a common member, and are not without, but within, each other. Advance in thinking, a new cognition, cannot originate by the syllogism; it is merely the reflection upon the way in which we have attained, or could attain, to a judgment, the conclusion; no new insight is ever reached."[2] The two opposed views thus indicated do not necessitate conflicting or mutually exclusive processes. It is better to

---

[1] *Essay on Human Understanding*, Book IV, p. 7.
[2] See Ueberweg, *System of Logic*, etc., p. 345.

regard them, not as radically different types of inference, but rather as different phases of one and the same inferential process. We have seen that inference consists in interpreting the implications of the system to which the given in consciousness belongs. In the light of this definition we can best indicate the relative functions of induction and deduction in the process of inference. When the system can be considered as a whole, and is apprehended in its entirety, then it may become the ground upon which the inference is based, resulting in unfolding the necessary nature or relations of any of the parts considered in themselves, or in reference to the system as a whole. The procedure in such a case is from the nature of the whole system, to the nature of the several parts, and their existent relations, and this is deductive in its essential features.

On the other hand, when we know the various parts, and proceed from them as data to construct the system which their known nature and relations necessitate, it is induction, or procedure from elementary parts to the whole thus necessitated. From a knowledge of the planetary system we can infer the necessary positions of sun, moon, and earth at any required time, as, for instance, in the calculation of an eclipse. This is deduction. But when we begin with investigating the several movements of the different planets, and from them infer the necessary nature of the system of which they are parts, we have the process of induction. Such processes we see must be complementary, and mutually dependent. As Lavater says, "He only sees well who sees the whole in the parts, and the parts in the whole."

Moreover, the distinction between deduction and induction may be shown through their respective relations to the universal, which we have seen is the ground of inference. The question whose answer leads to the deductive process in reasoning, is, What does the universal necessitate? In induction, the question which starts the investigation is, Into what system may the given material properties or relations be constructed so as to reach a universal concept that will be consistent with itself and with the whole of knowledge which forms the world of consciousness? In this there is an analytical discrimination of the essential from the accidental elements, and the gathering together of the former into the complex whole which is the universal. Induction, therefore, is inference viewed from the side of the differences; deduction is inference viewed from that of the universal. For instance, we may investigate the characteristic features of a diamond, and find that a certain specific gravity, 3.53 as compared with water, is a constant and determining attribute, and as such must be incorporated as an essential element of the general concept diamond. We can then form the universal judgment, Whatever stones possess this specific gravity are diamonds. Their differences, regarding size, brilliancy, etc., may all be set aside as accidental, but the one constant determining feature indicates a oneness in which they all agree.

And so with the other essential attributes. After possessing such knowledge gained inductively, we may use it practically in a deductive manner; and it is so used in discriminating between true and imitation stones, as described in the following process: "Diamonds, rubies, and sapphires are now tested by floating to prove their genuineness. The liquid used has five times the density of water, and is composed of double nitrate of silver and thallium. The tests are rapidly made, as all stones of the same nature have the same specific gravity, while none of the bogus ones have the same weight as those they are made to imitate."

Another view of the relation of induction to deduction may be gained by calling attention to the difference of significance between the terms, a "truth" and a "fact." A fact carries with it only the special and individual character of the particular occurrence in which it is manifested. A truth, however, is always universal in its very nature, admitting of universal application, and capable of illustration in an indefinite number of different facts which embody its essence. In deduction we have given some truth of universal nature that leads to individual facts that may be subsumed under it. In induction, we interpret a fact or a number of facts in the light of their universal implication, on the ground that there can be no such thing as an isolated fact, but every fact must have some relation to a universal to which it must be referred.

While considering the distinctions between induction and deduction, we must not overlook their mutual dependence. We cannot proceed in deduction irrespective of induction, because the universal upon which the deductive process is based arises in the majority of cases from a previous induction. It is true that the universal term may be in a proposition that is known *a priori*, as the axioms of geometry and certain space and time postulates; but a very small proportion of major premises can be said to have such an origin, and their resulting conclusions have very slight material significance. Deduction that reaches other than purely abstract and formal conclusions must rest upon induction for the material to form its premises. We find this even in the technical construction of the syllogism, where, for instance, the question of the distribution of the terms is raised. We may insist that a certain middle term is distributed, as it is the subject of an universal affirmative proposition; but then the further question naturally suggests itself, How do we know that the proposition in question is really a universal? Its material significance alone tells us that we may write it as an *A* or *I* proposition, as the case may be. The matter is a function of the form, and the form a function of the matter. They cannot be separated, in fact, unless we conceive reasoning as a purely formal process of determining a conclusion, irrespective of the truth or falsity of the premises. If we regard the premises as given, and we accept them with unquestioning credence, the deduction is purely formal; so, also, if the various terms are expressed by letters *A*, *B*, *C*, etc., and devoid of any material significance. Any process of reasoning based upon a slavish acceptance of premises can only reach artificial and even false results. In the actual experiences of life our premises are not made for us. They must be constructed by us through our interpretation of reality. Disregard of this has brought formal logic into much disrepute, and it has often degenerated into the barren discussion of logical puzzles and quibbles. Grant a person any premises he may choose to assume, irrespective of an inductive test of their validity, he can prove black white and white black.

On the other hand, induction is dependent upon deduction; for we cannot reason from particular instances to a universal proposition, unless we assume as basis of the whole inductive process some postulate which has real universal significance. Otherwise, we reach only a high degree of probability, but not necessity; a rude generalization, but not universality. When we assert some such general statement as this, that arsenic always acts as a poison, we have based the universal character of the proposition upon an underlying postulate that is understood even though it is not expressed, such as the uniformity of nature, that under identical conditions we always look for identical effects. This will be discussed later more in detail; it is referred to at this point merely to illustrate the deductive basis of induction. Bradley insists that there can be no such thing as induction, because it always rests upon an implied universal which gives to the process as a whole a deductive character.[1] His criticism has the force only of proving that induction cannot be independent of deduction. This dependence does not, however, necessarily vitiate the integrity of induction as a mode of the inferential process. Lotze has placed special emphasis upon this dependemce of induction upon deduction. He says: "It is the custom in our day to

[1] Bradley, *Principles of Logic*, p. 342.

collect into one body the numerous operations which assist us in ascending from particulars to generals, or to call this inductive logic, and to set it against the deductive or demonstrative logic along with much disparagement of the latter. Such disparagement rests on a mistake. The inductive methods, it is certain, are the most effectual helps to the attainment of new truth, but it is no less certain that they rest entirely on the results of deductive logic." [1]

Moreover, in induction the results obtained and formulated in general propositions may be extended and often modified by a deduction which is based upon them as major premises; for the deduction thus proceeding from them reveals new instances which conform or perhaps modify the simple inductive results themselves. What is popularly called a hasty generalization, if made a major premise of a syllogism, will often lead us astray through the deductions drawn from it. As soon as we are aware of this, we return to question the validity of the generalization, whose weakness is not appreciated until thus tested and revealed. Thus deduction serves to extend and correct the results of induction, and at the same time it itself is dependent upon the results of inductive generalization for the material to form its premises. We come to see therefore how intimately associated these two processes are in actual reasoning. For convenience of illustrating their individual characteristics, they may be considered as separate, and each investigated as an independent mode of inference. But they are in reality mutually related and dependent, and are always found manifesting their functions together. In any course of reasoning concerning the conduct of our everyday affairs, or in scientific investigation, — anywhere, indeed, outside of the artificial examples of logical text-books, — we reason both inductively and deductively in one complex process.

[1] Lotze, *Logic*, p. 288. See also Bosanquet, *Logic*, Vol. II, p. 119.

CHAPTER II

THE ESSENTIALS OF INDUCTION

WE now proceed to a more precise determination of the nature of induction. Its point of view in all reasoning has reference to concrete instances. They are the data, and from them general propositions are to result. The procedure is from given facts to laws which are the ground and explanation of these facts. We are here however at once struck with the evident break in the course of our reasoning. Procedure from the particular to the universal cannot be a continuous process. There is a gap somewhere. The conclusion contains more than the premises. In deduction, we are proceeding from the greater to the less, and we experience no violation of our logical sense; but at once we appreciate the difficulty which attends the reverse process from the less to the greater.[1] Here we soon reach a point where we pass beyond the sphere of our experience to the generalization which necessarily embraces far more than our experience. This is the so-called inductive leap; or it is sometimes referred to as the inductive hazard. But is this a leap in the dark — a wild guess concerning all that lies beyond the sensuous sphere of our immediate experience? This would be the case, were we compelled to use the mere data of experience as sole ground for our inferences. John Stuart Mill insists that nothing whatever is given in consciousness but particular sensations, and these are but subjective states of feeling, and with no assurance of any definite correspondence with the external world. With such purely empirical data it is impossible to proceed to truths of

[1] See p. 107.

universal validity. It is necessary to postulate some universal truth which the mind through strictly *a priori* considerations is constrained to formulate, and which will serve to bridge the gulf between the particular and the universal.

This postulate has been variously expressed by different authors, yet with substantially the same significance in all. In the older logic, it is put under the convenient formula of the uniformity of nature; that is, that beyond the sphere of experience, phenomena will behave in the same manner under like conditions, as in the sphere of immediate observation and experiment. In the modern logic this is somewhat differently expressed. The phrase "uniformity of nature," being somewhat indefinite and implying a point of view purely objective, is not used. Modern writers have omitted it largely from their terminology. Lotze says: "The logical idea upon which induction rests is by no means merely probable, but certain and irrefragable. It consists in the conviction based upon the principle of identity, that every determinate phenomenon M can depend upon only one determinate condition, and accordingly that, where under apparently different circumstances or in different subjects P, S, T, U, the same M occurs, there must inevitably be in them some common element Σ which is the true identical condition of M, or the true subject of M."[1] We have a somewhat similar description of the basis of the inductive process given by Sigwart: "The logical justification of the inductive process rests upon the fact that it is an inevitable postulate of our effort after knowledge that the given is necessary, and can be known as proceeding from its grounds according to universal laws."[2] Bosanquet considers as the basis of inductive inference that which he calls the postulate of knowledge, that "the universe is a rational system, taking 'rational' to mean not only of such a nature that it can be known by intelligence, but further of such a nature that it can be known and handled by our intelligence."[3]

---

[1] Lotze, *Logic*, p. 102. [2] Sigwart, *Logic* (Eng. trans.), Vol. II, p. 289.
[3] Bosanquet, *The Essentials of Logic*, p. 166.

I have quoted these passages from Lotze, Bosanquet, and Sigwart, that we may appreciate the modern tendency to derive the inductive postulate from an epistemological source; namely, that our knowledge must be consistent throughout with itself, part to part, and parts to whole, and that the world for us is the world as constructed by our knowledge. Whatever is given in consciousness must belong therefore in the one place where it appropriately and necessarily belongs. Here also there must be a place for everything, and everything in its place. There must be a uniformity of consciousness; that is, the primary postulate and the uniformity of nature is secondary to this, and implied in it. This postulate may also be expressed as follows: What is once true is always true. Here "true" is used in the sense of the universal significance of a fact. Whenever a concrete instance is present in consciousness, its existence must be considered as necessitated by some antecedent which can satisfactorily account for it, and which can at the same time be appropriately adjusted to the whole of our knowledge in interpreting it. Bosanquet says that "ideally speaking, every concrete real totality can be analyzed into a complex of necessary relations."[1] These necessary relations of course have a universal significance, and therefore in every concrete instance, if we can rightly interpret it, we may discern the universal element which is contained in it, and gives it a place and meaning in the world as cognized by us. Nature, after all, is only another word for the world as we know it.

There is a sense in which induction may be regarded as the inverse process of deduction. In deduction the problem is concerned with the question, What does the universal necessitate? In induction, the instance is given, and the problem is, What universal can be discovered which could give rise to the instance in question? This view of induction is especially associated with the name of Jevons, whose

[1] Bosanquet, *Logic*, Vol. II, p. 82.

inductive system is described as the inverse of deduction. He calls it the deciphering of the hidden meaning of natural phenomena.[1] The name commonly used to designate this view of induction is that of "reduction," originally suggested by Duhamel.[2] This process was known to the old logicians, who called it "Method," to denote the process of hunting for middle terms by the aid of which a given conclusion could be proved.[3] Like all inverse processes, it is by itself an indeterminate one.

Given, All A is B, and
All B is C,

we infer by the direct process of deduction that

All A is C.

But in the indirect or inverse process we have given A is C, and the problem, to find a middle term which necessitates such a conclusion, is an indeterminate one. There may be a number of middle terms. This is analogous in one respect to the method of integral calculus; while differentiation leads to a definite result, the inverse process of integration leads to an indeterminate result. So also we multiply two numbers, producing one determinate result; but inversely, when we have given a certain number, and ask what factors multiplied together could produce this number, we may reach several different solutions. The answer is indeterminate. Professor Jevons, in his scheme of inductive inference, falls back upon probability to indicate which of several possibilities is the most likely one in the given case.[4] But before the inverse operation can result in determinate results, the given terms such as A and C must be subjected to some analysis in order that their material signification may give suggestion as to the nature

---

[1] Jevons, *Principles of Science*, p. 124.
[2] Duhamel, *Methodes*, Vol. I, p. 24.
[3] Venn, *Empirical Logic*, p. 361.
[4] Jevons, *Principles of Science*, p. 219.

of the middle term. For instance, a man is found dead, washed ashore by the tide; the natural supposition would be that he met his death by drowning. And yet it might possibly happen that the man died through injuries inflicted by blows, or by poison, or heart failure. The attendant circumstances and bodily indications must suggest the most probable cause to account for the given effect. Venn criticises Jevons' view of induction, that is, making it the inverse process of deduction, on the ground that it is purely a formal process, and therefore can lead only to indeterminate results.[1]

It is always possible, however, to make some analysis of the material significance of the data, as has been above indicated, which relieves the purely formal processes from the indefiniteness of the results. Bosanquet criticises Jevons' theory of inductive inference, in that the hypothesis proposed to account for the given in reality can at best be only highly probable.[2] However, Venn, Lotze, Bosanquet, Sigwart, all allow a place to the inverse function of all inductive reasoning; their contention, however, is this, that it does not funish an adequate account of the whole matter.[3]

It is interesting to note that Whewell's theory of induction corresponds in the main to this idea of reduction, or inverse process. He finds in induction a twofold operation of the mind, consisting in the colligation of facts and the explication of conceptions. By the colligation of facts he refers to that insight which is able to see the connections and relations which necessarily exist between the different phenomena present in consciousness; and by explication of conceptions he refers to the appropriate fitting in of these related facts to some conception of the mind which most readily accounts for them.[4] Such a process is merely the

---

[1] *Empirical Logic*, p. 359.   [2] Bosanquet, *Logic*, Vol. II, p. 175.
[3] Venn, 361; Bosanquet, Vol. II, p. 175; Sigwart, Vol. II, p. 203, 289. Lotze, *Outlines of Logic*, p. 93.
[4] Whewell, *Philosophy of the Inductive Sciences*, pp. 172, 202.

reading of given facts backward to their origin, or substantially an inverse process, where the procedure is from the given concrete to the explanation of the same in terms of the universal to which it can be most appropriately referred. So also Mill's account of procedure by hypothesis presents characteristics similar to this process of reduction.

The end of induction is to discover a law having objective validity and universal application. There is a distinction which must be noticed and clearly kept in mind; namely, the distinction between a law and a rule. Induction seeks a law, and not a rule. A law expresses the essential and universal relations subsisting between given phenomena, eliminating entirely all accidental and local coloring. A law has objective validity, and preserves a constant nature. There can be only one law in reference to one and the same connection of facts. A rule however is subjective, dealing with the individual's attitude to phenomena, rather than an explanation of the essential features of the phenomena themselves. It often is determined in the concrete by that which is external, local, and accidental. There may be many rules, varying with many minds and many tastes. Fundamental and universal laws of political economy become maxims and rules in different communities. The laws of morality, universal and immutable, become rules of conduct in individual experience, admitting of wide difference of opinion and diversity of application.[1] In the processes of induction, therefore, the law is the desideratum, and not the rule.

Law however is used rather loosely in our ordinary terminology. Law as used in jurisprudence has a meaning quite different from law as used in physical science. And so, also, the laws of biology, the laws of political economy, the laws of ethics, are referred to with different shades of meaning in each sphere. However ambiguous may be the significance of "law" in ordinary thought and usage, never-

[1] Lotze, *Logic*, p. 335.

theless in induction it has a constant and a simple significance, which, if carefully adhered to, will avoid confusion and obscurity as well, in our inferential processes and results. Law in induction is always in the form of an hypothetical universal: —

If A is, B is.

It does not assert what has happened, but what should happen under certain conditions. Given the antecedent A, a certain determinate consequent B is always necessitated. The relation is constant and invariable, and therefore has a universal significance.

Induction holds a peculiar and important place in our everyday life, because it has to do with the analytical treatment of instances as they appear in experience. The large part of our conscious thinking has to do with the concrete, the raw-material of experience; this, induction alone can handle. Leonardo da Vinci's maxim was "to begin with experience and by means of it to direct the reason."[1] Thus the superstructure of knowledge is raised day by day. The given is continually being interpreted and referred to its appropriate place, as the stones of the quarry are hewn and fitted into their proper position in the building for which they have been designed. There are certain individual experiences which it is impossible to determine through our syllogistic forms. They cannot be judged deductively. There is no general category under which they can be subsumed. They may be formally illogical if thus expressed, and yet admit of direct investigation and experiment in the inductive manner, for the purpose of disclosing the law underlying them and as yet unknown.

It often happens that through indifference or indolence we are content to refer many phenomena to long-established and convenient categories, which, if investigated independently, we would find could not possibly be so treated. The

[1] Ueberweg, *Logic*, p. 42.

convenient pigeon hole, because near at hand, receives much that does not properly belong there. It is the office of induction to investigate anew the old material, and then to reclassify in accordance with the revised generalizations which such investigations may necessitate.

The procedure by induction is in keeping with the scientific spirit of the day, — to interpret the phenomena of nature as given, and not to anticipate nature through preconceptions, and wrest fact in order to fit theory. It comes to the sources in nature with empty vessels, to draw and carry away that which nature alone can give.

CHAPTER III

TYPES OF INDUCTIVE INFERENCE

THE process of induction, as we have seen, is a procedure from given instances to the discovery of the law which underlies them, and which is the ground of the connection of the various attributes and relations that unite in the one concrete whole. Viewed from the standpoint of the direction of the process, we have found that it is always toward some general expression of individual experiences, and in this respect it is the inverse of deduction, which proceeds from the general to the particulars which are embraced in it. There is however another and important point of view that should not be overlooked. We have to consider the mode of the process as well as its direction; not merely the result to be attained, but also the peculiar manner of realizing the same must be considered. Difference in method here gives rise to various kinds of inductive inference. The end proposed in all is to generalize our experiences as they occur in the concrete and particular. When I find a given phenomenon, A, given in consciousness, and characterized by several distinctive features among which I note specially the mark B, the question at once most naturally suggests itself, Is there a reasonable expectation that I shall always find B as an inseparable accompaniment of A, so that I can assert confidently that whenever A is found, B also will be found? There are three ways of satisfying ourselves as to the existence of any constant rather than coincidental connection between antecedent and consequent, as A and B. These give rise to three different methods of inductive research, and they are as follows:—

I. The Method of Enumeration.
II. The Method of Analogy.
III. The Method of Scientific Analysis, or search after causal connection.

Failure to distinguish between the three methods has given rise to confusion in the definition of and corresponding reference to inductive inference; some authors use induction in one, and some in another of these senses. It is necessary to discriminate carefully, and to maintain a strict consistency in the usage of the terms as defined.

I. *The Method of Enumeration.* — We observe the various instances in which certain attributes, as A and B, are conjoined in our experience. We count them in the sense of noting to what extent they accumulate without noticing any exception to what seems at least an invariable connection. We do not necessarily count by precise enumeration reaching a numerically definite result. We notice merely to what extent the observed instances of like nature accumulate; that is, whether a few, a considerable number, or a very large number. The mere number of instances produces a certain psychological impression, whatever may be their logical force. This is brought about through the laws of association, and creates an expectation of a continuous repetition of the experience in question. This arises from a natural tendency of the mind to generalize. We observe that crows are black; and the increasing number of confirming instances goes far to establish a connection between the crow and its color which seems to have universal validity. The enumeration of instances may lead us to any one of three results: —

1. We may meet with no exception whatsoever, until the scope of observation completely embraces the sum of all possible instances. This is complete enumeration, and when enumeration reaches this limit, it passes over into deductive reasoning, by virtue of the logical canon that

TYPES OF INDUCTIVE INFERENCE 185

whatever is true of the parts is true of the whole distributively; that is, provided the summation of the parts has been an exhaustive one. We assert that all the sheep of a given flock are white; for we have observed each separately, and no one has been missed in the count. So, also, the judgment that all planets move around the sun, resulting from an enumeration of the planets one by one. It is possible also to have a perfect induction with an infinite enumeration of parts. This is possible in two cases, as pointed out by Beneke.[1] First, when the parts are connected together continuously in space. This occurs in geometrical demonstration when the inference, based upon the simple figure it refers to, is extended to all figures falling under the like definition. And second, when the parts are not continuously connected, if it can be proved syllogistically that what is true of a definite nth part, must also be true for the $(n+1)$th part.

Perfect induction also embraces arithmetical method and computation. Here the whole, which is the sum of the facts in each case, is a totality or universal whose differences, which are all separate and distinguishable, are yet homogeneous and equal.[2] There is no qualitative differentiation of parts, only a quantitative one. The total is the sum of the units, and each unit is like every other one. If we have one hundred units making a totality, the one that may be the twenty-seventh is precisely like the sixty-seventh. It is a case where each one counts for one and no one for more than one, in an absolutely literal sense.

It has been urged against perfect induction that it affords no new information, and, therefore, its results are not valuable. However, the summation of particulars in abbreviated forms is always an advantage. It is a labor-saving process to the mind. It enables the mind to retain a large number of facts by throwing them into one and the same

---

[1] Quoted by Ueberweg, *Logic*, p. 482.
[2] Bosanquet, *Logic*, Vol. II, p. 54.

category; and it facilitates arithmetical processes by convenient comprehending of units within a totality.

2. The second result that is possible, is that, in counting instances, our enumeration should prove incomplete. From the necessities of the case, we are often not able to observe the entire sphere of possible occurrences and cover the whole ground. It may be that beyond the sphere of our experience, the constant connection between certain phenomena may be disturbed by the appearance of some variable factor of which we have been wholly ignorant. It is the possibilities beyond the sphere of observation which render uncertain the results of our count. We are sure as far as we have observed; but we have not gone far enough perhaps. Such results, formulated in general propositions, are termed empirical laws; that is, generalizations from an experience necessarily limited.

3. We have still a third case; where in our enumeration of positive instances we meet with exceptions to a greater or less extent. Here we cannot even sum up the actual experience in terms of a generalization. There are outstanding exceptions which will invalidate it. We must, therefore, fall back upon the theory of probability and the calculation of chances, presuming that, in general, we will meet with the same proportion of exceptions to positive instances in the future, that we have already observed in the past. So we make, in our minds at least, comparative tables of positive cases over against exceptions, and reach a summary of the result in the form of a ratio, whose numerator will be the number of positive cases observed, and the denominator the total number of instances including positive instances and the corresponding exceptions. We observe that some cryptogamous plants possess a purely cellular structure; others, however, do not, being partially vascular. The probability that a new cryptogam will be cellular can be estimated only on the ground of the comparative number of known cryptogams which are cellular, as over against

the total number of cryptogams, both cellular and vascular, previously observed.[1]

II. *The Method of Analogy.* — Here, also, we start with the experience that A is characterized by the mark B. But there is additional knowledge of which we may avail ourselves in the generalization of some past experience already effected, such as the following: that A very closely resembles C, in that the two have many properties or attributes in common. The inference by analogy is that C also, as well as A, will have the mark B. It may be that we cannot examine C in a number of various instances to see in how many the mark B occurs. Our only resource is the inference which is based upon the known resemblances, or analogies. This kind of inference, for example, was employed by Sir Isaac Newton in a very interesting manner. He had observed that certain "fat, sulphureous, unctious bodies," such as camphor, oils, spirit of turpentine, amber, etc., have refractive powers two or three times greater than might be anticipated from their densities. He noticed also the unusually high refractive index of diamond, and from this resemblance, based upon similarity in reference to one attribute only, he inferred that diamond also would prove to be combustible. His prediction in this regard was verified by the Florentine Academicians in 1694.[2] Brewster made a striking comment upon Newton's inference, to the effect that if Newton had drawn a like analogy in reference to greenockite and octahedrite as he did concerning diamond, inasmuch as they, too, have a very high refractive index, he would have been wholly incorrect. This is an indication of the fact that argument by analogy is not conclusive.

Bosanquet has very strikingly expressed the essence of the analogical method in saying that "in analogy we weigh the instances rather than count them."[3] The distinction

[1] Jevons, *Principles of Science*, pp. 146, 147. [2] *Ibid.* p. 527.
[3] Bosanquet, *The Essentials of Logic*, p. 155.

between analogy and enumeration of instances lies in this, that in the former we count similar attributes in the contents of two instances, and balance them against the dissimilar or unknown. In induction by enumeration we count similar instances, considering them in their totality without examination and comparison of their respective attributes.

III. *The Method of Scientific Analysis.* — The instance in question, A, which is characterized by the mark B, is subjected to a vigorous analytical examination, to show that A and B are related through a causal connection. This analysis is effected either through a minute observation or by means of exact experiment. The end to be attained by such analysis is to separate a complex phenomenon into its several elements, by which process a causal connection may be revealed, whose very existence is disguised by the complexity of the phenomenon. For instance, the phenomenon of death following the taking of arsenic is an event so complex as to evade a precise determination of the causal relation. When analyzed into simpler elements, it is found that the immediate effect of arsenic upon the bodily tissues is to harden them so as to prevent their normal functioning. This is the causal ground of the death due to arsenic. Moreover, this analytic process, which may be appropriately called a material one, is supplemented by a formal process of negation; that is, an instance in which the suspected causal element is absent in the complex phenomenon under investigation, and the related effect, before observed, now no longer appears. This formal process acts as a check, and as a verification as well, of the material analysis of the phenomenon. For example, an antidote, as sesquioxide of iron, being administered, no death from arsenic occurs; and it is also observed that no hardening of the tissues has resulted, therefore the former result, hardening of tissues producing death, has been thus corroborated negatively by the fact that where no hardening of tissues has resulted, death does not follow.

We see at once the advantage of such a method over that of counting all instances where taking of arsenic has caused death. The latter is a phenomenally adjudged result; the former penetrates with analytic insight to the ground of the phenomenon itself. Thus one instance, if its parts and their manifold relations are adequately comprehended, may suffice for a universal conclusion based upon it. It is true, however, as remarked by Bosanquet, that "number of observations does, as a rule, assist analysis and contribute to eliminating error. Scientific analysis as such, however, does not deal with instances, but only with contents."[1]

In cases where the phenomenon does not reveal its component elements under observation, and it is impossible to subject it to experiment, the most likely cause of the effect in question is tentatively judged to be the real cause, until it can be verified in reality. This is procedure by hypothesis, and is always resorted to as preliminary to a subsequent experiment which is its test, or else in lieu of such an experiment when it is by the nature of the case precluded. It is a form of *ideal* analysis. The experiment is constructed mentally. The phenomenon is separated into what we would reasonably imagine its simpler elements would be. We are constrained to believe that if the hypothetical antecedent existed, it would be adequate to produce the effect. Although rising in the sphere of the imagination, it is that with which the mind is, for the time at least, satisfied as an explanation of the facts which demand some cause to account for them. Regarding induction as a process of reduction, hypothesis is the assumed universal or middle term, which will necessitate the phenomenon under investigation as its logical conclusion.

We will now proceed to a further examination of these methods, considered both singly and together.

1. They all proceed upon the supposition that what is given in consciousness has some necessary ground for its

[1] Bosanquet, *Logic*, Vol. II, p. 118.

being. In enumerative induction, there is some causal connection presupposed, yet in a very general and indefinite manner, and accompanied by no analysis of the various concepts either by a systematic observation or experiment. It is a vague sense of uniformity, which, when observed for many times, we feel will continue indefinitely. That which has happened often and not contradicted carries with it a certain convincing power by dint of bare repetition, especially to persons of narrow experience, and unaccustomed to discriminating observation. Ueberweg has made the following comment in reference to the so-called imperfect induction. "The conclusion is made universal with more or less probability, and the blank which remains over in the given relations of spheres is legitimately filled up partly on the universal presupposition of a causal-nexus in the objects of knowledge, partly on the particular presupposition that in the case presented such a causal-nexus exists as connects the subject and predicate of the conclusion. The degree of probability of the inductive inference depends in each case on the admissibility of this last presupposition, and the various inductive operations, the extension of the sphere of observation, the simplification of the observed conditions by successive exhaustion of the unessential, etc., all tend to secure its admissibility."[1]

Analogy likewise proceeds upon the assumption of an underlying cause among the observed phenomena, and this is more definitely in the foreground throughout the process than in that of induction by enumeration. Analogy is based upon the postulate that similar phenomena have similar causes; the greater the agreement of the various attributes of the different phenomena compared, the greater will be the resultant probability that causes capable of producing them as effects will be similar. The similarity of the lightning flash to the electric spark suggested to Benjamin Franklin the possibility that they were due to a like origin, and

[1] Ueberweg, *Logic*, pp. 483 f.

by experiment his analogical reasoning was actually confirmed, as is well known. Upon the theory that the world as it exists for us in knowledge forms a system, to some place in which every phenomenon given in experience must be appropriately and necessarily referred, it follows therefore that a simple experience devoid of any complexity of parts may fit into several possible places in our world of consciousness, and remain so far forth indeterminate. However, a complex phenomenon, with many parts intricately connected, will fit into one unique place only in the system to which it must be referred. It is like a key that will fit into only one lock. The presumption therefore is that any other phenomenon which resembles the first through much of its entire content, part for part, attribute for attribute, will also resemble it further as regards other attributes not yet examined, so that it will likewise fit into the peculiar place in the system of knowledge to which the first has been found to belong. There is always a strong probability that agreement in spheres of great complexity is not a mere coincidence, but the result of a causal relation. One characteristic of a system, which we have found to be the ground of inference generally, is the coördination of like things under one concept. Analogy therefore is based upon the view of causal connections within the system which comprises the world as given in consciousness.

In the third method, the causal relation is more prominent still, and the search for it characterizes the procedure employed. That which in the other methods may exist merely as a vague impression is here formulated and made the direct and sole object of research.

2. The three methods in the order here presented show an increasing prominence given to the causal connection in the phenomena of experience. And therefore they possess a relatively increasing scientific value. As the first has only indirect reference to the causal connection of its facts, it is the least trustworthy and has no claim as a scientific

method. It breaks down as soon as an exception is noted; and is even weakened by the fact that it is constantly menaced by the possibility at least of the appearance of an exception. "How do we know," says Green, "that the instances, with the examination of which we are always dispensing on the strength of the rule (that is, our generalization), might not be just what would invalidate it, if they were examined?"[1] We may arrive at the conclusion, based upon our observation and consequent record, that all sheep are white, and yet black sheep do occur, in every flock, as the proverb has it. According to Aristotle, the proposition that all swans are white, was a perfectly general one, and yet in recent times black swans have been discovered in Australia. Bacon's criticism upon this method has become classic: "Inductio quae procedit per enumerationem simplicem, res puerilis est et precario concludit et periculo exponitur ab instantia contradictoria et plerumque secundum pauciora quam par est et exiis tantummodo quae presto sunt pronunciat."[2]

The validity of this method of procedure depends largely upon the probability of our meeting and noticing exceptions were they to occur. As Lotze puts it: "A man who never observes a place of public resort but once in every seven days, and that on a Sunday afternoon, has no right to suppose, because it is crowded then, that it is as crowded on a week-day."[3] He is here in no position to note the exceptions even should they occur.

Analogy, unless confirmed by experiment, or upon the ground of resemblance established by a verifiable hypothesis, has no claim to be considered as a scientific method. There may be false analogies depending upon surface resemblances. A child might conclude that oil would put out fire because it so closely resembles water, which he knows can extinguish the flames. The difference between essential and accidental

---

[1] Green, *Philosophical Works*, Vol. II, p. 282.
[2] *Novum Organum*, i. 105.   [3] Lotze, *Logic*, p. 343.

agreement between phenomena can be revealed only when the underlying cause is ascertained.

The third method alone has scientific worth. True induction must be a continued search to discover a causal relation.

3. The two first processes fulfil their functions largely as tentative and suggestive methods. In enumeration of instances, we are often led to note resemblances which become the basis of analogy. And analogy suggests, in turn, hypothesis which is capable of verification through subsequent experiment.

The question may be put, "Which of the three processes is induction proper?". The fact is that it may involve all three, but it is not complete until it reaches the third, — the experimental method. Analogy is especially fertile in suggestion. Scientific minds most carefully trained and versed in scientific methods of research are often most keen in noting resemblances, and detecting analogies which become the basis of their experiments. Newton possessed that rare insight which, in spite of the manifest dissimilarity of the two phenomena, could yet discern an essential likeness between the fall of an apple and the gravitating force of the moon toward the earth.

4. It is also to be observed that the choice of method will depend largely upon mental habit. Some minds naturally or by special training and surroundings are given to experiment. They have a testing facility and inventive capacity. Others naturally are susceptible in an unusual degree to contrasts and resemblances. Others again are accustomed to accurate observation that is ever pushing beyond and seeking to extend its sphere. Thus we have a natural division of these methods according to psychical proclivities. The choice of method is often conditioned by the force of circumstances. Experiment is not always possible. Are all crows black? There is no connection between the general organism of the crow and its color that has thus far been

revealed through analysis or experiment. The only recourse is to number instances over the widest possible field. We say, moreover, that Mars may be inhabited; for it has an atmosphere similar to the earth and therefore capable of sustaining life. Analogy is the only guide in such a case, and it is impossible to verify it either by observation or experiment.

5. All the methods tend to one end, that of effecting a generalization of experience. The generalization may be either a numerically general one, or one expressed in terms of a generic concept.

(1) The former consists in the extension of several instances to their repetition under like conditions.

(2) The second consists in the extension of several instances to all cognate species under the same genus.

Examples of these two kinds of generalization are as follows: The general proposition that all sulphur is combustible is of the former kind; all instances are substantially of the same nature, and do not differ as distinguishable species under the same genus, but rather a repetition of like phenomena. The general concept in the above proposition is of the nature of an *infima species*. On the other hand, the proposition that all mammals are vertebrates, has the subject-term in form of a generic concept. Many species, differing widely among themselves, may be embraced under it.[1]

[1] Sigwart, *Logic*, Vol. II, pp. 310, 311.

CHAPTER IV

CAUSATION

WE have seen that induction as a truly scientific method consists in the analytical determination of the relations of cause to effect in any complex phenomenon, accompanied by a generalization of the result obtained. The final outcome of such a process is a universal concept which embodies a law, expressed in terms of a constant connection between antecedent and consequent. As Green has said, "The essence of induction consists in the discovery of the causes of phenomena."[1] A causal view of the universe gives rise to logical concepts, whereas a mythological view of the universe, as in ancient times, resulted in mere empirical concepts, which gave no assurance either of stability or invariability. It will be necessary therefore to determine more precisely the logical significance of the causal idea, which seems to underlie all inductive inference. This is no easy task. According to Clifford, "cause" has sixty-four meanings in Plato, and forty-eight in Aristotle.[2]

The causal idea has sometimes found expression in the phrase, the uniformity of nature, or it is often referred to as the doctrine of universal causation. These two phrases are often used interchangeably; this gives rise to confusion of thought, for their meanings are quite distinct.

Uniformity of nature, strictly interpreted, means that like antecedents, under precisely the same conditions, will be followed by like effects; this idea expresses one phase of causation, viz. its invariability.

---
[1] Green, *Philosophical Works*, Vol. I, p. 284.
[2] Clifford, *Lectures and Essays*, Vol. I, p. 149.

The doctrine of <u>universal causation</u>, however, expresses the impossibility of phenomena rising spontaneously, without an antecedent, or antecedents, sufficient rationally to account for them. The two ideas lie at the root of the causal idea. As Tennyson has put it: —

For nothing is that errs from Law.

Some confusion has also arisen from the failure to discriminate precisely between the philosophical and the purely logical questions relative to the general subject of causation. <u>Causation</u> may be viewed from three different points of view: —

1. What it is <u>phenomenally</u>, that is, as regards its physical aspects.

2. What it is <u>essentially</u>, as regards its real nature. This is a metaphysical question.

3. What it is in respect to its characteristic attribute of <u>invariability</u>. This is a purely logical question.

(1) As to the first, what is causation <u>phenomenally</u>? What is its purely physical significance? Investigations in this line have led to the doctrine of the <u>conservation of energy</u>. This is substantially the assertion that, in every event, no new energy is called forth which did not exist before potentially at least, nor can any energy be ultimately lost; nothing new is created, — there is only a change or transfer from one state or condition to another. Moreover, the sum total of energy in the universe is a constant quantity; it can neither be added to, nor subtracted from. There is an excellent illustration of this theory in the admirable chapter on "Conservation of Energy" by Professor Tait. I give it somewhat in full: "I allow an electric current to pass through a galvanic battery, and there is for the moment a certain quantity of zinc consumed, or, as we may put it, a certain quantity of potential energy in the battery has been converted into the kinetic energy of a current of electricity. That current of electricity passes round some yards of cop-

per wire, coiled round a bar of iron or a number of fine iron wires which are standing vertically inside this apparatus. The moment the current passes, these iron wires are converted into magnets, but, in consequence of the conservation of energy, while this is going on they weaken the current. The current of electricity becomes weaker in the act of making the magnet, but the moment the magnet springs into existence, it again is weakened, because, from the necessities of its position, its mere coming into existence necessitates the passage of a new current of electricity in another coil of wire which surrounds this externally, and finally this last current we can use to produce heat, or light, or sound."[1] In this cycle of changes we see how closely connected even disparate phenomena are, and how the appearance of energy in any one definite state is dependent upon its previous existence in some other state. The doctrine of conservation of energy, we shall see later on, may be suggestive as to the nature of the analytical treatment of cause and effect.

(2) The philosophical question as to the inner nature of causation met with one answer generally until the time of Hume; namely, that the idea of cause signified that the antecedent was efficient in producing the corresponding consequent, implying the transfer of power sufficient to bring about the effect. Hume, however, contended that in the greatest possible extent of our knowledge, all that we certainly know is this, that one event follows another. We have no ground for an assertion concerning the manner in which the sequence is effected, nor for assuming any real tie between them. Hume insisted that phenomena were conjoined, but never connected.[2] His opponents, as Kant and others, deny him, however, his fundamental position,—that the origin of the causal concept comes from experience alone. They urged that it has an *a priori* origin, a concept simple

[1] Tait, *Recent Advances in Physical Science*, pp. 76, 77.
[2] Hume, *Essay on Idea of Necessary Causation*.

and unanalyzable, given through intuitive insight; developed in the sphere of experience, but not dependent upon experience for its warrant. It is an interesting fact that the idea of the conservation of energy developed subsequent to Hume's time. It seems to give evidence which Hume insisted was not and could not be forthcoming; namely, concerning the idea of the antecedent as an efficient power. Through the modern doctrine, the impression of a transfer of real power is produced, though its mode and manner still remain a mystery.

(3) The logical aspect concerns not the phenomenal manifestation of cause and effect, nor their inner nature, but rather the element of invariability in causation. Two questions here suggest themselves: First, Is invariability a fact, — a constant element in causation? Second, How do we account for its existence? The first only has truly logical significance. The invariability of causation, that like antecedents under precisely the same conditions produce like effects, alone makes induction possible. Mill says that it is the belief in the uniformity of nature which stands as the ultimate major premise in every process of induction. Hume accepted it, and based inferences upon it, and never challenged it as a working basis as regards the affairs of everyday life. He acknowledged the element of invariability, and only denied the bond of connection. This element has peculiar logical significance: without it, it would be impossible to extend our knowledge beyond the seen and the heard, indeed that which is seen and heard would then have no meaning, and no basis for their interpretation and appreciation. Being assumed, however, as a logical postulate, we have a basis for induction, — a constant to be sought for and to be depended upon, in explanation of the past and in prediction of the future.

When we come to the second question, which is essentially a genetic one, how the belief in the uniformity of nature arose, we find two classes which answer respectively that the belief arose *a priori*, and on the other hand, from experience simply. The former is the opinion especially associated with the Scottish School of philosophy. Hume holds that it proceeds from a psychological law of custom or habit, — an unbroken line of mental associations inducing a belief within, concerning the uniformity of nature without. Mill has also a like empirical basis for a belief in the uniformity of nature; he holds that having observed uniformity in many experiences, in fact never contradicted, we generalize so as to cover a sphere beyond our experience. Moreover, we possess the consensus of testimony, coextensive with the history of humanity, of the indefinitely wide extent of the sphere of causation, and the accompanying characteristic of uniformity. His position is fortified by the fact that in the process of incomplete induction, its probability is strengthened where there has been exceptionally abundant scope for observation, so that there is the overwhelming conviction that if there had been a time or place where the law would prove untrue, it would have been noticed. Instead of universal causation, Mill and his followers make a more cautious statement, — causation as coextensive with the sum total of human experience. This is abundantly adequate to embrace all possible circumstances of practical inference. The immensely high degree of probability engenders a subjective certitude which in everyday conduct of affairs, and even in the more exact requirements of scientific investigation, is never questioned.

Preyer has given an interesting account of the extremely early appearance of the appreciation of the causal relation in the case of his child, "who, at the three hundred nineteenth day of its life, struck several times with a spoon upon a plate. It happened accidentally, while he was doing this, that he touched the plate with the hand that was free; the sound was dulled, and the child noticed the difference. He now took the spoon in the other hand, struck with it on the plate and dulled the sound again, and so on. In the evening the experiment was renewed with a like result. Evidently the function of causality had emerged in some strength, for it prompted the experiment. The cause of the dulling of the sound by the hand — was it in the hand or in the plate ? The other hand had the same dulling effect, so the cause was not lodged with the one hand. Pretty nearly in this fashion the child must have interpreted his sound-impression, and this at a time when he did not know a single word of his later language."[1]

The theoretical soundness of Mill's speculations, however, has a flaw, although the practical results may not be thereby invalidated. The inductive process, which is supposed to be a truly scientific method, and superior to induction by simple enumeration must, according to Mill, at the last analysis, rest upon a principle which is itself based upon an incomplete induction. A very fair and searching criticism of Mill is that of Venn's in his *Empirical Logic*.[2] Whately insists that the whole question concerning the nature of our belief in uniformity is irrelevant, as it is a purely psychological and not a logical one. Mansel holds a mediating position in insisting that the idea of universal causation is intuitive, while that of uniformity is necessarily empirical. Sigwart has very trenchantly criticised Mill in that " taking away with one hand what he gives with the other, he shows in the uncertainty of his views the helplessness of pure empiricism, the impossibility of erecting an edifice of universal propositions on the sand-heap of shifting and isolated facts, or, more accurately, sensations; the endeavor to extract any necessity from a mere sum of facts must be fruitless. The only true point in the whole treatment is one in which Mill as a logician gets the better of Mill as an empiricist; namely, that every inductive inference contains a universal principle; that if it is to be an inference and not merely an association of only subjective validity, the

[1] Preyer, *The Senses and the Will*, pp. 87, 88.
[2] Venn, *Empirical Logic*, p. 130.

transition from the empirically universal judgment All known A's are B to the unconditionally universal All that is A is B, can only be made by means of a universal major premise, and that only upon condition of this being true are we justified in inferring from the particular known A's to the still unknown A's."[1]

The whole tendency of the modern logic is to base the causal postulate upon a ground which is epistemological; namely, inasmuch as our knowledge is one and self-consistent throughout all its separate elements, there must be a corresponding invariability in the phenomena themselves, as there is in the system of knowledge which results from the interpretation of these phenomena. This is the general view of Sigwart, Bosanquet, Lotze, and Green.[2]

This view may be considered also as an expression of the Law of Sufficient Reason; namely, that there is an inherent characteristic of intelligence which demands that every element of consciousness must be referred to some other element for its explanation, and that it is only when the logical connection of ideas corresponds to a real causal connection, that the mind discovers a reason for its several experiences which is satisfying. It has been said by Ueberweg, as giving expression to this view: "The external invariable connection among sense phenomena is, with logical correctness, explained by an inner conformability to law, according to the analogy of the causal connection perceived in ourselves between volition and its actual accomplishment."[3]

There is a distinction that is of importance to note between the popular and the scientific idea of cause. The former is the outcome of the supposition that whatever immediately precedes the effect has evidently produced it, and that this is sufficient wholly to account for it. Such

[1] Sigwart, *Logic*, Vol. II, p. 303.
[2] *Ibid.*, Vol. II, pp. 119, 120; Bosanquet, *Logic*, Vol. II, pp. 220, 251; Lotze, *Logic*, p. 68; Green, *Philosophical Works*, Vol. II, p. 286.
[3] Ueberweg, *Logic*, pp. 281, 282.

an idea of causes leads, at the best, but to a loose and superficial determination of the relation between any antecedent and its consequent, and there is the danger, moreover, of a hasty inference which results in the fallacy of *post hoc ergo propter hoc*. In order to attain a true view of causation, we must especially attend to the extreme complexity of the causal connection. There is no such thing as a simple cause followed by a simple effect. The cause is always a combination of several elements, circumstances, and conditions; the effect is always manifold. This characteristic has been admirably presented in Mill's chapter on the "Plurality of Causes and the Intermixture of Effects."[1] It is well known that the variation in the height of a barometer is due partly to the variation of the atmospheric pressure, and partly to the variation of the expansion of the mercurial column due to heat. In exact determination, some experiment or calculation must precede, before there can be a discrimination between the elements of the joint effect. And so also, a number of circumstances may combine to restore an invalid to health, no one of which alone being capable of effecting his recovery.

The cause of any phenomenon has been defined by Mill, as also by Brown and Herschel, as the sum total of all its antecedents. This statement has been criticised, inasmuch as the sum total of all antecedents is indeterminate, and that there is no end to the possible ramifications in all directions which an exhaustive analysis of any complex cause will yield. However, the problem is one of reduction to simplest possible terms within the range of our powers of observation and experiment. There is much in the sum total of all the antecedents of any given effect which is irrelevant. It is the peculiar function of logical analysis to discriminate between the relevant and irrelevant. The temperature of the laboratory will not affect, one way or the other, experiments with falling bodies; but will essen-

[1] Mill, *Logic*, Book III, Chap. X.

tially influence certain chemical experiments, and must enter as one of the determining factors in the sum total of antecedents. It may be that certain elements of a complex whole may seem to us ultimate and unanalyzable, and yet be themselves systems of more or less complexity. There is always a limit to analysis, both experimental and mental. The analysis is to extend to the ultimate parts as far as possible. It is not an exact process, but a process which tends to exactness to the extent which the scope of finite intelligence will permit. The reason is not at fault so much as the natural limitations of observation and experimental analysis. The end of our research in causal analysis is to discover an invariable relation that can be expressed in the form of an hypothetical universal, — If A, then B.

In order to effect this, the complex A must be separated into its parts, a, b, c, etc., and the effective, and necessary, and indispensable element producing B must be determined. Suppose it proves to be a, it may be possible to subject this to further analysis, and to reduce it to simpler elements, such as x, y, z, etc., and x be found as the significant element of the real cause. Each analysis determines a narrower and still narrower sphere within which the cause lies. A man is shot. We say the bullet killed him; then the driving force behind the bullet; then the explosive power of the gunpowder; this in turn was occasioned by the combined chemical and mechanical energy of its ingredients whereby a solid is transformed into a gaseous substance many times its original bulk.

Sooner or later we must reach the end of our analysis, and the investigation be necessarily checked. No explanation is ultimate; we only transfer our point of view from a less to a more familiar sphere of interpretation. We do not feel the need of explaining the very familiar; though the most familiar is hardest satisfactorily to explain, because there is nothing simpler in whose terms we may paraphrase it. We feel this in giving a definition of terms whose meaning we best know, and which we most frequently use. Mr. Barrett, a former assistant at the Royal Institution, said of Faraday: "I well remember one day when Mr. Faraday was by my side, I happened to be steadying, by means of a magnet, the motion of a magnetic needle under a glass shade. Mr. Faraday suddenly looked most impressively and earnestly, as he said: 'How wonderful and mysterious is that power you have there! The more I think over it, the less I seem to know.' And yet, he who said this knew more of it than any living man." [1]

Although our knowledge is limited as in all cases of causation however simple, nevertheless, as far as it goes, the several elements are related logically, that is, necessarily and universally. We may only know in part, but still we know, and the world, as interpreted for us in knowledge, is a world of invariable sequences. The process of inductive analysis, therefore, consists in reducing a complex antecedent to its ultimate parts, in order to reveal the element or elements in it which may have caused the given effect. It sometimes happens that different elements in an antecedent may be considered severally as the cause, according to the psychological point of view as regards the interests of the investigator. It is not always that a scientific determination of the cause is required; it may be that all that is desired is a knowledge of that part of the antecedent which is most closely and prominently connected with the event in question. An inquiry may be started in reference to the cause of an epidemic in a community. One may discover the cause in the carelessness of sanitary engineers; another may say the cause lies in the poor construction of the sewerage; another says that the cause of the epidemic is a certain kind of bacilli. Each one is looking at the chain of events related as cause and effect; but they all look at different links of the same chain. One element, therefore, of a complex antecedent may be brought into more or less

[1] Gladstone, *Michael Faraday*, p. 180.

prominence as the efficient element of the cause, according as the point of view is shifted. If, in the search for the cause of phenomena, the sum total of antecedents were always given exhaustively, the explanation might become so loaded down with details as to burden the mind, and confuse rather than clear the understanding.

CHAPTER V

THE METHOD OF CAUSAL ANALYSIS AND DETERMINATION

It will be well to consider the various cases which will confront us in seeking to analyze a complex antecedent for the purpose of discovering its cause.

1. There are instances where cause and effect appear in evident sequence. There is an antecedent which is followed by a consequent. If A happens, then B will happen. Instances of this kind most readily yield themselves to the process of analysis, because a change in any given phenomenon is occasioned by the efficiency of the antecedent which may be observed in connection with the change itself. It is easier to note active than passive relations, the dynamic rather than the static. The attention is attracted and held by change. The bird flying across our path is observed, and the one perched upon the tree near at hand, however conspicuous may be its position, is passed by without any notice taken of it. It is easier to connect the moisture of the grass with falling rain, than when the same is occasioned by the dew. In one case, the causal relation is exhibited in operation; in the other, the connection is veiled. We find the grass wet; what preceded it we are not able to see. There are several instances of sequence among observed phenomena which must be carefully discriminated in order to avoid confusion of thought. They are as follows: —

(1) When we have A followed by B, and A ceases wholly while B endures for an appreciable time afterwards, or it may be permanently. A billiard ball strikes another, the

second goes on by virtue of the newly acquired energy transferred by impact from the first, which, however, stops altogether. I throw a ball which lodges on the top of a building; the effect produced lasts permanently, for the ball has gained a gravity potential due to the energy imparted to it by the initial throwing. The old formula, therefore, does not always hold: "Cessante causa cessat effectus."

(2) Cases where A ceases, and thereupon B immediately ceases also. If we cut off the supply of gas which feeds a flame, the flame at once disappears. There are cases, however, when an appreciable time must elapse in order that the transferred energy in the effect may be dissipated. When we shut our eyes the stimulus causing the perception is cut off, and the perception at once is at an end; however, there are cases where the stimulus being very strong, after-images are induced which remain for some time in the dark field after the eyes are closed.

(3) Cases where the antecedent is wholly inadequate to produce the effect, but whose function is merely to liberate potential energy already stored, and waiting an occasion for its active manifestation. A slight blow upon a piece of dynamite causes an explosion wholly disproportionate to the striking force employed. As is well known, heat is often an exciting cause of chemical action. In such cases the real cause is more or less concealed, while that which is apparent upon the surface is not a cause so much as an occasion of the phenomenon in question. I touch the pendulum and a clock starts and so continues for many hours; the swinging pendulum, however, is only the occasion of liberating the potential energy of the wound-up spring, and thence the power which runs the clock, pendulum, wheels, hands, and all.

2. We have also instances not so much of sequence as of concurrence. The planets revolve around the central sun; here the cause is constant, attended by constant

effect. The machine never runs down, nor has to be wound up.

3. Again there are instances of coexistence. These are more difficult to analyze, for the phenomena do not here appear as antecedent and consequent in the midst of changing conditions and circumstances. We have coexistence of two kinds: —

(1) Coexisting attributes in one and the same organism. They are always found together. They form one generic concept and are called by one name. Cows have horns, cloven feet, are ruminant, etc. Dogs have their distinct and constant characteristics. The orange has its correlation of color, taste, smell. And so we have the so-called "natural kinds," *i.e.* organisms presenting an unique and characteristic appearance, differentiated thereby from all others. There are also certain correlations of growth which present a constant relation between certain attributes, as the fact, however we may explain it, that cats with blue eyes are invariably deaf. There are, moreover, illustrations of the same in an inorganic sphere, as the law which connects the atomic weight of substances and their specific heat by an inverse proportion; or that other law which obtains between the specific gravity of substances in the gaseous state, and their atomic weights, they being either equal or the one a multiple of the other. In many cases, the bare fact of coexistence must be accepted without being able to explain the causal ground of it. The several elements present a constant association, and that is all that can be said about it. In other cases, however, a cause may be found, for instance, as regards the correlation of warm-blooded animals always possessing lungs; the connection between respiration and the generation of heat is found to depend upon chemical action as its causal basis.

(2) A relation of statics rather than dynamics, as, for instance, a pillar supporting a roof or arch is said to be the cause, in the sense of the sustaining cause, of the super-

structure. So also the cohesive force which holds together the particles of a stone. In such cases the energy inherent in the cause is of the nature of a stress and strain.

4. Under this head are embraced the phenomena of vital growth or development. These are the most difficult of all the causal problems to determine; for it is required to discover the inner necessity of essence, and how the succeeding stages of development unfold through the play of the central forces inherent in the very nature and being of the organism itself. Mill is content with classifying organisms as different natural kinds, and he is not concerned with the reason why there should be such and such kinds, nor does he attempt to discover any law concerning these natural correlations and the mode of their growth. In inductive analysis, our concepts must not merely grasp what the natural kinds are, but also what has determined them to be what they are. Darwin puts special emphasis upon the environment as affecting changes in organisms and producing differentiating modifications among species. This, however, must be considered not as sole factor, but one which is combined with inner needs and necessities. Moreover, Darwin has drawn attention to the fact that individual differences need scientific explanation as well as the common attributes, as, for instance, why some sheep are black, and why some pigeons are fantailed and others are not. In all such considerations we must not lose sight of the fact that there are two determining factors, — the inner necessity of development, and the external necessity of causality, as organisms are acted upon by their environment.[1]

5. Cases of collocation where no one element of the cause is efficient, but together they all combine to produce the effect. In searching for the cause, we must not only find a certain amount of energy capable of producing the effect, but we must also discover what peculiar arrangement of the elements concerned must exist before the energy in question

[1] Sigwart, *Logic*, Vol. II, pp. 322, 330, 331.

can become operative. Chalmers says that "the existing collocations of the material world are as important as the laws which the objects obey, that many overlook this distinction and forget that mere laws without collocations would have afforded no security against a turbid and disorderly chaos."[1] We would naturally say that the sole cause of water boiling at 212° is the enveloping heat; it has, however, been observed that on top of Mont Blanc, water boils at 180° instead of 212°. This indicates that, in addition to the fire, the atmospheric pressure is an element in the cause, very easily overlooked. Charcoal and diamond are of the same substance; a difference only in the arrangement of the molecules results in such radically different combinations. There are, in the main, three special kinds of collocations, as follows: —

(1) Cases of modifying circumstance. A strong wind blows down a tree; this would not have occurred had not the tree been hollow. The hollowness of the tree is here a coöperative circumstance that is combined with the efficient cause, — the force of the wind. An instance where arrangement of the elements concerned rather than their efficient energies is productive of the effect, is that of capillarity, the rising of liquid in a tube of exceedingly small bore. Here form is more essential to the effect than the expenditure of any visible energy.

(2) Cases in which certain negative conditions prevent the realization of the effect. The plants and shrubs die in a long drouth, because it does not rain. A train collides with another, because the red signal was not exposed as it should have been. A match will ignite gunpowder generally, but it fails to do so should the powder prove to be wet.

(3) There are also cases of counteracting causes, where the effect of cause A is not realized, as cause B neutralizes the force of cause A; as when an anchored boat will not

---

[1] Quoted by Jevons, *Principles of Science,* p. 740.

respond to the pull of the oar. Sometimes the cause is not wholly counteracted, or it may be the counteracting cause more than holds the positive cause in check, and is itself operative. The rise of a balloon in the air is due to the fact that the force of gravity is more than overbalanced by the expansive force of the gas within the balloon; one force pulling downwards, the other bearing up, and the latter prevailing.

Mechanical forces acting in combination admit of a resolution of their joint effect according to the theory of the parallelogram of forces. Chemical and vital forces cannot be treated in such a way at all. From the character of the elementary forces in mechanics, one can calculate their combination. In chemistry, however, when the elements are given, the resulting compound cannot be thus determined. So, also, in vital and mental phenomena, the necessarily complex nature of the elements involved prevents not only prediction of resulting combinations, but even adequate explanation of that which may be immediately given in consciousness.

It is necessary, in connection with these various instances of causal relations, to understand the different modes of the transfer of energy, which are as follows:—

(1) Molar or mechanical, as in the case of a billiard-ball transferring its energy to another through impact.

(2) Molecular, as heat, chemical and electrical and magnetic forces, light, etc. One passes into another, as chemical force producing electric, electric producing magnetic, or producing heat and light.

(3) Cases where mechanical force becomes molecular, as friction inducing heat; or cases where molecular becomes mechanical, as heat transferred into the driving power of an engine, or electricity applied as a motor. A precise determination of equivalents can be made between molar and molecular energy; as, for example, it has been found that it takes the same amount of energy to raise 772 pounds a

distance of one foot that it does to raise the temperature of one pound of water 1° F.; or the heat requisite to boil a gallon of freezing water would lift 1,389,600 pounds through a distance of one foot.

As a consequence of the doctrine of the transfer of energy, a causal law can be so stated as to express the fact that variations in the antecedents will call for the corresponding variations in the effect, as, for instance, such a law as the following: "Resistance in a wire of constant section and material is directly proportional to the length and inversely proportional to the area of the cross-section."[1] The neglect of quantitative determination of the proportionate variations of the antecedent and consequent was a glaring defect in the inductive systems both of Mill and of Bacon.

Through the representation of the various stages of such variation, it is also possible to establish the upper and lower limits beyond which the cause does not produce the corresponding effect; as in Weber's law concerning the relation of stimulus to sensation, that stimulus must increase geometrically in order that the sensations increase arithmetically. There is an upper and lower limit beyond which this proportion does not hold.

The doctrine of conservation of energy creates the impression of continuous change in causation, in which the effect unfolds out of the cause. We do not think of phenomena under this aspect as discrete events. More than ever, in the light of modern science, does the old saying obtain, "*Natura non facit saltum.*" We no longer look for catastrophic results in nature, but regard causation as a continuous transfer of potential energy into kinetic or actual energy.

We come now to the consideration of the method by which the causal analysis is mediated. This is effected through observation and experiment. Observation is something more than mere looking at phenomena: it means con-

[1] Jenkin, *Electricity and Magnetism*, p. 83.

centration of attention for the purpose of research; it means discriminating insight, an appreciation of likeness and difference; it means a penetration beneath surface appearances, and an apprehension of the essential features of the objects of perception. Experiment consists in modifying the elements which form the complex antecedent in order to observe the resultant effect upon the corresponding consequent. Forces may be added or subtracted; their intensity may be varied, increased, or decreased; the circumstances or conditions may be altered. Herschel speaks of observation and experiment, as passive and active observation respectively. When we interfere to change the course of nature, or to bring natural forces within the range of our observation, we are experimenting. Observation is preliminary to experiment, and suggests the lines along which experiment should proceed. An observation that sees the parts in the whole and the whole in the parts, is in itself an analysis of a phenomenon, in course of which process causal relations must be disclosed. The scientific spirit demands absolute veracity in observation. One ought not to be blind to facts even though they tend to contradict preconceived theories. Bacon has observed that "men mark when they hit, never mark when they miss." We must strive against a natural tendency to see things as we would have them, and not as they strictly are.

We must also carefully distinguish between observed facts, and inferences which we instinctively draw from these facts. Observation is preliminary to an inductive inference, therefore it must not itself involve an inference, or we should be arguing in a circle. An interesting illustration of the difference between observation and inference based upon it, is narrated in the life of Faraday: "An artist was once maintaining that in natural appearances and in pictures, up and down, and high and low, were fixed indubitable realities; but Faraday told him that they were merely conventional acceptations, based on standards often arbitrary. The disputant could not be convinced that ideas which he had hitherto never doubted, had such shifting foundations. 'Well,' said Faraday, 'hold a walking-stick between your chin and great toe; look along it and say which is the upper end.' The experiment was tried, and the artist found his idea of perspective at complete variance with his sense of reality; either end of the stick might be called upper, — pictorially it was one, physically it was the other." [1]

This indicates how readily our inferences and observations blend, and how difficult it is to separate them in consciousness. De Morgan has pointed out that there are four ways of one event seeming to follow another, or to be connected with it, without really being so: —

(1) Instead of A causing B, our perception of A may cause B. A man dies on a certain day which he has always regarded as his last through his own fears concerning it.

(2) The event A may make our perception of B follow, which otherwise would happen without being perceived. It was thought that more comets appeared in hot than cold summers; no account, however, was taken of the fact that hot summers would be comparatively cloudless, and afford better opportunities for the discovery of comets.

(3) Our perception of A may make our perception of B follow. This is illustrated by the fallacy of the moon's influence in the dissipation of the clouds. When the sky is densely clouded, the moon would not be visible at all; it would be necessary for us to see the full moon in order that our attention should be strongly drawn to the fact, and this would happen most often on those nights when the sky is cloudless.

(4) B is really the antecedent event, but our perception of A, which is a consequence of B, may be necessary to bring about our perception of B. Upward and downward currents are continually circulating in the lowest stratum of

[1] Gladstone, *Michael Faraday*, pp. 165, 166.

the atmosphere; but there is no evidence of this, until we perceive cumulous clouds, which are the consequence of such currents.[1]

There are certain natural limitations to observation, as things too minute to be seen, too swift to be carefully examined; there are sounds which some ears can detect, while others cannot, and shades that some eyes cannot discriminate. There are effects proceeding from certain causes that are so slight that we fail to observe them, and yet erroneously infer that they do not exist. Professor Tyndall has given a striking illustration of the difference of auditory power in two individuals; he says: "In crossing the Wengern Alp in company with a friend, the grass at each side of the path swarmed with insects which to me rent the air with their shrill chirruping. My friend heard nothing of this, the insect music lying quite beyond his limit of audition."[2] Much has been done by inventive skill to increase our powers of observation, and at the same time to render them more accurate, as the telescope, microscope, the vernier for precise measurement of minute differences of magnitude, the chronograph for time measurements, self-registering thermometers, the thermopile, galvanometers, etc. One of the chief problems of scientific method is to overcome natural limitations of observation through mechanical devices.

Observations on a large scale and over a considerable period of time must sometimes be taken in order to disclose tendencies as seen only in the average or the mean of the observed results. Thus meteorological, vital statistics, and others of a like kind, must extend over a large area, and embrace a large number of instances in order to reach results of any value. It is known that Tycho Brahé made an immense number of most exact records of the positions of the heavenly bodies with the aid of the best of astronomical

---

[1] Quoted by Jevons, *Principles of Science*, pp. 409-411.
[2] Tyndall, *On Sound*, pp. 73, 74.

instruments, and these records afterwards became the foundation of Kepler's laws and of modern astronomy.[1]

The faculty for accurate observation can be increased by acquiring the habit of examining carefully everything within the field of vision. We fail to see many things because we fall into the easy way of passing them by without noting their presence or appreciating their significance. It was said of Charles Darwin by his son that "he wished to learn as much as possible from every experiment, so that he did not confine himself to observing the single point to which the experiment was directed, and his power of seeing a number of other things was wonderful."[2] The open-eyed vision is the prime requisite for scientific investigation.

The limitations of observation naturally lead to experiment, whose special function is to so modify phenomena as to bring a suspected causal element more prominently into notice. This can be done by intensifying the force in question, or by neutralizing all other elements in combination with it, so that the sole effect of this force in actual operation can be observed. When the cause is not a simple element, but a combination, then the problem is to vary the conditions so that but one possible combination can be operative alone, and note the corresponding effect. Given a certain number of elements, the number of possible combinations is mathematically determinate, and can be tried *seriatim* until all possibilities are exhausted. Venn has given a long and interesting illustration of this in his *Empirical Logic*.[3] All combinations need not be tried, however; for many will be seen to be either impossible or irrelevant. The aim is to obtain an antecedent which shall consist either of a simple element, or a combination such that with its presence the effect in question is present also, but with its disappearance the effect is wanting.

[1] Gore, *The Art of Scientific Discovery*, p. 316.
[2] *Life and Letters of Charles Darwin*, Vol. I, p. 122.
[3] pp. 402 ff.

It is not sufficient to note merely the presence of an antecedent connected with a corresponding consequent; scientific determination consists also in proving the absence of the suspected cause in cases where the given effect is not present. This is called determination by negation. A proposition which is held affirmatively has only a vague significance; it must be determined within definite limits assigned to it by virtue of what it is not. Defining means to set limits to a term; these limits grow out of the nature of the thing itself. The negative judgment marks a transition always from that which is indefinite and incoherent to that which is definite and coherent.[1]

This may be illustrated in the concrete, when in dissection one is tracing a nerve; it is followed throughout its course by a series of negative judgments though they be unexpressed: This is not a nerve, but an artery; this is not a nerve, but a vein; this is not a nerve, but a filament, or shred of muscle, etc. So we rise through negative discrimination to a clear apprehension of an object under investigation. The original proposition must be readjusted with every new negative determination. It sometimes happens that the original proposition is completely negatived by the negative determination, sometimes again it is confirmed.

A proposition that has not been worked over through such a process has no real logical worth or scientific value. Therefore in the analysis of phenomena when the suspected cause and effect are combined in a proposition, it can at first be held only tentatively. It must be confirmed negatively, or else readjusted to conform to the negative requirements. Suppose we have given that A is followed by B as far as we have been able to observe. We may proceed by experiment to multiply instances of A's connection with B, but still the causal relation is not absolutely proved. We must go on to show that in all cases of not-A there is not-B, or in all cases of not-B there is not-A. Negative experiment pro-

[1] See p. 74.

duces the contrapositive, or the converse contrapositive, of the proposition under investigation, which deductively necessitates the validity of the original proposition.

This is substantially Mill's method of difference, that if an instance in which the phenomenon under investigation occurs, and an instance in which it does not occur, have every circumstance save one in common, and that one occurring only in the former, the circumstance in which alone the two instances differ is the effect or cause or a necessary part of the cause of the phenomenon. This method will be described later; it is the main inductive method, the others being largely modifications of it. A negative instance which is established concerning relations of not-A and not-B is absolutely conclusive, inasmuch as not-A is the contradictory of A, and not-B is the contradictory of B. They are mutually exclusive. No other possibility can be forthcoming, and the experimental analysis is exhaustive. Professor Tyndall gives the following account of an experiment to determine the cause of resonance. "I hold a vibrating tuning-fork over a glass jar eighteen inches deep; but you fail to hear the sound of the fork. Preserving the fork in its position, I pour water with the least possible noise into the jar. The column of air underneath the fork becomes shorter as the water rises. The sound augments in intensity, and when the water reaches a certain level, it bursts forth with extraordinary power. I continue to pour in water, the sound sinks, and becomes finally as inaudible as at first."[1]

From this it is inferred that a certain column of water of definite height is necessary to the production of the sound, for above and below the limits no sound is heard. This experiment also indicates that which is most important in causal determination, — a variation in cause accompanied by a variation in effect, as also a maximum and minimum as regards the intensity of the sound. Experiment proceeds

[1] Tyndall, *On Sound*, p. 172.

upon the supposition of the measurableness of phenomena, and seeks numerically expressible results in this regard. For instance, by different experiments, Tyndall proved that the length of the column of air which resounds to the fork in a maximum degree of intensity is equal to one-fourth of the length of the wave produced by the fork.[1]

The negative determination of a suspected connection of cause and effect must be precise in order to establish the causal relation with that degree of accuracy which is demanded in a truly logical and scientific method. Upon this point, Bosanquet has a very suggestive passage: "The essence of significant negation consists in correcting and confirming our judgment of the nature of a positive phenomenon by showing that *just when* its condition ceases, *just then* something else begins. The 'Just-not' is the important point, and this is only given by a positive negation within a definite system. You want to explain or define the case in which A becomes B. You want observation of not-B, but almost the whole world is formally or barely not-B, so that you are lost in chaos. What you must do is to find the point within A where A_1 which is B, passes into A_2 which is C, and that will give you the *just-not-B* which is the valuable negative instance."[2] For example, in Professor Tyndall's experiment, the significant negative instance was this, — when the water in the tube reached just that height when for the first time during the experiment no sound was audible. The discriminating observation that can mark and measure the precise point of transition from sound to no sound, has determined accurately the conditions necessary to produce the sound, and precisely define their limitations.

In all observation and experiment, the following possibilities should be kept before the mind in order to avoid a hasty conclusion in reference to a seeming causal connec-

[1] Tyndall, *On Sound*, p. 174.
[2] Bosanquet, *The Essentials of Logic*, p. 134.

tion. We may think that we have discovered the relation that if there is A, then there must be B, and the one therefore the cause of the other, but it may happen that

1. Both A and B are effects of another cause and are thereby related coördinately in reference to it.
2. A may be merely a liberating circumstance, or an invariable accompaniment of B.
3. A may not be the cause of B, but only an element of a complex collocation which is the cause of B.
4. Each separate instance of B may so differ as to respond to the action of A in a manner different from the others.
5. A may be related to B in a system of such a nature that the system in continuously developing new effects causes B, as the introduction of medicine into an organism whose forces are themselves effecting a healing process.
6. It is often very difficult to tell whether A is the cause of B, or B the cause of A, as in districts where drunkenness and poverty are prevalent, or cases of moral and intellectual feebleness. Which is the cause? and which the effect? In many cases such as these, the forces react upon each other, the effect tending to increase the intensity of the cause.
7. The connection of A and B may be one of mere coincidence, and not of a causal nature whatsoever. Newton was much impressed with the apparent connection between the seven intervals of the octave, and the fact that the colors of the spectrum divide into a like series of seven intervals. And yet there is no causal connection that can be proved to exist between the two.

The more we dwell upon these various possibilities, the more are we impressed with the extreme complexity in which the relation of cause and effect is involved. The investigator must bring to his research the spirit of patience and perseverance, as well as a clear vision and discriminating insight. Sir John Lubbock, in his observations upon the habits of ants, says that at one time he watched an ant from six in the morning until a quarter to ten at night, as she worked without intermission during all that time.[1] It is to such patient investigators that nature reveals her secrets.

[1] Sir John Lubbock, *Scientific Lectures*, p. 73.

CHAPTER VI

MILL'S INDUCTIVE METHODS — THE METHOD OF AGREEMENT

THERE are certain specific methods by which a supposed relation of cause and effect may be tested. Before applying any method however to concrete instances, there is naturally in mind some suspected causal relation which is the result of one or both of the two preliminary inductive processes. As we have seen, these primary processes in inductive inquiry are induction by simple enumeration, and induction by analogy. By the enumeration of the special cases in which we have found a significant coexistence or sequence, a causal relation is suggested as a possible or probable explanation. By analogy also a causal relation is suggested on the basis that a given phenomenon which in essential particulars resembles another phenomenon whose cause or effect is already known will, in all probability, have a like cause or effect. Enumeration and analogy thus suggest a probable explanation which is not as yet proved, but which ranks as a tentative hypothesis. The natural history, therefore, of the final product of the inductive process recognizes the initial stages of enumeration and analogy leading to some preliminary hypothesis, which is to be tested by one or more of the specific methods of scientific investigation. These methods have been formulated by John Stuart Mill and are especially associated with his name. They are as follows: —

    1. The Method of Agreement.
    2. The Method of Difference.
    3. The Joint Method of Agreement and Difference.

4. The Method of Concomitant Variations. 258
5. The Method of Residues. 271

The method of agreement consists in inferring the existence of a causal relation, when in a number of varying instances it is observed that the supposed cause is always accompanied by the phenomenon in question, as corresponding effect.

The method of difference is the comparing of an instance where the supposed cause is present, accompanied by the corresponding effect, with an instance having precisely the same setting, but where the supposed cause is withdrawn, the effect also disappearing; the inference of a causal relation is then permissible.

The joint method of agreement and difference is the comparing of instances where the supposed cause is present, with similar instances where it is absent; if the corresponding effect is present in the former, and absent in the latter, group of instances, a causal relation may be inferred. This differs from the method of difference, that in the latter the same instance, now with, and again without, the presence of the suspected cause, is the subject of observation; in the joint method it is a number of instances with, compared with a number of similar instances without, the presence of the supposed cause.

The method of concomitant variations consists in so modifying any given phenomenon that the supposed cause will vary in intensity; then a corresponding variation in the accompanying effect is evidence of a causal relation.

The method of residues consists in the analysis of a given complex phenomenon, in which all elements save one of the antecedent are known to be related severally in a causal manner to all elements save one of the consequent; then the residual element of the one may be regarded as the cause of the residual element of the other.

These methods, it is true, deal only with concrete

instances; but, in so far as these instances discover an underlying causal connection, they thereby furnish sufficient ground for a complete generalization, and warrant the inductive procedure from special cases to the universal.

We will now examine these methods more in detail. The brief outline above is intended merely to give a general idea of the methods, that it may lead to a better understanding of the more exact statement of their nature and characteristics.

The Method of Agreement. — The more precise statement of this method is given in the first canon of Mill, which is substantially as follows: —

If two or more instances of the phenomenon under investigation have only one circumstance in common, the circumstance in which alone all the instances agree is the probable cause (or effect) of the given phenomenon, or sustains some causal relation to it.

The above is based upon the causal axiom that the constant elements which emerge in any given series of similar phenomena are to be considered as connected in some manner with the cause of the phenomena; but that the variable elements are not connected with the phenomena in any causal manner whatsoever.

The method of agreement is illustrated in the investigation of the very common phenomenon of the transformation of substances from the solid to the liquid state. What is the one circumstance which is always present when we consider the melting of such widely different substances as butter, ice, lead, iron, etc.? In all instances, to whatsoever extent they may be multiplied, of the change from solid to liquid states, heat has been observed to be present, and is thereby indicated as the likely cause of the phenomenon in question. The method may be represented through the use of symbols which, according to Mill, are capital letters to denote antecedents, and smaller letters to denote corresponding consequents. Let the following be a number of different instances with the antecedents and consequents arranged in order, and represented as above indicated:—

$$ABC \ldots \ldots \ldots abc.$$
$$ADE \ldots \ldots \ldots ade.$$
$$AMN \ldots \ldots \ldots amn.$$
$$\text{etc.} \qquad\qquad \text{etc.}$$

By inspection of such a table of instances thus analyzed, and symbolically represented, it will be readily seen that A is the only element common to all the antecedents, while a is the only one common to all the consequents. The inference, therefore, is that A is the cause of a. It has been objected to this system of representation that it artificially arranges the elements of antecedent and consequent, as though there were a number of distinct cause-elements, each connected with a correspondingly distinct effect-element, and it produces the impression that it is quite an easy matter to see how these causal pairs are thus separately related.[1] As nature presents her phenomena to us, however, there is such complexity throughout, that the analysis cannot readily distribute part to part in appropriate causal relations. To avoid such an error in notation, I have adopted the following symbols, which will be used hereafter to describe the various methods. Let us take C as the letter to represent the supposed causal element, and S, the entire setting of accompanying circumstances; let e denote the corresponding effect, and s the sum total of the attendant consequences. The causal relation will be then indicated, according to the method of agreement, as follows:—

$$S + C \ldots \ldots \ldots s + e.$$
$$S' + C \ldots \ldots \ldots s' + e.$$
$$S'' + C \ldots \ldots \ldots s'' + e.$$

Here the setting changes throughout, as indicated by S, S', S'', etc., but C remains constant in the antecedents; also

[1] Venn, *Empirical Logic*, p. 411.

the corresponding setting in the consequents changes, as indicated by s, s', s'', etc., but e remains constant throughout. Such a notation does not attempt to represent just which parts of S cause corresponding parts of s, nor by what elements precisely S differs from S' and S'', etc. It does represent, however, the difference between the variable and constant elements of the table of instances which are arranged for comparison, and this is the key to disclose the causal relation.

As an example of this method, let us take the physical law that different bodies tend at the same time to absorb and to emit the same waves of light. It is known that every substance in burning gives its own lines in the spectrum analysis, sodium, for instance, producing a very bright line in the yellow portion of the spectrum in a definite locality (Line D, of Fraunhofer). If now, instead of burning sodium, we interpose the vapor of sodium in the path of the ray which should give a continuous spectrum, the phenomenon is completely reversed; at the exact point where there was a bright line in the spectrum, a dark line now appears. Thus the vapor of sodium, acting as a screen, absorbs the rays which it emits when it acts as the luminous source. A similar effect is observed in the case of vapors of iodine, of strontium, of iron, etc.; it may therefore be regarded as a phenomenon, admitting of generalization by induction.[1] This is according to the method of agreement; and we may make the following representation: —

Vapor of sodium acting as a screen $= S + C.$
Vapor of iodine acting as a screen $= S' + C.$
Vapor of iron acting as a screen $= S'' + C.$
Vapor of strontium acting as a screen $= S''' + C.$
etc. etc.

[1] Saigey, *The Unity of Natural Phenomena*, pp. 94, 95.

The corresponding consequents are: —

Reversing bright sodium line to dark $= s \;\; + e.$
Reversing bright iodine line to dark $= s' \;\; + e.$
Reversing bright iron line to dark $= s'' \;\; + e.$
Reversing bright strontium line to dark $= s''' \;\; + e.$
   etc.   etc.

Therefore we have: —

$$S \;\; + C \;\; \ldots \ldots \;\; s \;\; + e.$$
$$S' \;\; + C \;\; \ldots \ldots \;\; s' \;\; + e.$$
$$S'' \;\; + C \;\; \ldots \ldots \;\; s'' \;\; + e.$$
$$S''' \;\; + C \;\; \ldots \ldots \;\; s''' \;\; + e.$$
   etc.   etc.

In this the constant C of the antecedents is the vapor of any substance acting as a screen; the constant e is the reversal in each case of the bright line of the substance in the spectrum to the corresponding dark line of the same. From this it is inferred that the vapor of any substance acting as a screen absorbs exactly those rays which it emits when it acts as the luminous source.

It is of great importance that the instances selected for observation or experiment be as varied as possible, so that widely differing phenomena may be gathered together. Then if running through them all there is one common element observed among the antecedents, and one common element among the consequents, the greater the variation among the instances the more pronounced will be the significance of the constant elements. In the illustration given the substances which are so different as iron, strontium, sodium, iodine, etc., preclude the possibility of the resultant phenomenon described being due to the peculiar properties of any one metal, or group of metals. So many phenomena and so different in kind are taken as to eliminate the peculiarities attached to any one in particular. In this respect the method is one of elimination. By varying the instances the non-essential is eliminated, and the essential, which remains as the element common to all, is thereby emphasized, and differentiated from all attendant circumstances.

This method also is one of discrimination, of discerning the constant element under the various changing forms which it can assume, and as such it is similar to the logical process of the formation of a concept. The concept is the grasping of the universal element which is present through the particular and concrete manifestations of the same. Through them all there is the like common element which is the basis of the concept itself. So out of many particular instances the mind grasps the elements which are common to all, and considers them as related in a constant and therefore causal manner, which has in itself the character of a universal concept and so admits of being formulated in the form of a law universal, which is the end of all induction.

This method, moreover, is peculiarly adapted to observation, the collating of a number of instances, rather than to experiment. Instances cannot always be manufactured, and so it may be beyond the power of experiment to reproduce them. They can, however, always be the objects of research, and as such fall naturally into the field of observation.

The question may properly be asked at this point, How does this method differ from that of induction by simple enumeration? The latter we have seen is never satisfactory because the enumeration cannot be complete, and may be contradicted by an enlarged experience. This method however is superior in that it provides for more than simple enumeration of instances in which the phenomenon in question has occurred; there must be a corresponding analysis of the instances, accompanied by a discriminating insight to distinguish the essential from the unessential. Number of instances increases the probability that the variable elements have been eliminated, and enables the mind to concentrate upon the constant elements that remain and are thereby disclosed.

This method primarily admits of application to instances where a sequence is observable; that is, where antecedent can be distinguished from consequent by an appreciable time element. It is however possible to apply this method to the investigation of coexistences, where it may show that either the coexisting elements are related as cause and effect, or that in some causal manner they are the correlated effect of some cause sufficient to account for them both. Many instances may be adduced of the prevalence of poverty and crime associated together. This may indicate a causal relation between them, and yet a sequence cannot be observed of sufficient definiteness to indicate which is the cause, and which the effect. The problem is thus left indeterminate, with the suggestion of some other cause which may possibly account for them both. All that the method of agreement can attain, is by collecting a number of instances of diverse nature to indicate that in some way at least poverty and crime are connected by causal ties. The constant coexistence of attributes in one individual admits of a similar treatment and similar results. The fact of the high coloring of male butterflies in a large number of instances, in reference to a variety of species, indicates a constant relation between the fact of its being a male and the possession of brilliant coloring. This inseparable association indicates a causal relation, which, however, cannot be more precisely determined by this method. The full explanation of the phenomenon requires some supplementary hypothesis depending upon conditions not disclosed by this method, an hypothesis such that the high coloring has the special function of attracting the female butterfly and has been intensified and developed by natural selection.

The method of agreement is open to criticism at several points, and yet it must be at the beginning understood that this method does not rank as a final method. We shall soon see that in many cases it needs to be supplemented by the method of difference, in order either to confirm or to disprove its tentative results. The chief criticisms that have been made of this method may be summed up as follows: —

1. The cause indicated by the method of agreement is not thereby proved to be the sole cause of the phenomenon in question. We may gather together a number of varied instances where an extensive failure of crops in the summer has caused hard times during the winter following. And yet there may be, and as a fact there are, many other causes which engender periods of industrial depression. We may say, therefore, that this method is capable of establishing, tentatively at least, a universal proposition of the form, All x is y; it does not, however, attempt to give any indication, one way or the other, regarding the validity of the converse, All y is x. Knowing the limitations of a method does not by any means destroy its legitimacy as a method; it rather increases its efficiency within its proper sphere, by the more exact knowledge as to the precise extent of that sphere itself.

2. It is urged that while it is possible to recognize in most, if not in all, cases, the common element in the several effects of similar phenomena, it is not so easy a matter to separate the common element in the corresponding antecedents by the simple method of agreement alone. For instance, in Bacon's illustration of the investigation of the cause of heat, he cites such disparate phenomena as the sun's rays, friction, combustion, etc. The element of heat is readily discernible through them all; but what is the common element which operates as cause in each case? There is the difficulty. Sigwart illustrates this in the case of the phenomenon of death. The effect can be easily detected as similar throughout, but in all the antecedents the only property common to them all is life, and, therefore, we are led into the fallacy of attributing to life the cause of death.[1] We must therefore acknowledge that some phe-

[1] Sigwart, *Logic*, Vol. II, p. 341.

nomena may occur in such a variety and such a number of manifestations as to disguise the nature of the cause under the mask of a generality too indefinite to be recognized. In all such instances, the method of agreement must avail itself of suggestions received from some other source, as to the nature of the common element in the antecedents. Or, some minor circumstances attending the effect may indicate more precisely the nature of the cause, as, for instance, the peculiar symptoms associated with death by drowning, which differentiate it from death due to any other cause.

3. The common element in the antecedents may prove to be an unessential accompaniment of all the instances examined. Its presence, therefore, may have nothing whatsoever to do with the observed effects. A number of different medicines, for example, may produce a certain effect alike in all instances. The only common element that can be detected in the various medicines examined may be the alcohol which is used as the common vehicle of the different drugs, and yet its effect may be entirely inert as regards the medicinal qualities in question. The common element really efficient may be overlooked, and another common element which is easily discernible may nevertheless remain wholly inoperative. This difficulty may be overcome by a more thorough analysis of the phenomena observed, which may be attained by a judicious variation of the instances, so as to reveal, in turn, the precise effect of the various simple elements which together constitute the complex whole of the phenomenon in question. The defects of the method in this respect are, in a word, the defects of induction by simple enumeration.

4. The cause may be present in all the antecedents, and, notwithstanding the corresponding effect not appear, and this, not because the two are not related in a causal manner, but because the cause is neutralized by the associated elements which appear in combination with it in the various antecedents. For instance, diphtheria germs are the cause

of diphtheria, and have been found accompanying this disease in all cases which have been observed. And yet their presence is often noted when the disease itself does not develop. The tendency existing is counteracted by the condition of the organism at the time, so that the dread bacilli are inoperative and therefore harmless. As we have seen before, the presence of the effect necessitates the presence of the corresponding cause; but by no means is it always true that the presence of the cause necessitates the effect. The cause always produces the tendency at least, which however may be neutralized.

5. This method is often applied in a very careless way to the observations of persons who do not possess the power of accurate discrimination, and therefore observed coincidences are hastily assumed to be particular instances of an universal law. Such procedure leads to superstition and prejudice. It not only warps the judgment, owing to its illogical nature, but it also affects indirectly the man's moral view, as it implies a weakness in character as well as in mind. This criticism refers however to the abuse rather than the legitimate use of this method under such restrictions as have been already indicated.

The chief function of this method is that of suggestion. It indicates often only the possibility of the existence of a causal relation; in other cases it leads to an inference of high probability. In all cases however it marks merely the preliminary steps of an investigation which should be followed up by painstaking experiment. As it is the method of observation chiefly, it is natural that it should precede experiment; for it is only by reflection upon our observations that we discover the nature and relations of phenomena, which serve as data for subsequent experiment.

I have selected several illustrations to indicate the various fields of research in which this method of agreement has led to satisfactory results.

The first refers to the relation between the occurrence of

financial crises and the prevalence of over-production. Guyot, in his *Principles of Social Economy*, gives the following instances: An enormous consumption of capital in the United States in the seventies, for the construction of railroads, was followed by unusual commercial depression. Then the like outlay in India for railway construction by means of loans and taxes which absorbed the whole circulating capital of the Indian population was followed by a devastating famine and general commercial paralysis. Again in Germany there was an enormous consumption of capital in forts and armaments and general military equipment, bringing on the crisis of 1876–1879. England at the same time was unduly supplying circulating capital to the United States, Egypt, and her colonies, and a financial crisis was the result. Through all these varying instances and others of a like nature which might be added, the constant relation of overconsumption in the antecedents to the industrial depression evident in the effect indicates the one to be the cause of the other, either in whole or in part.

Again it is narrated in Brewster's *Treatise on Optics* that he accidentally took an impression from a piece of mother-of-pearl in a cement of resin and beeswax, and, finding the colors repeated upon the surface of the wax, he proceeded to take other impressions in balsam, fusible metal, lead, gum arabic, isinglass, etc., and always found the iridescent colors the same. His inference was that the form of the surface is the real cause of such color effects.[1] The common element which appears in all the antecedents is evidently the same form impressed upon each, which was originally received from the mother-of-pearl. The cause is moreover independent of the nature of the substance in each case which received the impression upon its surface, because such a variety of substances was chosen as to eliminate the individual nature of each as an influencing factor in the result. In this experiment we see the advantage of varying

[1] Quoted by Jevons, *Principles of Science*, p. 419.

the instances as far as possible for this very purpose of eliminating all irrelevant elements. Similar experiments have proved like results in reference to the colors exhibited by thin plates and films. Here the rings and lines of color have been found to be nearly the same whatever may be the nature of the substance. A slight variation in color is due to the refractive index of the intervening substance. With this exception, the nature of the substance is not operative in producing the color effect, but the form alone.

The celebrated scientist, Pasteur, in the year 1868 was carrying on his investigations as to the cause of the blight then devastating the silkworms of France. One of his experiments consisted in selecting thirty perfectly healthy worms from moths that were entirely free from the corpuscles, which latter are the germs of disease, or at that time suspected to be the germs of disease. Then, rubbing a small corpusculous worm in water, he smeared the mixture over the mulberry leaves. Assuring himself that the leaves had been eaten, he watched the consequences day by day. One after the other the worms languished; all showed evidences of being the prey of the corpusculous matter, and finally, within one month's time, all died. Pasteur's inference naturally was that the corpuscles had produced the death. Of course his results were not founded upon this experiment alone, but other experiments, carried on in many different ways, served to corroborate the causal relation which the experiment just described had suggested as at least highly probable.

In medicine also the method of agreement is often used with effect. Certain drugs are administered in a number of cases and the results noted. A uniform effect consequent upon the administration of a given drug indicates a causal connection capable of generalization. Not only are subjects in disease, but also in health, selected, and the effects upon both the normal and morbid natures compared. Thus a variation in instances is secured. If a number of different drugs produce like effects, the question at once suggests itself, What is the property common to them all? The method of agreement often gives some indication of this, when the elimination of the inert properties can be accomplished through a sufficient variation of instances. The difficulty lies, however, in this very thing, to so vary the instances as to disclose the efficient element present in them all. Various medicines present a complex nature of such a character that it is extremely difficult to discriminate the precise effects which the several component parts individually exercise.

The method of agreement is also used, perhaps unconsciously, in the conduct of the everyday affairs of life. Whenever different phenomena in our experience present certain characteristics of a constant nature, we are at once led to suspect a causal connection, and to start upon a more searching investigation of the same. Too often however the supplementary investigation is omitted, and the mind rests content with a few surface resemblances that lead to a hasty generalization without being more precisely and adequately determined.

CHAPTER VII

THE METHOD OF DIFFERENCE

The method of agreement, as we have seen, presents a causal relation as a suggestion, admitting of a high degree of probability it may be, but requiring to be tested by some more scientific method. This is accomplished by the method of difference. Here a phenomenon is observed, in which the supposed cause-element and effect-element appear; then while all other circumstances and conditions remain unaltered, the supposed cause-element is withdrawn, or its force adequately eliminated; the immediate disappearance of the supposed effect-element, consequent upon this, indicates a causal relation between the two. Or the experiment may be made in a different manner, but to the same end, that is, a phenomenon may be characterized by the absence of both cause-element and effect-element; then, if the introduction of the cause-element does not disturb the phenomenon in question, except immediately to produce the effect-element, the inference may be drawn that the one is the veritable cause of the other.

Canon of the Method of Difference. — If an instance in which the phenomenon under investigation occurs, and an instance in which it does not occur, have every circumstance save one in common, that one occurring only in the former; the circumstance in which alone the two instances differ is the effect, or it may be the cause, or a necessary part of the cause, of the phenomenon.

This method admits of manifold illustration in our everyday inferences. A person is asleep in the room with us, and we hear the loud noise of a slamming door, and observe the person at once awakening with a start and exclamation. We have no hesitancy in ascribing the awakening to the noise immediately preceding it. We observe again some one receiving a letter or telegram, and immediately upon opening it the face grows white with anxiety and fear, the hands tremble, and there are shown general symptoms of perturbation. The message received, we say, has caused the mental shock and physical accompaniments.

Or, taking a simple experiment in quite another sphere, it was observed by Boyle, in 1670, that an extract of litmus was immediately turned red by the introduction of an acid. This subsequently became a test for the presence of acids, the inference being that an acid has this capacity of changing the litmus to a red color from its original blue.

Professor Tyndall describes an experiment to prove that waves of ether issuing from a strong source, such as the sun or electric light, are competent to shake asunder the atoms of gaseous molecules, such as those of the sulphur and oxygen which constitute the molecule of sulphurous acid. He enclosed the substance in a vessel, placing it in a dark room, and sending through it a powerful beam of light. At first nothing was seen; the vessel containing the gas seemed as empty as a vacuum. Soon, along the track of the beam, a beautiful sky-blue color was observed, due to the liberated particles of sulphur. For a time the blue grew more intense; it then became whitish; and from a whitish-blue it passed to a more or less perfect white. Continuing the action, the tube became filled with a dense cloud of sulphur particles which, by the application of proper means, could be rendered visible.[1] In this series of continuous changes, we find the one antecedent giving the causal impulse to be the beam of light. It was the one element introduced which started the several changes leading to the appearance of the sulphur. The one, therefore, is to be regarded as the cause of the other.

[1] Tyndall, *Use and Limit of the Imagination in Science*, p. 33.

It is possible to represent this method by means of symbols in a manner similar to that of the method of agreement. Let C be the supposed cause and e the effect corresponding, while S and s denote the setting of antecedent and consequent respectively. We have, therefore, the following:—

$$S + C \quad . \quad . \quad . \quad . \quad . \quad . \quad . \quad s + e.$$

Then, withdrawing C, we have the absence of e.

$$S \quad . \quad . \quad . \quad . \quad . \quad . \quad . \quad . \quad . \quad s.$$

The inference then is that C is the cause of e. Or, we may have given

$$S \quad . \quad . \quad . \quad . \quad . \quad . \quad . \quad . \quad . \quad s.$$

Then if, adding C, we find that e also appears, represented by

$$S + C \quad . \quad . \quad . \quad . \quad . \quad . \quad . \quad s + e,$$

we infer that C and e have a causal connection.

In the method of agreement, a number of instances are taken agreeing only in the possession of two circumstances,—the cause and effect elements common to them all. In this method, only two instances are taken, and they must be precisely alike, with the one exception,—the presence of two circumstances in one, that is, the cause and the effect elements, and the absence of the same in the other. In the method of agreement, we compare the various phenomena to note wherein they agree; in the method of difference, we compare the two phenomena to note wherein they differ. The logical axiom underlying the two methods is substantially one and the same, differing only in its special adaptation in each case. The former method rests on the assumption, which must be accepted as a fundamental postulate, that whatever can be eliminated from the various instances is not connected with the phenomenon under investigation in any causal manner; and the method of differ-

THE METHOD OF DIFFERENCE

ence is based on the postulate that whatever cannot be eliminated is connected with the phenomenon by a causal law.

The method of difference is evidently the method by negation, which has already been indicated as the truly scientific process in induction. It is also preëminently the method of experiment rather than observation; for the withdrawal or introduction of forces can only be accomplished at will when we bring the phenomena under experimental control. At times nature herself may perform the experiment for us, and we stand simply as observers to note the results. This is especially the case in the catastrophic phenomena, such as volcanic eruption, earthquakes, etc. Generally speaking, however, the method of difference is the process of man's manipulation to secure purposed results in which a causal relation is disclosed.

A question naturally suggests itself, What is there to determine the precise mode of experiment? We may have given a concrete whole of extreme complexity. In our experiment, which element shall we proceed to eliminate, in order to note the result? An answer may be given us through suggestions received from the results of enumeration, analogy, or the method of agreement. If it is not possible to avail one's self of this contribution from another sphere of investigation, then the complex whole must be broken up, as far as possible, into its simplest component parts, and one after another these parts, singly, then in pairs, and all other possible combinations, caused to be withdrawn, or their force neutralized, and the results in each case noted, as to whether the effect under investigation disappears. The exhaustion of all possible combinations must yield some definite result. Suppose, for instance, there is a complex antecedent involving four separable elements, as A, B, C, D. Withdraw severally A, B, C, and D, noting results; then withdraw, in turn, AB, AC, AD, BC, BD, CD, that is, the possible combinations of four elements taken two at a time; then withdraw ABC, then BCD, ABD, and *ACD*, that is, combinations of four elements taken three at a time.[1] By such a process there will be disclosed whether one element alone or whether a combination of two or more have produced the effect under investigation. The practical difficulty in separating the elements of a complex whole, and withdrawing the several combinations from the whole, renders this process in many cases impossible. The cause, however, is generally suspected. It may be suggested, as we have seen, by the method of agreement, by analogy, or by that insight which at once declares certain combinations to be impossible and others irrelevant. There is generally a mental experiment in which the judgment rejects unlikely combinations, thus narrowing the field of investigation and furnishing a tentative hypothesis as a preliminary to the experiments proper.

The method of difference is open to various criticisms; the most important are the following: —

1. In applying this method, we may be easily misled, in supposing our two instances are precisely alike with the one exception of the presence or absence of the supposed cause, but in reality the instance may differ radically, and yet we may be unable to detect this. A patient may have medicine administered to him, and begin at once rapidly to recover, and yet the very taking of the medicine in itself may have made such a mental impression inducing confidence and hope that the real cause of the recovery may be due wholly to this mental reaction. Persons taking pills composed of inert substances have often given evidence of bodily effects wholly impossible to trace to the medicine itself. And yet this criticism is one of caution rather than of censure; for the defects are but difficulties which extreme care and insight may overcome.

2. It has been objected that this method may point out the cause in the concrete instance before the experimenter,

[1] This process has been illustrated and criticised at length in a striking manner by Venn, *Empirical Logic*, pp. 401 ff.

but that this furnishes no basis whatsoever for a wider generalization that the effect in question is always produced by this cause. Sigwart has illustrated this objection by the instances in which typhus fever has been traced to the drinking of impure water.[1] The causal relation may be fully established in the cases investigated, but the universal proposition does not follow that wherever typhus fever appears, impure water has been drunk. This objection applies especially to cases of extreme complexity, where proximate causes alone can be discovered, and their ultimate nature which may appear in various forms is not revealed; for instance, the impure water is not in itself the ultimate cause of the typhus fever. It contains the poison germs, the real cause; they may be introduced into the system in some other way. Care therefore should be taken to reveal the cause in and by itself, and not the cause of the cause. The objection, therefore, may be in a measure overcome. To effect a generalization of logical validity, it is necessary to supplement the method of difference by hypothesis and subsequent verification, which will be described later on.

3. This method may lead to error in cases where the supposed causal element is regarded as the cause in its entirety, when it is in reality but a part of the cause. If one should plant seed in a garden and water only one-half of the plot, and it should follow that only the watered part brought forth the leaf and flower, then an inference according to the method of difference might be drawn that the water caused the sprouting of the young plants. And yet it must be regarded simply as contributory to the real cause. Such a difficulty may be obviated by a careful discrimination in the analysis of the phenomenon investigated.

4. Sometimes a liberating cause may be revealed by a strict interpretation of the method of difference, when the real cause is more obscure, and may be overlooked. A stone may strike a can of dynamite, and the explosion which

[1] Sigwart, *Logic*, Vol. II, p. 420.

occurs may be traced to the impact of the stone. It is the one element of difference introduced in the sphere of the observed phenomena, with the consequent result. The force existing as a potential is naturally obscure, and apt to elude observation. Therefore, whenever a cause disclosed by the method of difference seems to be out of all proportion to the effect, it at once suggests the probability that a potential force not discerned by our powers of observation has been the real cause, and the former a conditioning cause merely. Another illustration of this is the experiment of Priestley, which led to his discovery of oxygen in 1774. He placed some oxide of mercury upon the top of quicksilver in an inverted glass tube filled with that metal and standing in mercury; he then heated the oxide by means of a glass lens and the sun's rays, and obtained a gas, which he called "nitrous air," afterwards designated as oxygen. The heat in this case was the sole element of difference between the two instances, one in which there was no gas, and the second after application of the heat, when the gas was present. Here the heat must be regarded as the liberating and not in any sense the producing cause. Again, as Lotze says, "the fact that with the destruction of a single part of the brain a definite psychical function ceases, is no proof that just this single part was the organ which alone produced that function."[1]

In addition to the difficulties attending this method, which have been enumerated and which have to do with the logical theory of the method, there are also difficulties of a practical nature which arise in the actual application of this method in experimental inquiry. They are as follows: —

1. Care must be taken that, in the two phenomena compared, with and without the supposed cause, there shall not be an interval of time elapsing, in which period some other cause might be introduced unknown to the investigator, and yet capable of producing the result, or else of neutralizing

[1] Lotze, *Logic*, p. 322.

some force that is present and itself capable of producing the result. For instance, if a chemical compound be left for an appreciable time, we may notice certain changes and be able to assert positively that no new element has been introduced, and yet the action of the air may in itself have been sufficient to work these changes. When the two phenomena to be compared can be presented for inspection simultaneously, this difficulty is obviated. This is illustrated in an experiment devised to exhibit the presence of light effects in the spectrum beyond the violet rays; that is, beyond the place where the spectrum seems to end. A sheet of paper is taken, the lower part of which is moistened with a solution of sulphate of quinine, while the upper part remains dry. Let the image of the solar ray fall upon this sheet; the spectrum preserves at the top of the sheet in the dry portion of the paper its ordinary appearance, while in the moistened portion a brilliant phosphorescence appears beyond the region of the violet rays. Here the dry and wet portions are simultaneously presented, and there is but one point of difference between the two. The inference, therefore, is readily drawn that the solution of sulphate of quinine is a substance sensitive to the ultra-violet portion of the sun's rays, the phosphorescence being the effect of these rays upon the solution.

2. Extreme care must be taken that, in the withdrawing of any element in the course of the experiment, no other element is inadvertently introduced, and that, in adding any element, no existing element or combination of elements is destroyed, or their effect neutralized. Mr. Venn has admirably illustrated this difficulty, and I give the following quotation in full from him: "We suppose that when we have put a weight into one pan of a pair of scales we have done nothing more than this, or can at any rate by due caution succeed in doing nothing more. But if we exact the utmost rigidity of conditions, we easily see that we have done a great deal more. Our bodies are heavy, and there-

fore the mere approach to the machine has altered the magnitude and direction of the resultant attraction upon the scales. Our bodies are presumably warmer than the surrounding air; accordingly, we warm and therefore lighten the air in which the scales hang, and if the two scales and their contents are not of the same volume, we at once alter their weight as measured in the air. Our breath produces disturbing currents of air. Our approach affects the surface of the non-rigid floor or ground on which the scales stand, and produces another source of disturbance, and so on through the whole range of the physical forces." [1]

In the Report of the British Association, 1881, an account is given of Professor G. H. Darwin's experiments to measure the lunar disturbance of gravity at the Cavendish Laboratory by means of an extremely delicate pendulum. It was found that approaching the pendulum in order to observe its reading, the surface level of the stone floor on which the instrument stood was deflected by the weight of the observer. As he stood to take the reading, the shifting of his weight from one leg to the other was perceptible; so it became necessary to observe the reading by a telescope from a distance, or to adopt some similar plan.[2]

Faraday was able at will to produce or remove a magnetic force, through the revealed properties of the electromagnet. Many of his experiments would have been impossible if it had been necessary to remove a cumbersome magnet and reinstate it again and again in his experiments. The electromagnet however could produce or destroy the presence of magnetic force without any incidental perturbations. Thus Faraday was enabled to prove the rotation of circularly polarized light by the fact that certain light ceased to be visible when the electric current of the magnet was cut off, and instantly reappeared when the current was reëstablished. Faraday says of the experiment himself: "These

[1] Venn, *Empirical Logic*, p. 416.
[2] Quoted by Venn in *Empirical Logic*, p. 419.

phenomena could be reversed at pleasure, and at any instant of time, and upon any occasion, showing a perfect dependence of cause and effect." [1]

3. In some cases it is impossible to remove an element which is supposed to be the cause of an effect under investigation. Its removal might cause the destruction or the impairing of the whole phenomenon. The force therefore that cannot be eliminated must be neutralized by an equal and opposing force. For instance, the force of gravity cannot be eliminated; it must therefore be counterbalanced by some device of the investigator. In chemistry the removal of an element from a compound may be impossible without destroying utterly the compound itself; in such a case also a neutralizing agent must be introduced. Darwin wished to prove that the odor of flowers is attractive to insects irrespective of the attraction of color. He therefore covered certain flowers with a muslin net, and still the insects were attracted to the flowers although the color was thus concealed.[2]

The following illustrations may serve further to exhibit the various features of the method of difference: —

Mr. Robert Mallet gives the following interesting account of his visit to Faraday: "It must be now eighteen years ago when I paid him a visit, and brought some slips of flexible and *tough* Muntz's yellow metal, to show him the instantaneous change to complete brittleness with rigidity produced by dipping into pernitrate of mercury solution. He got the solution and I showed him the facts; he obviously did not doubt what he saw me do before and close to him; but a sort of experimental instinct seemed to require he should try it himself. So he took one of the slips, bent it forward and backward, dipped it, and broke it up into short bits between his own fingers. He had not before spoken. Then he said, 'Yes, it *is* pliable, and it *does*

---

[1] *Experimental Researches in Electricity*, Vol. III, p. 4.
[2] Darwin, *Cross and Self Fertilization*, p. 374.

become instantly brittle.'"[1] Here the experiment with and without the significant antecedent and consequent indicates the causal relation, especially as the instantaneous effect precludes the possibility of the operation of any other cause.

Another experiment of Faraday's is that of his investigation of the behavior of Lycopodium powder on a vibrating plate. It had been observed that the minute particles of the powder collected together at the points of greatest motion, whereas sand and all heavy particles collected at the nodes, where the motion was least. It occurred to Faraday to try the experiment in the exhausted receiver of an air-pump, and it was then found that the light powder behaved exactly like heavy powder. The inference was that the presence of air was the condition of importance, because it was thrown into eddies by the motion of the plate, and carried the Lycopodium powder to the points of greatest agitation. Sand was too heavy to be carried by the air.[2]

Sir John Lubbock gives an account of experiments performed upon insects to prove that the sense of smell is in some way connected with their antennæ. One experiment was performed by Forel, who removed the wings from some blue-bottle flies and placed them near a decaying mole. They immediately walked to it, and began licking it and laying eggs. He then took them away, and removed the antennæ, all other circumstances remaining the same as before, after which, even when placed close to the mole, they did not appear to perceive it. Another experiment similar to this was tried by Plateau, who put some food of which cockroaches are fond on a table and surrounded it with a low circular wall of cardboard. He then put some cockroaches on the table; they evidently scented the food, and made straight for it. He then removed their antennæ, after which, as long as they could not see the food, they

[1] Gladstone, *Michael Faraday*, p. 175.
[2] Jevons, *Principles of Science*, p. 419.

failed to find it, even though they wandered about quite close to it.[1]

Another experiment is that of Graber to prove the sense of hearing in insects. He placed some water-boatmen (*Corixa*) in a deep jar full of water, at the bottom of which was a layer of mud. He dropped a stone on the mud, but the beetles, which were reposing quietly on some weeds, took no notice. He then put a piece of glass on the mud, and dropped a stone on to it, thus making a noise, though the disturbance of the water was the same as when the stone was dropped on the mud. The water-boatmen, however, then at once took flight.[2]

An illustration of the method of difference occurs in the so-called *blind experiments,* which are often made in chemistry especially. As Professor Jevons has described such an experiment: "Suppose, for instance, a chemist places a certain suspected substance in Marsh's test apparatus and finds that it gives a small deposit of metallic arsenic, he cannot be sure that the arsenic really proceeds from the suspected substance; the impurity of the zinc or sulphuric acid may have been the cause of its appearance. It is therefore the practice of chemists to make what they call blind experiments, that is, to try whether arsenic appears in the absence of the suspected substance. The same precaution ought to be taken in all important analytical operations. Indeed it is not merely a precaution, it is an essential part of any experiment. If the blind trial be not made, the chemist merely assumes that he knows what would happen."[3]

---

[1] Lubbock, *On the Senses, Instincts, and Intelligence of Animals,* p. 45.
[2] *Ibid.,* p. 75.   [3] Jevons, *Principles of Science,* p. 433.

CHAPTER VIII

THE JOINT METHOD OF AGREEMENT AND DIFFERENCE

It has already been shown that the method of difference is sometimes not available, inasmuch as it may be neither possible nor practicable to remove from the phenomenon to be investigated the suspected causal element without destroying the phenomenon itself. Sometimes, too, it is impossible even to neutralize the effect of the causal element if it is allowed to remain as an integral part of the phenomenon. This is especially the case in all vital phenomena, and also in many chemical phenomena. Therefore another method is resorted to, which is known as the joint method of agreement and difference. Inasmuch as the suspected causal element cannot be removed, we must select another phenomenon as much like the former as possible, which is however characterized by the absence of the causal element. By the simple method of difference, two instances only need be compared, the one with and the other without the causal element, but agreeing precisely in every other particular. In the joint method, the instances with and without the causal element differ, it may be, in several particulars. A number of varying instances must therefore be selected so as to eliminate the possibility of any of these differing characteristics being the cause in question. Therefore two sets of instances are collected and compared. The one set comprises all the positive instances having the presence of the supposed causal element, and the second set consists of the negative instances having the supposed causal element absent altogether. The validity of the method depends upon the similarity of the two sets of instances. As the similarity increases, the method approximates to the simple method of difference.

The Canon of the Joint Method. — If several instances in which the phenomenon occurs have only one circumstance in common, while several instances in which it does not occur have nothing in common save the absence of that circumstance; the circumstance in which alone the two sets of instances differ, is the effect, or cause, or a necessary part of the cause, of the phenomenon.

The symbolical representation of this method may be exhibited as follows, using a similar notation to that employed in the previous methods: —

I. Table of positive instances.

$$S + C \ldots\ldots s + e.$$
$$S' + C \ldots\ldots s' + e.$$
$$S'' + C \ldots\ldots s'' + e.$$
$$S''' + C \ldots\ldots s''' + e.$$
etc.   etc.

II. Table of negative instances.

$$S_{I} \ldots\ldots s_{I}.$$
$$S_{II} \ldots\ldots s_{II}.$$
$$S_{III} \ldots\ldots s_{III}.$$
etc.   etc.

In the two sets of instances, the following conditions must be observed in order to render the method valid: —

1. $S + C, S' + C, S'' + C, S''' + C$, etc.,

must be so varied that they reveal but one constant element, common to them all, as C. It may be that S will resemble S' in more marks than the one, namely C, and this may be true of any two or more instances; however, taken all together, they must possess but the one common element C.

2. In the same way S_{I} may resemble S_{II} in more marks than merely the absence of C and so for any two or more

instances in the series $S_{\prime}$, $S_{\prime\prime}$, $S_{\prime\prime\prime}$, etc. However, the one characteristic common to them all must be the absence of C.

3. If in the instances chosen an element is common to all in addition to C, or in the second set its absence, then additional instances must be added to the tables both positive and negative in order to secure this all-important condition of elimination through suitable variation.

4. Moreover, the two series, positive and negative, must have their settings similar. $S_{\prime}$, $S_{\prime\prime}$, $S_{\prime\prime\prime}$, etc., must resemble S', S'', S''', etc.; otherwise the negative instances would not be significant.[1] They must be chosen from the same sphere as the positive, in order that they may be similar. It is possible to multiply negative instances *ad infinitum*, which, however, would furnish no ground for any inference, because they would be wholly irrelevant to the problem under investigation.

5. If $S_{\prime}$ is so similar to S' as to be identical with it, and also $s_{\prime}$ passes over into s'; then we have the method of difference in its pure form:—

$$S' + C \quad \ldots \ldots \ldots \quad s' + e.$$
$$S' \quad \ldots \ldots \ldots \ldots \quad s'.$$

Here the setting, instead of being similar in the two cases, is the same in each.

The following is an experiment of Sir John Lubbock's concerning the sense of smell in insects, which I have chosen as illustrating this method of inductive research. He took a large ant and tethered her on a board by a thread. When she was quite still, he brought a tuning-fork into close proximity to her antennæ, but she was not disturbed in the least. He then approached the feather of a pen very quietly, so as almost to touch first one and then the other of the antennæ, which, however, did not move. He then dipped the pen in the essence of musk and did the same; the antenna was slowly retracted and drawn quite back. He

[1] See p. 75.

then repeated the same with the other antenna, and with like result. Care was taken throughout not to touch the antennæ. Lubbock then repeated the experiment with a number of different ants, and using various substances. The results in all cases were the same, and the inference was naturally drawn that the antennæ possessed the sense of smell. In these experiments various substances were taken having nothing in common save the odor of musk that had been placed upon them.

. In some cases it is not possible to discover positive instances in which the only common element is the suspected cause. In such cases the method is not conclusive in its results, although it may attain a high degree of probability, if all the common elements save the suspected cause-element are known to be irrelevant, or can in any other way be proved to have no influence whatsoever upon the result. For instance, an illustration is often given of this method, which fails in the manner just described. A man is attempting to discover whether a particular article of food disagrees with him. He notices several occasions, a large number if you please, when he has eaten this particular kind of food, and has soon after experienced distress. These are the positive instances. This peculiar distress has never been experienced when he has abstained from the food in question. The inference is that this food has caused the distress. In the various instances, however, the sole element in common is not merely the taking or not taking the food. The person's whole bodily organism is common to all the instances. Within it, unforeseen complications, independent of this article of food, might have caused the trouble. In such cases a large number of instances must be resorted to in order to render the possibility of a coincidence out of the question.

So also in such cases as the treatment of any given disease in a hospital. An experiment may be tried in the treatment, say, of typhoid fever. One ward may be subjected to a particular kind of treatment, and another ward not subjected to that treatment. If recovery is hastened in the one and retarded in the other case, an inference may be drawn as to efficacy of this treatment. In these instances again, while they are all different patients, still the nursing, surroundings, etc., are common to them all. It must be shown that these are present both in the negative and positive instances, and equally capable of accomplishing the effect if they had been real causes. They may therefore be eliminated in comparing the two sets of instances, because common both to the negative and positive cases. In this also resort must be had to the number of instances in order to eliminate chance coincidences. The presence of common elements in excess of the common causal element may be represented according to the symbolical notation of the joint method, by the introduction of another symbol x. Let x stand for that which is common to all instances in addition to the common element C. We then have: —

I. Set of positive instances.

$$S + C + x \ \ldots\ \ldots\ \ldots\ s + e.$$
$$S' + C + x \ \ldots\ \ldots\ \ldots\ s' + e.$$
$$S'' + C + x \ \ldots\ \ldots\ \ldots\ s'' + e.$$
$$S''' + C + x \ \ldots\ \ldots\ \ldots\ s''' + e.$$
$$\text{etc.} \qquad\qquad\qquad \text{etc.}$$

II. Set of negative instances.

$$S_{I} + x \ \ldots\ \ldots\ \ldots\ s_{I}.$$
$$S_{II} + x \ \ldots\ \ldots\ \ldots\ s_{II}.$$
$$S_{III} + x \ \ldots\ \ldots\ \ldots\ s_{III}.$$
$$\text{etc.} \qquad\qquad\qquad \text{etc.}$$

We observe x in all instances both positive and negative. Being present when the effect occurs and when it does not, indifferently, we can at once infer that x is not the whole cause of e. However, it may have united with C in the first set of instances to produce the effect e, so that C without x, or some part or parts of x, could not alone produce the effect e. In all such cases the exact force of x must be estimated in some other way. If x is extremely complex, or subject to change from forces emanating from within itself, as in the case of organic phenomena, then it becomes extremely difficult to determine x; and consequently the method of agreement and difference does not yield as exact results. As long as the force of x remains unknown, it becomes the source of possible disturbance, which may wholly vitiate the results attained.

Mr. Darwin, in his experiments upon cross and self fertilization in the vegetable kingdom, placed a net about one hundred flower heads, thus protecting them from the bees and from any chance of fertilization by means of the pollen conveyed to them by the bees. He at the same time placed one hundred other flower heads of the same variety of plant where they would be exposed to the bees, and, as he observed, were repeatedly visited by them. Here we have the two sets of instances, in one the flowers accessible to the bees, and in the other, not accessible. He obtained the following result. The protected flowers failed to yield a single seed. The others produced 68 grains' weight of seed, which he estimated as numbering 2720 seeds. Cross-fertilization as the cause in this case is thus proved. The common element in all these instances, however, is not merely the presence in one case and the absence in the other of the bees; there is also the element of the common plant structure running through all of the two hundred instances. This element is, however, of such an unvarying nature in all the instances, and the number observed so many as to eliminate the possibility of any given plant structure possessing unobserved peculiarities sufficient to produce the result in question. It may therefore be considered as an inert element as regards the effects noticed in the one and absent in the other set of instances.

Sir John Lubbock, in his researches concerning the different functions of the two kinds of eyes in insects, illustrates the joint method in its general features. The two kinds of eyes are the large compound eyes, situated one on each side of the head, and the ocelli, or small eyes, of which there are generally three, arranged in a triangle between the other two. He wished to determine the precise function of the small eyes, the ocelli; and he has gathered together the following facts. Plateau has shown that caterpillars, which possess ocelli, but no compound eyes, are very short-sighted, not seeing above one to two centimetres. He has also proved by experiments that spiders, which have ocelli but no compound eyes, are very short-sighted; they were easily deceived by artificial flies of most inartistic construction, and even hunting spiders could not see beyond ten centimetres (four inches). Lubbock experimented on this point with a female spider, which, after laying her eggs, had rolled them into a ball, and had enveloped the whole with a silken bag which she carried about with her. Having captured the female and having taken the bag of eggs from her, he placed it on a table about two inches in front of her. She evidently did not see it. He then pushed it gradually towards her, but she took no notice till it nearly touched her, when she eagerly seized it. He then took it away a second time, and put it in the middle of the table, which was two feet four inches by one foot four, and had nothing else on it. The spider wandered about for an hour and fifty minutes before she found it, apparently by accident. He then took it away again and put it down as before, when she wandered about for an hour without finding it. Like experiments were tried with other spiders and with the same results. Plateau also experimented with scorpions which had ocelli and no compound eyes. They appeared scarcely to see beyond their own pincers. Moreover, the ocelli are especially developed in insects, such as ants, bees, and wasps, which live partly in the open light and partly in the dark recesses of nests. Again, the night-flying moths all possess ocelli. On the other hand, however, they are entirely absent in all butterflies, with but one exception, according to Scudder, namely, the genus Pamphila. Forel varnished the compound eyes of various insects which had ocelli as well. The latter however he allowed to remain in their natural state. Inasmuch as their habits of flight required powers of vision in these insects extending to a considerable distance, it happened that when placed on the ground they made no attempt to rise; while, if thrown into the air, they flew first in one direction and then in another, striking against any object that came in their way, and being apparently quite unable to guide themselves. They flew repeatedly against a wall, falling to the ground, and unable to alight against it, as they did so cleverly when they had their compound eyes to guide them. All these instances, taken together in their positive and negative aspects, led Sir John Lubbock to infer that the ocelli were useful in dark places and for near vision, while the compound eyes were for the light and more distant vision.[1]

Another illustration of this method may be found in Darwin's account of the extreme tameness of the birds in the Galapagos and Falkland islands. I quote some extracts from his narrative, in which it will be seen that Darwin's inferences follow from his comparison of the positive and negative instances before him. He says: "This tameness of disposition is common to all the terrestrial species of these islands in the Galapagos Archipelago; namely, to the mocking-thrushes, the finches, wrens, tyrant flycatchers, the dove, and carrion-buzzard. All of them often approached sufficiently near to be killed with a switch, and sometimes, as I myself tried, with a cap or hat. A gun is here almost superfluous; for, with the muzzle, I pushed a hawk off the branch of a tree. In Charles Island, which had been colonized about six years, I saw a boy sitting by a well with a

[1] Lubbock, *On the Senses, Instinct, and Intelligence of Animals*, pp. 175 ff.

switch in his hand, with which he killed the doves and finches as they came to drink. He had already procured a little heap of them for his dinner; and he said that he had constantly been in the habit of waiting by this well for the same purpose. The Falkland Islands offer instances of birds with a similar disposition. The snipe, upland and lowland goose, thrush bunting, and even some true hawks, are more or less tame. The black-necked swan is here wild, and it was impossible to kill it. It however is a bird of passage, which probably brought with it the wisdom learned in foreign countries.

"From these several facts, we may, I think, conclude that the wildness of birds with regard to man is a particular instinct directed against *him* and not dependent on any general degree of caution arising from other sources of danger; secondly, that it is not acquired by individual birds in a short time, even when much persecuted, but that in the course of successive generations it becomes hereditary. With domesticated animals we are accustomed to see new mental habits or instincts acquired and rendered hereditary, but with animals in a state of nature it must always be most difficult to discover instances of acquired hereditary knowledge. In regard to the wildness of birds towards man, there is no way of accounting for it except as an inherited habit; comparatively few young birds, in any one year, have been injured by man in England, yet almost all, even nestlings, are afraid of him; many individuals, on the other hand, both at Galapagos and at the Falklands, have been pursued and injured by him, but yet have not learned a salutary dread of him."[1]

I have given this quotation somewhat at length in order to show the method of a great investigator in the realm of nature; and that it may be seen how naturally he falls into the method of comparing positive and negative sets of instances relative to the object of research. The animal and

[1] Darwin, *Voyage of a Naturalist*, Vol. II, pp. 172 f.

vegetable kingdoms are especially adapted to the application of this joint method, and therefore it is in biology that it is most frequently employed and where it has yielded the most fertile results.

The advantage of the joint method over the simple method of agreement is that it largely eliminates the possibility of there being any other cause of the given phenomenon than the one disclosed by the operation of this method. The method of agreement, as we have seen, often fails of a definite result owing to the plurality of causes. The joint method tends to indicate the one and only cause, and when the instances are rigorously selected according to the conditions of the canon, there is a high degree of probability that the sole cause is discovered. Mr. Mill at this point claims too much for the method in insisting that it gives a certainty regarding the sole cause, when the requirements are perfectly realized. It is impossible to realize the requirements perfectly. In selecting the negative instances, we are never sure that we have compassed the entire sphere of *significant* negative instances. We may, however, attain results highly probable in this regard, though they may not reach an absolute certainty. Such a statement is more moderate in its expression, and practically it assures as satisfactory results.

CHAPTER IX

THE METHOD OF CONCOMITANT VARIATIONS

The method of concomitant variations is a process of determining a causal relation when, as an element in an antecedent varies in intensity greater or less, there is observed a corresponding or concomitant variation in the consequent.

Canon of the Method of Concomitant Variations. — Whatever phenomenon varies in any manner, whenever another phenomenon varies in some particular, is either a cause or an effect of that phenomenon, or is connected with it through some fact of causation.

The latter clause of this canon provides for that circumstance in which the varying elements may both be concomitant effects of a common cause. When we are assured of the absence of any possible common cause to which we can assign the two phenomena as effects, then they must be related between themselves as cause and effect. A simple illustration of this method is the rise of the mercury in the thermometer owing to the increase of heat; its fall, whenever there is decrease of heat. One varies as the other concomitantly, and we infer a causal relation that we at once proceed to generalize without hesitation.

The symbolical representation of this method is as follows: —

$$S + C \quad \ldots \ldots \quad s + e.$$
$$S + C \pm dC \quad \ldots \ldots \quad s + e \pm de.$$
$$\text{etc.} \qquad\qquad \text{etc.}$$

Then C is the cause of e.

I have used dC and de to denote the increments or decrements of the cause and effect respectively. This method is used generally when the method of difference is impossible, owing to the fact that the supposed causal element cannot be made to vanish wholly. In all such cases a variation of the element is resorted to, and the corresponding result observed. Heat is relative and not absolute, as also the height of mercury in the tube. The relation is determined, therefore, by variations, greater and less. This method is also used to supplement the results of other methods by which a causal relation has been determined, but not in exact quantitative terms. It may be known that a certain phenomenon C is always the cause of a certain effect e, and the method of concomitant variations will then be of use in determining precisely how much of a variation in C will cause a specified variation in e. A law finds scientific expression only when stated in terms of exact quantitative relation between variations in antecedent and consequent. We may express the law of universal attraction in a vague way that bodies always attract each other, and the greater attraction when the bodies are nearer together, and the larger they are. But this statement needs to be recast in terms exhibiting the precise quantitative variation, — bodies attract each other directly as the product of their masses, and inversely as the square of their distance. It is evident that the special function of this method of concomitant variations consists in just this quantitative determination. In one respect, therefore, it may be regarded as a substitute for the method of difference, and in another way as a supplement to the method of difference in leading to quantitatively determinate results.

The quantitative variation between antecedent and consequent may be either direct or inverse variation. The former is when one increases as the other increases, or when one decreases as the other decreases. The inverse is when one decreases as the other increases, or *vice versa*. This may be expressed symbolically

$$S + C \pm dC \quad \ldots \quad s + e \mp de.$$

We have, for instance, Boyle's law as regards the variation of volume of gases according to the pressure; that is, when we double the pressure, we halve the volume. This may be proved experimentally. The method also was used by Ricardo to prove his law that the rate of profits varies in inverse ratio to the rate of wages. We have also the tendency observed in respect to increase of crimes when there is decrease of opportunities for labor.

The expression of a law in terms of the quantitative relation between antecedent and consequent may be facilitated by a graphic representation of the same, through corresponding abscissæ and ordinates. The varying antecedents, for instance, may be laid off on the axis of X, and each several consequent represented by the corresponding ordinate. The resulting curve thus obtained will represent the law of their mutual relation. If the equation of the curve can be determined, it will represent the mathematically exact expression of the law in question. If this is not possible, it may prove at least suggestive of the law which otherwise might have remained concealed. This graphical method is especially useful in dealing with physical phenomena. "If the abscissæ represent intervals of time, and the ordinates corresponding heights of the barometer, we may construct curves which show at a glance the dependence of barometric pressure upon the time of day. Such curves may be accurately drawn by photographic processes on a sheet of sensitive paper placed behind the mercurial column, and made to move past it with a uniform horizontal velocity by clockwork. A similar process is applied to the temperature and electricity of the atmosphere, and to the components of terrestrial magnetism."[1]

The method of concomitant variation has the advantage of the psychological impression which it makes. The mind is more susceptible to the perception of variation in forces where the change is apparent to the senses, than to the perception of a constant force, whose constant character thereby conceals its nature and function from the senses. Synchronous changes attract the attention, and admit of ready comparison, as we follow out the variations from point to point. We may ring a bell in a vacuum, and detect no sound whatsoever, and then allow the air to enter gradually. We notice that as the air enters more and more freely, the sound grows louder and louder. The relation of cause and effect is thus demonstrated to the senses in the most vivid manner possible. The variations are exhibited side by side, and thus, presented together in their concomitant relation, produce the deeper impression.

This method is of special advantage in all experiments where the intensity of the forces can be varied at will and the consequent effects exhibited in some palpable manner. The determination of the heat rays in the solar spectrum is accomplished by this method. The spectrum may be received upon a plate pierced with a narrow slit, through which the rays can act upon a thermo-electric pile, which will indicate by deflections of a needle the varying intensity of the heat in the several rays of the spectrum. Now, move the slit through the whole extent of the spectrum, beginning with the violet portion. While in the violet, the indigo, the blue, and even the green, the needle of the thermoscopic apparatus will be deflected but slightly, it will indicate an amount of heat increasing as the slit crosses the yellow, next the orange, then the red; and then beyond the red, and entering the dark portion of the spectrum, we find the greatest deflection of all. The maximum of heat is

[1] Thomson and Tait, *Elements of Natural Philosophy*, Vol. I, p. 119.

therefore in a region beyond the observation of the senses when unaided by experimental device; and yet revealed conclusively by this method.[1]

Professor Tyndall performed a very interesting experiment to prove that the cloud of darkness surrounding flames of great heat was due to the fact that the heat consumed the floating motes in the air which serve to scatter the light which is visible only when thus diffused. The phenomenon which he endeavored to explain was somewhat as follows: Beneath a beam of electric light, a red-hot poker was placed, and from it black wreaths as of smoke were seen to ascend. A large hydrogen flame being employed, it produced whirling masses of darkness far more copiously than the poker. Of this Professor Tyndall remarked: "Smoke was out of the question; what then was the blackness? It was simply that of stellar space; that is to say, blackness resulting from the absence from the track of the beam of all matter competent to scatter its light. When the flame was placed below the beam, the floating matter was destroyed *in situ*; and the air freed from this matter rose into the beam, jostled aside the illuminated particles, and substituted for their light the darkness due to its own perfect transparency. Nothing could more forcibly illustrate the invisibility of the agent which renders all things visible. The beam crossed, unseen, the black chasm formed by the transparent air, while at both sides of the gap the thick-strewn particles shone out like a luminous solid under the powerful illumination."[2] Such being the phenomenon and Professor Tyndall's explanation, it will be seen that he proceeded according to the method of concomitant variations in the following experiment of many which he performed to substantiate this theory: —

A platinum tube with its plug of platinum gauze was connected with an experimental tube, through which a pow-

[1] Saigey, *The Unity of Natural Phenomena*, p. 61.
[2] Tyndall, *Fragments of Science*, p. 280.

erful beam could be sent from an electric lamp placed at its end. The platinum tube was heated till it glowed feebly but distinctly in the dark. The experimental tube was then exhausted, and filled with air that had passed through the red-hot tube. A considerable amount of floating matter which had escaped combustion was revealed by the electric beam.

Then the tube was raised to a brighter redness and the air permitted to pass slowly through it. Though diminished in quantity, a certain amount of floating matter passed into the exhausted experimental tube.

The platinum tube was rendered still hotter; a barely perceptible trace of the floating matter now passed through it. The experiment was repeated, with the difference that the air was sent more slowly through the red-hot tube. The floating matter was totally destroyed. The platinum tube was now lowered until it bordered upon a visible red heat. The air, sent through it still more slowly than in the last experiment, carried with it a cloud of floating matter. Professor Tyndall's commentary upon this experiment is as follows: "If, then, the suspended matter is destroyed by a bright-red heat, much more is it destroyed by a flame whose temperature is vastly higher than any employed in this experiment. So that the blackness introduced into a luminous beam where a flame is placed beneath it is due, as stated, to the destruction of the suspended matter."[1]

Professor Tyndall also supplemented this experiment by one which was according to the joint method of agreement and difference. He prepared oxygen so as to exclude all floating particles, and found that when blown into the beam, darkness was produced; also that hydrogen, nitrogen, carbonic acid, and coal-gas, when prepared in a similar way, each produce darkness when poured or blown into the beam. These instances, combined with various positive instances of

[1] Tyndall, *Fragments of Science*, pp. 283, 284.

illumination of mote-strewn currents of air, illustrate the method of agreement and difference.

An additional experiment, according to the method of difference, was as follows: Professor Tyndall placed an ordinary glass shade in the air with its mouth downward. This permitted the track of the beam to be seen crossing it. Letting coal-gas, or hydrogen, enter the shade by a tube reaching to its top, the gas gradually filled the shade from the top downward. As soon as it occupied the space crossed by the beam, the luminous track was instantly abolished. Lifting the shade so as to bring the common boundary of gas and air above the beam, the track flashed forth. After the shade was full, he inverted it; thereupon the gas passed upward like a black smoke among the illuminated particles.[1]

The method of concomitant variations is not only capable of illustration by laboratory methods and devices; it finds abundant illustration as well in the realm of nature, where observation alone becomes the instrument of investigation and where experiment is impossible or impracticable. Lyell, in his *Principles of Geology*, gives a very interesting account of the alternate elevation and subsidence of the temple of Jupiter Serapis, at Pozzuoli, on the Bay of Naples.[2] It is situated in proximity to several volcanoes, Vesuvius, however, being at some distance. It has been observed that there is a certain connection between each era of upheaval, and a local development of volcanic heat; and on the other hand, between each era of depression, and the local quiescent condition of volcanic phenomena. Before the Christian era, when Ischia was in a state of eruption, and Avernus and other points in the Phlegræan fields were celebrated for their volcanic character, it was observed that at that time the ground on which the temple stood was several feet above water. Vesuvius was then regarded as a spent volcano. After the Christian era, Vesuvius became active and then

[1] Tyndall, *Fragments of Science*, pp. 284, 285.
[2] Chapter XXX.

scarcely a single eruption occurred in Ischia or around the Bay of Baiæ. It was observed that at that time the temple was sinking. Vesuvius then became quiet for five centuries preceding the eruption of 1631, and during that period the Solfatara was in eruption in 1198, Ischia in 1302, and Monte Nuovo was formed in 1538. Then the foundations of the temple were observed to be rising again. Vesuvius became active after that, and has continued so ever since, and during this time the temple has been subsiding. The inference is that as the subterranean heat increases, and lava forms without obtaining an easy vent like that afforded by Vesuvius, the surface is elevated, but when the rocks below are cooling and contracting, the pent-up fire being withdrawn in the eruption of the great Vesuvius, then there is a corresponding subsidence.

The observation of concomitant variations is furthermore illustrated in Darwin's researches concerning the formation of coral reefs, as regards the question which some naturalists have raised as to which part of the coral reef is most favorable to the growth of coral.[1] He adduces the following facts, most of which are the direct result of his observations: "The great mounds of living Porites and of Millepora round Keeling atoll occur exclusively on the extreme verge of the reef, which is washed by a constant succession of breakers. At the Marshall Islands the larger kinds of coral which form rocks measuring several fathoms in thickness prefer the most violent surf. The outer margin of the Maldiva atolls consists of living corals, and here the surf is so tremendous that even large ships have been thrown, by a single heave of the sea, high and dry on the reef, all on board thus escaping with their lives. In the Red Sea the strongest corals live on the outer reefs and appear to love the surf. From these facts it is certain that the strongest and most massive corals flourish where most exposed. The less perfect state of the reef of most atolls on the leeward

[1] Darwin, *Coral Reefs*, pp. 87 f.

and less exposed side, compared with its state to the windward, and the analogous case of the greater number of breaches on the rear sides of those atolls in the Maldiva Archipelago, which afford some protection to each other, are obviously explained by this circumstance." There seems to be here a combination of the method of agreement with that of concomitant variations. And such a combination may be employed to advantage in cases where the phenomena under investigation show forces under varying degrees of intensity; the causal relation is more apparent, and the possibility of fortuitous coincidence is largely eliminated if a number of instances can be collected in which the forces manifest themselves in varying degrees. Accumulation of instances, showing concomitant variations in the forces observed, corresponds to the actual variations which in an experiment are effected by the investigator himself. In such observed instances, however, we cannot always have before us the variations expressed continuously. There are evident gaps that must be interpolated mentally. In experiment however of whatever nature, the degrees of intensity can be exhibited continuously, one degree merging into another through inappreciable increments. There is thus a gradation which has no gaps to be filled, and the psychological impression is thereby heightened.

By the method of concomitant variations it is possible also to represent to the mind the magnitude of an unknown force, or unobservable force, by a comparison with the intensity of a known force which lies within the sphere of observation. For instance, Mr. Darwin gives an interesting account in his narrative of the finding near the shores of the Plata a group of vitrified siliceous tubes which had been formed by lightning entering loose sand. The internal surface of such tubes is completely vitrified, glossy, and smooth, and the tubes themselves are generally compressed, and have deep longitudinal furrows so as closely to resemble a shrivelled vegetable stalk, or the bark of an elm or cork tree. Their circumference is about two inches, but in some fragments which are cylindrical and without any furrows, it is as much as four inches. Judging from the uncompressed fragments, the measure or bore of the lightning proved to be about one inch and a quarter. In contrast with the force of lightning as thus revealed in its effects, Mr. Darwin cites some experiments performed in Paris by an artificial force of great magnitude indeed and yet with results that seem insignificantly small in comparison. He says: "At Paris, M. Hatchette and M. Beudant succeeded in making tubes in most respects similar to these fulgurites by passing very strong shocks of galvanism through finely powdered glass: they failed, however, both with powdered felspar and quartz. One tube, formed with pounded glass, was very near an inch long, namely, .982, and had an internal diameter of .019 of an inch. When we hear that the strongest battery in Paris was used, and that its power on a substance of such easy fusibility as glass was to form tubes so diminutive, we must feel greatly astonished at the force of a shock of lightning, which, striking the sand in several places, has formed cylinders in one instance at least thirty feet long, and having an internal bore, where not compressed, of full an inch and a half; and this in a material so extraordinarily refractory as quartz!"[1]

The method of concomitant variations may be used in regard to phenomena whose nature is such as seemingly to indicate a constant law of variation, and yet inferences based thereupon lead to false results. It is therefore well to note some of these instances by way of general precaution in applying this method.

1. It does not necessarily follow that having observed two forces varying in a constant ratio through several concomitant modifications, the same ratio will be preserved indefinitely through all subsequent changes. Water contracts as it is cooling. Suppose we begin to note this con-

[1] Darwin, *Voyage of a Naturalist*, Vol. I, pp. 76 f.

tinued contracting of water from 100° F. to 90°; we naturally expect to find it continuing through 90° to 80°. And as we observe, we find our expectations confirmed. And so on through to 40°, we find that water continues to contract. It is, therefore, most natural for us to expect to find water contracting at 39°. But just at this point in the series, there is a break in the continuity of variation; at 39° water begins to expand and so continues until it passes into the solid form at the freezing-point. The same also is illustrated in Weber's law, already mentioned, which expresses the quantitative relation between the stimulus and the corresponding sensation. The law is that the force of the stimulus must increase geometrically, in order that the intensity of the sensation should increase arithmetically. This law, however, breaks down towards the upper or lower limits, with a stimulus of slight degree of intensity and with one of extreme intensity. We find also an increase of temperature as we proceed towards the centre of the earth of about one degree to every fifty-three feet of descent. This by no means warrants us in inferring that this ratio continues constant to the very centre itself. In certain phenomena, moreover, there are natural limits, as in sound, for example, where the pitch rises as the number of vibrations increases. At a certain point, varying according to different individuals, increase of vibrations gives no resulting sound whatsoever; and so there is a lower limit,—vibrations may decrease to a point beyond which no sound is heard.

An illustration of this fallacy, though not strictly of the method of concomitant variations, is given by Jevons. He takes the following series of prime numbers: 41, 43, 47, 53, 61, 71, 83, 97, 113, 131, etc. It will be seen that they all agree in being values of the general expression $x^2 + x + 41$, where we put for x the successive values of 0, 1, 2, 3, 4, etc. For instance, let $x = 0$ in $x^2 + x + 41$, we get 41; let $x = 1$ in the same, we get 43; when $x = 2$, we get 47; and so on.

It seems as though we could keep this up indefinitely, producing an increasing series, always of prime numbers. It is found, however, that if we take $x = 40$, in the formula $x^2 + x + 41$, we shall have $40 \times 40 + 40 + 41$, which equals 1681, and this number is the square of 41 and therefore not a prime number. At this point the law breaks down.[1]

In the sphere of political economy also we might be led into an easy yet false inference. Suppose a certain farm yield 500 bushels of corn with a given amount of expenditure and labor. We might think that if we double the expenditure and labor, we will also be able to double the results, and obtain a yield of 1000 bushels as over against the 500 of the previous year. Here, however, what is known as the law of decreasing returns obtains; to double the product it may be necessary to triple or quadruple the labor and expense. "Thus in the production of any plot of land there is a point of equilibrium, which marks an impassable limit, not of course a limit which could not be passed if it were wished, but one that no one wishes to pass, because there is nothing to be gained by so doing."[2]

To know that such false inferences are at least possible in the application of this method of concomitant variations to the unknown regions beyond our experience, may serve at least to keep us on guard under similar circumstances.

2. There are certain phenomena moreover in which an increased intensity of the force in question may give rise to incidental effects which tend to neutralize the chief effect to be attained. For instance, an overdose of arsenic causes violent contractions of the stomach so that its contents are immediately ejected, and thus the system is relieved of the noxious substance.

3. Two elements in a given phenomenon may vary together constantly and yet they may not be related at all as

---

[1] Jevons, *Principles of Science*, p. 230.
[2] Gide, *Political Economy*, p. 325.

cause and effect, but appear as coincidental effects of one and the same cause. It has been observed that the occurrence of the aurora borealis has been accompanied by pronounced magnetic disturbances. It, however, cannot be inferred that the former has been the cause of the latter; they are probably the varied effects of some widely operating magnetic force.

The precaution above mentioned has already been referred to as provided for in the canon of this method which states that the observed concomitant variation may indicate not always a direct causal element between the two varying elements, but that they are at least connected with the phenomenon under investigation through some fact of causation.

CHAPTER X

THE METHOD OF RESIDUES

The method of residues consists in the analysis of a given phenomenon based upon previous inductions, through which it has been determined that certain elements in the antecedent have caused certain elements in the consequent; the inference is then drawn, that the remaining elements of the antecedent are necessarily the cause of the remainder of the consequent. It is a method of elimination of the known relations so as to simplify the complex character of the phenomenon and disclose the relations that are unknown in the light of a causal connection which we are constrained to believe must obtain.

The Canon of the Method of Residues. — Subduct from any phenomenon such part as is known by previous inductions to be the effect of certain antecedents, and the residue of the phenomenon is the effect of the remaining antecedents.

The symbolical representation is as follows: —

$$\text{Given } S + C \quad \ldots \ldots \quad s + e.$$

If it is known that there exists already the causal relation

$$S \quad \ldots \ldots \ldots \quad s,$$

we may then infer that C is the cause of e. In this, C may be simple or complex; if it is simple, the causal relation established is expressed in its simplest terms and is therefore a determinate result. If however the residue C is complex, it must be reduced by experimental analysis to its simplest elements, and their relation to the elements into which e can be analyzed further determined.

The most striking illustration of this method, and one of the most brilliant achievements of science as well, is the discovery of the planet Neptune by Adams and Le Verrier, working on the problem independently and reaching the same result. These astronomers had observed certain perturbations in the planet Uranus. It did not keep in its proper orbit as determined by their mathematical calculations based upon the presence of the known stellar bodies. It behaved as though beyond its orbit was an outer planet, whose presence alone could account for the observed perturbations. Adams and Le Verrier then proceeded to calculate the exact position of such a disturbing body as determined by the nature and magnitude of the perturbations of Uranus. The telescope was then pointed to the exact point in the heavens, as thus indicated, and the planet Neptune was revealed to the eye according to the determination of far-reaching prophecy, which confidently asserted that it must be there.

The method of residues is really a deductive method based upon the law of sufficient reason; so many elements on the one hand producing so many elements on the other; if, then, a part of the former can be checked off as cause of a part of the latter, then the remainder on the one hand must be the cause of the remainder on the other. This is pure deduction. For we ask, Why are we constrained to account for the remainder on one side by the remainder on the other? The only possible answer is that it *must* be accounted for within the system to which it is referred; and but one part therein is left which can possibly account for it, because all the others are specifically determined in the known effects which they have produced. This method, however, has a proper place among the inductive methods, inasmuch as it is based on previous inductions, and leads to investigations that can be prosecuted only by the various inductive processes of experiment.

When the residue of the antecedent is a simple element,

and no other possible causal element can lie concealed from our observation, then the inference is simple and conclusive. A difficulty, however, may present itself, owing to the fact that the residual element is apt to be complex and leave the phenomenon still indeterminate, or there may be a lurking element unnoticed by us which is the real cause in question. The function of this method is, therefore, largely suggestive. It says the effect is not wholly accounted for by the known causal elements; there is a residue unaccounted for, and its cause is to be sought in the residue of the antecedent, and if it is thought that the whole of the antecedent is comprehended, the question is started, May there not be unobserved circumstances of the antecedent that further experiment will be calculated to reveal? In many cases, therefore, this method must be supplemented by some other experimental method in order to secure more precise determination, generally the method of difference. It often happens in investigations in chemistry, astronomy, and physics, that the actual phenomena vary in greater or less degree from their expected behavior according to established theory. This must lead either to a reconstruction of theory, or to a search for some unobserved force sufficient to account for the discrepancy. Herschel was the first to point out the significance of such discrepancies in scientific research, and he called them *residual phenomena*.

An illustration of such a situation and the solution of the problem thus presented is that of Sir Humphry Davy's experiments upon the decomposition of water by galvanism. "He found that besides the two components of water, oxygen and hydrogen, an acid and alkali were developed at the two opposite poles of the machine. As the theory of the analysis of water did not give reason to expect these products, they were a *residual phenomenon,* the cause of which was still to be found. The insight of Davy conjectured that there might be some hidden cause of this portion of the effect; the glass containing the water might suffer partial decomposition, or some foreign matter might be mingled with the water, and the acid and alkali be disengaged from it, so that the water would have no share in their production. Assuming this, he proceeded to try whether the total removal of the cause would destroy the effect produced. By the substitution of gold vessels for the glass, without any change in the effect, he at once determined that the glass was not the cause. Employing distilled water, he found a marked diminution of the quantity of acid and alkali evolved; yet there was enough to show that the cause, whatever it was, was still in operation. The impurity of the water, then, was not the sole, but a concurrent, cause. He now conceived that the perspiration from the hands touching the instruments might affect the case, as it would contain common salt, and an acid and alkali would result from its decomposition under the agency of electricity. By carefully avoiding such contact, he reduced the quantity of the products still further, until no more than slight traces of them were perceptible. What remained of the effect might be traceable to impurities of the atmosphere decomposed by contact with the electrical apparatus. An experiment determined this; the machine was placed under an exhausted receiver, and when thus secured from atmospheric influence, it no longer evolved the acid and alkali."[1]

By means of the suggestions incident upon this method, Bunsen, in 1860, discovered two new alkaline metals, caesium and rubidium. He was examining alkalies produced by the evaporation of mineral water from Dürkheim. The flame of these salts was examined by the spectroscope. Bunsen discovered several bright lines which he had never noticed before, and which he knew could not be produced by potash or soda, whose corresponding lines were in close proximity. He then subjected the mixture to a searching analysis and succeeded in obtaining two new alkaline substances. When he had separated them, he then tested them

[1] Gore, *The Art of Scientific Discovery*, pp. 432, 433.

by the method of difference, by which he found that they were capable of producing the lines at first noticed; but when withdrawn, the lines instantaneously disappeared.

Thomson and Tait, in their *Elements of Natural Philosophy*, have the following reference and illustration of this method. "When, in an experiment, all known causes being allowed for, there remain unexplained effects (excessively slight it may be), these must be carefully investigated, and every conceivable variation of arrangement of apparatus, etc., tried; until, if possible, we manage so to exaggerate the residual phenomenon as to be able to detect its cause. It is here perhaps that in the present state of science we may most reasonably look for extensions of our knowledge; at all events, we are warranted by the recent history of natural philosophy in so doing. Thus, to take only a very few instances, and to say nothing of the discovery of electricity and magnetism by the ancients, the peculiar smell observed in a room in which an electrical machine is kept in action was long ago observed, but called the 'smell of electricity,' and thus left unexplained. The sagacity of Schönbein led to the discovery that this is due to the formation of ozone, a most extraordinary body, of enormous chemical energies; whose nature is still uncertain, though the attention of chemists has for years been directed to it."[1]

Another illustration of this method is seen in the comparison of the observed and calculated positions of Encke's comet. It was found that the comet returned a little sooner than it should have done, the period regularly decreasing from 1212.79 days, between 1786 and 1789, to 1210.44 between 1855 and 1858. The inference has been that there is a resisting medium, as the ether, filling the space through which the comet passes. What the resisting medium is, and its nature, is of course a matter of conjecture as far as revealed by this method alone. The method merely indi-

[1] Thomson and Tait, *Elements of Natural Philosophy*, Vol. I, pp. 113 f.

cates some resisting medium to account for the observed discrepancy.[1]

Herschel has observed that all great astronomical discoveries have been disclosed in the form of residual differences. The practice was introduced by Halley, when astronomer royal, of comparing systematically the positions of the heavenly bodies as actually observed with what might have been expected theoretically. His reductions of the lunar observations gave a series of residual errors, extending from 1722 to 1739. These were carefully tabulated, and formed the basis for certain modifications of the lunar theory.[2]

A discrepancy was observed by Newton between the theoretical and actual velocity of sound; the former being 968 feet per second, and the latter 1142. Newton's experiments and calculation were both inaccurate; nevertheless, a real discrepancy has been proved to exist, the theoretical being 916 and the real velocity 1090 feet per second. In 1816 La Place showed this difference to be due to the heat evolved by the sudden compression of the air during the propagation of the sound wave, the heat having the effect of increasing the elasticity of the air, and therefore appreciably accelerating the sound impulse.

It sometimes happens that in repeating an experiment, we are confronted with evidently different results. Then, we may be sure, the experiment has been carelessly or inaccurately performed; or else there are some disturbing causes not observed by us. On the other hand, however, if there is no likelihood of coincidence on repeated trials, yet, nevertheless, a marked agreement is noticed in the results of various trials, the mind should be at once alert to discover the hidden cause of such agreement, and possibly may be led to new truths of great importance. The following illustration is given by Thomson and Tait: "With a very good achromatic telescope a star appears to have a sensible disc. But, as it is observed that the discs of all stars appear to

[1] Jevons, *Principles of Science*, p. 570. [2] *Ibid.*, p. 572.

be of equal angular diameter, we of course suspect some common error. Limiting the aperture of the object-glass increases the appearance in question, which, on full investigation, is found to have nothing to do with discs at all. It is, in fact, a phenomenon due to diffraction of light."[1]

It was said of Darwin that in his researches the residual phenomena were always the special objects of his attention. His son, Francis Darwin, says of him: "There was one quality of mind which seemed to be of special and extreme advantage in leading him to make discoveries. It was the power of never letting exceptions pass unnoticed. Everybody notices a fact as an exception when it is striking or frequent, but he had a special instinct for arresting an exception. A point apparently slight and unconnected with his present work is passed over by many a man almost unconsciously, with some half-considered explanation, which is in fact no explanation. It was just these things that he seized upon to make a start from. In a certain sense there is nothing special in this procedure, many discoveries being made by means of it. I only mention it, because, as I watched him at his work, the value of this power to an experimenter was so strongly impressed upon me."[2] This is striking testimony as to the practical worth of this method as an instrument of research.

This method has also been applied to the more practical usage of examining the refuse of manufactured and other products in order to discover some concealed utility. The analysis of coal-tar refuse has led to the discovery of many valuable substances that have proved of use in the arts, and in medicine as well. Glauber, the eminent chemist, and a discoverer of several chemical compounds, said he made it a rule to examine what every other chemist threw away.

[1] Thomson and Tait, *Elements of Natural Philosophy*, Vol. I, p. 114.
[2] F. Darwin, *Life and Letters of Charles Darwin*, Vol. I, p. 125.

CHAPTER XI

PREDICTION AND VERIFICATION

WHEN our inductive methods have finally led us to formulate some universal law or principle, we are then able to use the same as a major premise upon which to ground further deductions, and so to apply the results of inductive research to new fields not as yet investigated. Mr. Mill calls this procedure the deductive method of reasoning. Inasmuch however as it is founded upon some previous induction, it would seem more fitting to designate it as the inducto-deductive method. It is essentially a combined process of induction and deduction.[1] This so-called inducto-deductive method consists of three stages as follows: —

1. Obtaining by the inductive methods already described, the evidence of some existing causal connection, tentatively expressed in the form of a universal law.

2. Regarding this universal law as the basis for subsequent deductions, by which we gain a knowledge of the nature of unknown phenomena, as necessitated by the conditions of this law.

3. Verifying the results thus obtained by their correspondence with the phenomena as actually observed. Where this correspondence is wanting, then either the law has not been correctly expressed, or there must have been some error in our deduction based upon it. When we are assured that the latter is not the case, then a discrepancy between the theoretically deduced result and the actual facts as observed, always discredits our original induction. This

[1] See pp. 171 f.

method of verification serves as a check upon hasty generalization, on the one hand; and on the other, it serves to extend our knowledge into unknown regions, and is valuable as a means of scientific prediction. In the development of scientific knowledge, it has been a potent factor in enlarging the bounds of knowledge beyond the sphere of immediate observation.

This combined process of reasoning is the one commonly employed by us all. Induction and deduction are not separate processes, but, as before remarked, they are complementary factors in the one actual process of reasoning. We are continually using our inductions as a deductive basis, inferring how things should be before they are really seen; and, when seen, at once instinctively comparing prior inference with present fact, we are either confirmed in our reasoning process, or compelled to discard our previous inference as false or inadequate as the case may be. Our world, the world of knowledge, is built up of the seen, and the unseen as well, because necessitated by inferences growing out of the seen which we are constrained to make; the unseen which we thus are continually building into the seen and regarding it as though the actually known, we are however from time to time compelled to alter, and here and there tear down what we have too rashly builded, as the structure is put to the test of verifying fact.

This method of prediction and verification was used to decide between inferences drawn by Newton and Huyghens respectively, regarding the nature of light. Newton's observations led him to infer that light consisted of particles of matter shot out from the sun. Huyghens insisted that light consisted in the propagation of some kind of disturbance in the manner of a wave-motion. Newton's theory being taken as established, it would necessitate that light on entering a denser body of water, being refracted more nearly in a direction perpendicular to the surface, should, accordingly, move faster in the denser body than in the rarer one outside. On the other hand, according to Huyghens's theory, the opposite effect should take place, — light being refracted towards the vertical at the horizontal surface of a dense body such as water, its velocity in the dense body should be less than its velocity in the rare body. The experiments separately made by Fizeau and Foucault, both gave the result that in water light moves slower than in air, and therefore the theory of Huyghens, which was in accord with such a fact, was verified, and the theory of Newton, which was radically out of harmony with such a fact, was discredited.[1]

We cannot theorize concerning nature to any considerable extent without resorting to nature again to correct aberrations of reason, and the false fancies of the imagination. Theory, if correctly formulated, will always lead to a representation of facts as they are; just as facts as they are, if rightly interpreted, will always lead to correct theory.

The following are illustrations of the value of this method in predicting results before unknown.

"Halley had the glory of having first detected a periodic comet in the case of that which has since borne his name. In 1705, Halley explained how the parabolic orbit of a planet may be determined from three observations; and joining example to precept, himself calculated the positions and orbits of twenty-four comets. He found, as the reward of his industry, that the comets of 1607 and 1531 had the same orbit as that of 1682. And here the intervals are nearly the same, namely, about seventy-five years. Are these three comets then identical? In looking back into the history of such appearances, he found comets recorded in 1456, in 1380, and 1305; the intervals are still the same, — seventy-five or seventy-six years. It was impossible now to doubt that they were the periods of a revolving body, its orbit a long ellipse, not a parabola. If this were so, the

[1] Tait, *Recent Advances in Physical Science*, pp. 65, 66.

comet must reappear in 1758 or 1759. Halley began his laborious calculations and predicted that the comet would reach its perihelion April 13, 1759, but claimed the license of a month for the inevitable inaccuracies of a calculation in which, in addition to all other sources of error, was made in haste, that it might appear as a prediction. The comet justified his calculations and his caution together; for it arrived at its perihelion on March 13, 1759." [1]

Another illustration of a like nature is the prediction of Faraday, based upon Wheatstone's experimental proof that the conduction of electricity required time; namely, "that if the conducting wires were connected with the coatings of a large Leyden jar, the rapidity of conduction would be necessarily lessened." This prediction was made in 1838 and was not verified until, sixteen years later, a submarine cable was laid beneath the English Channel. A considerable retardation of the electric spark was then detected by Siemens and Latimer Clark. Faraday at once pointed out that the wire surrounded by water resembles a Leyden jar on a large scale: so that each message sent through the cable verified his remark of 1838." [2]

In Pasteur's experiments with silkworms already referred to, he made a prediction in 1866, when, having inspected fourteen parcels of eggs intended for incubation, and having examined the moths which produced these eggs, he wrote out the prediction of what would occur in 1867, and placed the prophecy as a sealed letter in the hands of the mayor of St. Hippolyte. In 1867, the cultivators communicated to the mayor their results. The letter of Pasteur was then opened and read, and it was found that in twelve out of fourteen cases there was absolute conformity between his prediction and the observed facts. Many of the groups had perished totally; the others had perished almost totally; and such was Pasteur's prediction. In two out of the

[1] Whewell, *History of Inductive Science*, 3d ed., Vol. II, p. 182.
[2] Jevons, *Principles of Science*, p. 543.

fourteen cases, instead of the prophesied destruction, half an average crop was obtained.[1]

Another interesting illustration concerns Darwin's speculations regarding the formation of coral reefs and atolls. Before Darwin wrote on the subject, it was generally believed that the coral atolls were formed by the coral polypes growing upon submerged volcanic craters. Darwin insisted that as the polypes cannot live below a depth of 100 feet, and are killed by exposure to sunshine and air, and could not therefore have grown upward from the vast depths to which the coral masses extend, each atoll must have begun as a fringing-reef about an island almost touching the shore, and with only a narrow and shallow channel of water between; and then became a barrier reef, that is, one with a wider and deeper channel of water separating from the shore, owing to the slow but progressive subsidence of the island round which the polypes first began to build. Then with the further and complete subsidence of the island beneath the water, there remained a ring of coral with a central lagoon forming the so-called atoll. Darwin says in his *Autobiography* that the main features of his theory were conceived while on the voyage, and that even previous to seeing a true coral reef.[2] He says: "No other work of mine was begun in so deductive a spirit as this, for the whole theory was thought out on the west coast of South America, before I had seen a true coral reef. I had only to verify and extend my views by a careful examination of living reefs. But it should be observed that I had during the two previous years been incessantly attending to the effects on the shores of South America of the intermittent elevation of the land, together with denudation and deposition of sediment. This necessarily led me to reflect much on the effects of subsidence, and it was easy to replace in imagination the continued deposition of sediment by the

[1] Tyndall, *Fragments of Science*, pp. 291, 292.
[2] *Life and Letters of Charles Darwin*, 1887, Vol. I, p. 58.

upward growth of corals. To do this was to form my theory of the formation of barrier reefs and atolls."

It will thus be seen that Darwin's deduction was based upon previous inductions in other spheres, the result of his own observation; he also tells us in the same connection, that he had, in the preparation of his work on *Coral Reefs*, spent twenty months of hard labor, reading every work on the island of the Pacific and consulting many charts. He thus made the widely extended observations of other men tributary to his inferences concerning coral-reef formations. Dr. Williams says of Darwin's insight in this particular: "He saw more clearly than his precursors had done the validity of the dictum of Johannes Müller in this, and indeed all his works, that the most important truths in natural science are to be discovered, neither by the mere analysis of philosophical ideas, nor by simple experience, but by *reflective experience*, which distinguishes the essential from the accidental in the phenomena observed, and thus finds principles from which many experiences can be derived."[1] This is a very satisfactory and striking account of what may be styled the combined inducto-deductive temper of mind, and especially as embodied in so eminent a student of nature as Darwin.

Bacon insists that anticipations of nature are sources of innumerable errors, and that the truly scientific method consists in an interpretation of nature as it is revealed to the perception through direct observation and experiment. It is, however, largely through these "anticipations" that progress in science is attained. There may be anticipations which are considered final, and all attempts at verification regarded as unnecessary and even as impertinent. Results deductively attained are then asserted with dogmatic insistence, as though possessing the convincing power of facts themselves; and all appeal to controverting or exceptional cases are set aside, without even so much as a respectful

[1] Darwin, *Coral Reefs*. Prefatory note by Dr. J. W. Williams, p. ix.

hearing. Such anticipations of nature rightfully fall under the scornful reprehension of a Bacon. But there are other anticipations which serve as a spur to a more penetrating observation, and more painstaking experiment, in order to square theory to facts. Such anticipations are the glory of science!

Suppose such anticipations are disproved by subsequent experiment or observation; they have served a high purpose in suggesting investigation along lines which otherwise would have remained unthought of. Anticipations alone are barren; anticipations leading to verification are productive of valuable results. To this the history of scientific thought bears abundant testimony. Professor Clifford has made the power of prediction one of the essential characteristics of scientific thought. He says, in his essay on the *Aims and Instruments of Scientific Thought*, that "the difference between scientific and merely technical thought is just this: Both of them make use of experience to direct human action; but while technical thought or skill enables a man to deal with the same circumstances that he has met with before, scientific thought enables him to deal with different circumstances that he has never met with before."[1] He cites two illustrations, which are admirable examples of scientific prediction. The first relates to the suggestion of Fleeming Jenkin, regarding structural bracing. It had been known before that in an arch every part is compressed or pushed by other parts; and every part of a chain is in a state of tension, that is, pulled by the other parts. In many cases these forms are united in the common girder, which consists of two main pieces, of which the upper acts as an arch, and is compressed, while the lower one acts as a chain and is pulled. "Now," says Professor Clifford, "suppose that any good, practical engineer makes a bridge or a roof upon some approved pattern which has been made before. He designs the size and shape of it to suit the opening

[1] Clifford, *Lectures and Essays*, Vol. I, p. 128.

which has to be spanned; selects his material according to the locality; assigns the strength which must be given to the several parts of the structure, according to the load which it will have to bear. There is a great deal of thought in the making of this design, whose success is predicted by the application of previous experience; it requires technical skill of a very high order, but it is not scientific thought. On the other hand, Mr. Fleeming Jenkin designs a roof consisting of two arches braced together, instead of an arch and a chain braced together; and, although this form is quite different from any known structure, yet before it is built he assigns with accuracy the amount of material that must be put into every part of the structure in order to bear the required load, and this prediction may be trusted with perfect security. What is the natural comment on this? Why, that Mr. Fleeming Jenkin is a *scientific* engineer."[1]

The second illustration which Professor Clifford gives is as follows: "You know that if you make a dot on a piece of paper, and then hold a piece of Iceland spar over it, you will see not one dot, but two. A mineralogist, by measuring the angles of a crystal, can tell you whether or no it possesses this property without looking through it. He requires no scientific thought to do that. But Sir William Rowan Hamilton, the late astronomer royal of Ireland, knowing these facts, and also the explanation of them, which Fresnel had given, thought about the subject, and he predicted that by looking through certain crystals in a particular direction we should see not two dots, but a continuous circle of dots. Mr. Lloyd made the experiment and saw the circle, a result which had never been even suspected. This has always been considered one of the most signal instances of scientific thought in the domain of physics. It is most distinctly an application of experience gained under certain circumstances to entirely different circumstances."[2]

[1] Clifford, *Lectures and Essays*, Vol. I, pp. 127, 128.
[2] *Ibid.*, Vol. I, pp. 128, 129.

There is also an indirect method of prediction, varying somewhat from the one already described and yet similar to it. It is called prediction by inversion of cause and effect. There are many cases in which cause and effect are related in a reciprocal manner, so that not only will the cause produce the effect, but the effect, operating as a cause, will bring about the original cause as an effect, it may be in a modified form but clearly recognizable as such. Professor Tyndall said of Faraday that "the strong tendency of his mind to look upon the reciprocal actions of natural forces gave birth to his greatest discoveries."[1] For instance, Oersted had proved that an electric current will produce magnetism, and Faraday, taking this as a suggestion, inferred that magnetism might produce an electric current; in the year 1831 he devised a suitable experiment of introducing a bar-magnet into a coil of insulated copper wire, and then withdrawing the magnet whilst the two ends of the wire were connected with a distant galvanometer, which indicated the presence of the electric current. Thus, his inference received substantial verification.[2]

It has, moreover, been found that when a given cause produces a certain effect, then if the effect be produced in some other manner, the process will tend to produce the original cause, but inverted as regards its direction or nature. For instance, it is known that heat will expand gases; now, if a gas be relieved of the pressure of the vessel enclosing it, it will expand by virtue of its own elastic power, producing, however, cold in the surrounding atmosphere. So also heat will cause a bar of iron to expand. Dr. Joule proved that if iron were expanded by mechanical force, it would be accompanied by cold. Inasmuch as india-rubber is related to heat in an opposite manner to that of iron, being contracted by heat instead of expanded, we would, according to the law above expressed, naturally expect that a mechanical ex-

[1] Tyndall, *Fragments of Science*, p. 338.
[2] Gore, *The Art of Scientific Discovery*, p. 594.

pansion of india-rubber would give heat, and a contraction produce cold. An experiment may be tried by suddenly stretching a rubber band while the middle part is in the mouth; when stretched, it grows warm; when relaxed, it seems cold.[1]

Again, as heat will melt many substances, if we can reduce the same substance from the solid to the liquid state, we would expect, as a result, the opposite of heat, namely, cold. This occurs in all freezing mixtures; as the affinity of salt for water causes it to melt ice, thus producing cold in the surrounding atmosphere, sufficient to freeze cream or other similar substance, inasmuch as, passing from solid to liquid, water absorbs heat from all substances near it; this absorption producing artificial cold surrounding it. The reciprocal action of heat and cold is illustrated in an interesting experiment described by Tait.[2] He took a bar of ice, supported horizontally at either end, and over the middle of the bar he put a fine wire, and put equal weights to the two ends of the wire. The wire gradually, by the action of the weights, cut through the bar of ice, and yet it was observed that the path of the wire was instantly replaced by the freezing again of the melted portion produced by the pressure, and when the wire had wholly traversed the entire thickness of the bar, the bar itself was intact, and even stronger along the line of the cutting than before. The explanation of this experiment is that inasmuch as heat melts ice, then when ice is melted by pressure, as in this case of the weighted wire, cold, the opposite of heat, is induced; thus, as the wire was forced by the weights into the ice, the pressure upon the ice melted it, making it colder, so that the water produced, passing around the chilled wire, and being thus relieved of pressure, froze again.

Faraday predicted certain magnetic phenomena by this method, which are specially interesting as illustrations of

[1] Jevons, *Principles of Science*, p. 545.
[2] Tait, *Recent Advances in Physical Science*, pp. 99, 100.

this kind of prediction. It seems that Arago had observed in 1824 that the number of oscillations which a magnetized needle makes in a given time, under the influence of the earth's magnetism, is very much lessened by the proximity of certain metallic masses, and especially of copper. Employing the latter substance in an experiment upon a magnetized needle, he succeeded in reducing the number of its vibrations in a given time from three hundred to four. Taking the experiment as a basis for his inference, Faraday predicted that since the presence of a metal at rest stops the oscillations of a magnetic needle, the neighborhood of a magnet at rest ought to stop the motion of a rotating mass of metal. He therefore proceeded to put his inference to the test of actual experiment, by suspending a cube of copper to a twisted thread which was placed between the poles of a powerful electromagnet. When the thread was left to itself, it began to spin round with great velocity, but stopped the moment a powerful current passed through the electromagnet.[1] Again, as heat applied to the junction of two metallic bars, as antimony and bismuth, produced an electric current, it was inferred that if an electric current was made to pass through such a junction, it would produce cold, and such proved to be the case.[2]

In the general process of verification, it often happens that seeming exceptions occur which are direct contradictions of the law we are attempting to prove. And it is in dealing with such cases that one's power of discrimination is most fully taxed. It is necessary to make a most careful distinction between seeming and real exceptions. Professor Jevons has given a very exhaustive classification of the different kinds of exceptional phenomena, which it is well to have in mind, in order to know in any investigation the various possible complications that may rise.[3] The exceptional phenomena, as given by Jevons, are: —

[1] Ganot, *Physics*, pp. 797, 798. [2] Jevons, *Principles of Science*, p. 547.
[3] See Jevons, Chapter XXIX, in his *Principles of Science*, on "Exceptional Phenomena."

1. Imaginary, or false exceptions; that is, facts, objects, or events which are not really what they are supposed to be.

2. Apparent but congruent exceptions, which, though apparently in conflict with a law of nature, are really in agreement with it.

3. Singular exceptions, which really agree with a law of nature, but exhibit remarkable and unique results of it.

4. Divergent exceptions, which really proceed from the ordinary action of known processes of nature, but which are excessive in amount or monstrous in character.

5. Accidental exceptions, arising from the interference of some entirely distinct but known law of nature.

6. Novel and unexplained exceptions, which lead to the discovery of a new series of laws and phenomena, modifying or disguising the effects of previously known laws without being inconsistent with them.

7. Limiting exceptions, showing the falsity of a supposed law to some cases to which it had been extended, but not affecting its truth in other cases.

8. Contradictory, or real, exceptions, which lead us to the conclusion that a supposed hypothesis or theory is in opposition to the phenomena of nature, and must therefore be abandoned.

It will be seen that among so many possibilities of interpretation an exception does not necessarily prove the rule, as the old adage would have it; nor does the exception, on the other hand, necessarily disprove the rule or law. It must be in each case strictly and adequately interpreted, which requires a penetrating sagacity and a thorough knowledge of the phenomena under investigation.

In the process of verification, the question naturally suggests itself: How many verifying instances are sufficient to determine the universal validity of a given law? This question will be recognized as an old difficulty, now presented in another form; but in reality it is the perplexing problem of determining the logical ground of induction. What is our warrant for proceeding from known and verified instances to unknown phenomena, of the same kind it is true, but as yet beyond the pale of our experience? The warrant for our generalization does not lie wholly in the number of verifying instances. In addition to the effect which mere number produces in confirming our belief, there is the confidence which we feel in the constancy of the order of nature, and which we are constrained to assume as a fundamental postulate.[1] Therefore, we say that the verifying facts must be of such a number, and of such a nature as well, that they give evidence of a uniformity which transcends all supposition of mere coincidence, and compels us to attribute it to the uniformity of nature itself, in which we find a warrant for our generalization. As Professor Clifford has remarked: "The aim of scientific thought is to apply past experiences to new circumstances. The instrument is an observed uniformity in the course of events. By the use of this instrument it gives us information transcending our experience, it enables us to infer things that we have not seen from things that we have seen; and the evidence for the truth of that information depends on our supposing that the uniformity holds good beyond our experience."[2]

In extending knowledge and predicting results beyond the sphere of experience, modern scientific investigation is largely indebted to the principles and methods of mathematics. Mathematical laws, applied to the data given in sense-perception, give indications of the necessary relations that must exist in the observed phenomena, and all that they involve. Thus, that which is given directly in consciousness is supplemented by that which is given indirectly as mathematically necessitated. The mathematico-experimental method in physics has led to very rich and important results which have proved practically its efficiency as a scientific method.

[1] See Sigwart, *Logic*, Vol. II, p. 348.
[2] Clifford, *Lectures and Essays*, Vol. I, pp. 131, 132.

CHAPTER XII

HYPOTHESIS

THE inductive process cannot proceed to any great extent or attain satisfactory results without the aid of some hypothesis. An hypothesis is a supposition regarding the cause of a phenomenon, which we make either as preliminary to an experiment which will prove or disprove the supposition, or in lieu of an experiment or systematic observation, when such are impossible owing to the peculiar conditions of the phenomenon itself. We see therefore that the framing of hypotheses has a double function. First, considered as preliminary to experiment, — we found that in cases where two, three, or more elements enter into a complex antecedent, it is impossible often, and always impracticable to test the various possible combinations separately in order to note their different results. The combinations in complex phenomena are indefinitely great, and the isolation of certain elements in order to estimate the exact result of the combined force of the other combinations is extremely difficult and often impossible. Therefore the mind discards some combinations as irrelevant, others as impossible, and selects one perhaps as the most likely cause of the given effect. This selective function of the mind, therefore, indicates the line of experiment in a determinate manner and does not leave the phenomena to indeterminate and haphazard investigation.

Consider, for instance, so eminent an experimenter as Charles Darwin, so fertile in all kinds of experimental resources; yet it is said of him that every experiment was the result of a tentative theory, thought out in advance of all actual test and by a sagacious insight into the necessary conditions of the interrelated phenomena before him. His son, Francis Darwin, says of him in his *Reminiscences:* "He often said that no one could be a good observer unless he was an active theorizer. It was as though he were charged with theorizing power ready to flow into any channel on the slightest disturbance, so that no fact, however small, could avoid releasing a stream of theory, and thus the fact became magnified into importance. In this way, it naturally happened that many untenable theories occurred to him; but fortunately his richness of imagination was equalled by his power of judging and condemning the thoughts that occurred to him. He was just to his theories, and did not condemn them unheard; and so it happened that he was willing to test what would seem to most people not at all worth testing. These rather wild trials he called 'fool's experiments,' and enjoyed extremely. As an example, I may mention that, finding the cotyledons of Biophytum to be highly sensitive to vibrations of the table, he fancied that he might perceive the vibrations of sound, and therefore made me play my bassoon close to a plant. The love of experiment was very strong in him, and I can remember the way he would say, 'I shan't be easy till I have tried it,' as if an outside force were driving him."[1] Hypothesis and experiment were in the hand of Darwin like a two-edged sword, which he employed with rare skill and effect.

An hypothesis is to be regarded not only as the precursor of experiment, but it also functions as a method of explanation when actual verification is impossible. We see this constantly in our everyday life. We are compelled again and again to account for situations which occur that are impossible for us to reproduce in the form of an experiment, that we are able to observe but once. Some explanation is required to satisfy mental demands which are imperative in this regard. The explanation which seems

[1] *Life and Letters of Charles Darwin,* Vol. I, p. 126.

most in keeping with the sum of facts in our possession, is the hypothesis which we frame; so also in explaining the conduct of others by conjecture as to the most reasonable motives that will satisfactorily account for the same; such hypotheses we are constantly compelled to assume. We are not always able to perceive the relations existing between facts as they come into the sphere of our experience, and yet we are constrained to think of them as related; but in order to systematize them, we must supply mentally the *lacunæ* which appear in the phenomena as perceived. This supposition that is necessary to construct facts into a system is an hypothesis.

An illustration of an hypothesis suggesting systematic observation and experiment is found in the history of the discovery of vaccination by Jenner. It seems that while a mere youth, pursuing his studies at Sodbury, he chanced to hear a casual remark made by a country girl who came to his master's shop for advice. The smallpox was mentioned, when the girl said, "I cannot take that disease, for I have had cowpox."[1] This observation, expressing the common superstition of the simple country folk, appealed to Jenner's mind as an inchoate hypothesis. Seizing upon it as a suggestion of possible value, he proceeded to make diligent inquiries and careful observations, which finally led him to the discovery of vaccination.

An illustration of hypothesis as explanation of phenomena beyond the range of experiment is found in the hypothesis as to the source of the sun's energy. An enumeration of the different hypotheses advanced upon this subject is given by Tait in his *Recent Advances in Physical Science*.[2] "The old notion that the sun is a huge fire, or something of that kind, is one which will only occur to one thinking of the matter for the first time; but with our modern chemical knowledge, we are enabled to say that, massive as the sun is, if its materials had consisted of the very best materials for

---

[1] Gore, *The Art of Scientific Discovery*, p. 495.   [2] pp. 151 ff.

giving out heat, that enormous mass of some 400,000 miles in radius could have supplied us with only about 5000 years of the present radiation. A mass of coal of that size would have produced very much less than that amount of heat. Nor would the most energetic chemicals known to us, combined in proportion for giving the greatest amount of heat by actual chemical combination, supply the sun's present waste for even 5000 years. Therefore as we all know that geological facts, if there were no others, point to at least as high a radiation from the sun as the present, for at all events a few hundreds of thousands of years back,— and perhaps also indicate even a higher rate of radiation from the sun in old time than at present,— it is quite obvious that the heat of the sun cannot possibly be supplied by any chemical process of which we have the slightest conception.

"Now, if we can find, on the other hand, any physical explanation of this consistent with any present knowledge, we are bound to take it and use it as far as we can, rather than say: This question is totally unanswerable unless there be chemical agencies at work in the sun of a far more powerful order than anything we meet with on the earth's surface. If we can find a thoroughly intelligible source of heat, which, though depending upon a different physical cause from the usual one, combustion, is amply sufficient to have supplied the sun with such an amount of heat as to enable it to radiate for perhaps the last hundred millions of years at the same rate as it is now radiating, then I say we are bound to try that hypothesis first, and argue upon it until we find it inconsistent with something known. And if we do not find it inconsistent with anything that is known, while we find it completely capable of explaining our difficulty, then it is not only philosophic to say that it is most probably the origin of the sun's energy, but we feel ourselves constrained to admit it. Newton long ago told us this obligation in his *Rules of Philosophizing.* Now it is known that if we were to take a mass of the most perfect combustibles which we know, and let it fall upon the sun merely from the earth's distance, then the work done upon it by the sun's attraction during its fall would give it so large an amount of kinetic energy when it reached the sun's surface as to produce an impact which would represent six thousand times the amount of energy which could be produced by its mere burning.

"It appears, then, that our natural and only trustworthy mode of explaining the sun's heat at present, in time past, and for time to come, must be something closely analogous to, but not identical with, what was called the nebular hypothesis of Laplace, — the hypothesis of the falling together (from rudely scattered distribution in space) of the matter which now forms the various suns and planets. We find by calculation in which there is no possibility of large error, that this hypothesis is thoroughly competent to explain one hundred millions of years' solar radiation at the present rate, perhaps more; and it is capable of showing us how it is that the sun, for thousands of years together, can part with energy at the enormous rate at which it does still part with it, and yet not apparently cool by perhaps any measurable quantity.

"In confirmation of this, not only is the hypothesis itself capable of explaining the amounts of energy which are in question, but also recent investigations, aided by the spectroscope, have shown us that there are gigantic nebular systems at great distances from our solar system, in the process of physical degradation in that very way, by the falling together of scattered masses, and with numerous consequent developments of heat by impacts. What are called temporary stars form another splendid and still more striking instance of it, as where a star suddenly appears, of the first magnitude, or even brighter than the first, outshining all the planets for a month or two at a time, and then, after a little time, becomes invisible in the most powerful telescope. Things of that kind are constantly occurring on a larger or smaller scale, and they can all be easily explained on this supposition of the impact of gravitating masses."

Such a hypothesis, it will be seen, embraces all the facts observed in one self-consistent system. The other hypotheses are inadequate to account satisfactorily for the phenomena. The validity of this hypothesis lies in its being both adequate and congruent as well; experiment or corroborative observation being out of the question, we are, as Tait says, "constrained to admit it."

Mr. Darwin gives an enumeration and criticism of the different hypotheses which have been suggested to explain the extinction of the gigantic animals known to have existed upon the earth. His account will give an indication of the natural propensity of the mind to frame hypotheses concerning phenomena which lie outside the sphere both of observation and experiment. Mr. Darwin says: "It is impossible to reflect on the changed state of the American Continent without the deepest astonishment. Formerly it must have swarmed with great monsters; now we find mere pigmies compared with the antecedent allied races. The greater number, if not all, of these extinct quadrupeds, lived at a late period, and were the contemporaries of most of the existing sea-shells. What, then, has exterminated so many species and whole genera? The mind at first is irresistibly hurried into the belief of some great catastrophe; but thus to destroy animals, both large and small, in Southern Patagonia, in Brazil, on the Cordillera of Peru, in North America up to Behring's Straits, we must shake the entire framework of the globe.

"An examination, moreover, of the geology of La Plata and Patagonia leads to the belief that all the features of the land result from slow and gradual changes. It appears from the character of the fossils in Europe, Asia, Australia, and in North and South America, that those conditions which favor the life of the *larger* quadrupeds were lately coextensive with the world. What those conditions were, no one has yet even conjectured. It could hardly have been a change of temperature, which at about the same time destroyed the inhabitants of tropical, temperate, and arctic latitudes on both sides of the globe. In North America we positively know from Mr. Lyell that the large quadrupeds lived subsequently to that period when boulders were brought into latitudes at which icebergs now never arrive; from conclusive but indirect reasons we may feel sure that in the southern hemisphere the Macrauchenia also lived long subsequently to the ice-transporting boulder-period. Did man, after his first inroad into South America, destroy, as has been suggested, the unwieldy Megatherium and the other Edentata? . We must look at least to some other cause for the destruction of the little tucutuco at Bahia Blanca, and of the many fossil mice and other small quadrupeds in Brazil. No one will imagine that a drought, even far severer than those which cause such losses in the provinces of La Plata, could destroy every individual of every species from Southern Patagonia to Behring's Straits. What shall we say of the extinction of the horse? Did those plains fail of pasture which have since been overrun by thousands and hundreds of thousands of the descendants of the stock introduced by the Spaniards? Have the subsequently introduced species consumed the food of the great antecedent races? Can we believe that the Capybara has taken the food of the Toxodon, the Guanaco of the Macrauchenia, the existing small Edentata of their numerous gigantic prototypes? Certainly no fact in the long history of the world is so startling as the wide and repeated exterminations of its inhabitants."[1] Mr. Darwin's own hypothesis concerning this phenomenon is rather indefinite, but nevertheless as definite as the extreme complexity of the facts will allow. He says that there are certain causes operating in nature, their exact character remaining unknown, such that the too rapid increase of every species, even the most favored, is

[1] Darwin, *Voyage of a Naturalist*, Vol. I, p. 223.

steadily checked, producing in some cases rarity and in others extinction, if these causes operate with unusual efficacy. His hypothesis marks a tendency whose nature, nevertheless, remains concealed.

In all these widely differing hypotheses we see a certain mental constraint to offer some explanation, even though it be but a disguised confession of ignorance, as in Mr. Darwin's hypothesis.

An illustration of an hypothesis to explain observed phenomena that cannot be further tested is that given in the following instance cited by Professor Tyndall: "At Erith, in 1864, there occurred a tremendous explosion of a powder magazine. The village of Erith was some miles distant from the magazine, but in nearly all cases the windows were shattered; and it was noticeable that the windows turned away from the origin of the explosion suffered almost as much as those which faced it. Lead sashes were employed in Erith church; and these, being in some degree flexible, enabled the windows to yield to pressure without much fracture of glass. Every window in the church, front and back, was bent *inwards*. In fact, as the sound-wave reached the church, it separated right and left, and, for a moment, the edifice was clasped by a girdle of intensely compressed air, which forced all its windows inwards. After compression, the air in the church no doubt dilated, and tended to restore the windows to their first condition. The bending in of the windows, however, produced but a small condensation of the whole mass of air within the church; the force of the recoil was, therefore, feeble in comparison with the force of impact, and insufficient to undo what the latter had accomplished."[1] Here also is a set of conditions that must be satisfied by a correct hypothesis. The phenomenon was not capable of repetition by any experiment. Professor Tyndall, therefore, pictures to his mind what must have happened beyond that which was

[1] Tyndall, *On Sound*, p. 23.

observed, in order to account for the result which actually happened. He fills up the unseen from what he knows of the nature of sound-waves, and thus constructs one self-consistent system which includes both the seen and the unseen, the known and the unknown, the observed and the inferred.

It will be noticed in this and other illustrations of hypothesis, how large a part is played by the imagination. It is the imagination which fills out the vacant spaces in the picture of perception. With some, the function of imagination is associated with fancy rather than fact. It must, in this connection however, be clearly emphasized that the imagination which constructs hypotheses must be throughout in touch with fact. It must represent to the mind, not what fancy suggests, but what the known facts necessitate. The unseen is constructed out of the determining conditions of the seen. It is this deductive function of the imagination that gives to it a strictly logical significance. For instance, Professor Tyndall's reasoning concerning the Erith church was somewhat as follows: The windows are all bent inward, therefore the pressure must have operated on all sides from without, inward; such pressure could only occur upon the supposition that the sound-waves, separating right and left, wholly encompassed the church, etc. In each case, that which he pictured to his mind as happening, was regarded by him as actually necessitated by the facts as observed.

Professor Tyndall has most admirably discussed the *Scientific Use of the Imagination;* and his lecture under that title every student, both of logic or of science, should read. I quote one passage from it, which has special bearing upon what has just been said: "We are gifted with the power of Imagination, — combining what the Germans call *Anschauungsgabe* and *Einbildungskraft*, — and by this power we can lighten the darkness which surrounds the world of the senses. There are tories in science who regard imagination as a faculty to be feared and avoided rather than employed. They had observed its action in weak vessels and were unduly impressed by its disasters. But they might with equal justice point to exploded boilers as an argument against the use of steam. Bounded and conditioned by co-operant Reason, imagination becomes the mightiest instrument of the scientific discoverer. Newton's passage from a falling apple to a falling moon was, at the outset, a leap of the imagination. When William Thomson tries to place the ultimate particles of matter between his compass points, and to apply to them a scale of millimetres, he is powerfully aided by this faculty. And in much that has been recently said about protoplasm and life, we have the outgoings of the imagination guided and controlled by the known analogies of science. In fact, without this power our knowledge of nature would be a mere tabulation of coexistences and sequences. We should still believe in the succession of day and night, of summer and winter; but the soul of Force would be dislodged from our universe; causal relations would disappear, and with them that science which is now binding the parts of nature to an organic whole."[1]

In all the illustrations which have been given, and, in fact, in all examples of the framing of hypotheses, it will be seen that the mental functions specially in operation are those of analysis and synthesis, — a separation of the elements as far as possible into their simplest forms of expression, and the building them together into some one system whose unity lies in the assumed hypothesis. Mr. Venn has especially emphasized this aspect of hypothesis, and his chapter on this subject will well repay a careful reading.[2]

Every supposition however is not necessarily an hypothesis in the logical or scientific significance of that term. It will be necessary therefore to mention some of the requirements which a logical hypothesis should satisfy.

[1] Tyndall, *Use and Limit of the Imagination in Science*, p. 16.
[2] Venn, *Empirical Logic*, Chapter XVI.

1. An hypothesis should be plausible; that is, it should be no fanciful, or merely conjectural, explanation of the phenomena in question. The suppositions of the interference of spirits, or in a mythological age of the gods, to account for perplexing situations or obscure happenings, have no rank as hypotheses; so, also, Fate is often referred to as a convenient confession of ignorance in lieu of a satisfactory explanation. Spinoza has remarked upon this as follows: "They who have desired to find scope for the display of their ingenuity in assigning causes, have had recourse to a new style of argument to help them in their conclusions, namely, by reduction, not to the impossible or absurd, but to ignorance or the unknown, a procedure which shows very plainly that there was no other course open to them."

The difference between a scientific hypothesis and a popular explanation concerning the same phenomena may be found in Darwin's account of "a strange belief which is general amongst the inhabitants of the Maldiva atolls, namely, that corals have roots, and therefore that if merely broken down to the surface, they grow up again; but if rooted out, they are permanently destroyed. By this means the inhabitants keep their harbors clear; and thus the French governor of St. Mary's in Madagascar 'cleared out and made a beautiful little port at that place.'"[1] Their explanation, however, is purely fanciful, having no basis in fact. In contrast, Darwin's hypothesis to explain the facts in the case is of a logically scientific nature, and is as follows: Inasmuch as loose sediment is injurious to the living polypifers, and as it is probable that sand would accumulate in the hollows formed by tearing out the corals, but not on the broken and projecting stumps, therefore in the former case the fresh growth of coral might be thus prevented by the deposited sediment.

2. The second requirement is that the hypothesis must be capable of proof or disproof. This does not demand a test

[1] Darwin, *Coral Reefs*, p. 89.

by experiment necessarily; for that, as we have seen, may be impossible. It does, however, require that some facts should be forthcoming that will either confirm the hypothesis or disprove it. There are cases, however, as Lotze suggests, whose very nature precludes the possibility of proving or disproving the hypothesis framed to account for them. For instance, the very common and simple hypothesis of regarding the stars, which are apparently but small points of light, as bodies of vast size, only very remote from us, is in itself incapable of being either refuted or confirmed by subsequent discovery. Lotze says: "We must abide content if our hypotheses are thinkable and useful, if they are capable of explaining all interconnected appearances, even such as were still unknown when we constructed them, if, that is to say, they are indirectly confirmed by the agreement of all that can be deduced from them in thought with the actual progress of experience. But if we would be so fortunate as to find an hypothesis which will not lack this subsequent confirmation, we must not simply assume anything that can be barely conceived as real; we must only assume that which, besides being thinkable, conforms, so to speak, to the universal customs of reality, or to the special local customs which prevail in that department of phenomena to which the object we are investigating belongs."[1]

It is to be specially observed that while the requirement of proof of an hypothesis may be waived in the sphere of phenomena where proof is manifestly impossible, still, where proof is available, an hypothesis must never be so framed as to render the required test either impossible or impracticable.

3. The hypothesis must be adequate. It must cover all the facts in the case. An outstanding fact which it cannot explain is sufficient to controvert such an hypothesis. A knowledge of the distinction between postulate and hypothesis, and of the relation which nominally exists between

[1] Lotze, *Logic*, p. 353.

the two, will help us to appreciate more clearly the force of this requirement of adequacy. As defined by Lotze, a postulate "expresses the conditions which must be set up, or the ground of explanation which must be given by some reality, force, or event, before we can think the phenomenon in the form in which it is presented to us; it thus requires or postulates the presence of something that can account for the given effect. An hypothesis is a conjecture which seeks to fill up the postulate thus abstractly stated by specifying the concrete causes, forces, or processes out of which the phenomenon really arose in this particular case, while in other cases maybe the same postulate is to be satisfied by utterly different though equivalent combinations of forces or active elements."[1] According to this distinction as applied to the problem of the source of the sun's energy, the postulate would be the sum of conditions which require explanation; namely, the tremendous radiation of heat extending through thousands and thousands of years. The postulate therefore requires a force adequate to supply for so long a period so great an amount of energy. We found that ordinary combustion of the most highly combustible materials would not, as an hypothesis, satisfy the conditions which obtain in the postulate; nor would the liberation of chemical energy stand as an hypothesis adequate to satisfy the postulate; the hypothesis of impact of masses upon the sun's surface from immense distances presents a force sufficient to meet the requirements of the postulate. Moreover we see in this illustration how the hypothesis is a particular and concrete expression of the conditions expressed in general and abstract terms in the postulate. The essential characteristic therefore of the hypothesis is that it shall perfectly satisfy all the conditions expressed in the postulate.

The hypothesis that nature abhorred a vacuum, in order to account for the rise of water in a tube or pump, was seen

[1] Lotze, *Logic*, pp. 349, 350.

to break down utterly when it was found that the water did not rise beyond some thirty-three feet. The demand of the postulate in the case was a force of precisely such magnitude that it would balance a column of water thirty-three feet in height. This force, precisely satisfying the conditions of the postulate, is found in the hypothesis that the atmospheric pressure is such a magnitude as to exert a pressure equivalent to a column of water some thirty-three feet in height. The strength of the hypothesis lies in its exact and appropriate fitting into the facts of the problem.

Another illustration of the fitting of hypothesis to postulate, and one where the conditions of the postulate are extremely complex, I have chosen from Mr. Wallace's work, *On Natural Selection:* "There is a Madagascar orchis — the *Angrœcum sesquipedale* — with an immensely long and deep nectary. How did such an extraordinary organ come to be developed? Mr. Darwin's explanation is this. The pollen of this flower can only be removed by the base of the proboscis of some very large moths, when trying to get at the nectar at the bottom of the vessel. The moths with the longest proboscis would do this most effectually; they would be rewarded for their long tongues by getting the most nectar; whilst, on the other hand, the flowers with the deepest nectaries would be the best fertilized by the largest moths preferring them. Consequently the deepest-nectaried orchids and the longest-tongued moths would each confer on the other an advantage in the battle of life. This would tend to their respective perpetuation, and to the constant lengthening of nectaries and proboscis. In the *Angrœcum sesquipedale* it is necessary that the proboscis should be forced into a particular part of the flower, and this would only be done by a large moth burying its proboscis to the very base, and straining to drain the nectar from the bottom of the long tube, in which it occupies a depth of one or two inches only. Now let us start from the time when the nectary was only half its present length, or about six inches, and was chiefly fertilized by a species of moth which appeared at the time of the plant's flowering, and whose proboscis was of the same length. Among the millions of flowers of the *Angræcum* produced every year, some would always be shorter than the average, some longer. The former, owing to the structure of the flower, would not get fertilized, because the moths could get all the nectar without forcing their trunks down to the very base. By this process alone the average length of the nectary would annually increase, because the short-nectaried flowers being sterile, and the long ones having abundant offspring, exactly the same effect would be produced as if a gardener destroyed the short ones, and sowed the seed of the long ones only; and this we know by experience would produce a regular increase of length, since it is this very process which has increased the size and changed the form of our cultivated fruits and flowers. But this would lead in time to such an increased length of the nectary that many of the moths could only just reach to the surface of the nectar, and only the few with exceptionally long trunks be able to suck up a considerable portion. This would cause many moths to neglect these flowers, because they could not get a satisfying supply of nectar, and if these were the only moths in the country, the flowers would undoubtedly suffer, and the further growth of the nectary be checked by exactly the same process which had led to its increase.

"But there are an immense variety of moths, of various lengths of proboscis, and as the nectary became longer, other and larger species would become the fertilizers, and would carry on the process till the largest moths became the sole agents. Now, if not before, the moth would also be affected; for those with the longest prosboces would get the most food, would be the strongest and most vigorous, would visit and fertilize the greatest number of flowers, and would leave the largest number of descendants. The flowers most completely fertilized by these moths being those which had the longest nectaries, there would in each generation be, on the average, an increase in the length of the nectaries, and also an average increase in the length of the probosces of the moths; and this would be a *necessary result* from the fact that nature ever fluctuates about a mean, or that in every generation there would be flowers with longer and shorter nectaries, and moths with longer and shorter probosces than the average. I may here mention that some of the large Sphinx moths of the tropics have probosces nearly as long as the nectary of *Angrœcum sesquipedale.* I have carefully measured the proboscis of a specimen of *Macrosila cluentius* from South America, in the collection of the British Museum, and find it to be nine inches and a quarter long. One from tropical Africa (*Macrosila morganii*) is seven inches and a half. A species having a proboscis two or three inches longer could reach the nectar in the longest flowers of *Angrœcum sesquipedale,* whose nectaries vary in length from ten to fourteen inches. That such a moth exists in Madagascar may be safely predicted;[1] and naturalists who visit that island should search for it with as much confidence as astronomers searched for the planet Neptune, — and I venture to predict they will be equally successful."[2]

I have given this quotation at length in order to indicate not only the fitting of hypothesis to the facts observed, but also the large and important part performed by the imagination in reproducing along parallel lines the natural history of the orchid and moth. The hypothesis reaches back over an indefinitely long past, by virtue of the necessities observed in the present, and in accordance with well-established analogies and approved inductions. The function of the imagination especially prominent is that of

[1] It is interesting to note that since Mr. Wallace wrote the above, Kirby, in his *European Moths and Butterflies,* makes mention of one of the *Sphingidæ* with a proboscis *twelve* inches long!

[2] Wallace, *On Natural Selection,* pp. 271-275.

its deductive insight, which is able to picture to the mind the inevitable results of this and that condition as furnished by the postulate, and then to fit such necessitated results into one self-consistent system, with nothing left unexplained, incongruous, or contradictory.

Another illustration of an hypothesis covering a large number of complex facts is that of the fertilization of certain flowers by means of the wind. As given by Sir John Lubbock, we have the following facts and the corresponding explanation of them: "Wind-fertilized flowers, as a rule, have no color, emit no scent and produce no honey, and are regular in form. Color, scent, and honey are the three characteristics by which insects are attracted to flowers. Again, as a rule wind-fertilized flowers produce much more pollen than those which are fertilized by insects. This is necessary, because it is obvious that the chances against any given pollen grain reaching the stigma are much greater in the one case than in the other. Every one has observed the showers of yellow pollen produced by the Scotch fir. Again, it is an advantage to wind-fertilized plants to flower early in the spring before the leaves are out, because the latter would catch much of the pollen, and thus interfere with its access to the stigma. Again, in these plants the pollen is less adherent, so that it can be easily blown away by the wind, which would be a disadvantage in most plants which are fertilized by insects. Again, such flowers generally have the stigma more or less branched, or hairy, which evidently must tend to increase their chances of catching the pollen."[1] There is here a structural adaptation of these plants to the circumstances designed to explain them, so that the consequent self-consistent system thus formed carries with it the weight of conviction.

There are some explanations which do not perfectly correspond to reality, and yet, when their nature is known, they may be profitably used, not to represent reality, but to assist

[1] Lubbock, *Scientific Lectures*, pp. 9, 10.

the mind by an *approximate* representation to better appreciate the facts as they really are related one to another. These so-called "fictions" are useful, especially in mathematics. We suppose, for instance, inscribed and circumscribed polygons of a circle, with ever-increasing number of sides, gradually approaching and becoming coincident finally with the curve itself. This latter we know to be impossible, and yet we may treat that which happens only approximately as though really happening, merely as an aid to the imagination; and a fiction, if always so understood, may thus prove helpful in the representation of reality more clearly to our minds.

4. The hypothesis moreover should involve no contradiction. This is clearly a requirement that is deductive rather than inductive, depending upon the fundamental principle of contradiction lying at the basis of the deductive system of logic.

5. The hypothesis should be as simple as possible. No involved explanation that mystifies rather than clears the difficulties presented can rank as a true hypothesis. *Simplex veri sigillum.* This requirement, of course, cannot in all cases be strictly complied with; for the phenomena to be explained may present such a degree of complexity that a simple hypothesis would be altogether out of the question. For instance, the hypothesis of a substance filling the universe, and pervading all particles of matter, however solid and closely knit together, a substance itself more solid than steel, and more elastic as well, such a supposition seems not only too involved, but also even to belie the ordinary judgments of common sense. And yet this undulatory hypothesis is more and more confirmed by every advance of science in the knowledge of the phenomena of light and heat.

It sometimes happens that the very failure of an hypothesis forms a substantial contribution to the progress of thought, leading to the readjustment of a received theory, or stimulating research in order to discover the true in place of the false hypothesis. As Mr. Tait says: "We all know that if there had not been a pursuit after the philosopher's stone, chemistry could not yet have been anything like the gigantic science it now is. In the same way we can say, that modern physics could not yet have covered the ground it now occupies had it not been for this experimental seeking for the so-called perpetual motion, and the consequent establishment of a definite and scientifically useful negative."[1] The circular theory of the orbits of the planets, while incorrect, yet made the transition easier from the hypothesis of circular motion to that of motion in an elliptical orbit, which is the true theory. It often happens that an hypothesis may not be wholly wrong but may need correction, and this is often provided for, not by a total rejection of the hypothesis in question, but by supplementing it by so-called subsidiary hypotheses.

As to the tests of a correct hypothesis in addition to the fulfilment of the requirements already mentioned, Dr. Whewell has especially emphasized the importance of what he has styled a "Consilience of Inductions." An hypothesis receives a confirmatory strengthening of its validity, when it enables us to explain and determine cases not only of the same kind as the phenomena out of which the hypothesis itself has developed, but cases which arise in a sphere entirely different from that which gave material originally for the formation of the hypothesis. An hypothesis that can thus be carried into new territory as an effective instrument of research, is thereby doubly accredited. As Dr. Whewell remarks: "Accordingly the cases in which inductions from classes of parts altogether different have thus *jumped together*, belong only to the best established theories which the history of science contains. And as I shall have occasion to refer to this peculiar feature in their evidence, I will take the liberty of describing it by a particular phrase; and will term it the *Consilience of Inductions.*

[1] Tait, *Recent Advances in Physical Science*, p. 69.

It is exemplified principally in some of the greatest discoveries. Thus it was found by Newton that the doctrine of the attraction of the sun varying according to the inverse square of the distance, which explained Kepler's *Third Law*, of the proportionality of the cubes of the distances to the squares of the periodic times of the planets, explained also his *First* and *Second Laws*, of the elliptical motion of each planet; although no connection of these laws had been visible before. Again, it appeared that the force of universal gravitation, which had been inferred from the *perturbations* of the moon and planets by the sun and by each other, also accounted for the fact, apparently altogether dissimilar and remote, of the *precession of the equinoxes*. Here was a most striking and surprising coincidence which gave to the theory a stamp of truth beyond the power of ingenuity to counterfeit."[1]

When two rival hypotheses can be submitted to the test of an experiment which negatives one and confirms the other, such a testing is called an *experimentum crucis*. The name was first given by Bacon, and has met with universal acceptance in scientific phraseology. A crucial test, as decisive between the emission and the undulatory theory of light, is given in an experiment first tried by Father Grimaldi, a Bolognese monk, in 1665. If a shutter be pierced with a very small hole, and the luminous cone which passes through the orifice be examined, the cone will be found to be much less acute than would be expected, considering only the rectilinear transmission of the rays, as according to the emission theory. If there be interposed in the path of the luminous ray a second shutter, pierced with a hole also, it will be noticed that the rays of the second cone are even more divergent than those of the first. If the image of the orifice be received upon a screen, a white circle is seen surrounded by a dark ring, next a white ring, even more brilliant than the central portion, then a second dark

[1] Whewell, *Novum Organum Renovatum*, Book II, Chap. V, Art. 110.

ring, and finally another very faint white ring. If in the shutter with which the experiment is made, two very small holes are pierced at a distance from each other of one or two millimetres, and the two images received upon a screen in such a manner that they overlap each other, it is found that in the cuticular segment formed by the overlapping of the images, the circles are more obscure than in the part where they are separated. Thus by adding light to light darkness is produced.[1] These phenomena are now known to be consistent only with the undulatory theory, and directly in contradiction to the emission hypothesis.

M. Romanes performed several experiments upon bees which had the force of crucial tests of two opposed hypotheses: one, that bees possess a general sense of direction, irrespective of any special knowledge of their particular surroundings; the other, that they are guided in their flight by a knowledge of the localities which they have been wont to frequent. M. Romanes took a score of bees in a box out to sea, where there could be no landmarks to guide the insects home. None of them returned home. Then he liberated a second lot of bees on the seashore, and, none of these returning, he liberated another lot on the lawn between the shore and the house. None of these returned, although the distance from the lawn to the hive was not more than two hundred yards. Lastly, he liberated bees in different parts of the flower-garden on either side of the house, and these at once returned to the hive; and with repetition of the experiment, a similar result, even arriving at the hive before he himself had time to run from the place where he had liberated them to the hive. As the garden was a large one, many of them had to fly a greater distance, in order to reach the hive, than those liberated on the front lawn. Their uniform success, therefore, in finding their way home so immediately was no doubt due to their special knowledge

[1] Saigey, *The Unity of Natural Phenomena*, p. 66.

of the flower-garden, and not to any general sense of direction.[1]

The hypothesis that leads to verification by experiment represents true scientific procedure, and that which has actually been the most effective instrument of research in all the various spheres of human investigation. The old controversy between Mill and Whewell admits of a ready adjustment in this regard. Whewell emphasized discovery as the heart of the system of induction, leading to the framing of hypotheses whose chief test was not experimental so much as the capability of accounting for the given phenomena. Mill, on the other hand, insisted that logic was essentially proof, and not discovery. He, accordingly, emphasized the experimental testing by means of his several methods, as being the all-important part of the inductive method. He had little concern for the origin of the suggestions as to the most likely causal elements in the midst of a complex phenomenon. The primary function of logic, according to him, is merely to prove or disprove. The ideas of Whewell and Mill are not necessarily contradictory; they can be regarded as mutually supplementary, which gives us a true account of the ideal logical method, where hypothesis suggests the line of experiment, and experiment in turn confirms hypothesis. In such a method, as can be seen in the illustration given, there is a blending of deductive and inductive reasoning, which is the general characteristic of all actual processes of thought. As Sigwart has so admirably put it: "Without quickness of combination, by which we can call up a number of possible analogies and apply them to the unexplained case; without a happy power of divination which is guided by unanalyzable associations to discover that analogy which embraces most aspects of the event; finally, without imagination to construct connections for which the only ground may be a hidden

[1] Lubbock, *On the Senses, Instincts, and Intelligence of Animals*, pp. 269, 270.

similarity, our thoughts, if compelled to proceed strictly according to method, would frequently be condemned, by the impossibility of discovering in this way a sufficiently grounded connection, to complete stagnation. But the fact is in no way contrary to the nature of induction; it is a necessary consequence of it. We cannot even begin the process of inference without making general assumptions; and the general proposition which we get by summing up a number of instances is really a hypothesis, to which, it is true, we are led clearly and certainly in this case. But between these most general presuppositions, upon which all induction is grounded, and the simplest cases to which they can be applied, there is a wide region within which the hypotheses which are always necessary for induction can only be formed tentatively, in order to give some definite direction to investigation, to serve in our analysis of phenomena into their elements as a means of breaking up complete phenomena on certain lines, and to invent the experiments which will make it possible to confirm or refute an opinion." [1]

[1] Sigwart, *Logic*, Vol. II, p. 423.

CHAPTER XIII

ANALOGY

ANALOGY as we have seen is a process of inference from a particular case to a particular.[1] Because they agree in certain respects, it is inferred that they will agree in other respects also. Such reasoning admits of various degrees of cogency, and in no case is it ever completely conclusive. It may give rise to an exceedingly high degree of probability, but nothing more. However the conclusion which analogy suggests as extremely probable may be submitted to the tests of one or more of the inductive methods, and thereby be satisfactorily proved. In that case, the particular case which was the starting-point of the analogical inference can then be regarded as the typical case which ranks as representative of the universal attained by the inductive investigation. One of the most important features of analogy is that while incomplete in itself, it nevertheless leads by suggestion to inductive experimentation which renders it complete or else discloses its points of weakness. As an instrument of discovery, analogy has played a very important role in scientific research. In 1845 Faraday discovered the magnetic rotary polarization of light; by analogical reasoning, Waitmann in the following year inferred that a similar result would be attained with a beam of heat, which was afterwards experimentally verified.

The so-called "natural kinds" furnish manifold illustrations of analogies. They possess numerous properties, some of them known and others unknown. Through large groups of them are found similar characteristics side by side with

[1] See p. 150.

manifest differences, and yet the similarities are so striking that often, when new properties are discovered in certain members of the group, there seems to be ground for inferring their existence in other members of the group also. Certain properties known to exist in potassium and sodium were inferred to be present in rubidium and cæsium; the carbonates of sodium and potassium are not decomposed by a red heat, and it was inferred that the same would prove true of the carbonates of rubidium and cæsium; and such proved to be the case. Some of the statements which are true of chlorine are found to be true of bromine and iodine. Mr. Gore, having found the molecular change in antimony electro-deposited from its chloride, he inferred and discovered the same in that deposited from its bromide and iodide. Sir Humphry Davy, having discovered that potassium might be isolated by means of electrolysis, immediately inferred and proceeded to prove by experiment that it would be possible also to isolate sodium and other substances having analogous properties.[1]

The principle of analogy lies at the basis of all classification, the separating and grouping together in appropriate divisions individuals which possess certain salient attributes in common.

Professor Jevons's definition of classification embodies at the same time a full statement of its exact logical significance as an instrument of research, and therefore I give it in full: "By the classification of any series of objects is meant the actual or ideal arrangement together of those which are alike, and the separation of those which are unlike, the purpose of this arrangement being, primarily, to disclose the correlations or laws of union of properties and circumstances, and secondarily, to facilitate the operations of the mind in clearly conceiving and retaining in the memory the characters of the object in question."[2] In

[1] Gore, *The Art of Scientific Discovery*, p. 522.
[2] Jevons, *Principles of Science*, p. 677.

describing the purpose of classification, the latter clause is more a psychological desideratum than logical; the former specification contains its logical purpose; namely, to disclose the correlations or laws of union of properties and circumstances. This may be illustrated in the grouping together of potassium, sodium, cæsium, rubidium, and lithium, and calling them the alkaline metals. This was done by virtue of the common characteristics in the midst of their individual peculiarities; namely, they all combine very energetically with oxygen to decompose water at all temperatures, and form strongly basic oxides, which are highly soluble in water, yielding powerful caustic and alkaline hydrates from which water cannot be expelled by heat; their carbonates are also soluble in water, and each metal forms only one chloride. The manifest advantage of classifying these metals together lies in its suggestive capacity, as we have already noted in illustrations above given. So many observed similarities suggest inferences by analogy; when, for instance, a new property is discovered in any one or two of the metals of this class, the idea immediately suggests itself that the same property may possibly extend over all the metals of the same class. Not only is such an idea suggested, but along with it there exists an antecedent probability that it will be realized actually.

An excellent illustration of the practical results attained through a scientific use of classification is found in Mr. Lockyer's researches on the sun.[1] As a guide to the elements to look for in the sun's photosphere, he prepared a classification of elements according as they had or had not been traced in the sun, together with a detailed statement of the chemical nature of each element. He was then able to observe that the elements found in the sun were, for the most part, those forming stable compounds with oxygen. He then inferred that the other elements which were known to form stable compounds with oxygen would, in all proba-

[1] Quoted by Jevons in *Principles of Science*, p. 676.

bility, be found present in the sun. Starting upon this suggested track, he succeeded in discovering five such metals.

Analogical inference carries special weight when it is based upon the principle of teleology; that is, when any observed phenomena seem to possess structural contrivances adapted to ends, similar in some degree at least to human contrivances designed to produce certain proposed ends. When this similarity is apparent, it suggests the possibility that an observed contrivance in nature may subserve ends beyond the possibility of observation, and which, therefore, may be inferred really to exist. We have seen that the ground of all inference lies in the representation of any given phenomena of consciousness as cohering in one system, which comprehends the several parts in a common unity of such a nature that, knowing some of the parts and their relations, we infer the character and function of other parts not known, and yet which that already known necessitates. And among the many kinds of relation that may obtain between part and part, or part and whole, the teleological is a very common one; and, moreover, by its nature necessitates certain consequences that lie beyond the sphere of observation, and yet, nevertheless, may very properly be supplied by inference. In other words, the causal connections in a system are not merely those of an efficient or a formal cause; they may, with a like force and suggestiveness, be considered in the light of a final cause; that is, the presence of means adapted to certain ends, or of organs adapted to certain necessary functions, or of contrivances of a mechanical nature as though designed for a specific purpose.

Janet has specially emphasized the importance and prevalence of this kind of inference, and, as an illustration of the cogency of inference based upon finality, he urges that the certitude which the belief in the intelligence of our fellow-men gives us is based upon analogical reasoning of this type; and that, moreover, this belief, resting upon such a basis, is one of the strongest beliefs which we possess.

He says: "Now, if we ask ourselves why we suppose that other men think, we shall see that it is in virtue of the principle of final causes. In effect, what is it that experience shows in the actions of other men, but a certain number of phenomena coördinated in a certain manner, and bound not only together, but also to a future phenomenon more or less remote? Thus, when we see a man prepare his food by means of fire, we know that this assemblage of phenomena is connected with the act of taking food; when we see a painter drawing lines on a canvas, we know that these apparently arbitrary acts are connected with the execution of a picture; when we see a deaf mute making signs which we do not understand, we believe that these gestures are connected with a final effect, which is to be understood by him to whom he makes them; in fine, when men speak, we see that the articulations of which a phrase is composed are coördinated to each other so as to produce a certain final effect, which is to awaken in us a certain thought and sentiment. Now we cannot see such coördinations, whether actual or future, without supposing a certain cause for them; and as we know by internal experience that with ourselves such coördinations only take place under the condition that the final effect is previously represented in our consciousness, we suppose the same thing in the case of other men; in a word, we suppose for them the consciousness of an end, a consciousness reflecting more or less, according as the circumstances more or less resemble those that accompany in ourselves the reflecting consciousness. Thus when we affirm the intelligence of other men, we affirm a truth of indisputable certitude; and yet we only affirm it on the ground of analogy, and of analogy guided by the principle of final causes."[1]

In this illustration of Janet's we have the idea of a system of coördinated parts especially prominent; and for a satisfactory account of the relations obtaining in such a system,

[1] Janet, *Final Causes*, pp. 113, 114.

it will be seen how indispensable it is to postulate the theory of final cause. This mode of inference finds a striking illustration in the famous discovery of Harvey, concerning the circulation of the blood. In the early part of the seventeenth century, while Harvey was his pupil, the celebrated anatomist, Fabricius Aquapendente of Padua, observed that many veins contain valves which lie open as long as the blood is flowing toward the heart. Harvey, learning of this fact, saw in it the suggestion of an adaptation of means to an end; namely, a contrivance so fashioned by nature as to permit the blood to flow always in one direction only, and to prevent its flow in an opposite direction. Observation of other portions of the circulatory mechanism led to a confirmation of the idea, and to the discovery of the circulation of the blood.[1]

Again, many flint substances have been discovered, as though curiously wrought with sharp edges, and a place as though designed for a handle with which to wield the stone as a weapon or a tool; it has been inferred from these general characteristics that the stones were so constructed by human effort, and used by human beings for the purposes for which they evidently seem to be adapted. This inference is based upon an analogy between the peculiar shapes of such stones, and known shapes designed and used by man.

This form of analogy has proved especially suggestive in researches regarding plant and animal life. Sir John Lubbock gives the following description of the common white dead-nettle with the explanation of its functions that is evidently a teleological inference: "The flower consists of a narrow tube, somewhat expanded at the upper end, where the lower lobe of the corolla forms a platform, on each side of which is a small projecting lobe. The upper portion of the corolla is an arched hood, under which lie four anthers in pairs, while between them and projecting

[1] Gore, *Art of Scientific Discovery*, p. 571.

somewhat downwards is the pointed pistil. At the lower end, the tube contains honey, and above the honey is a row of hairs almost closing the tube. Now, why has the flower this peculiar form? What regulates the length of the tube? *What is the use of this arch?* What lessons do these lobes teach us? What advantage is the honey to the flower? *Of what use* is the fringe of hairs? Why does the stigma project beyond the anthers? Why is the corolla white, while the rest of the plant is green? Similar questions may of course be asked with reference to other flowers. At the close of the last century, Conrad Sprengel published a valuable work, in which he pointed out that the forms and colors, the scent, honey, and general structure of flowers, have reference to the visits of insects, which are of importance in transferring the pollen from the stamens to the pistil. Mr. Darwin developed this theory and proved experimentally that the special service which insects perform to flowers, consists not only in transferring the pollen from the stamens to the pistil, but in transferring it from the stamens of one flower to the pistil of another."[1] The line of subsequent observation and experiment was thus originally suggested by the structural appearance of these flowers which seemed formed for some specific end. The questions, once started, — To what end? To what purpose? For what use? — led to the theory of Sprengel and the corroborative experiments of Darwin.

This is further illustrated in some very interesting flower structures, also described by Sir John Lubbock, which indicate peculiar contrivances for the destruction of insects. The peculiarity of formation first suggested some such end as this, which has since been proved by careful observation to be the case. "The first observation on insect-eating flowers was made about the year 1868 by Ellis. He observed that in *Dionœa*, a North American plant, the leaves have a joint in the middle, and thus close over, kill, and

[1] Lubbock, *Scientific Lectures*, pp. 1, 2.

actually digest any insect which may alight on them. Another case is that of *Utricularia,* an aquatic species which bears a number of utricles or sacs, which have been supposed to act as floats. Branches, however, which bear no bladders float just as well as the others, and there seems no doubt that their real use is to capture small aquatic animals, which they do in considerable numbers. The bladders, in fact, are on the principle of an eel-trap, having an entrance closed with a flap, which permits an easy entrance, but effectually prevents the unfortunate victim from getting out again. In the genus, *Sarracenia,* some of the leaves are in the form of a pitcher. They secrete a fluid, and are lined internally with hairs pointing downwards. Up the outside of the pitcher there is a line of honey glands which lure the insects to their destruction. Flies and other insects which fall into this pitcher cannot get out again and are actually digested by the plant." [1]

In the example where the idea of an eel-trap suggested the possible function of the similar structure in the plant, *Utricularia,* we find one of the most striking illustrations of this mode of analogical inference. It was an easy and natural transition from similarity of structure to similarity of function. To give an idea of the great number of teleological phenomena in the vegetable and animal world, and the wealth of possible suggestion stored away in these various structures, and disclosed by a sagacious analysis, I quote a remark of Sir John Lubbock's in commenting upon the variation of color and markings of caterpillars: " I should produce an impression very different from that which I wish to convey, were I to lead you to suppose that all these varieties have been explained or are understood. Far from it; they still offer a large field for study; nevertheless, I venture to think the evidence now brought forward, however imperfectly, is at least sufficient to justify the conclusion that there is not a hair or a line, not a spot or a color,

[1] Lubbock, *Scientific Lectures,* pp. 4, 5.

for which there is not a reason, — which has not a purpose or a meaning in the economy of nature."[1]

An illustration given by Darwin shows this mode of inference applied to the sphere of animal life also. He says: "The great size of the bones of the megatherioid animals was a complete puzzle to naturalists until Professor Owen lately solved the problem with remarkable ingenuity. The teeth indicate, by their simple structure, that these megatherioid animals lived on vegetable food, and probably on the leaves and small twigs of trees; their ponderous forms and great, strong, curved claws *seem so little adapted* for locomotion that some eminent naturalists have actually believed that, like the sloths, to which they are intimately related, they subsisted by climbing back downwards on trees, and feeding on the leaves. It was a bold, not to say preposterous, idea, to conceive even antediluvian trees with branches strong enough to bear animals as large as elephants. Professor Owen, with far more probability, believes that, instead of climbing on the trees, they pulled the branches down to them, and tore up the smaller ones by the roots, and so fed on the leaves. The colossal breadth and weight of their hinder quarters, which can hardly be imagined without having been seen, become, on this view, of obvious service, instead of being an encumbrance: their apparent clumsiness disappears. With their great tails and their huge heels firmly fixed like a tripod on the ground, they could freely exert the full force of their most powerful arms and great claws. Strongly rooted, indeed, must have been that tree which could have resisted such force! The Mylodon, moreover, was furnished with a long extensile tongue like that of the giraffe, which, by one of those beautiful provisions of nature, thus reaches, with the aid of its long neck, its leafy food."[2] Throughout we observe analogical inference based upon these teleological marks, and furnishing a basis for a satisfactory hypothesis.

[1] Lubbock, *Scientific Lectures*, pp. 66, 67.
[2] Darwin, *Voyage of a Naturalist*, pp. 106, 107.

We see what a wide field thus opens in the region of biology alone for the discovery of resemblances leading to the appreciation of the fuller teleological significance of plant and animal life.

In the illustrations given, both of the teleological and other forms of analogy, we notice that its chief logical function is that of suggestion of some hypothesis which may or may not be afterwards confirmed by subsequent experiment. Some of the most important discoveries of science have arisen from analogical suggestions. Sir John Herschel was led by observed analogies to predict certain phenomena afterwards verified experimentally by Faraday. Herschel had noticed that a screw-like form, known as helicoidal dissymmetry, was observed in three cases, namely, in electrical helices, plagihedral quartz crystals (that is, crystals having an oblique spiral arrangement of planes), and the rotation of the plane of polarization of light. As Herschel himself said: "I reasoned thus: Here are three phenomena agreeing in a *very strange peculiarity*. Probably this peculiarity is a connecting link, physically speaking, among them. Now, in the case of the crystals and the light, this probability has been turned into certainty by my own experiments. Therefore, induction led me to conclude that a similar connection exists, and must turn up, somehow or other, between the electric current and polarized light, and that the plane of polarization would be defected by magneto-electricity." Herschel thus anticipated Faraday's experimental discovery of the influence of magnetic strain upon polarized light.[1]

Another important discovery — the germ-theory of epidemic disease — was first suggested by an analogy. In the theory, as expressed by Kircher, and favored by Linnæus, and afterwards supported by Sir Henry Holland, its special strength, according to Professor Tyndall, "consisted in the perfect parallelism of the phenomena of contagious disease with those of life. As a planted acorn gives birth to an

[1] Jevons, *Principles of Science*, p. 630.

oak competent to produce a whole crop of acorns, each gifted with the power of reproducing the parent tree, and as thus from a single seedling a whole forest may spring, so, it is contended, these epidemic diseases literally plant their seeds, grow and shake abroad new germs, which, meeting in the human body their proper food and temperature, finally take possession of whole populations."[1]

The theory of evolution was first suggested to Mr. Darwin by the analogous phenomena observed in artificial selection and breeding. The transition to natural selection was easily made, especially as, on reading Malthus, *On Population*, he conceived the idea of a struggle for existence as the inevitable result of the rapid increase of organic beings. This idea necessitated the natural selection, which he needed to account for results similar to the artificial selection, and thus his theory grew out of an analogy as its beginning. Moreover, in the development of the theory in its manifold details, other analogies proved also suggestive. For instance, there is the supposed analogy between the growth of a species and the growth of an individual. It supposes, for example, as Professor Clifford has put it, "that the race of crabs has gone through much the same sort of changes as every crab goes through now, in the course of its formation in the egg, — changes represented by its pristine shape utterly unlike what it afterwards attains, and by its gradual metamorphosis and formation of shell and claws."[2]

The germ-theory of putrefaction, first suggested by Schwann, received confirmation through certain resemblances noted by Professor Lister between fermentation and putrefaction. In his *Introductory Lecture* before the University of Edinburgh, Professor Lister called attention to the fact that fermentation and putrefaction present a very striking parallel. In each a stable compound — sugar in one case, albumen in the other — undergoes extraordi-

---

[1] Tyndall, *Fragments of Science*, p. 287.
[2] Clifford, *Lectures and Essays*, p. 86.

nary chemical changes under the influence of an excessively minute quantity of a substance which, regarded chemically, would be considered inert. It was pointed out also by Professor Lister in this connection, that, as was well known, one of the chief peculiarities of living organisms is that they possess extraordinary powers of effecting chemical changes in materials in their vicinity out of all proportion to their energy as mere chemical compounds. Such being the facts in the case, and, moreover, the fermentation of sugar being generally allowed to be occasioned by the presence of living organisms, Professor Lister's inference was that putrefaction was due to an analogous agency.[1]

A discovery in quite a different sphere, that of mathematics, leading to the branch of analytical geometry, was first suggested to Descartes through observing the resemblances existing between geometry and algebra. In a similar manner, Boole was led, by the resemblances noted between algebra and logic, to give expression to the same in a system which he called the laws of thought, and which has become the basis of a general or symbolic logic.

While there are thus unquestionable evidences of the value of analogy as a form of inference, there are also cases of false analogy unfortunately so numerous as to discredit the process wholly in some quarters. It will be well, therefore, to indicate some of the requirements of true analogy:—

1. In the first place the resemblance must be a preponderating one; that is, the phenomena compared must show a more striking agreement than difference. Some writers have balanced agreement against difference upon a purely numerical basis of comparison, forming what may be called an analogical ratio, with points of similarity forming the numerator, and the points both of similarity and difference, plus the unknown, that is, the total number, forming the denominator. Such a representation of the force of

[1] Tyndall, *Fragments of Science*, pp. 300–302.

an analogy is given by Mill, Bain, and others. I think, however, that this representation is apt to be misleading in producing the impression that the mere number of points of agreement, irrespective of their significance, is the chief feature of analogy. Whereas it is the weight of the agreeing attributes, and not the number, that counts. As has been before said, in analogy we weigh instances, and do not count them. The analogical ratio expressed numerically, as above, is really equivalent to the ratio of probability which will be described in the following chapter. I have therefore changed the usual wording of this requirement, so that it reads, the resemblances must be more striking and more significant than the differences. This provides for cases when perhaps a few points of resemblance will be of such a nature as to outweigh many points of difference in the total estimate.

This requirement also excludes all fanciful analogies and all resemblances resting upon a figurative rather than a real basis. For instance, the advocates of annual Parliaments in the time of the Commonwealth, urged their case on the analogical ground that a body politic is similar to a living body and that serpents annually cast their skin, which, being no doubt for a beneficial purpose, might well be imitated.

2. In noting the points of resemblance between two phenomena, all circumstances which are known to be effects of one cause must therefore be regarded not as many, but as one. For instance, two chemical oxides may be compared; the effects common to each may be due to the presence of the oxygen which each contains, and therefore must not be regarded in the light of independent marks of similarity.

3. If we infer by analogy that a substance possesses a certain property which we know is incompatible with some one or other known properties of the substance, the analogy is at once discredited. We may infer that the moon is inhabited, by virtue of the many points of resemblance

between the moon and the earth. However, the fact that the moon has no atmosphere necessary to sustain life, at once makes such an argument based upon analogy wholly out of the question.

4. There are certain special requirements referring to that particular form of analogy which is based upon teleological considerations. They are as follows: —

a. This principle must never be used as an argument against an observed fact, or an established law of nature. While this precaution is not necessary at the present time, in scientific circles at least, still there was a time when its counsel was sorely needed. When in astronomy it was proved that there were suns gravitating around other suns, without our solar system, this was objected to upon the following ground, as given by one Nicholas Fuss, a celebrated astronomer, at the end of the eighteenth century: "What is the good of some luminous bodies revolving round others? The sun is the only source whence the planets derive light and heat. Were their entire systems of suns controlled by other suns, their neighborhood and their motions would be *objectless*, their rays *useless*. The suns have no need to borrow from strange bodies what they themselves have received as their own. If the secondary stars are luminous bodies, *what is the end* of their motives?"

There is, moreover, another abuse of the principle of final causes, which has also historic interest rather than any present pertinence; namely, opposing certain false teleological ideas to established discoveries or inventions, with a mistaken zeal, in defence of a Divine Providence. For instance, at the time of Jenner's great discovery, an English physician, Dr. Rowley, said of smallpox: "It is a malady imposed by the decree of heaven, and vaccination is an audacious and sacrilegious violation of our holy religion. The designs of these vaccinators appear to defy heaven itself, and the very will of God." The introduction of winnowing machines into Scotland met with bitter opposition on the ground that the winds were the work of God, and that the wind thus artificially raised was a veritable "devil's wind," as they were wont to call it. Sir Walter Scott, in *Old Mortality*, has the old Mause say to her mistress: "Your ladyship and the steward are wishing Cuddie to use a new machine to winnow the corn. This machine opposes the designs of Providence, by furnishing wind for your special use, and by human means, in place of asking it by prayer, and waiting with patience till Providence itself sends it."

b. Final causes should never be employed to explain phenomena which do not exist. As M. Florens has said: "We must proceed not from final causes to facts, but from facts to final causes; that is, we should not superimpose final causes upon phenomena. We must see them in phenomena themselves, and we must not arbitrarily project a teleological idea, purely subjective, upon an objective ground. ' Thus in ancient times, Hippocrates is said to 'have admired the skill with which the auricles of the heart have been made *to blow the air into the heart.*' "

c. We must distinguish accidental from essential marks of finality, and not be led into fanciful or far-fetched analogies. Voltaire has expressed such a defect when in satire he made that famous remark, "Noses are made in order to bear spectacles."

Bernardin de Saint-Pierre says: "Dogs are usually of two opposite colors, the one light, the other dark, in order that whenever they may be in the house, they may be distinguished from the furniture, with the color of which they might be confounded. . . . Wherever fleas are they jump on white colors. This instinct has been given them, that we may the more easily catch them." And again the same writer says: "The melon has been divided into sections by nature, for family eating."[1] All such grotesque inferences will give

[1] The illustrations upon the abuse of final causes I have taken from Janet's admirable chapter, — Chapter VIII of Appendix.

an idea of how readily the imagination will run riot if allowed to remain uncurbed by the reason.

5. Analogy should never be regarded as having more weight than that of extremely high probability, even in cases seemingly most conclusive. Its true function as we have seen is suggestive, leading to hypothesis and experiment, and it needs this supplementary proof. It was an inference based on analogy, for instance, which suggested the probability that the Binomial Law, having proved to be valid as regards the second, third, and fourth powers, might also be extended to the fifth, and so on to the other powers indefinitely. This suggestion offered no real basis, however, upon which the Binomial Theorem could rest; it needed mathematical demonstration to confirm and generalize its expression in the special cases already experimentally tested, so as to cover all possible exponents, both positive and negative, fractional and integral.

So also the discovery of the circulation of the blood was first suggested to Harvey, as has been said, by analogical considerations upon observed teleological phenomena. Harvey, however, was not content with this suggestion merely. He was led to experiment upon the veins and arteries; he tied an artery and vein, and carefully observed the mechanical effects upon the two sides of the tied parts. Experiments of this nature, with close observation and study, were kept up most diligently, and with rare perseverance, for *nineteen* years, before he had traced the entire course of the blood through all parts of the human body, and, in a manner wholly satisfactory to himself, verified the first statement of this theory.

CHAPTER XIV

PROBABILITY

There are certain phenomena of such a nature that their antecedents, being extremely complex, cannot be adequately comprehended by observation, however searching it may be; nor can they be subjected to any analysis that will disclose the causal elements to which the effect in question is due. Moreover, with seemingly the same antecedents, the event sometimes happens, and sometimes does not; and even with antecedents associated with an event as cause and effect respectively, nevertheless the event does not occur as we should naturally expect, while with antecedents associated with the contradiction of the event as cause and effect respectively, we find the occurrence of the event quite contrary to what we should naturally expect. The evidence of a constant connection between antecedent and consequent, that we have found in so many cases which we have examined, is here wholly lacking. Regularity has been replaced by irregularity respecting such phenomena. For instance, I throw dice repeatedly; the antecedent shaking of the box, and tossing the dice upon the table, is about the same each time, at least the difference cannot be determined, and yet the results vary with each successive throw. The causal determination in each case is so complex as to be beyond computation; the initial position of the dice, the force of their ejection from the box, the height of the box above the table when they leave it, the inequalities of the table itself, a variation between the physical and geometrical centres of gravity of the dice, etc., all these make the antecedent so complex that a slight variation in any one of these conditions will affect the result. We find, therefore, double sixes at one time, a three and four at another, and so on indefinitely.

Or, again, it sometimes happens that with perfect sanitary conditions a contagious disease will appear, that has always been regarded, and that correctly, as due to imperfect sanitation; or, an entire disregard of sanitary requirements and of all the laws of health may yet give rise to no disease of special moment. Certain conditions of temperature, atmospheric pressure, velocity and direction of the wind, may one day bring storm and rain, and as far as observation can detect, similar conditions may again bring fair weather. So, also, the rise and fall in stock and money markets is extremely susceptible to the varying conditions of indefinitely complex forces wholly beyond all powers of determination or of prediction. Such phenomena present a problem which the methods of inductive inquiry cannot deal with. Observation is not far-reaching enough to provide the data for the solution of the problem, and, even if it were, our methods of computation and determination are not sufficiently adequate to solve problems of so many terms and of so complex a nature.

The experimental methods are designed to test causes suggested by analogy, or by mental analysis; but in such phenomena as these, the problem is not simply to find a causal connection. The causal connection may be established beyond all reasonable doubt, and yet the cause obtains in the midst of so complex a setting that the problem is really this, — to determine whether a cause, whose exact nature may be known or unknown, will prove operative or inoperative. The cause may be always present and even its exact nature may be known, and yet the complex circumstances attending it may be of such a character that one alone, or two or more combining, may neutralize the operation of the cause, and on the other hand a slight variation of the combined circumstances may promote and even accelerate the operation of the cause in question. The problem then is to determine how often the event happens, and how often it fails of happening, the complex and indeterminate antecedent being present in all the instances examined.

When we begin to count instances, we are reminded that we must be in the near neighborhood of the sphere of enumerative induction. Enumerative induction, it will be remembered, treats instances by noting the number of observed coincident happenings of the antecedent and consequent under investigation, no attempt being made to analyze their respective contents, or to determine a causal connection more definitely by means of any one or more of the inductive methods of research and verification. The result of such an investigation may be formulated in a proposition of the form, Every A is B. This, strictly interpreted, has the force of, Every A that has been observed is B. The enumeration of the kind of instances which we are discussing in this chapter, however, differs from this in that the observation leads to a twofold result, — a set of instances in which it is observed that the A's *are* B's also, another set however in which the A's *are not* B's. These instances are of such a nature that the observed A is an antecedent so extremely complex that the element within it, which is a cause capable of producing B, may either be absent without producing an appreciable change in the general nature of A, or, being present, may be neutralized by some other element of A itself. The result gives a basis for a probable inference only; and the nature of that inference will depend upon the preponderance of the observed happening, or of the failure of the event under investigation.

The probability attached to such an inference, however, is different from the probability which characterizes the nature of enumerative induction. In the latter, when the observation has been widely extended and no exceptions noted, it is usual to say the result expressed in the proposition, Every A is B, has the force of a high degree of probability. In the instances, however, whose investigation shows the result that some A's are B's, and some not, and yet where the former, for instance, far outnumber the latter cases, then it may be inferred that the A's which in future we may meet with will probably be B's; and the degree of probability expressed in such a proposition is commensurate with the preponderance of the number of observed affirmative instances over the negative. Here the probability refers to the validity of an inference concerning certain *particular* instances, be they many or be they few, which lie beyond the sphere of our present knowledge; in enumerative induction, the probability is attached to the *universality* of the proposition affirmed as a result of observation that has not so far detected an exception. In the former case, the question of the universality of the result is conclusively answered, and that in the negative; there can be no universal proposition possible, as some instances give A and B together, others give A with the absence of B; and the question of probability that here arises, therefore, refers to individual cases not yet examined, as to whether they severally will more likely correspond to the set of affirmative, or to that of the negative, instances already noted.

The comparison of the number of happenings with that of the failures of an event affords a basis for three kinds of inference, all of them in the sphere of probability.

1. We find in such a comparison a basis for the calculation of the probability of a particular event happening, in case there is a repetition of the circumstances which, in former cases, have sometimes produced the event, and sometimes have failed to produce it. If, according to former observation, the event has happened, let us say, seven times, and failed three, the probability, expressed numerically, of its happening again is $\frac{7}{10}$. The rule is, to express the

probability of an event, take as numerator the number of times which the event has been observed to occur, and as denominator the total number observed, both of happening and failure; the fraction thus expressed will represent the probability of the event happening. The counter-probability may be represented by the number of observed failures of the event divided by the total number of cases observed. The counter-probability, plus the probability, evidently is equal to unity. If, therefore, the probability is unity, the counter-probability will equal zero; that is, the probability in that case has merged into certainty. Zero, therefore, represents absolute impossibility. All fractions between the limits zero and one represent varying degrees of probability from impossibility at one extreme to certainty at the other.

Not only may there be this inductive basis for the calculation of probability, arising from actually observed instances; there may be also a deductive calculation of probability based upon the known structure or nature of the phenomena themselves in advance of any observation as to their actual behavior. For instance, we say the probability of a penny turning up heads is $\frac{1}{2}$. Knowing the form of the penny and that there are but two possibilities, heads or tails, and there being no reason why one should more likely turn up than the other, we say there is one chance favorable to heads as over against the two chances which represent the total number of possibilities under the existing circumstances. With a die, in the form of a perfect cube, we say there is one chance of its turning up the face marked 1, as over against the six chances represented by the six faces, the total number; here the probability is $\frac{1}{6}$. Thus the basis for the calculation of probability may be a theoretical as well as an empirical one.

In the estimate of the probability of an event in the actual conduct of affairs, we seldom express that probability numerically. I would say that we express a degree of probability adverbially rather than numerically; that is, we say an event is *quite* probable, or it is *very* probable, or it is *extremely* probable. The fact is that, as regards most phenomena, we do not keep an exact or even approximate memorandum of the number of happenings compared with that of the failures. We rather classify our observations in terms of more or less. For instance, certain circumstances we observe produce about as many failures as happenings of an event; other circumstances produce far more happenings than failures; others far less, and so on. Consequently we receive certain psychological impressions of varying degrees of intensity according to the preponderance of happening over failure, or *vice versa;* this impression becomes the basis for estimating the probability in question, and the degree of that probability is commensurate with the intensity of the original psychological impression arising from concepts of more or of less. In such a sphere, however, as that devoted to the interests of betting, gambling, pool-selling, book-making, etc., probabilities are estimated according to statistical observations and theoretical considerations, whose conditions are expressed numerically; and the amount risked in each case is strictly estimated according to the exact ratio of probability to counter-probability under the existing circumstances.

The estimation of probability in terms of a greater or less degree is however more usual, and applicable to the conduct of human life generally. It has special force and utility as a mode of inference, when the observed instances so far outnumber the exceptions as to create an impression of such a high degree of probability as to approximate practical if not theoretical certainty. For instance, it has been noted over a wide field of observation, that a second attack of scarlet fever is extremely rare. Exceptions have occurred and therefore by enumerative induction it is impossible to generalize the universal proposition that a second attack will never occur. It is however possible to assert with somewhat positive assurance that it is highly probable that a person will be exempt from a second attack.

Or, you hear that a person, whose name is unknown to you, has met with an accident in the city of New York, resulting fatally. You are not alarmed, and perhaps the possibility does not even suggest itself to you, that the unknown person may prove to be a member of your own family, or a friend who at the time is known to be in New York. The probability against such a suggestion is so large as to preclude even the thought of it. Suppose, however, the accident occurred at one of the suburban stations. Your knowledge that your friend rides on one of the suburban trains each day to and from town, may be the ground of some anxiety, because in this case the range of possibilities is materially narrowed. Suppose, moreover, that the station where the accident occurred is at the village where your friend resides, your anxiety receives an additional increment; and, again, suppose it is at the hour at which your friend ordinarily reaches this station, there is then increased apprehension on his account. Thus, as further knowledge limits the number of total possible cases, the denominator of the probability fraction is continually decreasing, and therefore the probability itself continually increases, until it has developed from a fraction of insignificant proportions to one which is suggestive of great anxiety and suspense.

2. The comparison of failure and happening of events based upon observation, or theoretical considerations of structure and nature, leads also to inferences concerning large numbers of instances considered together. If a memorandum is kept of the number of times an event has happened, and the number of times it has failed, and the total number of instances examined be sufficiently great, then the resulting ratio of favorable instances to the total number will be found approximately repeated, if a second set of an equal number of instances be likewise examined. There is a law of tendency whereby nature seems to repeat

herself even when the attendant circumstances of an event are most complex, and beyond all powers of accurate determination. As the result of observations extending over thousands and thousands of instances, it is affirmed that about one-fourth of the children born in the world die before the age of six years, and about one-half before the age of sixteen. Take a group of ten children, the ratios would perhaps be deviated from very materially; in a group of a hundred the deviation is apt to be less; in a group of a thousand, still less; and in a group of one hundred thousand, the ratios as above given would be substantially realized. The approximation would be so near that the error would be insignificant as compared with total number of cases. The following law, therefore, expresses this tendency, — that while in a small number of instances there is irregularity in the observed ratio between the number of times a given event has happened and its failures, still in a large number of instances this ratio tends toward a constant limit. This is clearly seen in the pitching of a penny; 10 throws might very possibly result in 7 heads and 3 tails; in 100 throws, however, the ratio expressing the result as to heads and tails observed will be much nearer $\frac{1}{2}$ than in the former case; while if 1000 or 10,000 throws be observed, the result will approximate the ratio $\frac{1}{2}$. The comparison of observed cases with the number given by the calculation of the probabilities in question has been made by Quetelet, also by Jevons. Their results are most significant and interesting. Quetelet made 4096 drawings from an urn containing 20 black balls and 20 white. Theoretically, he should have drawn as many white as black balls, 2048 each; the actual drawings resulted in 2066 white balls and 2030 black. Jevons made 20,480 throws of a penny; the theoretical result should have been 10,240 heads; the actual result was 10,353 heads.

The tendency towards a constant ratio in aggregates containing a considerable number of instances is strikingly illustrated in the record of baptisms taken from an old parish register in England. The number of male baptisms registered to every 1000 female ran as follows for the respective years from 1821 to 1830: 1048, 1047, 1047, 1041, 1049, 1046, 1047, 1043, 1043, 1034. We see with what surprising accuracy the constant ratio was repeated substantially, year after year. This tendency to approximate a constant ratio is seen even in such indeterminate events as railroad accidents. Here the causes producing the accidents are so numerous, so diverse, so complex and extending over so large an area, — as, for example, the whole of the United States, — that we should think that the results would exhibit so many variations from any definite ratio as absolutely to elude all attempts at accurate determination. The figures on pages 339 and 340, however, given by the Interstate Commerce Commission, indicate results wonderfully corresponding for year after year.

An examination of these figures will disclose the fact that there is a striking approximation to an accurately proportionate distribution of the number of accidents, of the killed and of the injured, throughout these several years. It will be noticed, also, that the distribution among employees, passengers, other persons, etc., tends toward a regularity that is remarkable when we consider the extreme complexity of the circumstances that must combine to produce these results. A like regularity seems to pervade every department of life. The total number of crimes is approximately the same, year after year; the annual death-rate, the apportionment of deaths, moreover, to the several diseases as their evident causes, the number of missent letters that reach the Dead-Letter Office at Washington each year, the annual number of suicides, of divorces, all these diverse events indicate a regularity, in the long run, as regards their numerical estimate.

The results which are thus attained regarding aggregates cannot be stated as probable results merely. If a sufficiently

RAILROAD ACCIDENTS IN THE UNITED STATES

(As reported by the Interstate Commerce Commission, Washington, D.C.)

YEAR ENDING JUNE 30.	EMPLOYEES. Killed.	EMPLOYEES. Injured.	PASSENGERS. Killed.	PASSENGERS. Injured.	OTHER PERSONS. Killed.	OTHER PERSONS. Injured.	TOTAL. Killed.	TOTAL. Injured.
1888	2070	20,148	315	2158	2897	3682	5282	25,888
1889	1972	20,028	310	2146	3541	4135	5823	26,309
1890	2451	22,396	286	2425	3598	4206	6335	29,027
1891	2660	26,140	293	2972	4076	4769	7029	33,881
1892	2554	28,267	376	3227	4217	5158	7147	36,652
1893	2727	31,729	299	3229	4320	5435	7346	40,393

The total number of passengers carried was 593,560,612 in 1893, as against 560,958,211 in 1892, being an increase of 32,602,401. Casualties at stations, highway crossings, and trespassers upon tracks are included in above table under the heading "other persons."

340 INDUCTIVE LOGIC

KIND OF ACCIDENT.	EMPLOYEES.		PASSENGERS.		OTHERS.					
					Trespassing.		Not Trespassing.		Total.	
Year ending June 30, 1893.	Killed.	Injured.	Killed.	Injured.	Killed.	Injured.	Killed.	Injured.	Killed.	Injured.
Coupling and uncoupling	433	11,227	...	...	...	...	...	...	...	...
Falling from trains and engines	644	3,780	...	...	...	...	...	...	...	...
Overhead obstructions	73	444	...	...	...	...	...	...	...	...
Collisions	247	1,491	68	772	32	38	14	64	46	102
Derailments	153	867	22	774	25	43	4	42	29	85
Other train accidents	125	650	10	157	84	124	7	19	91	143
At highway crossings	32	43	2	15	163	179	431	870	594	1049
At stations	117	1,258	65	568	379	409	75	143	454	552
Other causes	903	11,919	132	943	2990	3216	116	288	3106	3504
Total	2727	31,729	299	3229	3673	4009	647	1426	4320	5435

Train accidents for twenty-one years ending December 31, as computed by the *Railroad Gazette*.

KIND OF ACCIDENT.	1893.	1892.	1891.	1890.	1889.	1888.	1887.	1886.	1885.	1884.	1883.	1878-82.*	1873-7.*
Collisions	996	1062	1137	1041	749	804	700	501	464	445	630	417	295
Derailments	1212	1165	1204	1004	759	1032	705	641	681	681	926	646	709
Other accidents	99	100	103	101	61	99	86	69	72	65	84	46	61
Total	2307	2327	2444	2146	1569	1935	1491	1211	1217	1191	1640	1109	1065

* Average per year for five years.

large number of instances are taken, the result will be certain within a very small, and in many cases an insignificant, margin. In estimating the probability of a single event, the question is whether it will happen or not happen, and the element of uncertainty is therefore prominent. In dealing with aggregates, however, no such element of uncertainty enters; the question is not whether or not there will be certain results, the question concerns rather the degree of exactness with which the results will approximate a definite ratio. And the law of tendency is, that the larger the number of instances, the greater will be the approximation to an accurate and definite result.

This is especially illustrated in the numerous insurance companies, whose business is conducted upon the basis of an approximately constant death-rate. For instance, the general procedure is somewhat as follows: Suppose 10,000 persons insure their lives at $1000 per individual, and the annual death-rate observed over a rude extent of territory, and including a very large number of instances, amounts to 200 persons out of 10,000. The losses then to the insurance company will amount annually to $200,000 on such a basis. These losses, distributed among the 10,000 insuring in the company, would amount to $20 apiece. The company, therefore, has a numerical basis for calculating the amount which each person must pay in order to cover the annual losses and provide an assured revenue for the company.

I have, of course, stated the problem in round numbers, merely to illustrate in general the principle involved; the actual calculation is more complicated, because, in each particular case, the age of the individual and the varying death-rates for different years must be taken into account. The substantial standing of the innumerable insurance companies in our country bears witness to the fact that these enterprises are based upon a practical certainty regarding death-rates when applied to large aggregates. Chance is thus eliminated almost entirely; that which would be a serious risk as regards an individual is substantially void of all risk when large numbers are concerned.

Moreover, statistics covering different classes are often most valuable in indicating tendencies operative in the classes when compared one with another. According to M. Loua (*Economiste Français*, 1882, Vol. I, p. 179), the following are the figures of the annual mortality in Paris: —

The rich and well-to-do classes, 156 out of every 10,000 inhabitants.
The poor, 285 out of every 10,000 inhabitants.

So also, in England, the average duration of life among the wealthy classes is from 55 to 56 years; for the working classes it falls to 28 years, or even lower.[1] Such comparisons are significant in indicating underlying forces in society that otherwise might be overlooked, or, at least, not adequately appreciated, and which a limited observation could not accurately reveal. Mr. Darwin, after observing and experimenting upon a very large number of plants, found the following figures respecting the relative productivity of cross and spontaneously self-fertilized flowers: As regards the number of seeds per pod yielded by cross and self-fertilized flowers, the ratio was 100 to 41 respectively; the crossed seeds compared with an equal number of the spontaneously self-fertilized seeds were heavier, in the ratio of 100 to 88.[2] The ratios thus disclosed in examining a large number of instances could not have been gained by any experimental method adapted for dealing with individual instances. Although the cause is not quantitatively determined, a tendency of a constant nature toward a definite end is clearly indicated.

Race characteristics are often disclosed by comparative statistics, and the presence or absence of causes possessing moral significance are thus revealed which otherwise could

---

[1] Gide, *Political Economy*, p. 405.
[2] Darwin, *Cross and Self Fertilization*, p. 165.

not be determined with any considerable degree of definiteness. The following tables will indicate this:—

Suicides. — In European cities the number of suicides per 100,000 inhabitants is as follows: Paris, 42; Lyons, 29; St. Petersburg, 7; Moscow, 11; Berlin, 36; Vienna, 28; London, 23; Rome, 8; Milan, 6; Madrid, 3; Genoa, 31; Brussels, 15; Amsterdam, 14; Lisbon, 2; Christiania, 25; Stockholm, 27; Constantinople, 12; Geneva, 11; Dresden, 51. Madrid and Lisbon show the lowest, Dresden the highest, figure.

The average annual suicide rate in countries of the world per 100,000 persons living is given by Barker as follows: Saxony, 31.1; Denmark, 25.8; Schleswig-Holstein, 24.0; Austria, 21.2; Switzerland, 20.2; France, 15.7; German Empire, 14.3; Hanover, 14.0; Queensland, 13.5; Prussia, 13.3; Victoria, 11.5; New South Wales, 9.3; Bavaria, 9.1; New Zealand, 9.0; South Australia, 8.9; Sweden, 8.1; Norway, 7.5; Belgium, 6.9; England and Wales, 6.9; Tasmania, 5.3; Hungary, 5.2; Scotland, 4.0; Italy, 3.7; Netherlands, 3.6; United States, 3.5; Russia, 2.9; Ireland, 1.7; Spain, 1.4.

The causes of suicide in European countries are reported as follows: Of 100 suicides: Madness, delirium, 18 per cent; alcoholism, 11; vice, crime, 19; different diseases, 2; moral sufferings, 6; family matters, 4; poverty, want, 4; loss of intellect, 14; consequence of crimes, 3; unknown reasons, 19.

Homicides. — Italy takes the lead of European nations, with an average annual crop of murders of 2470, a ratio per 10,000 deaths of 29.4; Spain follows, with a ratio of 23.8, and 1200 murders; Austria, ratio of 8.8, and 600 murders; France, ratio of 8.0, and 662 murders; England, ratio of 7.1, and 377 murders. The figures, however, represent actual murders, not homicides from all causes, as do those in the United States table.

Illegitimacy. — Of each 1000 births, the number illegitimate, according to statistics published in London, 1892, were: Russia, 27; Ireland, 28; Holland, 33; England and Wales, 46; Switzerland, 47; Italy, 73; Norway, 74; Scotland, 79; Prussia, 80; France, 84; Hungary, 85; Belgium, 88; Denmark, 93; Sweden, 101; Saxony, 125; Bavaria, 141; Austria, 147. No accurate statistics for the United States exist. The lowest rate in Europe is that of Connaught, in Western Ireland, 7 per 1000. — *Dr. Albert Leffingwell, Summit, N.J.*

3. When phenomena indicate a marked departure from the ratio of frequency as determined by prior observation, or by theoretical considerations, then it is ordinarily inferred that a new cause has become operative, which was not before existent, or, whose effect had been neutralized. For instance, we would naturally expect a die to show the face three, on an average, about once in six throws. But if it repeatedly turns up three in succession, and no other number appears, or appears but rarely, we are warranted in inferring that the die is loaded. The number of homicides in the United States in 1894 far exceeded the annual number observed for the several years preceding. This discrepancy is easily accounted for by the fact that the natural number was swollen by the deaths caused by the strikers and rioters in the month of July of that year. So also a marked departure from the annual death-rate of such a city as New York is at once an urgent suggestion to the Board of Health to start investigations that will unearth the hidden cause that one is constrained to believe must be present. Such causes as defective drains, prevalence of epidemics, etc., are again and again found to accompany an increase of the average death-rate.

Under such circumstances, the method of investigation, when practicable, which should be pursued, is to endeavor to break up the total into smaller groups of a specific nature. Thus, if the death-rate for the year is appreciably increased, examine the death-rate per month. See if any month shows a marked departure from the average. If so, this will suggest a careful investigation of the circumstances and characteristics of the month in question. Or it may be possible to make a geographical distribution of the total over different sections of the city under investigation. Some special locality may indicate an unusually large death-rate. Investigation, therefore, at that point may reveal a lurking cause of disease, otherwise unnoticed.

By similar considerations, also, it is often possible to distinguish between a chance coincidence, and a determinate cause which may have produced the event in question. For, if the possibility of some one definite cause is considered out of the question, and the origin of the event is found among complex phenomena of such a number and variety that they may form an indefinite number of combinations, only one of which can possibly produce the event in question, then the probability that the event has actually been produced by such a chance combination is extremely small. We are then thrown back upon the other hypothesis, that, instead of one out of many possible combinations, there is some one determinate cause operative in the case. Its nature may not be definitely indicated, but at least the possibility of its presence is suggested.

This line of reasoning is illustrated in the following account of the discovery of the existence of iron in the sun, in the researches of Bunsen and Kirchhoff: "On comparing the spectra of sunlight and of the light proceeding from the incandescent vapor of iron, it became apparent that at least sixty bright lines in the spectrum of iron coincided with dark lines in the sun's spectrum. Such coincidences could never be observed with certainty, because, even if the lines only closely approached, the instrumental imperfections of the spectroscope would make them apparently coincident, and if one line came within half a millimetre of another, on the map of the spectra, they could not be pronounced distinct. Now the average distance of the solar lines on Kirchhoff's map is two millimetres, and if we throw down a line, as it were by pure chance, on such a map, the probability is about $\frac{1}{2}$ that the new line will fall within one-half millimetre on one side or the other of some one of the solar lines. To put it in another way, we may suppose that each solar line, either on account of its real breadth, or the defects of the instrument, possesses a breadth of one-half millimetre, and that each line in the iron spectrum has a like breadth. The probability, then, is just $\frac{1}{2}$ that the centre of each iron line will come by chance within one millimetre of the centre of a solar line, so as to appear to coincide with it. The probability of casual coincidence of each iron line with a solar line is in like manner $\frac{1}{2}$. Coincidence in the case of each of the sixty iron lines is a very unlikely event if it arises casually, for it would have a probability of only $(\frac{1}{2})^{60}$ or less than one in a trillion. The odds, in short, are more than a million million millions to unity against such a casual coincidence. But on the other hypothesis, that iron exists in the sun, it is highly probable that such coincidences would be observed; it is immensely more probable that sixty coincidences would be observed if iron existed in the sun, than that they should arise from chance. Hence, by our principle, it is immensely probable that iron does exist in the sun."[1]

This principle is also illustrated in instances of circumstantial evidence. In such cases, the observed combination of so many diverse circumstances, even as regards an indefinite number of minor details, precludes the hypothesis of casual coincidence, and suggests some one definite cause that will prove a unifying principle of explanation of all the attendant circumstances. As Mr. Justice Bullen says: "A presumption which necessarily arises from circumstances is very often more convincing and more satisfactory than any other kind of evidence. It is not within the reach and compass of human abilities to invent a train of

[1] Jevons, *Principles of Science*, pp. 244, 245.

circumstances which shall be so connected together as to amount to a proof of guilt without affording opportunities to contradict a great part, if not all, of these circumstances."

The following account, taken from *The New York Law Journal,* illustrates the probative force of circumstantial evidence: —

In Nicholas v. Commonwealth (March 1895, 21 S. E. R. 364) the Supreme Court of Appeals of Virginia sustained a conviction of murder, the criminal agency being established by circumstantial evidence. The following extract from the opinion presents the main facts which implicated the defendant: —

"On the 8th day of December, 1892, Philip Norman Nicholas, the plaintiff in error, one James Mills, and his wife, Anna A. Mills, and their three small children, were living in the upper part of Henrico County, on a farm known as the 'Wickham Place,' about one mile from James River. Nicholas was the renter of this farm, and cultivated it on shares. He was himself, however, chiefly engaged as a trapper, having a number of traps set along both sides of the river. He employed James Mills, with whom he lived, and one William Judson Wilkerson, as sub-tenants, to do the farm work, for a portion of his share of the crops. Wilkerson lived with an aged mother in a small house very near to Mills's house — near enough to see into the windows of one house from the other. Philip N. Nicholas, the prisoner, was an unmarried man, and lived in a room of the house occupied by James Mills and his family. The evidence shows that on the night before the drowning, the prisoner, James Mills, and William J. Wilkerson were together at the house of Mrs. Wilkerson, the latter's mother, and there arranged and determined upon a trip across the river the next morning, to take a bee tree. This expedition was suggested, planned, and carried out by the prisoner. Wilkerson was very unwilling to go, and finally consented at the suggestion of his mother, who said that, as Mr. Nicholas seemed so anxious for him to go, he had better do so. Mills was unwilling to go unless Wilkerson went. Wilkerson said he would rather plough than go. The prisoner replied, 'If you will go, you shall not lose anything.' In the course of conversation which resulted in this expedition being agreed upon, both Mills and Wilkerson stated, in the presence of Nicholas, that they could not swim, and were very much afraid of water; that they did not like water more than knee-deep. The fact that they could not swim was generally known to their friends. It is further shown that it was the habit of Nicholas to go every morning, early, to the river, to examine his traps. And it appears from the evidence that on the morning of the day the drowning occurred he went to the river about daylight, and returned about breakfast time, and, when questioned about it, said: 'I did not go to my traps this morning. I was sick.' He afterwards told Mrs. Wilkerson he did not catch anything. Everything being in readiness to carry out the plan for the day, these three men started from home about nine o'clock in the morning, equipped with everything necessary for taking the bee tree; having with them two buckets holding two and one-half to three gallons each for the honey, two axes, one hatchet, and a piece of netting to protect the person from the bees. The boat used belonged to one Joseph Bruin, and on their way to the river an uncle of the owner was asked if they might use the boat, and was told they could get the key which unlocked the boat from its fastening to the bank from Bruin, the owner. The prisoner replied that he had a key of his own, and had often used it before without permission. It appears that they landed on the Chesterfield side of the river, at a point one mile and a half from where any one lived, and proceeded to the bee tree, which was one mile from the point of landing. Investigation showed that there were no tracks about the point of landing but those of the three men going from and returning to the boat. It further appears from the statement of the prisoner that after reaching the tree they concluded not to cut it, because it was a large tree, near the main road, and might get them into trouble, and for the further reason that the hole was small, and it might not have any honey in it anyhow. The tree was afterwards cut by order of the Magistrate and found to be full of honey. It further appears that the boat was a small one, about ten feet long and about two and one-half feet wide, and that both in going over and returning the prisoner sat in the extreme rear of the boat, with his face to the front, and that Wilkerson and Mills sat in front of him, with their faces to the front and their backs to the accused. This position of the parties the prisoner admitted very reluctantly, when questioned about it. When returning, and about fifty yards from the Henrico shore, the boat suddenly filled with water, and Mills and Wilkerson were drowned, and the prisoner swam to shore. The next day the Magistrate of the district was notified of the occurrence, and an investigation was set on foot. The boat was gotten out of the water, and it was found that immediately under the seat where Nicholas sat there were three holes, freshly bored with an inch and a half auger. The evidence of the owner of the boat shows that on Tuesday evening, the 6th of December, he used his boat, and it was sound. It was taken by Nicholas for this fatal trip Thursday morning, the 8th of December. Further investigation discovered fresh pine shavings corresponding to size of the holes and to the wood the boat was made of, which had been thrown into the water, but had drifted upon the shore near the point where the boat had stood fastened to the Henrico side. There were also found corn-cobs which had been cut to exactly fit the holes in the boat, which had also drifted to the same point. It was shown that the prisoner had in his possession an auger just the size of the holes. This the prisoner at first denied, but afterwards said that it must be about the place somewhere. Diligent search was made for the auger, but it was never found.

"Taken together, the case is an interesting illustration of the conclusive probative force of circumstantial evidence, provided there is enough of it. The old saying that 'murder will out' is almost unexceptionally true as to murders of elaborate stealth and complexity of detail. Once let a clue be obtained to the chain of causation and motive, and the mystery unravels almost of itself. It is quite natural that most of the elaborately planned murders of recent times should have been by poison. And the Harris, Buchanan, and Meyer cases in New York disclose how comparatively easy detection and conviction are in crimes of such class. It is significant that two of the greatest enigmas in American criminal annals during the last quarter of a century have been the Nathan murder and the Borden murder. In both cases the killing was done not by methods calculated to conceal the agency of a murderer, but in the most primitive and brutal manner. No traceable physical clue to any particular person was left, and we are inclined to believe that in both cases the connection of the murderer with the crime was merely casual or accidental."[1]

In the various illustrations which have been given we find that the theory of probability provides a method of dealing with phenomena which cannot be subjected to the ordinary inductive methods. The phenomena are so complex that a specific cause cannot be determined, for the real cause in question is a correlation of many diverse forces, and if only a few instances are examined no causal connection will be disclosed; it is necessary, therefore, to deal with large numbers, statistical averages, etc., in order to detect an emerging relation of a causal character, expressed by a

[1] *The New York Law Journal*, Thursday, May 2, 1895.

constant ratio. This ratio once determined, it becomes a further test, as we have already seen, when the results widely depart from it, to suggest the presence of a new force outside of the combinations to which the effect would be naturally referred according to the indications of the probability-ratio. This latter mode of inference is akin to the method of residues, for the inference in question is based upon the fact that the probability-ratio will account for only a certain frequency of occurrence of the event under investigation; a marked excess must be accounted for by positing a definitely operative cause. And if an antecedent of such a nature is known to be present, the suggestion at once rises in our thought that this in all probability is the cause producing this excess in the results.

CHAPTER XV

EMPIRICAL LAWS

There is a class of laws which are intermediate between a universal, inductively grounded by scientific determination, and a law of tendency which expresses the probability of the happening of an event in spite of recognized exceptions. These are laws which have been observed to obtain under given conditions of time, place, and circumstance, and yet the causal relation not sufficiently determined to warrant a necessary extension of the same to a sphere beyond that wherein it has been observed to be operative. Such laws are known as Empirical Laws.

We have three classes of laws possessing varying degrees of probability. (1) The first is where there has been a scientifically determined causal connection between antecedent and consequent; and not only have no exceptions been noted, but the possibility of there being an exception has been eliminated by strict experimental methods. (2) The second is where the regularity of sequence has been broken by actual exceptions, and the result of the observations of instances gives an indication only of the relative frequency of occurrence and failure which will probably characterize other events of that nature. (3) The third class and, as has been said, an intermediate class, comprises all expressions of uniform sequence or coexistence, where no exception whatsoever has been noted, and yet there is no ground for necessitating a universal expression of the observed uniformity. There is here always a possibility of an exception appearing, or of an exception having been overlooked. This produces an element of uncertainty which pervades all phenomena of this sort.

There are several kinds of empirical laws, as follows: —

1. Where the causal relation is in process of scientific determination; a uniform connection between phenomena has been observed, and as yet has not been proved. All laws, finally determined as expressions of causal connection, pass through this empirical stage. Some expressions of uniform relations never pass beyond this stage, because, as we have seen, the nature of the phenomena may be such as to preclude all experiment or even indirect verification.

Empirical laws may become ultimate laws or derivative laws, as the case may be. Ultimate laws are those wherein the causal relation between a simple antecedent and its corresponding consequent has been scientifically determined in terms of their exact quantitative variation, and expressed in the simplest form possible. The derivative laws however as the name indicates, are more concrete expressions of the ultimate and simpler laws to which they are referred as special cases. An empirical law may be proved directly an ultimate law, or be proved a derivative law directly traceable to an ultimate law, as its basis, or logical ground. We may observe that a glass of ice-water always shows drops of moisture on its outer surface. This uniformity as thus expressed has the force only of an empirical law. No attempt having been made, as yet, to explain the presence of the moisture, its empirical nature is evident. But as soon as the moisture on the glass is traced to the condensation of the moisture in the atmosphere owing to the difference of temperature between the atmosphere and the cold surface of the glass, we have the empirical law becoming a derivative law; that is, the expression of a uniform sequence directly traceable to the more ultimate laws of the saturation and condensation of vapors. The progress of scientific and logically accurate thought is always marked, therefore, by the resolution of empirical generalities into derivative or ultimate laws.

2. The character of an empirical law is attached to the relation existing between antecedent and consequent, when that relation is a complex one in which a simple causal relation is so involved with other elements entering into combination with it, that its real nature is thus hidden and cannot readily be disclosed. This class includes all causal relations due to collocations of various kinds that are necessary to produce the required effect. As Mill has pointed out: "It is the nature of an empirical law that we do not know whether it results from the different effects of one cause or the effects of different causes. We cannot tell whether it depends wholly upon laws, or partly upon laws and partly upon a collocation. If it depends upon a collocation, it will be true in all the cases in which that particular collocation exists. But since we are entirely ignorant, in case of its depending upon a collocation, what the collocation is, we are not safe in extending the law beyond the limits of time and place in which we have actual experience of its truth. Knowing of no rule or principle to which the collocations themselves conform, we cannot conclude that because a collocation is proved to exist within certain limits of place or time, it will exist beyond those limits."[1]

There are many illustrations of such observed generalities where the effect is due largely, if not altogether, to collocations. The effect of certain medicines upon the human system, the opening and shutting of some flowers at certain hours of the day, the local action of tides at various places on the earth's surface, the adaptation of certain plants to a peculiar kind of soil, the reappearance of some chronic diseases, as hay-fever, at the same season each year, even to the very day of the month, — all such generalities have merely an empirical weight, and the effects mentioned are largely due to collocations that cannot be definitely determined. So

[1] Mill, *Logic*, Book III, Chap. XVI, § 4.

also certain laws or customs may have proved beneficial in the countries in which they have been tried, and yet, in countries where condition and circumstance are radically different, they may fail wholly of beneficial results. There may be also certain industrial circumstances which in one country might be conducive to prosperity, and in another country to adversity. Certain agricultural methods which in one section of the country tend to an increase of productive power, in another might prove a complete failure. A governmental policy may in one country lead to unparalleled success; in another, however, a like policy might lead to disastrous results.

The famous formula of Malthus, that population tends to increase in a geometrical progression, whilst the means of subsistence can only increase in an arithmetical progression, can have only an empirical force. Its extension into an indefinite future is unwarrantable. As is known, production has increased enormously and at a ratio vastly greater than any contemplated by Malthus as at all in the range of possibility. Many causes, on the other hand, may combine to check the rapid increase of population. The collocations here are so complex as to defy any definite prediction. This is true of all tendencies which are due to present social conditions; the conditions themselves may so vary in time to come as to change totally the accepted generalizations of to-day. Their empirical character is therefore most evident.

3. A third class of empirical laws comprises all those generalizations which represent a correlation of properties in the same individual. In all such cases no causal relation has been specifically determined between the properties themselves, or between the properties and the whole in which they coinhere. Outside of our experience, the properties observed might be materially changed, and yet not affect the integrity of the concept in general. A proposition such as, All swans are white, can have only empirical

force; for beyond our experience, the discovery of black swans would forbid the proposition being regarded in the light of a universal. Many properties of substances are thus referred to the nature of the substance itself as their ground, and yet because the exact causal relation is not determined, the connection can be considered only as an empirical one. In other words, reference to some ground as explanation of a phenomenon, without explaining why or how such reference is made, has always the force of an empirical law only. The following are empirical generalizations of this nature: Copper is ductile; steel is elastic; glass is brittle and transparent; the compound silicates of alkalies and alkaline metals are transparent; and other instances of like nature that can be multiplied indefinitely.

In the sphere of biology, Mr. Spencer has drawn attention to the fact that "during the era in which uniformity of many quite simple inorganic relations was still unrecognized, certain organic relations, intrinsically very complex and special, were generalized. The constant coexistence of feathers and a beak, of four legs with an internal bony framework, are facts which were, and are, familiar to every savage. Did a savage find a bird with teeth, or a mammal clothed with feathers, he would be as much surprised as an instructed naturalist. Now these uniformities of organic structure, thus early perceived, are of exactly the same kind as those more numerous ones later established by biology. The constant coexistence of mammary glands with two occipital condyles to the skull, of vertebræ with teeth lodged in sockets, of frontal horns with the habit of rumination, are generalizations as purely empirical as those known to the original hunter. The botanist cannot in the least understand the complex relation between papilionaceous flowers and seeds borne in flattened pods; he knows these and like connections simply in the same way that the barbarian knows the connections between particular leaves and particular kinds of wood."[1] Such knowledge as Mr. Spencer here describes is a knowledge of the coexistence of two phenomena in their totality which resist all attempts to analyze into their component parts. Moreover, laws which are but general descriptions of correlated events have the same force as the descriptions of coinhering attributes of substances. They, too, rank as empirical generalizations. The successive stages in the growth of a plant from seed to flower and fruit, the embryonic as well as the post-natal developments in animal life, the habits and instincts of animals,—all these are descriptive generalizations without any attempt at causal determination.

4. All generalizations expressed in terms of probability only, because of known exceptions, rank as empirical laws. Here, even in the time, place, and circumstance of observation, the law has not been found always valid. The significance of an empirical law, if we allow this latter class to be included under them, is evidently that of the contradictory of a law which is the result of a causal determination. Every generalization not causally determined is then to be regarded as an empirical law. There is, however, a narrower usage of the term which does not include this latter class; namely, a restriction of the term empirical law to signify the expression of a relation which has been found constant throughout the sphere of observation, and yet where there exists no known causal ground by reason of which we would be warranted in inferring the continuation of this relation in a sphere beyond that already observed. We might add that with this there is also the expectation, greater or less, according to the circumstances attending the phenomena, that the generalized experience will be further confirmed by subsequent observation in a wider sphere. This restricted meaning of an empirical law is the one generally understood, unless it is implied to the contrary.

[1] Spencer, *Classification of the Sciences*, p. 53.

An empirical uniformity generally results from the method of agreement. Observed instances, even so selected as to vary the antecedents as much as possible, cannot alone establish a law of uniformity that shall have universal validity. The method of agreement, we have seen, needed to be supplemented by the method of difference if possible, or by an hypothesis capable of subsequent verification. An empirical law is, therefore, due either to some deficiency in method, or to the natural limitations of our knowledge.

The element of uncertainty attached to all inferences depending upon the extension of an empirical law into unknown territory, it has been insisted upon, may apply equally as well to all inferences depending upon the results of the inductive methods even when most scientifically determined. It is contended that even a causal relation, however firmly grounded, and however simple may be its nature, nevertheless presents an empirical character. It may give assurances of a high degree of probability, but can never produce absolute certitude in our minds. Mr. Venn, for instance, has styled his work on induction, *Empirical Logic*, that by the title he might indicate his point of view in this regard. He says in the preface to his work: "By the introduction of the term empirical into the title, I wish to emphasize my belief that no ultimate objective certainty, such as Mill, for instance, seemed to attribute to the results of induction, is attainable by any exercise of the human reason." Regarded in this light, all laws are empirical.

The distinction, however, between empirical laws in the sense generally understood, and laws expressing causal relations scientifically determined, is a real distinction, and a significant one as well. And this must not be overlooked; and it cannot be obliterated by any shifting of the point of view. For, to doubt the validity of an empirical law when extended to a sphere beyond that which has been observed, casts a reflection merely upon one's ability adequately to determine the connections existing between the various elements involved in the particular phenomena under investigation. This is, however, no confession of inability to discover the causal connections of phenomena in general, in such a manner as to determine laws of universal validity. To say that all laws have only empirical significance is to reflect upon the basal postulates of knowledge. Our world is the world as we know it, the world of our consciousness. To discredit the uniformities and regularities therein existing, and which find expression in universal laws, is to discredit that which we feel obliged to think in order that our world of knowledge regarded as a system may remain consistent with itself, part to part, and part to whole. We must, therefore, regard an empirical law not as the final form of knowledge, or the goal of inductive research, but rather as marking a transition stage toward complete causal determination. And even when, owing to the nature of certain phenomena, we are not able to pass beyond this transition stage of empirical determination, nevertheless, such instances by contrast bear unimpeachable testimony to the fact that there are other phenomena of such a nature that it is possible to subject them to an analysis which will disclose causal connections of such a character as to form a basis for the formulation of universal laws.

CHAPTER XVI

INDUCTIVE FALLACIES

A CONSIDERATION of the various kinds of inductive fallacies, and their characteristic features, may be regarded as the obverse representation of the general theory of induction. From the one point of view we consider the positive conditions of true inductive inference; from the obverse point of view we regard the various breaches of these inductive conditions. The discussion of fallacies, therefore, indicates no progress in the elucidation of the subject under consideration; it rather serves to emphasize distinctions and requirements already indicated by presenting them in a new light, and from a different angle. The subject of fallacies is generally treated by exhibiting through various illustrations the cases in which the positive conditions of inductive inference have failed of satisfactory fulfilment. Such illustrations of the infringement of the requirements of valid induction, I have endeavored to incorporate in the body of the text in connection with the exposition of the various conditions and requirements themselves. In this chapter I shall attempt to indicate those fallacies especially which are due to the psychological disturbance of our normal logical processes. An enumeration of these tendencies, partly psychological and partly logical, may serve to impress upon us the danger of falling into easy errors, to which the human mind generally is liable. These errors emerge in the various mental processes. They are as follows: —

    I. Errors of Perception.
    II. Errors of Judgment.
    III. Errors of the Imagination.
    IV. Errors of the Conceptual Processes.

I. *Errors of Perception.* — Observation is the instrument of research preëminently, in all inductive inquiry. Experiment is but a method for increased facility and accuracy of observation. We may say therefore that all the data of inductive inference are furnished by this one process, observation. Any derangement of our powers of observation will affect the nature of the data, and therefore the nature of the results of induction. It becomes therefore all important that we should be appraised at least of the various circumstances whose tendency it is to operate in the midst of the perceptive processes as disturbing forces. We have the following possibilities of error in the sphere of perception: —

1. Errors due to a failure to take in the whole field of vision. There may be portions omitted which possess a determining significance as regards the object of investigation. Thus exceptions may be overlooked that might have an important bearing upon some received hypothesis; or a fact might be passed by which, if known, would prove highly suggestive. Various devices have been employed to enlarge the sphere of observation beyond the natural limits of the senses. As, for instance, sounds which are inaudible to us may be detected by means of a sensitive flame; the telescope, the microscope, serve to render the distant near, and the small large. It had been noted that there was a sudden elongation of an iron wire at a particular temperature whilst under longitudinal strain during the act of cooling from a red heat; an additional circumstance was noted by Professor Barrett when performing the experiment in a darkened room, namely, that at the moment of elongation the wire suddenly evolved heat, and exhibited a visible and conspicuous momentary glow of redness.[1] This circumstance it would be impossible to note unless in a darkened room. Thus, a prominent characteristic of scientific observation is the endeavor to extend continually the sphere of

[1] Gore, *The Art of Scientific Discovery,* p. 321.

observation. Here also much depends upon the mental habit. There are some who naturally see wider and farther than others. And it is absolutely necessary that the true observer should cultivate with all assiduity such a habit when it is not a natural possession. There is a slovenliness in observation which gives to the inferences based upon its results a color of indefiniteness and inaccuracy, and which proves a fertile source of error.

It also often happens, that, owing to the mind being prepossessed by a certain idea or theory, research will be thereby restricted to a limited region, and neighboring regions be wholly overlooked. An open-eyed vision, in spite of all preconceptions or prejudices, is the prime requisite for securing from all quarters the greatest possible array of facts that may in any way tend to the formation of a clearer and more adequate judgment.

2. A second error of observation arises from an opposite mental habit, a failure properly to concentrate the attention upon the relevant facts and so to discriminate as to exclude from consciousness, for the time being at least, all irrelevant details. The lack of such a discriminating faculty leads either to error, or to the dearth of all significant results. It is necessary to avoid either extreme, so that there may be a sweeping survey of all the possible facts relevant to the subject under investigation, combined at the same time with a concentration of attention that is the prerequisite of a deep insight into the inner connections and interrelations of these facts. There must be a depth as well as a wideness of vision.

There are also errors arising from a failure to note significant differences in phenomena that present striking surface resemblances. Here the closest scrutiny is necessary. The older chemists could not distinguish potash from soda; baryta and strontia were formerly confounded together, so also potash and cæsia. Throughout the whole realm of scientific research, it should be ever kept prominently in mind that surface differences may hide essential resemblances, and that surface resemblances may hide essential differences.

3. Errors may arise from apperceptive projection. Here the objective elements of perception combine with the subjective, so that the complete perception may contain elements which do not correspond with reality. The mind thus projects upon the field of vision its own coloring. We see often that which we wish to see, and fail to see that which we do not wish to see. When palladium was originally made known to the public, Chenevix proceeded to examine it, prepossessed with the idea that it was an alloy of some two known metals. This idea was so projected upon his experiments, that he at last came to the conclusion that it was a compound of platinum and mercury. Chenevix was led into an error of observation, as was afterwards proved by Dr. Wollaston, who himself had obtained palladium from the solution of crude platina in aqua regia.[1] This error of observation was due to the fact that he approached the experiments with a fixed idea in his mind as to what they should prove; and being determined to see evidences of this in the phenomena, he unconsciously read into them that which was not really there.

II. *Errors of Judgment.* — These errors occur in the interpretation of the data of perception. For that which is observed must be referred to its appropriate place in the body of knowledge regarded as a system, in which, part must fit to part, and part to whole. Inaccurate reference results in manifest imperfections and incongruities in that part of the system of knowledge to which the reference has been made. And the inferences based thereupon are naturally affected by this fundamental error of judgment. These errors are as follows: —

1. Errors due to false associations. Here, where artificial or superficial associations are interpreted as though they

[1] Gore, *The Art of Scientific Discovery.*

were real causal connections, the mistake may prove most serious. The most fertile source of such fallacies is the wrong interpretation of space and time associations, regarding mere contiguity in space and time as evidence of causal connection. Under this head may be classed the fallacies, *non causa pro causa* and *post hoc ergo propter hoc*. Prosperity, for instance, following the enactment of certain industrial or tariff measures, is often attributed as the effect of the same, merely because they appear in striking sequence. However, it may be that the prosperity has followed in spite of the laws and not on account of them.

2. Errors of judgment due to emotional perturbations. When the intellect is deflected from its true pointing by passion, or prejudice, or superstition, or any strong emotion, the consequent judgment is the resultant of two forces, rather than the expression of one. As Bacon says: "The human understanding resembles not a dry light, but admits a tincture of the will, and passions which generate their own systems accordingly; for man always believes more readily that which he prefers; his feelings imbue and corrupt his understanding in innumerable and sometimes imperceptible ways."[1]

The necessity of judging in a "dry light," as far as possible, is especially emphasized in the ethical positions of Adam Smith, and later of Mr. Sidgwick. Adam Smith contends that one's duty must be estimated from the standpoint of an impartial spectator and critic. That is, man must, as it were, step out of himself, leaving feeling behind, and judge of himself and of his duty from a purely objective point of view. So also Mr. Sidgwick says that one of the chief difficulties in the utilitarian position, namely, the discrepancy between the egoistic and altruistic claims upon our activities, cannot be harmonized satisfactorily, when stated as a problem of mere feeling. Here again man must eliminate feeling and judge of himself merely as one among many,

[1] Bacon, *Novum Organum*, Book I, Aphorism XLIX.

where each counts for one and no one for more than one. In the light of pure reason he may be able to see that the good of all is his highest good. But when that dry light is colored by feeling, such judgment is impossible.

Faraday, in his *Observations on Mental Education*, has borne testimony directly to the necessity of eliminating feeling from our judgments. He says: "The tendency to deceive ourselves regarding all we wish for should be kept in mind, and the necessity also of resistance to these desires. The force of the temptation which urges us to seek for such evidence and appearances as are in favor of our desires, and to disregard those which oppose them, is wonderfully great. In this respect we are all more or less active promoters of error. I will simply express my strong belief that that point of self-education which consists in teaching the mind to resist its desires and inclinations until they are proved to be right, is the most important of all, not only in things of natural philosophy, but in every department of daily life."[1]

3. Errors of judgment due to the common frailties of human nature. Such errors Bacon has styled "Idols." His enumeration is not only complete, but is classic in its way, and therefore I quote it at this place: "Four species of idols beset the human mind, to which, for distinction's sake, we have assigned names, calling the first Idols of the Tribe, the second Idols of the Den, the third Idols of the Market, the fourth Idols of the Theatre.

"The formation of notions and axioms on the foundation of true induction is the only fitting remedy by which we can ward off and expel these idols. It is, however, of great service to point them out; for the doctrine of idols bears the same relation to the interpretation of nature as that of the confutation of sophisms does to common logic. The idols of the tribe are inherent in human nature, and the very tribe or race of man; for man's sense is falsely asserted

[1] Gladstone, *Michael Faraday*, p. 128.

to be the standard of things; on the contrary, all the perceptions, both of the senses and the mind, bear reference to man and not to the universe, and the human mind is like those uneven mirrors which impart their own properties to different objects from which rays are emitted, and distort and disfigure them.

"The idols of the den are those of each individual, for everybody (in addition to the errors common to the race of man) has his own individual den or cavern which intercepts and corrupts the light of nature, either from his own peculiar and singular disposition, or from his education and intercourse with others, or from his reading, and the authority acquired by those whom he reverences and admires, or from the different impressions produced on the mind as it happened to be preoccupied and predisposed, or equable and tranquil, and the like; so that the spirit of man (according to its several dispositions) is variable, confused, and as it were actuated by chance; and Heraclitus said well that men search for knowledge in lesser worlds, and not in the greater or common world.

"There are also idols formed by the reciprocal intercourse and society of man with man, which we call idols of the market, from the commerce and association of men with each other; for men converse by means of language, but words are formed at the will of the generality, and there arises from a bad and unapt formation of words a wonderful obstruction to the mind. Nor can the definitions and explanations with which learned men are wont to guard and protect themselves in some instances, afford a complete remedy, — words still manifestly force the understanding, throw everything into confusion, and lead mankind into vain and innumerable controversies and fallacies.

"Lastly, there are idols which have crept into men's minds from the various dogmas of peculiar systems of philosophy, and also from the perverted rules of demonstration, and these we denominate idols of the theatre; for we regard all the systems of philosophy hitherto received or imagined, as so many plays brought out and performed, creating fictions and theatrical worlds. Nor do we allude merely to general systems, but also to many elements and axioms of sciences which have become inveterate by tradition, implicit credence, and neglect."[1]

All such tendencies, as thus presented by Bacon, clog and hamper the normal functioning of the judgment. The mind must be alert and on guard to eliminate such fatal seeds of error.

III. *Errors due to the Imagination.* — Here the imagination supplies inner connections and relations, lying beyond the sphere of observation, in order to explain the nature of the observed phenomena themselves. The danger here is that the elements supplied in order to make the self-consistent whole do not correspond to reality. The system, regarded as a mental construction, may be complete in all of its coördinated parts, and nevertheless possess no objective reality. Under this head fall all loosely constructed hypotheses. In the framing of an hypothesis in general, the imagination functions very largely. It is the inner vision that represents to the mind the things not seen. Moreover, the imagination is peculiarly liable to error, and to swing clear of the trammels of fact, and in the region of pure fancy construct systems that rest upon no solid basis of reality. These dangers in detail have been pointed out in the chapter on hypothesis.

The most fertile source of error, however, arises from that natural elation of mind upon the discovery even of slight confirming evidence of the truth of the assumed hypothesis. This enthusiasm is apt to magnify unduly an inadequate verification, and to rest satisfied in an hypothesis that is grounded upon an insufficient basis. Thus, since the year 1770, more than forty discoveries of new elementary substances have been announced to the world by enthusi-

[1] Bacon, *Novum Organum*, Book I, Aphorisms XXXIX, etc.

astic experimenters, and, in all cases, their discoveries have been proved to be absolutely worthless. For instance, it was confidently announced that Torbern Bergmann, in 1777, had extracted from diamonds what he considered to be a new earth, and called it "terra nobilis." Wedgwood, in 1790, discovered "australia" in sand obtained from the continent of that name; but Hatchett proved it to be merely a mixture of silica, alumina, oxide of iron, and plumbago. In 1805 Richter discovered "niccolanium"; it was afterwards proved to be a mixture of iron, cobalt, nickel, and arsenic. These instances are but a few of the many which characterize the history of chemical research, and stand as conspicuous witnesses of the danger of divorcing fancy from fact.

The imagination however properly constrained is most potent in suggesting possible causal relations, in constructing hypotheses, in devising methods of experiment in order to verify them, and in forming universal concepts in which all the particulars of observation must coinhere. Davy and Faraday were both conspicuous in this mental characteristic. And to this source their eminent discoveries may be traced. Dr. Whewell says, for instance, of Faraday: "In discovering the nature of voltaic action, the essential intellectual requisite was to have a distinct conception of that which Faraday expressed by the remarkable phrase, '*An axis of power having equal and opposite forces.*' And the distinctness of this idea in Faraday's mind shines forth in every part of his writings. He appears to possess the idea of this kind of force with the same eminent distinctness with which Archimedes in the ancient and Stevinus in the modern history of science possessed the idea of pressure, and were thus able to found the idea of mechanics. And when Faraday cannot obtain these distinct modes of conception, he is dissatisfied and conscious of defect."[1]

It is indeed a touch of genius that enables one to grasp

[1] Whewell, *History of Inductive Sciences*, Vol. III, 3d ed., p. 147.

and formulate a central idea that will unify and also universalize a large body of seemingly disconnected and incongruous facts. But such an idea must be the expression of the relations actually obtaining, and no subjective fancy projected upon the phenomena themselves, however clever or ingenious such an imaginative creation may be. If one were asked what is the most efficient instrument of scientific research, the answer must be, "The Imagination!" And if one were asked what is the most fertile source of error, the answer likewise must be, "The Imagination!" It must also be remembered that it is not sufficient merely that an hypothesis should be in harmony with the facts in the case; it must be proved, also, that the facts are connected with the hypothesis through necessary links.

And it is well, also, to bear this in mind when arguing against a rival hypothesis that may have been advanced by an opponent who has claimed for it only the possibility of its validity, and who has not affirmed its necessity. It is manifestly unfair, as well as fallacious, to deny the possibility of the hypothesis merely by indicating certain uncertainties connected with establishing it. To contradict possibility, one must prove the hypothesis impossible. Regarding such a conflict between rival hypotheses Ueberweg suggestively comments as follows: "In cases of this kind, it is one of the hardest of scientific and ethical problems to give fair play to one's opponent. Our own prejudices are sure to influence us. Yet the effect of the influence of another's standpoint, when it is reached, is of immense value in scientific knowledge. Polemic easily leads to exasperation; it is easy both to abuse it and to let it alone because of dislike to the conflicts which it produces; but it is difficult to recognize it, and use it in the right sense as the necessary form which the labor of investigation always takes. Man never attains to a scientific knowledge of the truth without a rightly conducted battle of scientifically justifiable hypotheses, the one against the other: the scientific guidance of this battle is the *true dialectic method.*"[1]

IV. *Errors of the Conceptual Processes.* — This class of errors arises in the formation of general concepts and their expression in universal laws. The natural tendency of the mind to generalize often leads to ill-considered results. The universal unites many differences into an identity, and the mind will readily minimize the differences in order to form a desired universal; thus disparate attributes may be incorrectly coördinated in one and the same system. Herschel has remarked that hasty generalization is the bane of science. And Bacon has said our intellects want not wings, but rather weights of lead to moderate their course.

The method of agreement, when relied upon to the exclusion of further experimental determination, is a fertile source of error in this respect. The possibility of a plurality of causes should be ever kept prominently in mind. One readily assigns an effect to a causal element which is only partially its cause; the consequent generalization is, therefore, incorrect. For instance, it often happens that activities of young animals are described as instinctive and congenital; and universal propositions are founded thereupon. And yet it may be that the activities referred solely to instinct are due partially to imitation. In order to avoid this error and eliminate the factor of imitation, investigators in this line are accustomed to study the activities of animals hatched in incubators and purposely kept from all of their kind. This illustration will serve to show the precautions that must be taken in order to eliminate all possible error from the data which the process of generalization constructs into universal forms. So also inaccuracies in any of the other inductive methods lead to gross errors in the consequent generalizations based upon them.

Under this head, also, are the fallacies resulting from the extension of empirical laws to spheres beyond the experience

[1] Ueberweg, *A System of Logic,* etc., p. 509.

which they embody and express. This source of error is especially illustrated in laws expressing some quantitative relation between antecedent and consequent; it is a natural supposition in such cases, and yet a misleading one oftentimes, that a simple proportional relation will exist between phenomena of the same nature, but with greater or lesser magnitude, as the case may be. Bacon gives the following illustrations of this fallacy: "Suppose a leaden ball of a pound weight, let fall from a steeple, reaches the earth in ten seconds, will a ball of two pounds, where the power of natural motion, as they call it, should be double, reach it in five? No, they will fall almost in equal times, and not be accelerated according to quantity. Suppose a drachm of sulphur would liquefy half a pound of steel, will, therefore, an ounce of sulphur liquefy four pounds of steel? It does not follow; for the stubbornness of the matter in the patient is more increased by quantity than the activity of the agent. Besides, too much as well as too little may frustrate the effect,—thus, in smelting and refining of metals it is a common error to increase the heat of the furnace or the quantity of the flux; but if these exceed a due proportion, they prejudice the operation, because by their force and corrosiveness they turn much of the pure metal into fumes, and carry it off, whence there ensues not only a loss in the metal, but the remaining mass becomes more sluggish and intractable. Men should, therefore, remember how Æsop's housewife was deceived, who expected that by doubling her feed her hen should lay two eggs a day; but the hen grew fat and laid none. It is absolutely unsafe to rely upon any natural experiment before proof be made of it, both in a less and a larger quantity."[1]

Another fallacy of the same order often occurs in the inference concerning the interpolated elements of a series whose successive values have not all been observed. The inference extends the nature of the known to the unknown

[1] Bacon, *Advancement of Learning*, Book V, Chap. II, p. 190.

parts, and presumes that the intermediate links between actually observed parts of the series are in accordance with the general nature of the latter. Such inferences very often give correct results, as, in the plotting of a curve, some salient points may be determined according to observed quantitative variations, and the remaining portions supplied, as upon the above supposition. This extension to cover intermediate and unobserved instances may, however, be sometimes very fallacious. For a force may be assumed to be such that its effects increase steadily, and it may be that they operate periodically; interpolation upon one assumed basis when the other is the true one would of course introduce grave errors. To eliminate such errors, devices have in many cases been resorted to by which a self-registering apparatus will record all successive values of the phenomena under investigation.

Under the fallacies of hasty generalization naturally fall all provincialisms which arise from a narrow nature and habit of mind. The local traditions and superstitions, the prevailing winds, the social customs and manners, are taken as types of a universal experience. The inferential widening of the circle of a limited experience is always provocative of false inference and misleading results.

We have also false analogies which consist in the extension of our experience of certain phenomena that we have observed to be alike in some respects to include other attributes not observed, concerning which we assume a corresponding similarity; the abuse of final causes may be regarded as a special case of false analogy. Moreover, a tendency to consider causation in the light exclusively of final causes has often retarded the advance of science, in withdrawing the attention and energies of the investigator from a search after physical causes, as, for instance, among the ancients it was declared that the leaves of the trees are to defend the fruit from the sun and wind. Resting satisfied in such an explanation, the precise function of the leaves in the economy of the plant's growth was not further investigated, and thus progress was impossible.

Again, incorrect classification is a source of error. In grouping together disparate phenomena, we have a basis for forming a generic concept that will include incompatible species, or, in other words, a universal that will have evident exceptions. Moreover, if the classification is partial, the resulting laws based upon it will have only empirical force.

I have endeavored in this chapter to indicate errors that are mainly psychological in their origin, for two reasons. In the first place, such errors operate as disturbing forces in the midst of purely logical processes. The data of inference are psychological as regards their source, and errors thus originating affect the inference based upon them, appearing in the final result as logical fallacies. An error of observation becomes an error in the judgment that is based upon the original perception, and perdures in the hypothesis, classification, etc., founded on that judgment, and finally emerges in the conclusions based upon these processes. In the second place, the fallacies that are purely formal, and in the strict sense logical, are not as apt to deceive and mislead the mind. In the material data especially lurk the germs of fallacy. On the theory that it is wiser and also more logical to stamp out an error in its incipiency, I have placed special emphasis upon the various psychological processes as initial sources of error. Moreover, it is more rational to deal with errors of process rather than flaws of product. A machine that turns out imperfect articles could have its imperfections rectified by repairing each article thus produced; or the machine itself could be readjusted so as to produce the articles without flaw. It is needless to say which method is the more logical, and most satisfactory, as well.

The desideratum is accurate and comprehensive observation; a discriminating judgment formed in the "dry light" of reason; an imagination that has deep insight into the heart of surface appearances; and powers of generalization which transcend observed phenomena by adequately interpreting them.

CHAPTER XVII

THE INDUCTIVE METHODS AS APPLIED TO THE VARIOUS SCIENCES

The nature of each separate science will determine certain peculiarities of method for that science; and its peculiar method will be largely a matter of growth, as experience accredits or discredits the various results which its operation may attain. It will thus be corrected or supplemented according as it stands the test of achieved results. There are, however, some general features, and especially some natural limitations of the inductive methods, that may be properly indicated.

I. In the first place, the nature of the method used, and its efficiency, as measured by its results, will be found to vary as the nature of the phenomena themselves. Some phenomena admit of analysis and determination by experiment. Instead of attempting to determine the relation of a complex antecedent to a complex consequent, the antecedent is first separated into its component parts, and each element is tested alone in order to disclose its precise effect. The relation can then be expressed between the simple antecedent and simple consequent, as a causal connection; and it admits, moreover, of a quantitative determination as well. Such a method of procedure by analytical experiment enables us to rise to laws having universal validity. This method is characteristic, especially, of the physical sciences, because the phenomena readily admit of resolution into component parts, and the isolation of one simple force so as to determine its total effect. The physical forces are most readily adaptable to experiment. They therefore afford the widest field for the application of the experimental method of inductive inquiry. Moreover, we may readily predict the results of a combination of simple forces, when we know the laws governing their component elements. The inducto-deductive method, therefore, becomes especially efficient in extending the domain of the physical sciences. Here, also, mathematical analysis and calculation is most valuable as an aid to experimental investigation, and in determining quantitative relations as necessitated by the mathematical laws to which the data gathered inductively must conform.

There are however sciences which present phenomena of such a high degree of complexity that an analysis of a complex whole into its separate parts or elements of force is impossible. Moreover, the phenomena cannot be analyzed so that a certain part of the complex whole can be indicated as the complete antecedent, and the remaining portion as the entire consequent. The difficulty therefore is twofold; it is impossible to separate the complex whole into two other complex wholes, antecedent and consequent, and still further impossible to separate such antecedent and consequent, even if they could be determined, into their simplest component parts. The phenomena presented are here not in the form of a sequence so often as in that of coexistence, as in the sciences of botany, zoölogy, and the like. Here the methods of analogy and classification must be resorted to, and we obtain descriptive laws as the result.

The forces manifested in the processes of vital growth are especially difficult to determine by experiment; for they not only operate to produce certain effects, but are conserved in the effects so as to produce certain other effects in a process of continuous construction. Separation by mechanical analysis means instant cessation of the process itself. Dissection means death. Here then is a natural limitation. Moreover, the laws of development are further modified by external changes. The result of the inner force and the outer influences working together complicates the problems to such an extent that the pure inductive methods are well-nigh impossible of application. Resort is then had to determination by statistical methods. Large groups of plants and animals are examined for the purpose of noting tendencies disclosed in the aggregate, but hidden as regards their manifestation in the individual. Here of course classification is an aid in disclosing similarities and differences that may suggest hypotheses to explain certain dominant characteristics.

We may moreover have merely permanent effects presented in perception, the cause having ceased to act long since. Thus in geology we have facts that have been caused, it is true, but the causes can be discerned only as manifested in the effects, and, therefore, they can be determined only by the method of hypothesis, which may lead to verification or not, as the case may be. Again, certain sciences may suggest problems which concern the explanation or significance, not of particular phenomena within the sphere of that science, but rather the interpretation of the whole body of phenomena which the science in question comprehends. The problem is not solved, therefore, by any attempt in the way of analysis by experiment, but rather in the way of synthesis through hypothesis, that is, the ideal construction of a whole which will unify and account for all facts, or, in other words, the disclosing of the system which underlies and coördinates the various particular manifestations. This is especially illustrated in the problems which geology and biology present concerning the interpretation of their respective phenomena regarded in the light of their totality. Astronomy also presents a mass of seemingly chaotic phenomena, and yet the aim of this science is to reduce them all to some one self-consistent system.

For instance, Mr. Spencer remarks concerning the general nature of biological study: "In like manner biology is the elaboration of a complete theory of life in each and all of its involved manifestations. If different aspects of its phenomena are investigated apart, if one observer busies himself in classing organisms, another in dissecting them, another in ascertaining their chemical compositions, another in studying functions, another in tracing laws of modification, — they are all consciously or unconsciously helping to work out a solution of vital phenomena in their entirety, both as displayed by individual organisms and by organisms at large."[1]

Mr. Spencer, as we have seen in the chapter on division, makes the distinction between investigation of particular causal relations on the one hand, and, on the other, the interpretation of the total phenomena of a science, as the basis for his classification of the sciences.

The division of Herbert Spencer can only be accepted in a general way as indicating predominant characteristics of the two kinds of sciences. It will not do to lay down hard and fast lines here, for every science presents two kinds of problems; the first, to determine particular causal relations; the second, to coördinate all such relations into a self-consistent system which will unify all separate and individual instances. For instance, take the phenomena of light in physics; particular problems as regards intensity, velocity, composition of light, etc., present themselves; then an underlying problem, How explain all the phenomena of light upon some one single basis regarding the essential nature of light? Hence arose the emission and undulatory theories of light, and all phenomena bearing upon the theory were marshalled in support of one and of the other, until the conflict was conclusively decided. And again, the theory of light, the theory of electricity, the theory of heat, etc., suggest still another problem, How unify all the separate theories in one all-comprehensive theory to which the separate phenomena may be alike referred? thus every science presents particular problems, and a general problem as well. And herein

[1] Spencer, *Classification of the Sciences*, pp. 19, 20.

lies a suggestion that all investigators in any branch of science would do well to bear in mind. Specialization in any one line of particular problems should always lead to a consideration of the relations of these particular problems to the general system of which they are parts. Specialization that does not thus supply its own corrective by the natural insistence of the mind to interpret the particular in the light of more general laws, tends to narrowness of mind and barren results.

II. In reference to method in the sciences it must be observed also that in certain phenomena the simple theory, which regards the causal connection as a transfer of energy according to the doctrine of the conservation of energy, is further complicated by certain variations and modifications of the energy in the process of transference. When, for instance, a billiard-ball strikes another, and the second ball, by virtue of the impact, receives the energy of the initial moving ball transferred to it, the problem is simplified by the fact that the motion of the first is easily traceable in the second, being a transfer of energy which manifests itself in the same manner in the two cases. However, the problem is complicated at once when in chemistry, for instance, the two combining elements form a third in which the characteristic features of the former are wholly lost in the new form. Here is likewise a transfer of energy, which may have mechanical equivalents, it is true, and yet so radical a change of form accompanies the transfer that it complicates the problems which arise in this science. We have seen how the combined inducto-deductive method often predicts events and the nature of phenomena not yet observed. And yet this becomes most difficult whenever transfer of energy is accompanied by a change in the peculiarities of its manifestation as well. Knowledge of the nature of two elements, and all their separate characteristics, will not be sufficient data for any prediction as to the nature of the compound. Thus chemistry confronts a natural difficulty as regards method, which does not affect physical science generally.

Another difficulty appears in psychology, for here stimuli from the outer world, expressed in terms of physical energy and quantitatively determined, produce psychical reactions, that cannot be expressed in physical terms. And, on the other hand, processes of ideation produce muscular activities, that may be estimated in physical terms. It has been urged that here the theory of conservation of energy breaks down, that the transferred energy is wholly accounted for by the nerve and brain modifications, and that the psychical accompaniments are wholly unaccounted for upon this basis. They stand out as unexplored remainders.

This objection is met in two ways. One is that the physical and psychical are, as it were, two closed circles, and while simultaneous in their functioning do not mutually interact. This is the theory of the so-called "psychophysical parallelism." It necessitates metaphysical explanations and postulates that seem to complicate rather than simplify the difficulties. The second is the more reasonable, that psychical activity may be radically different from physical and yet the two capable of reacting upon each other, so as to liberate the potential activities in either sphere, and thus initiate a series of causally connected phenomena. Such a theory is buttressed by substantial analogies in the physical sphere itself; namely, that in many phenomena the impinging force is so modified, by the reaction due to the nature of the substance acted upon, as to lose, to all observation at least, its original characteristic features. For instance, friction passes over into electricity because of the nature of the substance that is rubbed; thunder sours cream, and thus sound vibrations cause effects wholly incongruous to them.

These illustrations might be multiplied through all the realm of physical science. They are so many as to prepare us for realizing the possibility, at least, that physical excitations may produce psychical phenomena in the sense that the outer stimulus calls into activity psychical energies, that thus stirred, manifest themselves according to the forms of their own nature, rather than the forms of the physical phenomena exciting them. Upon such a theory we may proceed, by observation and experiment, to measure duration, intensity, etc., of mental reactions responding to external stimuli. As regards the method here employed, the series is considered as one and complete, so that physical excitations are traced, as it were, through an unbroken causal chain to their psychical effects, and *vice versa*. On the theory of two closed circles, it is difficult to indicate a logical method of experimental inquiry, unless it be further postulated that activities in the one, according to its kind, may induce modifications of the other according to its kind. This reservation is generally insisted upon.

III. It sometimes happens that the phenomena of one science are to be interpreted in the light of the results of another science. Thus the laws of one science become guiding principles in investigating the causal relations existing in another sphere. This can only be done when there is some similarity between the phenomena of the two sciences. This method is especially illustrated in historical explanation. The problem presents a mass of events that must be coördinated in a system wherein their several causal relations will be exhibited. And not merely must detached epochs be proved interrelated as regards the events occurring in them, but here, also, the special problems give rise to a general problem, to discover in the whole the underlying philosophy of history, and to determine the several historical tendencies in one system whose characteristic features will reveal the fact that "through the ages one increasing purpose runs."

To solve the special and the general problems of history, recourse is had to an analysis of events on the basis of well-established psychological results. The phenomena of history are substantially the activities of man, both in his individual and collective capacities. Events being given, an hypothesis concerning the motives, and ends which actuated them, is framed upon the supposition that men ordinarily are impelled by similar motives under similar circumstances, in order to achieve similar ends. Here the analogies drawn between men of the present and men of the past, or between men moving in the ordinary routine of everyday life and men whose acts may be epoch-making, furnish a basis for historical interpretation. We say that a series of events, perhaps of a very complicated nature, can be explained only by an hypothesis that a well-defined purpose and a strong determined will were fashioning them and moving through them to an end that was in the chief actor's mind from the beginning. And so the rise of social habits, customs, traditions, laws, the religion, the government, and national institutions of a people have an origin in psychical and not physical elements, a deeper understanding of whose nature and all that it necessitates tends to a clearer elucidation of the problems therein presented. The knowledge of man, the microcosm, is a guiding thread amid the bewildering mazes of the macrocosm. It is possible, of course, for the imagination of the historian to lead him to wander far afield, and invent fanciful motives, purposes, public policies, etc., to explain given events. However, here, as in the physical and other sciences, the hypotheses framed must meet the general requirements and conditions of a valid hypothesis.

IV. There has been a growing tendency in sciences regarded as solely or largely deductive, to correct and supplement the traditional method and results by a more searching inductive inquiry. This is especially true of political economy. The deductive method proceeded to build up a body of doctrine composed of inferences necessitated by a few fundamental premises. The premises were such as the following: The principal motive of action is self-interest; the earth, as man's great supply-house, is limited in extent and productivity; the physical and psychological tendencies of man lead him to multiply his own species with a rapidity which, if not counteracted by obstacles, would bring about an unlimited increase of population. All economic laws were thus deduced from some such fundamental propositions as these. The results of this deductive method, however, have been brought to the bar of another method for searching examination and judicial sentence. In 1848 Hildebrand, and Knies in 1853, with Roscher in 1854, set forth the principles of the historical school of political economy. They held that an inductive inquiry must be started in order to estimate the physical, ethnical, and historical conditions of a nation and its stage of civilization. These forces, correctly assessed, will give the economic conditions of a particular period of history, or of a particular nation. This is not the place to criticise the tenets of this school, but merely to point out the fact that its influence has been potent in correcting and supplementing the results obtained in a purely deductive manner.

Deduction may give the joint effect of universal psychological impulses, operative under certain natural conditions of environment, etc., provided no disturbing force is present. But the question here is not whether a certain cause, if acting alone, will produce a certain effect; but whether counteracting causes will be present, or modifying causes, as the case may be. To estimate the results of collocations and not simple causes becomes, as we have seen, a complex problem. For its solution recourse must be had largely to statistical methods whereby large aggregates reveal tendencies that are actual and not theoretical merely.

In a similar way, the historical school of jurisprudence, associated with Savigny, has influenced the so-called philosophical school in demonstrating that results theoretically determined by deduction are constantly modified by the real conditions and limitations of each particular nation's life. The influence of this school is indicated by a significant fact, that when Hegel wrote his theory of law (*Rechtslehre*) he paid more regard to the historical formation of states than did the earlier theorists of natural law.[1]

Again, another illustration of the growing prevalency of inductive method is found in the modern psychological method. The sole method was considered from time immemorial to be that of introspection. Its results, however, were meagre; the method itself was indefinite and lacked certainty and uniformity. Inductive inquiry therefore proceeded by its own methods to secure and interpret material in other and various fields. As Professor Ladd says: "The method of psychological science is peculiarly introspective and analytic of the envisaged phenomena called states of consciousness. But it is far broader and more effective than it could be if it were merely introspective. It pushes its analysis of the genesis of the phenomena as far back as possible, by the use of experimental methods, and methods of external observation applied to the whole process of mental evolution (study of infants, of primitive man, and of the lower animals, — evolutionary and comparative psychology). It interprets the psychological life of the individual mind in the light of knowledge gathered concerning the psychical development of the race (the psychological study of literature, society, art, religion, etc.). It lays peculiar emphasis upon abnormal and pathological phenomena of the nervous and mental life (psychiatry, hypnotism, phenomena of insanity and of the criminal classes, etc.). It takes account of the rise and fall of particular forms of psychological theory (the history of psychology). It strives to transcend experience by hypothetical principles of explanation. But in the employment of all these methods this science differs in no important respect from the sciences which deal wholly with physical phenomena. It is only the use of introspection for the possession, and, to some extent at least, for the analysis, of

[1] Bluntschli, *The Theory of the State*, p. 69.

its objects, which makes psychology, as respects its method, different from the other sciences."[1]

In the above, we see that inductive inquiry lays all possible fields of research under tribute to the one end of explaining and correlating psychical phenomena. The systems of ethics also, which are founded upon an *a priori* basis, are becoming more indebted to empirical investigations which have given a richer content to the strictly formal ethic. Advanced psychological research, the study of race characteristics, tribal customs, habits, law, religion, etc., the indications of moral progress, — all give material which, if interpreted by right hypotheses, will throw light upon the theory of ethical principles regarded merely from a speculative point of view. We may conclude, therefore, that the inductive method and the deductive are not mutually exclusive processes. They may be so combined as mutually to strengthen one another. What Bluntschli says of jurisprudence may be applied equally as well to all sciences that claim some *a priori* basis: "The old strife between the philosophical and historical schools in Germany has altogether ceased. Peace was made as early as 1840. Since then it is recognized on all sides that the experiences and phenomena of history must be illumined with the light of ideas, and that speculation is childish if it does not consider the real conditions of the nation's life."[2]

It will be seen how important a factor historical data become in all the sciences that deal with human volition and activities. Whatever hypothesis may be framed, it must correspond to these data, because they represent actual conditions that must be coördinated in a self-consistent system, and their nature and relations must admit of satisfactory interpretation.

[1] Ladd, *Introduction to Philosophy*, p. 116.
[2] Bluntschli, *The Theory of the State*, p. 70.

CHAPTER XVIII

HISTORICAL SKETCH OF INDUCTION

SOCRATES (470–399 B.C.). — We find the beginnings of inductive inquiry in the Socratic or *maieutic* method, that art of mental midwifery by which conceptions were to be delivered from the mass of individual experiences and opinions in which they lie concealed. The Socratic procedure in the formation of conceptions is to question every particular view, and estimate it by bringing together analogous cases, and discovering their natural connections, so as to explicate the general notion which it contains, and thus proceed from comparison of particulars to the framing of general propositions. Socrates's generalizations were many of them hasty, and in his desire to formulate a general conception he overlooked exceptions and minimized difficulties, but in his method there were the germs of truly scientific procedure. The sphere of his method was, however, limited, as he applied it only to the illumination of ethical controversies.

Plato (427–347 B.C.). — Plato enriched the Socratic method of induction by removing its limitation to ethical inquiry. Plato was especially concerned with investigating the relations of his "ideas" to each other, and this led to the apprehension of the logical relations between conceptions, especially as regards their subordination and coördination. This forms a basis for classification, — Plato's division of class-concepts or logical genera into their species is a prominent feature of his method. He also suggests the hypothetical method of treating the relations of concepts; namely, to examine a tentatively proposed conception by developing all the possible consequences that would follow from its union with known conceptions. This is in keeping with the inducto-deductive method of Mill and the modern logicians.

Aristotle (384–322 B.C.). — Aristotle's name is especially, and it may be said almost exclusively, associated with deductive logic and syllogistic reasoning. Although he did not develop fully the inductive logic, he nevertheless did not ignore it, in some of its essential features at least. He acknowledged the necessity of investigating the starting-point of deduction, namely, the ultimate grounds of proof, and of the principles of explanation. This process he called dialectic. It is a double process that proceeds from the particulars given in perception, and from the ideas current in customary opinion, to discover the general, and then from the general to deduce the particular, which is thereby verified in the process. The former procedure is the reverse of the deductive, and is epagogic or inductive. Induction, according to him, is a syllogism in which the inference that the major belongs to the middle, is mediated through the minor directly; and not indirectly through the middle. Thus, to use Aristotle's illustration, the investigation of the connection between the absence of gall in animals and longevity in a number of instances, as in man, horse, mule, etc., may disclose their coexistence.[1] They are then united directly without mediation of a middle term. If we had given the universal proposition to start with, Whatever animal has no gall is long-lived, and the minor premise that man, horse, mule, etc., are animals having no gall, then the conclusion would follow, therefore they are long-lived. This is the deductive syllogism. The inductive method, on the other hand, starts from particular observation that the horse which has no gall is long-lived, so also the mule, so also man, etc.; therefore, without any middle term, a coexistence is taken as equivalent to a causal relation between these

[1] Aristotle, *Prior Analytics*, II. xxiii.

attributes, and the inference is drawn that all animals having no gall are long-lived. Such an inference is valid syllogistically, however, only on the assumption that the instances examined comprise the whole class having the attributes under investigation. This inductive syllogism, therefore, expresses inferences only of complete enumeration.

The form of such a syllogism is as follows: —

Let $S =$ minor term,
$P =$ major term,
$M =$ middle term.

This, that, and the other S is P.
This, that, and the other S is all M.
∴ All M is P.

Here it will be observed that the particular instances comprising the minor term S, when summed up, equal the middle term. There is no inference in this if we have regard to the strict sense in which the word is used. Aristotle, indeed, considered the only scientific induction to be the so-called perfect induction, and says that to generalize many experiences of the same kind is admissible only when there is no contrary case. The thought that the proof of causal connection enables us to generalize is stated by Aristotle, but, as Ueberweg says, it "does not attain to a fundamental significance in his logical theory."[1]

The Precursors of Bacon. — The revolt against the scholasticism of the Middle Ages and the fetters of the Aristotelian logic was many-voiced, culminating, however, as regards the emphasis placed upon induction as a scientific method, in the works of Francis Bacon.

Foremost among the early champions of inductive inquiry we find Roger Bacon, born in 1214, a Franciscan monk, yet devoted heart and mind to the cause of science. His *Opus Majus* was published first in 1733 by Dr. S. Jebb, principally from a manuscript in the library of Trinity College,

[1] Ueberweg, *Logic*, p. 479.

Dublin. This work is characterized by a spirit of protest against authority in general, and that of Aristotle and his logic especially. He recommends mathematics and experiment as the two great instruments of scientific investigation. In this particular it is interesting to note his anticipation of the modern mathematico-physical modes of scientific inquiry. The following quotation will give an indication of his spirit and aims: —

"Experimental science, the sole mistress of speculative sciences, has three great prerogatives among other parts of knowledge: First, she tests by experiment the noblest conclusions of all other sciences; next, she discovers, respecting the notions which other sciences deal with, magnificent truths to which these sciences of themselves can by no means attain; her third dignity is, that she by her own power, and without respect of other sciences, investigates the secrets of nature."[1]

Leonardo da Vinci (1452–1519). — Leonardo combined in one personality many brilliant talents, being eminent as sculptor, painter, architect, engineer, astronomer, and natural philosopher. His works, unpublished, exist in manuscripts in the library of the Institute at Paris. He expresses himself very clearly and emphatically concerning the relation of experience to speculation: "Theory is the general; experiments are the soldiers. We must consult experience, and vary the circumstances till we have drawn from them general rules; for it is she who furnishes true rules. But of what use, you ask, are these rules? I reply, that they direct us in the researches of nature and the operations of art. They prevent our imposing upon ourselves and others, by promising ourselves results which we cannot obtain. But see the absurdity of men! They turn up their noses at a man who prefers to learn from nature herself rather than from authors who are only her clerks."[2] This latter

[1] Whewell, *Philosophy of the Inductive Sciences*, Vol. II, p. 369.
[2] *Ibid.*, Vol. II, p. 369.

remark is similar in its reference to the epithet of Galileo, applied to men whose knowledge comes wholly from books and not from observation; namely, "paper philosophers."

Bernardinus Telesius (1508-1588). — His work, entitled *De Rerum Natura*, anticipated, in some degree at least, the *Novum Organum* of Bacon. Bacon himself says of him: "We think well concerning Telesius, and acknowledge him as a lover of truth, a useful contributor to science, an amender of some tenets, the first of recent men." Telesius set for himself a high aim and purpose, but in the application of his method he was not so fortunate, being dominated in his researches by speculation rather than the results of experimental inquiry. As to his professed method, he announces in the title of his *De Natura* that "the construction of the world, the magnitude and nature of the bodies contained in it, are not to be investigated by reasoning, which was done by the ancients, but are to be apprehended by the senses and collected from the things themselves." And in the Proem of the same work he says in a like strain that "they who before us have inquired concerning the construction of this world, and of the things which it contains, seem indeed to have prosecuted their examination with protracted vigils and great labor, but never to have looked at it. For, as it were, attempting to rival God in wisdom, and venturing to seek for the principles and causes of the world by the light of their own reason, and thinking they had found what they had only invented, they made an arbitrary world of their own. We then, not relying on ourselves, and of a duller intellect than they, propose to ourselves to turn our regards to the world itself and its parts."

Following Telesius, and of his school, was Thomas Campanella (1568-1639). He was a contemporary of Bacon, and, under the influence of Telesius, early conceived the idea of an inductive method of research. At the age of twenty-two, he published a work whose character may be judged by its title, — "Thomas Campanella's Philosophy demonstrated to the senses, against those who have philosophized in an arbitrary and dogmatical manner, not taking nature for their guide; in which the errors of Aristotle and his followers are refuted from their own assertions and the laws of nature; and all the imaginations feigned in the place of nature by the Peripatetics are altogether rejected; with a true defence of Bernardin Telesius of Cosenza, the greatest of philosophers; confirmed by the opinions of the ancients, here elucidated and defended, especially those of the Platonists."

The ideas of Bacon, with their impetus to the inductive method of research, were not only anticipated by writers of books; but actual discoveries by zealous investigators were turning the attention of the thinking world to nature and her secrets. There was an illustrious line of pioneers in this undiscovered country. There was Andrew Cæsalpinus (1520–1603), the founder of the science of botany; and earlier, Copernicus (1473–1543), advancing his heliocentric theory; and Gilbert (1540–1603), the court physician of Elizabeth and James, conducting with untiring perseverance his investigations of the nature of magnetism and electricity. Kepler, born ten years after Bacon, 1571, and Galileo, born in 1564, and their contemporary, Tycho Brahé, born in 1546, formed a triumvirate of scientific power and brilliancy, made resplendent by the glory of the heavens itself. It must be remembered, too, that at this time a new world had been discovered across the seas; the recent inventions of gunpowder, of the mariner's compass, and of the art of printing, all tended to stimulate the thought of the world, and usher in a new epoch in the history of civilization.

Francis Bacon (1561–1626). — Bacon's inductive system is given, for the most part, in the *Novum Organum*. The title of this work was in itself a protest against Aristotle and his logic, implying that Aristotle's *Organon* was now out of date and was to be superseded by the new. Bacon insists that all knowledge of nature has for its end the disclosing of the causes of things. According to the Aristotelian scheme, causes are formal, material, efficient, or final. Bacon is only concerned with the formal causes. For, he says, all events have their ground in the "forms" of things. By the form of a thing, he meant its essential nature. Where he uses the form we may well supply the word law. To discover the forms of phenomena, it is necessary, according to Bacon, to collect as many instances as possible in which the phenomenon under investigation appears; together they form a *tabula præsentiæ*. In like manner, the instances in which the phenomenon is lacking are grouped in a *tabula absentiæ;* and a third group must be formed,— a *tabula graduum* in which the variations of intensity in the phenomena are compared with the varying intensity of other phenomena. The problem is then to be solved by a process of exclusion (*exclusio*); that is, the rejection or exclusion of the several qualities which are not found in some instance where the given quality is present, or are found in some instance where the given quality is absent, or are found to increase in some instance where the given quality decreases, or to decrease when the given quality increases. By this process an indication will be given by which an hypothesis may be framed, and finally verified by subsequent observation and experiment. In the sketch of this method it will be seen that his three tables of instances closely resemble the methods of agreement, of difference, and of concomitant variations. They, however, lack the precision of the later formulation of these methods. There is no hint at a systematic selection and variation of the instances; and no requirement, as in the method of difference, that two instances shall be so experimentally determined that they will agree in every point save the given phenomenon, which is present in the one and absent from the other. Bacon, however, made a substantial contribution to the method of induction in general, in insisting upon the examination of instances themselves, and in ascending from them quite gradually the scale of the more general up to the most general, and in this he entered a vigorous protest against hasty generalization.

As to the manner of certifying the hypothesis formed after the process of collecting and sifting instances, Bacon has no recourse to deduction based upon the hypothesis and consequent verification. He seems to despise mathematical method as an ally of inductive inquiry; and therefore has no place in his scheme for the prediction of new phenomena by means of calculation. Of his nine divisions of aids to induction, he completed only the first, — Prerogative Instances. Of the instances which he enumerates, twenty-seven in all, only a few have any bearing directly upon the inductive method proper. Two sets of these instances may be considered as a crude statement of the methods of agreement and difference; the Solitary Instances, which either exhibit a phenomenon without any of its usual accompaniments or which agree in everything except some particular phenomenon, and Migratory Instances, where qualities are produced in bodies by evident causes, as, for instance, the producing of whiteness by pounding glass, also by stirring water into froth. These instances however as exhibited by Bacon lack precision and the possibilities of accurate determination of causal connections. The only other group of instances having special inductive significance is that of the *Instantia Crucis;* as before mentioned, such instances are valuable in deciding between rival hypotheses. With all the deficiencies of Bacon's method, however, his service to the thinking world is indisputable, in emphasizing the need of investigating phenomena themselves as a corrective of fanciful speculations, and in his vigorous warnings against prejudice, against intellectual indolence, against subjection of the mind to the trammels of authority, and against over hasty generalizations.

Locke (1632–1704). — Locke applied the method of Bacon

to the objects of inner experience. He declared that the data of all knowledge come from sensation, or sense-perception, and from reflection, and that there are no "innate ideas," and therefore no starting-point for *a priori* speculations. The method that had been found useful in actual discoveries, such as those of Newton, Kepler, and others, Locke insisted would prove productive also of rich results in the intellectual sphere.

Isaac Newton (1642-1727). — Scientific method was gradually formulating itself in the actual pursuits of scientific investigation, — not thought out as much as worked out, and its efficiency tested and confirmed by results. Newton gives form to that which was a result of many experiments, and of a mass of various experiences, in his Rules of Philosophizing (*Regulæ Philosophandi*) prefixed to the *Principia*.

These rules are as follows: —

1. The first rule is twofold; —
a. "Only real causes are to be admitted in explanation of phenomena."
b. "No more causes are to be admitted than such as suffice to explain the phenomena."

2. "In as far as possible, the same causes are to be assigned for the same kind of natural effects."

3. "Qualities that can neither be increased nor diminished in intensity, and that obtain in all bodies accessible to experiment, must be considered qualities of all bodies whatsoever."

4. "In philosophical experiment, propositions collected from phenomena by induction are to be held, notwithstanding contrary hypotheses, as either exactly or approximately true, until other phenomena occur whereby they are either rendered more exact or are proved liable to exceptions."

Newton's celebrated saying, "Hypotheses non fingo," was originally a protest against the supposition of the existence of occult or imaginary causes to explain phenomena, notably the Cartesian explanation of the celestial movements by vortices. Hypotheses of a different nature, and rationally grounded, did not fall under Newton's reprehension.

Sir John Herschel (1792–1871). — Herschel's *Discourse on the Study of Natural Philosophy* was published in 1832. John Stuart Mill reviewed this book in the *Examiner*, and was evidently impressed and influenced by it. Herschel's design was to make the methods of science more explicit. These are contained in nine " propositions readily applicable to particular cases, or rules of philosophizing."

Of these propositions, the second, seventh, eighth, and ninth present substantially the experimental methods as afterwards more precisely formulated by Mill. These methods, however, he regards simply as means to discovery, and not methods of proof. Of the remaining propositions, the first is a more precise statement of Bacon's principle of exclusion, and is the foundation of the joint method of agreement and difference. The third proposition is that "we are not to deny the existence of a cause in favor of which we have a unanimous agreement of strong analogies, though it may not be apparent how such a cause can produce the effect, or even though it may be difficult to conceive its existence under the circumstances of the case." The fourth is that "contrary or opposing facts are equally instructive for the discovery of causes with favorable ones." The fifth recommends the "tabulation of facts in the order of intensity in which some peculiar quality subsists." The sixth rule insists upon the investigator keeping prominently in mind the possibility that "counteracting or modifying causes may subsist unperceived," and that this fact may be the means of explaining many apparent exceptions.

Herschel also emphasizes the necessity of combining induction and deduction in complicated inquiries; and, further, he explains the nature of empirical laws, as also the nature and tests of hypotheses. We can now see that the body of inductive principles begins at length to assume final form and proportion.

Whewell (1795–1866). — Dr. Whewell published his *Philosophy of the Inductive Sciences* in 1840, containing his system of induction. His method involves two principal processes, — the colligation of facts and the explication of conceptions. The investigator is to gather all the facts at his disposal, and upon them he is to superinduce a conception which will unify them, or colligate them. He says these conceptions are supplied by the mind, while facts are supplied by the sense. This however is a distinction that separates so widely the spheres of the particular facts, and the general conceptions, that upon such a basis a union of the two as explaining one by the other would be artificial and with no corresponding bond of reality. The colligating conception does not exist in the mind before or apart from its existence in fact. The attempt to fit facts to ready-made conceptions is of the nature of guesswork. Kepler's nineteen guesses regarding planetary orbits is an instance of attempting to superinduce conceptions upon a mass of facts. It is not a truly scientific or logical procedure, and the great danger of applying it lies in the fact that the mind all too readily tends to mould facts into the forms of prior conceptions.

"The Methods employed in the Formation of Science," the title of his concluding chapter, are three, as follows: Methods of Observation, Methods of Obtaining Clear Ideas, and Methods of Induction. The last principally concerns our present purposes. The methods of induction are methods of discovery rather than proof; save the last, which is one of the experimental methods. They are, the method of curves to express graphically the graduated results of several observations; the method of means, and the method of least squares, both designed to eliminate accidental accompaniments of constant causes by striking an average of several observations; and the method of residues. Whewell's method may be characterized in brief as a method of discovery rather than proof.

John Stuart Mill (1806–1873). — Mill's *Logic*, published in 1843, was essentially a method of proof rather than a method of discovery. His aim in formulating the methods in vogue in experimental science, was to discover the precise modes of their operation in order to apply the same in investigating the various mental, moral, social, and political phenomena. Bacon in the *Novum Organum* had asserted that this inductive method was applicable to the intellectual and moral sciences. This was no doubt suggestive to Mill, as it had been to Locke. Whately's *Logic*, published in 1827, influenced Mill, and was the means of turning his attention to logical studies. Whately's book was reviewed by Mill, when only twenty-one, in the *Westminster Review*. The revival in logical interest at this time and the departure from scholastic traditions have been traced to the influence of Edward Copleston, tutor at Oxford, and afterwards Bishop of Llandaff. Whately's work represented the first-fruits, and Mill's the richer and riper product of this revival of logic. It is a matter of more than passing interest to note that one of Whately's most active collaborators in the work was John Henry Newman, so that, as Professor Minto says, "the common room of Oriel, which Mr. Froude describes as the centre from which emanated the High Church Movement, may also be said to have been the centre from which emanated the movement that culminated in the revolution of logic."

Mill's special office as regards induction consists in his crystallizing the principles and practices of the scientific investigators who had caught and reflected the spirit of modern research. The formulated methods of inductive logic, substantially as given by Mill, have become the recognized methods of all investigation that is actuated by a scholarly spirit and a scientific habit. Mill's contributions to the inductive logic have been so largely drawn from and so frequently referred to in the composition of this book, as to need no further comment here. The works of the more recent writers, as Lotze, Sigwart, Bosanquet, Jevons, Venn, etc., have also been noticed in the body of the text. Their work is largely critical, and no distinct inductive system is especially associated with any of their names.

LOGICAL EXERCISES

LOGICAL EXERCISES

PART I

1. (a) All A is B.
   All B is C.
   ∴ All C is A.

   (b) All A is B.
   No A is C.
   ∴ No C is B.

   (c) All A is B.
   All C is B.
   ∴ All C is A.

   (d) Some A is B.
   No A is C.
   ∴ Some C is not B.

2. The atmosphere cannot be a conductor of electricity; for metals are conductors of electricity, and the atmosphere is of course not a metal.

3. If there is to be any appreciation of German literature, one must be conversant with the German language.
   A certain man has a knowledge of the German language.
   ∴ He appreciates German literature.

4. Whatever is opposed to our industrial prosperity is to be regarded as a serious evil.
   All European wars are serious evils.
   ∴ They are opposed to our industrial prosperity.

5. All patrons of the arts and sciences are public benefactors.
   No poor men are patrons of the arts and sciences.
   ∴ No poor men are public benefactors.

6. All democrats are hostile to the bill.
   All beet-sugar men are hostile to the bill.
   ∴ All beet-sugar men are democrats.

7. Given A is B, to prove B is A.
   Now B is either A or not A.
   If B is not A, then by what is given we have the syllogism,

   A is B.
   B is not A.
   ∴ A is not A, which is absurd.

   Is this reasoning correct or not?

   — *Professor Jastrow.*

8. The courageous are confident and the experienced are confident. Therefore the experienced are courageous.

9. If the door were locked, the horse would not be stolen; but the horse is not stolen; therefore the door must have been locked.

10. Given the major premise, If an engineer sees a danger signal, he will stop the train. What can be inferred from the several minor premises as follows: —

(a) He saw a danger signal.
(b) He did not see a danger signal.
(c) He stopped the train.
(d) He did not stop the train.

11. All dishonest men are immoral, and as a certain man is confessedly immoral, it follows that he must be dishonest.

12. All members of the finance committee are members of the executive committee. No members of the library committee are members of the finance committee; therefore no members of the library committee are members of the executive committee.

13. Given the major premise, If the game is lost, we lose the championship. What follows as the result of the several minor premises?

(a) The game is lost.
(b) The game is won.
(c) The championship is lost.
(d) The championship is won.

14. Given, x, y, z, P, Q, R, so that

(a) Of x, y, z, one and only one is true.
(b) Of P, Q, R, one and only one is true.
(c) If x is true, P is true.
(d) If y is true, Q is true.
(e) If z is true, R is true.

Prove,   If x is false, P is false.
If y is false, Q is false.
If z is false, R is false.

— *Keynes's Logic.*

15. I am sure that he must have known of the plan; for only members of the committee knew of it, and he was a member of the committee.

16. A certain man will make an excellent electrical engineer; for he is a good mathematician.

17. If he insists upon the present policy, he will fail; but he is willing to give up this policy and therefore he will succeed.

18. Only those messages which are prepaid will be delivered. This message has been prepaid; and therefore it will be delivered.

19. If a is b, c is d; if c is d, e is f; if e is f, g is h. What inferences are possible if you have given that c is d? What inferences, if e is not f?

20. A is nearer than B; B is nearer than C; therefore A is nearer than C.

21. All who were pledged voted for him.
A certain man was not pledged.
∴ He did not vote for him.

22. Because the poor who have cows are the most industrious, the way to make them industrious is to give them cows. — *Malthus.*

23. Governor McKinley charges that the democratic party believes in taxing ourselves. I'm afraid, gentlemen, we must admit this charge. We stand disgraced in the eyes of mankind if we cannot and if we do not support our own government. We can throw that support on other people only by beggary or by force. If we use the one, we are a pauper nation; if we use the other, we are a pirate nation. — *Congressman William L. Wilson of West Virginia.*

24. If the plate found had been originally on the outside of the ship, I should have judged that there must be green paint on it; but I couldn't find green paint on that part of the plate.—*Maine Court of Inquiry.*

25. Question: Can you imagine a 10-inch charge bursting inside of a tank? Would they look like that? [Showing a split tank.]

Answer: If a 10-inch charge burst inside of a tank, there would be nothing left of the tank. It would be blown into small pieces.

26. No one of the crowd would by himself stoop to so mean an act, and, therefore, I am quite sure that as a body they would not do it.

27. Our rule in the Philippines is unjust; for it is manifestly unjust to tyrannize over an inferior people.

28. A few years ago there appeared an unusual number of spots on the sun, and there followed immediately a very severe famine in India. It would seem that such variations in the nature of the sun had something to do with the consequent failure of the crops.

29. There should be no restriction of debate in the United States Senate, because freedom of speech is one of our most sacred privileges.

30. Each member of a certain board is liable to err in judgment, therefore as a body the chance of error is multiplied, and consequently is so much the greater.

31. It would be greatly to our advantage as a people were we to have a silver standard, for the prosperity of the people would be increased.

32. The expedition was destined to fail, because it started on Friday.

33. These men are traitors because they are opposed to the war, and opposition to the war is an opposition to the government, and opposition to the government is traitorous.

34. The combination which has been formed need not be feared, for all of its members are exceedingly weak and inexperienced.

35. That writer must be a follower of Plato; for all followers of Plato are idealists, and he is an idealist.

36. The philosophy of Naturalism, if regarded from the practical side, is insufficient; if from the speculative side, it is incoherent. Therefore it fails to justify itself. — *Mr. Balfour in Foundations of Belief.*

37. It is possible to have in thought the conception of the most perfect Being. This conception implies the reality of such a Being; for if the most perfect Being as thus conceived has no real existence, then it would be possible to conceive of a still more perfect Being which should possess reality, and thus the former would not be the most perfect Being possible. — *Anselm's Ontological Argument.*

38. Students who are free to choose their studies will, as a rule, select the easiest; therefore the easiest courses will be largely attended, or, conversely, the much-chosen courses will include all the easiest.

39. If there had been no portent of the Wilson-Gorman bill, there would have been no panic in 1893, no consequent revenue deficit, no need to issue bonds in time of peace, no addition to the national debt, no resulting 16-to-1 free silver craze, and no chance for the ring of silver Senators to bestride the financial legislation of the country.

40. The following is an excerpt from a letter written to one of our daily journals : —

I am in favor of free silver. First — Because I believe it to be right.

Second — Because it is constitutional and democratic, and right here I may say that for thirty-two years I have voted the democratic ticket.

Washington and Jefferson (the father of Democracy) bequeathed to the American people in 1792 the legacy that the dollar of $371\frac{1}{4}$ grains of pure silver was the unit of value. This legacy was ever kept sacred and preserved until 1873, when Congress destroyed the unit of value that had stood the test for over eighty years of American independence, and substituted a unit that seems to be acceptable to the Rothschilds of England and America.

From the effects of that outrage, the work, no doubt, of men who did not fully understand what they were doing, the people have never recovered. They can still see its effects by comparing the reduction in value of all property during recent years with the steady increase in value which took place before silver was demonetized.

The value of nearly everything that a man owned was depreciated by the demonetization of silver, but then there was no depreciation in any debt that he owed; on the contrary his debts increased because gold appreciated when made the only redemption money of the country, and consequently it took more labor and products to get the gold with which to pay his debts.

The people can also see the effects of the demonetization of silver by comparing the number of strikes and lockouts we have had since 1873 with the number we had for eighty years before. They can see its effect by comparing the number of trusts of the last fifteen years with the number we had before silver was demonetized. Before 1873 labor had little cause to organize for protection. America was the asylum for the oppressed of all nations, and American labor was the best paid and the most contented in the world. How is it now, and how has it been, on the average, since the old American policy of "live and let live" was abandoned at the behest of the comparative few who control the gold of the world? Instead of being those to whom the oppressed of other nations come for "fair play," we are a part of the world's great throng which is trying to get "fair play" for themselves.

The masses of our country are little, if any, better off, all things considered, than those of the most favored of the over-populated countries of the old world. It was not always thus, and it will not long continue to be so if the voters will turn a deaf ear to the plutocrats and their agents, the time-serving politicians, who tell them that silver money would be "dishonest" money unless measured by the gold standard which these same plutocrats have substituted for the old gold and silver standard which we used until 1873.

41. Luxurious expenditure is a good thing for laborers, as it increases the demand for labor.

42. Payment of interest on a public debt, so far as it is confined to the citizens of one country, neither enriches nor impoverishes the country, but is a payment of money from the right hand to the left.

43. A great fire tends to increase wages, as it creates employment to replace the devastated district.

44. A dense population implies a high rate of natural increase; hence (apart from immigration) the birth-rate in a city is higher than in the country.

45. As a thing is generally sold for more than it is worth, or for

less, one of the parties to an exchange commonly is a loser by the transaction.

46. An increase in the amount of money tends to lower the rate of interest, for interest is paid for the use of money.

47. Exchange between two traders in the same community commonly results in a profit to both. Such exchange is preferable to exchange where one of the parties is an outsider, because only one profit is realized by the community in the latter case.

48. The two following syllogisms are after the Stoic manner:—

(*a*) Nihil est tam contra naturam quam turpitudo.
Nihil est tam secundum naturam quam utilitas.
∴ In eadem re utilitas et turpitudo esse non possunt.

(*b*) Quod honestum est, id est aut solum aut summum bonum.
Quod autem bonum est id certe utile.
∴ Itaque, quidquid honestum, id utile.

— *Cicero, De Officiis, III. viii, 35.*

49. There is no such thing as innate knowledge. As it is evident that new-born children, idiots, and even the great part of illiterate men have not the least apprehension of the axioms alleged to be innate, the advocates of innate ideas are obliged to assume that the mind can have ideas without being conscious of them. But to say a notion is imprinted on the mind and at the same time to maintain that the mind is ignorant of it, is to make this impression nothing. If the words, *to be in the understanding,* have any positive meaning, they signify to be perceived and to be understood by the understanding: hence, if any one asserts that a thing is in the understanding and yet not understood by the understanding, and that it is in the mind without being perceived by the mind, it amounts to saying that a thing is and is not in the understanding. — *Locke, Essay on Human Understanding.*

50. There are some philosophers who imagine we are every moment intimately conscious of what we call our Self; that we feel its existence and its continuance in existence; and are certain, beyond the evidence of a demonstration, both of its perfect identity and simplicity. Now, it is evident that there must be some one impression that gives rise to every real idea. But self or person is not any one impression, but that to which our several impressions and ideas are supposed to have a reference. If any impression gives rise to the idea of self, that impression must continue invariably the same through the whole course of our lives; since self is supposed to exist after that manner. But there is no impression constant and invariable. Pain and pleasure,

grief and joy, passions and sensations succeed each other and never all exist at the same time. It cannot, therefore, be from any of these impressions or from any other that the idea of self is derived; and consequently there is no such idea. — *Hume, A Treatise on Human Nature.*

51. According to the common view external objects — tables, trees, horses, dogs — have an existence quite independent of the mind which perceives them, and our ideas of them are copies or resemblances of these things without us. Berkeley, however, combats this view with the following argument: Either those external objects or originals of our ideas are perceivable or they are not perceivable. If they are, then *they* are ideas and we have gained our point; but if you say they are not, I appeal to any one whether it be sense to assert a color is like something which is invisible; hard or soft like something intangible; and so of the rest. — *Principles of Human Knowledge.*

52. Motives are good or bad only on account of their effects; good on account of their tendency to produce pleasure, or avert pain; bad on account of their tendency to produce pain or avert pleasure. Let a man's motive be ill-will, — call it even malice, envy, cruelty, — it is still a kind of pleasure that is his motive; the pleasure he takes at the thought of the pain which he sees, or expects to see, his adversary undergo. Now even this wretched pleasure, taken by itself, is good: it may be faint; it may be short; it must at any rate be impure; yet while it lasts and before any bad consequences arrive, it is as good as any other that is not more intense. — *Bentham, Principles of Morals and Legislation.*

53. It is in accordance with the traditional policy of the United States that we should possess and develop colonies; for the states were themselves originally a group of colonies, and our territories have always been a most important feature of the growing power of the nation, and territory is only another name for colony.

54. All that we know or conceive are our own ideas. When, therefore, you say all ideas are occasioned by impressions in the brain, do you conceive this brain or no? If you do, then you talk of ideas imprinted in an idea causing that same idea, which is absurd. If you do not conceive it, you talk unintelligibly, instead of forming a reasonable hypothesis. — *Berkeley, Hylas and Philonous.*

55. What proves the soul to be matter — exceedingly fine matter, of course — is the influence exercised upon it by the body in fainting, anæsthesia, and delirium, in cases of injury and disease, and, above all, the fact that the advance and the decline of the soul correspond to analogous bodily conditions. The intellectual faculties are weak in

the period of childhood; they grow strong in youth, and gradually decay in old age. Sickness causes a serious reaction upon the soul; without the body the soul has no power to manifest itself. Nay, more than that, the dying man does not feel his soul gradually withdrawing from one organ to another, and then finally making its escape with its powers unimpaired; he experiences a gradual diminution of his mental faculties. — *Epicurus.*

56. *Consequens est: Si orator est, homo est. Inconsequens est: Si homo est, orator est. Repugnans: Si homo est, quadrupes est.*
— *Augustine, De Doct. Christ.*, II, 34.

57. The Greeks honored the gods and also the actors who took part in scenic games (often debasing) in honor of the gods. The Romans excluded such actors from citizenship on the ground that their calling was degrading. Augustine reasons as follows:—

Proponunt Graeci: Si tales dii colendi sunt, tales homines honorandi. Adsumunt Romani: Sed nullo modo tales homines honorandi sunt. Concludunt Christiani: Nullo modo igitur dii tales colendi sunt. — *De Civ. Dei*, II, 13.

58. Bain, in *Senses and Intellect* (p. 374), argues that "the conjoint experience of the senses and the movements appears to me to furnish all that we possess in the notion of extended matter. The association between sight and locomotion, or between touch and the movements of the arm, tells us that a given appearance implies the possibility of a certain movement; that a remote building implies a continuance of our walking exertions to change its appearance into another that we call a near view; and the power of moving, the scope for moving, exhausts every property in the idea of empty space. We estimate it first by our own movements, and next by other movements measured in the first instance by our own, as, for example, the flight of a bird, the speed of a cannon ball, or the movement of light. The mental conception that we have of empty space is scope for movement."

Professor Baldwin, in the *Handbook of Psychology* (Vol. I, p. 136), criticises the above as follows: "Now, if the idea of space enters through the intensive feeling of muscular contraction, there is more in our conclusion than in our premises, and we have an *ignoratio;* if, on the other hand, the sensation is one of movement proper, extension has already entered and we need no association; this is a *petitio.*"

59. In mediæval times it was held that Venus or that Saturn was inhabited, not because any one could devise, with any degree of probability, any organized structure which would be suitable for animal existence on the surfaces of those planets, but because it was conceived that the greatness or goodness of the Creator, or His wisdom, or some

other of His attributes, would be manifestly imperfect if these planets were not tenanted by living creatures. — *Whewell.*

60. That God is, the Bible affirms. Whatever the Bible affirms is true, because it is from God, and declares it is impossible for God to lie. Therefore the existence of God is surely proved.

61. No species of agnosticism is unrelated to its genus. No agnosticism with a special reference or limited sphere is without reference to the agnostic idea, spirit, and aim. On the contrary, every kind of agnosticism tends towards agnostic completeness. Agnosticism in any form is of the nature of agnosticism in every form. — *Flint, Agnosticism,* p. 311.

62. The propounders of what are called the "ethics of evolution" adduce a number of more or less interesting facts, and more or less sound arguments in favor of the origin of the moral sentiments in the same way as other natural phenomena, by a process of evolution. I have little doubt, for my own part, that they are on the right track; but as the immoral sentiments have been no less evolved, there is, so far, as much natural sanction for the one as the other. The thief and the murderer follow nature just as much as the philanthropist. — *Huxley, Evolution and Ethics.*

63. There is another fallacy which appears to me to pervade the so-called "ethics of evolution." It is the notion that because, on the whole, animals and plants have advanced in perfection of organization by means of the struggle for existence and the consequent survival of the fittest; therefore men in society, men as ethical beings, must look to the same process to help them towards perfection. — *Huxley.*

64. A profound study of the *system of protection* has taught us this syllogism, upon which the whole doctrine reposes : —
    The more men work the richer they become ;
    The more difficulties there are to be overcome, the more work ;
    Ergo, The more difficulties there are to be overcome, the richer they become. — *Bastiat, Economic Sophisms.*

65. The shopkeeper thrives only by the irregularities of youth; the farmer by the high prices of corn; the architect by the destruction of houses; the officers of justice by lawsuits and quarrels. Ministers of religion derive their distinction and employment from our vices and our death. No physician rejoices in the health of his friends, nor soldiers in the peace of his country; and so of the rest. Therefore carelessness, calamity, pestilence, disease, and even death are economic blessings. — *Montaigne.*

66. Restrictive laws always land us in this dilemma : Either you admit that they produce scarcity, or you do not. If you admit it, you

avow by the admission that you inflict on the people all the injury in your power. If you do not admit it, you deny having restricted the supply and raised prices, and consequently you deny having favored the producer. — *Bastiat.*

67. When products such as coal, iron, corn, or textile fabrics are sent us from abroad, and we can acquire them with less labor than if we made them ourselves, the difference is a free gift conferred upon us. The gift is more or less considerable in proportion as the difference is more or less great. It amounts to a quarter, a half, or three-quarters of the value of the product when the foreigner only asks us for three-fourths, a half, or a quarter of the price we should otherwise pay. It is as perfect and complete as it can be, when the donor (like the sun in furnishing us with light) asks us for nothing. The question, and we ask it formally, is this: Do you desire for our country the benefit of gratuitous consumption, or the pretended advantages of onerous production? Make your choice, but be logical; for as long as you exclude as you do, coal, iron, corn, foreign fabrics *in proportion* as their price approximates to *zero*, what inconsistency would it be to admit the light of the sun, the price of which is already at *zero* during the entire day? — *Bastiat.*

68. To hear the roaring of the sea as one does, one must hear the parts which compose its totality, that is, the sound of each wave, . . . although this noise would not be noticed if the wave were alone. One must be affected a little by the movement of one wave, one must have some perception of each several noise, however small it be. Otherwise one would not hear that of 100,000 waves, for of 100,000 zeros one can never make a quantity. — *Leibniz.*

69. Mr. Spencer, in his exposition of the doctrine of evolution, is guilty of the amazing fallacy of supposing that, because the laws of energy are everywhere present, they are everywhere sufficient to explain what we see; which is much the same as assuming that, because a painter's palette, like his finished canvas, shows us a mixture of colors laid on with a brush, therefore what sufficed to produce the one would equally suffice to produce the other. — *Professor Ward, Naturalism and Agnosticism.*

70. No one can believe what he does not understand; therefore there are no mysteries in true religion.

71. Christianity is necessarily modified by the growth of civilization and the exigencies of the times; therefore the Catholic priesthood, though necessary in the Middle Ages, may be superseded now.

72. There are rights of conscience such that every one may lawfully advance a claim to profess and teach what is false and wrong in mat-

ters religious, social, and moral, provided that it seems absolutely true and right to his private conscience; therefore individuals have a right to preach and practise polygamy.

73. There is no such thing as a national or state conscience; therefore no judgments can fall upon a sinful nation.

74. The civil power has no positive duty in a normal state of things to maintain religious truth; therefore blasphemy and Sabbath-breaking are not rightly punishable by law.

75. The civil power may dispose of church property without sacrilege; therefore Henry VIII committed no sin in his spoliations.

76. The civil power has the right of ecclesiastical jurisdiction and administration; therefore parliament may impose articles of faith on the church or suppress dioceses.

77. The people are the legitimate source of power; therefore universal suffrage is among the natural rights of man.

78. Virtue is the child of knowledge and vice of ignorance; therefore education, periodical literature, travelling, ventilation, drainage, and the arts of life, when fully carried out, serve to make a population moral and happy.

79. Unbelievers use the antecedent argument from the order of nature against our belief in miracles. Here, if they only mean that the fact of that system of laws, by which physical nature is governed, makes it antecedently improbable that an exception should occur in it, there is no objection to the argument; but if, as is not uncommon, they mean that the fact of an established order is fatal to the very notion of an exception, they are using a presumption as if it were a proof. — *Newman, Grammar of Assent.*

80. Gibbon mentions five causes to account for the establishment of Christianity, — the zeal of the Christians, inherited from the Jews, their doctrine of a future state, their claim to miraculous power, their virtues, and their ecclesiastical organization. He thinks these five causes, when combined, will fairly account for the event; but he has not thought of accounting for their combination. If they are ever so available for his purpose, still that availableness arises out of their coincidence, and out of what does that coincidence arise? — *Newman.*

81. Bentham was clearly the victim of a common delusion. If a system will work, the minutest details can be exhibited. Therefore, it is inferred, an exhibition of minute detail proves that it will work. Unfortunately, the philosophers of Laputa would have had no more difficulty in filling up details than the legislators of England or the United States. — *Leslie Stephen, The English Utilitarians.*

82. The "rights of man" doctrine confounds a primary logical canon

with a statement of fact. Every political theory must be based upon facts as well as upon logic. Any reasonable theory about politics must no doubt give a reason for inequality and a reason, too, for equality. The maxim that all men were or ought to be "equal" asserts correctly that there must not be arbitrary differences. Every inequality should have its justification in a reasonable system. But when this undeniable logical canon is taken to prove that men actually are equal, there is an obvious begging of the question. — *Leslie Stephen.*

83. I shall offer this one mark whereby prejudice may be known. He that is strongly of any opinion must suppose (unless he be self-condemned) that his persuasion is built upon good grounds, and that his assent is no greater than what the evidence of the truth he holds forces him to; and that they are arguments and not inclinations of fancy that make him so confident and positive in his tenets. Now if, after all his profession, he cannot bear any opposition to his opinion — if he cannot so much as give a patient hearing, much less examine and weigh the arguments on the other side — does he not plainly confess, it is prejudice governs him? And it is not the evidence of truth, but some lazy anticipation, some beloved presumption that he desires to rest undisturbed in. For, if what he holds be as he gives out, well fenced with evidence, and he sees it to be true, what need he fear to put it to the proof? — *Locke, The Conduct of the Understanding.*

84. When Mill urges us to choose the higher rather than the lower pleasures, then either the so-called "higher" pleasure is actually, as pleasure, so preferable to that called "lower" that the smaller amount of the one would be more pleasurable than the largest amount of the other; or else the higher is called higher and is to be preferred to the lower — even though the latter may be greater as pleasure — because of a quality belonging to it over and above its character as pleasant feeling. The former verdict would be, in the first place, paradoxical, and in the second place would give up Mill's case by reducing quality to a quantitative standard. According to the latter verdict, the characteristic upon which the distinction of quality depends, and not pleasure itself, becomes the ethical standard. — *Sorley, Ethics of Naturalism.*

85. Every one desires happiness; virtue is happiness; therefore every one desires virtue. — *Aristotle.*

86. The principles of justice are variable; the appointments of nature are invariable; therefore the principles of justice are no appointment of nature. — *Aristotle.*

87. It is no doubt true that if a law be universal, it will be confirmed by all our experiments; therefore, when all our experiments fail to detect an exception, we may regard the law as true universally.

PART II

1. When a coin and a feather are dropped simultaneously in the receiver of an air-pump, the air being left in, the feather flutters to the bottom after the coin; but, when the air is pumped out of the receiver, the coin and the feather, being dropped at the same instant, reach the bottom of the receiver together.

2. If a beam of the sun's light is passed through a prism, a colored band nearly five times as long as it is broad results. Newton tried several experiments in which he varied the size of prism, and the quality of the glass; he also passed the beam through various parts of the same prism, and tried other minor suppositions. But in all these cases there was the same color effect produced.

3. Nitrogen obtained from various chemical sources is of uniform density; in 1894, Lord Rayleigh and Professor Ramsay, noting the fact that atmospheric nitrogen is about one-half per cent heavier, were led to the discovery of a hitherto unknown substance which received the name of *argon*.

4. If the earth were 9500 miles in diameter instead of 8000, this increase would give two-thirds increase in bulk, and a corresponding increase of density due to the greater gravitative force; the mass would be about double what it is. But with double the mass, the quantity of gases of all sorts attracted and retained by gravity would probably have been double, and in that case there would have been double the quantity of water produced, as no hydrogen would then escape. But the surface of the globe would be only one-half greater than at present, in which case the water would have sufficed to cover the whole surface several miles deep.

5. Wherever the winds blow over extensive areas of water on to the land, especially if there are mountains or elevated plateaus which cause the moisture-laden air to rise to heights where the temperature is lower, clouds are formed and rain falls. But where the land is of an arid nature and much heated by the sun, the air becomes capable of holding still more aqueous vapor, and even dense rain-clouds disperse without producing any rainfall.

6. Very thin sheets of white light proceeding from various incandescent substances are passed through incandescent hydrogen, and the emergent light is then separated into its constituent elements by a prism. In the spectra thus obtained it is found that there are invariably dark lines occupying precisely the same relative position. But trying similar experiments with any other element than incandescent hydro-

gen, the lines obtained never occupy the same positions in the spectrum as the lines in question.

7. (a) Hawksbee in 1715 first noticed that by striking a bell in the receiver of an air-pump, the bell was heard when the receiver was full of air; but when the receiver was exhausted, no sound was heard.

(b) Also, it was found that as the air was gradually admitted into the receiver, the sound of the bell grew louder and louder.

8. The following are the results of a series of experiments conducted by Dr. Wells in order to discover the cause of dew : —

(a) Moisture bedews a cold metal or stone when we breathe upon it. The same appears on a glass of ice-water, and on the inside of windows when sudden rain or hail chills the external air; the inference is that when an object contracts dew, it is colder than the surrounding air.

(b) No dew is deposited on a piece of metal which has been polished, but on the same metal unpolished dew is deposited copiously. Therefore the deposit of dew is affected by the kind of surface which is exposed.

(c) With various kinds of polished metals, no dew is deposited; but with various kinds of glass, having highly polished surfaces, dew is deposited. Therefore, the deposit of dew is affected also by the kind of substances themselves.

(d) In general, it has been found that those substances are most strongly dewed which conduct heat worst, while those which conduct heat well resist dew most effectively.

(e) Again, substances of close firm texture, as stones and metals, have less dew, while substances of looser texture, as cloth, wool, velvet, eider-down, cotton, have more dew. But substances of loose texture resist the passage of heat, therefore the more these substances resist the passage of heat the greater the deposit of dew.

(f) All instances in which much dew is deposited have this feature in common : they either radiate heat rapidly or conduct it slowly. All instances in which no dew or very little is deposited have in common the opposite feature.

(g) The property of radiating heat rapidly, or conducting it slowly, signifies that the body in question tends to lose heat more rapidly from the surface than it can be restored from within. And this in turn renders the body colder than the surrounding air. Therefore a body colder than the surrounding air precipitates the dew upon it.

(h) It is known by direct experiment that for any given degree of temperature, only a limited quantity of water can remain suspended in the state of vapor, and this quantity grows less and less as the temperature diminishes. Therefore if there is already as much vapor suspended as the air will contain at its existing temperature, any lowering of the temperature will cause necessarily a portion of the vapor to be condensed and become water.

(*i*) It is possible by cooling the surface of any body to find some temperature lower than that of the surrounding air, at which the dew begins to appear.

(*j*) It is observed that dew is not deposited on cloudy nights, but if the clouds withdraw and leave a clear opening a deposition of dew immediately begins. Dew formed in clear intervals disappears when the sky becomes thickly overcast. Now a clear sky is nothing but the absence of clouds, and it is a known property of clouds that they keep up the temperature of exposed surfaces by radiating heat to them. We see that the disappearance of clouds will cause these surfaces to cool, and cold surfaces, as has been shown, condense the moisture of the air in the form of dew.

9. To the Editor of *The Tribune*.

Sir: In your issue of Sunday, February 7, is an article entitled "Results of Antitoxin Treatment." After quoting statistics showing a remarkable decrease in the mortality from diphtheria treated with antitoxin, as compared to diphtheria treated without antitoxin, you say:—

"The one point now in doubt, and, it must be confessed, in serious doubt, is the effect of antitoxin itself upon the human system. In many cases this has seemed to be injurious, if not fatal. Patients have been cured of diphtheria, only to suffer from declining vitality and a train of grievous disorders sometimes baffling the physicians' skill and ending in death. Are they caused by antitoxin?"

Before the antitoxin treatment was dreamed of it was a common occurrence — more common than now — for a patient to be "cured of diphtheria" and then to "suffer from declining vitality," etc., all too frequently "ending in death."

But no one ascribed these post-diphtheritic fatalities to the treatment. They were, very properly, believed to be the result of the action of the poison of diphtheria upon the cells of the body. There can be no doubt that this toxin (poison) has the power seriously to affect, and even to destroy, certain tissues. Therefore it is common for diphtheria to be accompanied or followed by palsies, Bright's disease, neuritis, anæmia (declining vitality), etc.

A child who has had diphtheria is liable to suffer from the deleterious effects for months or even years. That these results are due to the toxin of diphtheria and not to the antitoxin is very clearly shown by the fact that the mortality and the serious after-effects are so much less when the antitoxin is used early in the disease than when it is used in the last stages thereof, *i.e.* when the antitoxin is administered early the poison is destroyed before it has had time to do extensive injury.

10. Further explanation is needed of the extraordinary increase[1] in deaths from consumption in this state as shown by the annual report of the State Board of Health. There were 361 more deaths by consumption reported in 1899 than in 1898, and the number was 419 more than the average for the preceding twenty-one years. The increase in deaths from acute lung diseases is also noteworthy, and as the same conditions which give rise to the latter are likely to produce fatal termination in chronic cases, the connection between the two is perhaps not difficult to establish. There must, however, have been some special cause for the unusual mortality from diseases of the lungs.

The hypothesis may be advanced that there was no real increase over past years, but that the apparent increase is due to fuller and more accurate reports. This can hardly be accepted as a plausible explanation, since the system of gathering mortuary statistics last year was the same that had been employed for a number of years previously, and is as complete as can be devised to secure accuracy. The cause must be looked for elsewhere, and it will probably be found by a careful study of the atmospheric and climatic conditions existent during the year just ended. The winter was not one of more than ordinary severity, but attended with sudden and sharp variations of temperature, always trying upon persons of weak lungs. There was much snow and slush, filling the air with moisture, and during the late winter and early spring dense fogs were frequent. The spring months were also marked by rapid changes in temperature, while during the summer cool nights following hot days were the rule.

Considerable light might be thrown on the matter by noting whether the increase in deaths was general throughout the state or confined to certain localities; whether there was any difference between the region adjacent to the sea-coast and the more remote sections, where the influence of the ocean upon the climate is not so marked. The reports from city and country might also be compared.

11. To the philosopher the state is a human organism, a human person; but if so, the human spirit which lives in it must also have a human body, for spirit and body belong to one another, and between them make up the person. In a body which is not organized and human, the spirit of man cannot truly live. The body politic must therefore imitate the body natural of man. The perfect state is, as it were, the visible body of humanity. — *Bluntschli, Theory of the State.*

12. In the Yale-Princeton intercollegiate debate in 1895, Yale con-

tended that the *referendum* had failed in Switzerland, and therefore, in all probability, would fail in the United States. On the other hand, Princeton maintained that the *referendum* had succeeded in Switzerland, and therefore, in all probability, would succeed in the United States. Supposing the premise true in each case, which position is the stronger?

13. We may observe a very great similitude between the earth which we inhabit and the other planets. They all revolve around the sun as the earth does, though at different distances and in different periods. They borrow all their light from the sun as the earth does. Several of them are known to revolve round their axis like the earth, and by that means have a like succession of day and night. Some of them have moons that serve to give them light in the absence of the sun, as our moon does to us. They are all, in their motions, subject to the same law of gravitation as the earth is. From all this similitude, it is not unreasonable to think that these planets may, like our earth, be the habitation of various orders of living creatures. — *Reid, Intellectual Powers.*

14. Some remarkable observations of the French astronomer, M. Camille Flammarion, have been recently reported, which go to show that within certain limits the radiations of heat from the sun vary quite regularly during the eleven and a half year sun-spot cycle, and that these variations of solar heat apparently cause some definite changes in the natural phenomena of the earth. For instance, his figures prove that when sun spots are most numerous (as in 1893), migratory birds return to any given place earlier in the year than usual; and, on the contrary, when spots are at a minimum, they do not come back until a much later date. These phenological researches corroborate previous evidence, proving that after the sun has been abnormally agitated — erupting enormous tongues of flame one hundred thousand miles high, which frequently form directly over the spots — the earth receives more heat; and when (as was the case in 1898) the sun is comparatively calm and spotless he is less fiery, and hence slightly less influential on our globe.

Because the well-known periodic changes of solar activity are not followed by corresponding synchronous changes in the earth's atmosphere, many scientists deny that there is any connection — forgetting that effects generally lag far behind their causes and that nature seldom accomplishes her work at a leap. Professor Von Bezold, the German meteorologist, expresses the view generally accepted by astronomers, when he says: —

"It is not inconceivable if we should find the explanation of that remarkable periodicity in the temperature of whole zones, demonstrated by Koeppen in 1873, which without doubt indicates a close connection with the processes on the sun's surface, although the irregularities in the times of occurrence of the maximum and minimum temperatures, amounting to years of delay in certain zones, seem at first sight to prove that there is no such connection."

15. If a small jet of steam is sent into two large glass receivers, one filled with ordinary air, the other with air which has been filtered by passing through a thick layer of cotton-wool, so as to keep back all particles of solid matter, the first vessel will be instantly filled with condensed, cloudy-looking vapor, while in the other vessel the air and vapor will remain perfectly transparent and invisible.

16. It is a very suggestive fact that most of the stars belonging to the Milky Way have spectra of the solar type, which indicates that they are of the same general constitution as our sun, and are also at about the same stage of evolution; and this may well have arisen from their origin in a great nebulous mass situated at or near the centre of the galactic plane, and probably revolving round their common centre of gravity. — *Wallace, Man's Place in the Universe.*

17. If the moon had been destined to be merely a lamp to our earth, there was no occasion to variegate its surface with lofty mountains and extinct volcanoes, and cover it with large patches of matter that reflect different quantities of light and give its surface the appearance of continents and seas. It would have been a better lamp had it been a smooth piece of lime or of chalk. It is therefore prepared for inhabitants, and similarly all other satellites are also inhabited. — *Sir David Brewster.*

18. A chemist, as Mill observes, analyzes a substance, and assuming the accuracy of his results, we at once infer a general law of nature from "a single instance." But if any one from the beginning of the world has seen that crows are black, and a single credible witness says that he has seen a gray crow, we abandon at once a conjunction which seemed to rest upon invariable and superabundant evidence. Why is a "single instance" sufficient in one case, and any number of instances insufficient in the other?

19. What is the explanation of the following quotation from Schopenhauer: "False judgments are frequent, false conclusions very rare."

20. Stahl, a contemporary of Newton, supposed that all combustible substances contain a common element, or fire principle, which he called phlogiston, and which escapes in the process of combustion. But when it was observed that zinc and lead and sundry other sub-

stances grow heavier in burning, it seemed hardly correct to suppose that anything had escaped from these substances. To this objection the friends of the fire principle replied that phlogiston might weigh less than nothing, that is, might be endowed with a positive property of levity, so that to subtract it from a body would increase the weight of the body.

21. In all unhealthy countries the greatest risk of fever is run by sleeping on shore. Is this owing to the state of the body during sleep, or to a greater abundance of miasma at such times? It appears certain that those who stay on board a vessel, though anchored at only a short distance from the coast, generally suffer less than those actually on shore. — *Darwin in Voyage of Naturalist.*

22. That the period of the tide should be accidentally the same as that of the culmination of the moon, that the period of the highest tide should be accidentally the same as that of the syzygies, is possible *in abstracto;* but it is in the highest degree improbable; the far more probable assumption is, either that sun or moon produce the tide, or that their motion is due to the same grounds as the motion of the tide.

23. In measuring the velocity of sound by experiments conducted at night with cannon, the results at one station were never found to agree exactly with those at the other. Moreover, it was noticed that on the nights when the discordance was greatest, a strong wind was blowing nearly from one station to the other.

24. M. Melloni, observing that the maximum point of heat is transferred farther and farther towards the red end of the spectrum, according as the substance of the prism is more and more permeable to heat, inferred that a prism of rock salt, which possesses a greater power of transmitting the calorific rays than any known body, ought to throw the point of greatest heat to a considerable distance beyond the visible part of the spectrum; and his prediction was verified by subsequent experiment.

25. During the middle of the eighteenth century Bonnet and Spallanzani discovered that the horns, tails, legs, eyes, or even head of some creatures, if cut off, would grow again. The tail and legs of a salamander were removed and reproduced themselves eight times in succession. By means of a number of experiments it has been found that the more simple the structure of an animal is, the more do its several parts possess a power of independent existence, and that in the more complex animals, the derangement of one part much more affects the action of the entire organism.

26. Professor Jevons has observed that economic crises have occurred at regular intervals of about ten years. This ten-year periodicity,

moreover, seems to correspond to a similar periodicity of bad harvests; and the cause of this seems to be a decennial periodicity in the spots on the sun.

27. What is the significance of the remark of Chevreul, the French scientist: "Every fact is an abstraction."

28. Also of the following remark of M. Espinas: "If human activity was incompatible with the order of things, the act of boiling an egg would have to be regarded as a miracle."

29. It had long been known that grasshoppers and crickets have on their anterior legs two peculiar, glassy, generally more or less oval, drumlike structures; but these were supposed by the older entomologists to serve as resonators, and to reënforce or intensify the well-known chirping sounds which they produce. Johannes Müller was the first who suggested that these drums or tympana act like the tympana of our own ears, and that they are really the external parts of a true auditory apparatus. That any animal should have its ears in its legs sounds, no doubt, *a priori*, very unlikely, and hence probably the true function of this organ was so long unsuspected.— *Sir John Lubbock.*

30. In simple fracture of the ribs, if the lung be punctured by a fragment, the blood effused into the pleural cavity, though freely mixed with air, undergoes no decomposition. Why air introduced into the pleural cavity through a wounded lung should have such wholly different effects from that entering directly through a wound in the chest was to me a complete mystery until I heard of the germ-theory of putrefaction, when it at once occurred to me that it was only natural that air should be filtered of germs by the air-passages, one of whose offices is to arrest inhaled particles of dust and prevent them from entering the air-cells. — *Professor Lister.*

31. If the lungs be emptied as perfectly as possible and a handful of cotton-wool be placed against the mouth and nostrils, and you inhale through it, it will be found on expiring this air through a glass tube that its freedom from floating matter is manifest. The application of this is obvious: if a physician wishes to hold back from the lungs of his patient, or from his own, the germs, or virus, by which contagious disease is propagated, he will employ a cotton-wool respirator. — *Professor Tyndall.*

32. In the desert of North Africa, where neither trees, brushwood, nor even undulation of the surface afford the slightest protection to its foes, a modification of color in animals which shall be assimilated to that of the surrounding country is absolutely necessary. Hence, without exception, the upper plumage of every bird, whether lark,

chat, sylvian, or sand-grouse, and also the fur of all the smaller mammals and the skin of all snakes and lizards, is of one uniform isabelline, or sand color. — *Wallace.*

33. Darwin, in investigating the difference in weight between cross and self-fertilized plants, found that the six finest crossed plants averaged 108.16 ounces, whilst the six finest self-fertilized plants averaged only 23.7 ounces, or as 100 to 22.

34. Bees incessantly visit the flowers of the common broom, and these are adapted by a curious mechanism for cross-fertilization. When a bee lights on the wing-petals of a young flower, it is slightly opened, and the short stamens spring out, which rub their pollen against the abdomen of the bee. If a rather older flower is visited for the first time (or if the bee exerts great force on a younger flower), the keel opens along its whole length, and the longer as well as the shorter stamens, together with the much elongated curved pistil, spring forth with violence. The flattened spoonlike extremity of the pistil rests for a time on the back of the bee, and leaves on it the load of pollen with which it is charged. As soon as the bee flies away, the pistil instantly curls round, so that the stigmatic surface is now upturned and occupies a position in which it would be rubbed against the abdomen of another bee visiting the same flower. Thus, when the pistil first escapes from the keel, the stigma is rubbed against the back of the bee, dusted with pollen from the longer stamens, either of the same or another flower; and afterwards against the lower surface of the bee, dusted with pollen from the shorter stamens, which is often shed a day or two before that from the longer stamens. If the visits of bees are prevented, and if the flowers are not dashed by the wind against any object, the keel never opens, so that the stamens and pistil remain enclosed. Plants thus protected yield very few pods in comparison with those produced by neighboring uncovered bushes, and sometimes none at all. — *Darwin.*

35. Baron Zach received a letter from Pons, a successful finder of comets, complaining that for a certain period he had found no comets, though he had sought diligently. Zach, a man of much sly humor, told him that no spots had been seen on the sun for about the same time — which was true — and assured him that when the spots came back, the comets would come with them. Some time after that he got a letter from Pons, who informed him, with great satisfaction, that he was quite right, that very large spots had appeared on the sun, and that he had found a fine comet shortly after. — *De Morgan's Budget of Paradoxes.*

36.	If Tellus winged be,
	The earth a motion round ;
	Then much deceived are they
	Who nere before it found.
	Solomon was the wisest,
	His wit nere this attained ;
	Cease, then, Copernicus,
	Thy hypothesis vain !
	— *Sylvanus Morgan*, 1652.

37. Weather Forecaster Dunn has prepared a chart showing the number of deaths from grip in New York City during the period from March 22 to May 16, 1891, establishing the relation between the death-rates and weather conditions during the grip epidemic of that year. Mr. Dunn has made a careful study of records of the disease, and selected the epidemic of 1891 as being the time when the grip was most pronounced.

He has apparently demonstrated that the weather is an important factor in the mortality of grip cases. He says that humidity or moisture in the air seems to be the most important element in causing the disease to spread. There is a corresponding increase of deaths with increasing humidity.

The fatality is most marked when the humidity is at its maximum and there is a sudden fall of the temperature. This is shown by the record of April 21, when the death-rate from grip was the highest ever known. During the twenty-four hours of that day 250 deaths were reported. On April 1 and April 30 the death-rate was also high. These were days following a sudden fall in temperature.

All through the epidemic the charts show an increasing death-rate with high or increasing humidity. The higher the humidity and the more sudden the fall in temperature, the greater was the number of deaths. When the temperature and the humidity dropped at the same time, there was a decrease in the death-rate, as Mr. Dunn points out by several examples. He says that the lesson to be learned from his chart is that those suffering from an incipient attack of the grip should be most cautious of the cold, humid days that immediately follow the warm, damp ones.

38. If in a reservoir, immersed in water, the air be compressed to the extent of ten atmospheres, and supposing that now, when the compressed air has acquired the temperature of the water, it be allowed to act upon a piston loaded by a weight, the weight is raised. At the same time the water becomes cooler, showing that a certain quantity

of heat had disappeared in producing the mechanical effort of raising the weight.

39. That the feeling of effort is largely, if not entirely, of peripheral rather than central origin, appears from such experiments as the following: —

Hold the finger as if to pull the trigger of a pistol. Think vigorously of bending the finger, but do not bend it. An unmistakable feeling of effort results. Repeat the experiment, and notice that the breath is involuntarily held, and that there are tensions in the other muscles. Repeat the experiment again, taking care to keep the breathing regular and the other muscles passive. Little or no feeling of effort will now accompany the imaginary bending of the finger. — *Ferrier.*

40. As to the nature of petrified shells, Quirini conceived that as earthy particles united in the sea so as to form the shells of Mollusca, the same crystallizing process might be effected on the land; and that in the latter case the germs of the animals might have been disseminated through the substance of the rocks, and afterwards developed by virtue of humidity.

41. Voltaire suggested that the marine shells found on the tops of mountains are Eastern species dropped from the hats of pilgrims as they returned from the Holy Land.

42. The epicyclical theory of the heavens was confirmed by its predicting eclipses of the sun and moon, configurations of the planets, and other celestial phenomena.

43. Arfvedson discovered lithia, by perceiving an excess of weight in the sulphate produced from a small portion of what he considered as magnesia present in a mineral he had analyzed.

44. We see among the nebulæ (which are diffused along the Milky Way) instances of all degrees of condensation, from the most loosely diffused fluid to that separation and solidification of parts by which suns and satellites and planets are formed; and thus we have before us instances of systems in all their stages, as in a forest we see trees in every period of growth. — *Laplace.*

45. It had been deductively inferred from the Copernican theory that the planets, Venus and Mercury, ought to pass through phases, like the moon, and the telescope revealed this to be the case.

46. Werner, says Sir Charles Lyell, had not travelled to distant countries; he had merely explored a small portion of Germany, and conceived, and persuaded others to believe, that the whole surface of our planet, and all the mountain chains in the world, were made after the model of his own province.

47. Scheiner was a monk; and on communicating to the superior

of his order the account of the spots on the sun, received the reply: "I have searched through Aristotle, and can find nothing of the kind mentioned: be assured, therefore, that it is a deception of your senses, or of your glasses."

48. When we are told that a man has become deranged from anxiety or grief, we have learned very little if we rest content with that. How does it happen that another man, subjected to an exactly similar cause of grief, does not go mad? — *Maudsley*.

49. It was a general belief at St. Kilda that the arrival of a ship gave all the inhabitants colds. Dr. John Campbell took pains to ascertain the fact and to explain it as the effect of effluvia arising from human bodies; it was discovered, however, that the situation of St. Kilda renders a northeast wind indispensably necessary before a ship can make the landing.

50. Chrysippus maintained that cock-fighting was the final cause of cocks, these birds being made by Providence in order to inspire us by the example of their courage.

51. Touch in succession various objects on the table. A paperweight, if metallic, is usually cold to the touch; books, paper, and especially a woollen table-cover, comparatively warm. Test them by means of a thermometer, and there will be little or no difference in their temperatures. Why then do some feel cold, others warm, to the touch? The sense of touch does not inform us directly of temperature, but of the rate at which our finger gains or loses heat. As a rule, bodies in a room are colder than the hand, and heat always tends to pass from a warmer to a colder body. Of a number of bodies, all equally colder than the hand, that one will seem coldest to the touch, as the metallic, which is able most rapidly to convey away heat from the hand. — *Tait*.

52. One of Joule's experiments concerning the mechanical value of light is as follows: He compared the heat evolved in the wire conducting a galvanic current when the wire was ignited by the passage of the current with that evolved when with an equal current it was kept cool by immersion in water. These experiments showed a small but unmistakable diminution of the heat when light also was given out. — *Tait*.

53. It is an illusion in psychology and a corruption of logic to take the conditions which occasion the logical operations of thought for the operations themselves. There is only one delusion more desperate still, — to imagine that a complete physical theory of the nervous system will explain that which is itself the condition of any theory being possible at all. — *Lotze*.

54. During the retreat of the Ten Thousand a cutting north wind blew in the faces of the soldiers; sacrifices were offered to Boreas, and the severity of the wind immediately ceased, which seemed a proof of the god's causation.

55. It has been shown by observation that over-driven cattle, if killed before recovery from their fatigue, become rigid, and putrefy in a surprisingly short time. A similar fact has been observed in the case of animals hunted to death, cocks killed during a fight, and soldiers slain in battle. The contrary is remarked when the muscular exercise has not been great or excessive.

56. A correct analysis of lapis lazuli was suspected to be erroneous because there seemed to be nothing in the elements assigned to it, which were silica, alumina, soda, sulphur, and a trace of iron, to account for the brilliant blue color of the stone.

57. According to the theory that the earth has but a thin crust, it is still substantially a liquid globe, and therefore, under the attractive influence of the sun and moon, it ought to behave like a yielding liquid. According to Hopkins, Thomson, and others, the earth in all its astronomical relations behaves like a rigid solid, — a solid more rigid than a solid globe of glass, — and the difference between the behavior of a liquid globe and a solid globe could easily be detected by astronomical phenomena. — *Le Conte*.

58. Many years ago I was struck with the fact that humblebees, as a general rule, perforate flowers only when these grow in large numbers near together. In a garden where there were some very large beds of *Stachys coccinea* and of *Pentstemon argutus*, every single flower was perforated; but I found two plants of the former species growing quite separate with their petals much scratched, showing that they had been frequently visited by bees, and yet not a single flower was perforated. I found also a separate plant of the *Pentstemon*, and saw bees entering the mouth of the corolla and not a single flower had been perforated. In the following year (1842) I visited the same garden several times: on the 19th of July humblebees were sucking the flowers in the proper manner, and none of the corollas were perforated. On the 7th of August all the flowers were perforated, even those on some few plants of the salvia, which grew at a little distance from the great bed. On the 21st of August only a few flowers on the summits of the spikes of both species remained fresh, and not one of these was now bored. Again, in my own garden every plant in several rows of the common bean had many flowers perforated; but I found three plants in separate parts of the garden which had sprung up accidentally, and these had not a single flower perforated. General

Strachey formerly saw many perforated flowers in a garden in the Himalaya, and he wrote to the owner to inquire whether this relation between the plants growing crowded and their perforation by bees there held good, and was answered in the affirmative. Hence it follows that the red clover and the common bean when cultivated in great masses in fields, *Erica tetralix* growing in large numbers on heaths, — rows of the scarlet kidney-bean in the kitchen garden, — and masses of any species in the flower garden are all eminently liable to be perforated. The explanation of this is not difficult. Flowers growing in large numbers attract crowds of insects. They are thus stimulated to work quickly by rivalry. Also many flowers have their nectaries dry, which is most quickly discovered by biting holes in them.

— *Charles Darwin.*

59. The seat of sensation is in the heart, as it is in the centre of the body; the brain is cold in order that it may counteract the heat of the heart. In order to temper the coldness of the brain, blood is conveyed to the membrane which envelopes it by means of veins or channels. But, lest the heat so conveyed should injure the brain, the veins, instead of being large and few, are small and many, and the blood conveyed, instead of being copious and thick, is thin and pure. — *Aristotle.*

60. The lungs of a fox must be a specific for asthma, because that animal is remarkable for its strong powers of respiration. — *Paris' Pharmacologia.*

61. Galileo discovered, by the use of his telescope, the four small satellites which circulate round Jupiter. It was then inferred that what happened on the smaller scale might also be found true of the larger planetary system.

62. The first step toward the discovery of photography was the knowledge that visual light caused a chemical change in iodide of silver. The second step was to fix in permanent position the portion of the substance changed by the light, while the unchanged portion was removed.

From what is known of the chemical elements and their compounds, it seems highly probable that numerous compounds may exist which are sensitive in the same way to waves of entirely different lengths from those that produce vision. Even with the salts of silver it has long been known that the range of wave-lengths capable of producing photographic effect is much greater than the visual range; and that the wave-lengths which produce the maximum physiological effect (light) are not the same as those that produce the maximum photographic effect.

It has been shown by Professor S. R. Langley that flint glass is transparent to waves about four times as long as the longest in the visual range; and that rock-salt is transparent to a range below the red end of the visible spectrum twenty-nine times as long as the entire visual range. Glass is opaque to very short waves, its limit in that direction being nearly coincident with the visual limit. Quartz, on the other hand, is transparent to a range of short waves extending far beyond the visual limit, but is opaque to very short waves. May not these substances prove valuable in this new field of actinography, as quartz trains have proved in photographing the ultra-violet spectrum?

Should the report of this discovery (Röntgen's) be confirmed, we cannot fail to accord the highest praise to this new triumph of science, and to predict a development of the new field of actinography that may prove of greater importance than photography.

From the analogy between this form of radiant energy and dark heat it might appropriately be called "dark light." — *The Electrical World.*

63. As to the theory of geyser-eruption, the following principles have been established. The boiling-point of water rises as the pressure increases, being 293° for a pressure of four atmospheres. Also, if the pressure be diminished when the water is under very strong pressure, the water will immediately flash into steam. Moreover, if the circulation is impeded, as when the water is contained in long, narrow, irregular tubes, and heated with great rapidity, the boiling-point will be reached below while it is far from this point in the upper part of the tube. Therefore at the moment of eruption the boiling-point for the lowest depth is actually reached. The water there being transferred into steam, the expanding steam would lift the whole column of water in the tube, causing an overflow. This would diminish the pressure in every part of the tube, and consequently a large quantity of water before very near the boiling-point would flash into steam and instantly eject the whole of the water in the pipe, the steam rushing out immediately afterwards. The premonitory cannonading beneath is evidently produced by the collapse of large steam-bubbles rising through the cooler part of the water of the tube. — *Bunsen's Theory.*

64. Mackenzie's theory of geyser-eruption is that the geyser pipe is connected by a narrow conduit with the lower part of a subterranean cave, whose walls are heated by the near vicinity of volcanic fires. The water rising above the opening of the conduit, and changing into steam, and having no way of escape, would, through pressure thus caused, be forced up the pipe, the steam rushing after it. Professor Le Conte says of this theory: If there were but one geyser, this would

be considered a very ingenious and probable hypothesis; for we may conceive of a cave and a conduit so constructed as to account for the phenomena. But there are so many geysers that it is inconceivable that all of them should have caves and conduits so peculiarly constructed. This theory, therefore, is entirely untenable.

65. It has been found by experiment that a current moving at the rate of three inches per second will take up and carry along fine clay; moving six inches per second, will carry fine sand; eight inches per second, coarse sand the size of linseed; twelve inches, gravel; twenty-four inches, pebbles; three feet, angular stones of the size of a hen's egg. It will be readily seen that the carrying power increases much more rapidly than the velocity. For instance, a current of twelve inches per second carries gravel, while a current of three feet per second, only three times greater velocity, carries stones many hundred times as large as grains of gravel.

66. If wood be soaked in a strong solution of sulphate of iron (copperas) and dried, and the same process be repeated until the wood is highly charged with this salt, and then burned, the structure of the wood will be perserved in the peroxide of iron left. Also, it is well known that the smallest fissures and cavities in rocks are speedily filled by infiltrating waters with mineral matters. Now, wood buried in soil soaked with some petrifying material becomes highly charged with the same, and the cells filled with infiltrated matter, and when the wood decays the petrifying material is left, retaining the structure of the wood. In nature also there is an additional process, not illustrated by the experiment or by the example of infiltrated fillings. As each particle of organic matter passes away by decay, a particle of mineral matter takes its place, until finally the whole of the organic matter is replaced.

67. As to the origin of bitumen, the following observations have been made: Certain organic matters at ordinary temperature, in presence of abundant moisture, and out of contact of air, will undergo a species of decomposition or fermentation by which an oily or tarry substance, similar to bitumen is formed. In the interior of heaps of vegetable substance such bituminous matter is often found. Fossil cavities have been found in solid limestone containing bitumen, evidently formed by decomposition of the animal matter. So, also, shales have been found in Scotland, filled with fishes which have changed into bitumen.

68. Count Rumford in 1798 proved that the common notion that heat was a substance was false, by boring a large piece of brass, under great pressure of the borer, whilst the brass was in a gallon

of water; and at the end of two and one-half hours the water actually boiled.

69. Kenelm Digby's treatment of wounds was to apply an ointment, not to the wound itself, but to the sword that had inflicted it, to dress this carefully at regular intervals, and in the meantime, having bound up the wound, to leave it alone for seven days. It was observed that many cures followed upon this treatment.

70. When Pascal's barometer was carried to the top of Puy-de-Dôme, and the mercury in it fell, it was inferred that the fall of the mercury was due to the change in elevation. Before finally accepting this conclusion, the barometer was placed in exposed positions and in sheltered, when the wind blew and when it was calm, in rain and in fog; and these varying circumstances did not materially affect the result.

71. A French experimenter, Pouchet, thought he had obtained indubitable evidence of spontaneous generation. He took infusions of vegetable matter, boiled them to a pitch sufficient to destroy all germs of life, and hermetically sealed the liquid in glass flasks. After an interval, micro-organisms appeared. It seems that at a certain stage in Pouchet's process, he had occasion to dip the mouths of the flasks in mercury. It occurred to Pasteur, in repeating the experiments, that germs might have found their way in from the atmospheric dust on the surface of this mercury. And when he carefully cleansed the surface of the mercury, no life appeared afterwards in his flasks.

72. The causes to which the decay of the natives of New Zealand have been assigned are given as follows: drink, disease, European clothing, peace, and wealth. — *Journal of the Anthropological Institute.*

73. An eminent judge was in the habit of jocosely propounding, after dinner, a theory that the cause of the prevalence of Jacobinism was the practice of bearing three names. He quoted, on one side, Charles James Fox, Richard Brinsley Sheridan, John Horne Tooke, John Philpot Curran, Samuel Taylor Coleridge, Theobald Wolfe Tone. On the other hand there were William Pitt, John Scott, William Windham, Samuel Horsley, Henry Dundas, Edmund Burke. Moreover, the practice of giving children three names has been a growing practice, and Jacobinism has also been growing. The practice of giving children three names is more common in America than in England. In England, we still have a King and a House of Lords; but the Americans are Republicans. Burke and Theobald Wolfe Tone are both Irishmen; therefore the being an Irishman is not the cause of Jacobinism. Horsley and Horne Tooke are both clergymen; therefore the being a clergyman is not the cause of Jacobinism. Fox and

Windham were both educated at Oxford; therefore the being educated at Oxford is not the cause of Jacobinism. Pitt and Horne Tooke were both educated at Cambridge; therefore the being educated at Cambridge is not the cause of Jacobinism. The cause is, therefore, the having three names. — *Macaulay.*

74. The exotic *Pelargonia* have a peculiar herring-bone structure in the petals; moreover, the herring-bone structure is conjoined in the *Pelargonia* with the general characteristics of the *Geranieæ*. Also the flowers with such seed-vessels as our wild geraniums have the characters of *Geranieæ*. It is, therefore, exceedingly probable that our wild geraniums should have the peculiar herring-bone structure.

75. Colonies ought not to rebel against the mother country, since they are its children and children ought not to rebel against their parents.

76. Finding that the size of towns varies concomitantly with the size of the rivers on which they are built, an observer might infer that the size of the river was due to the size of the town.

77. An eminent author, writing on the work of the English Church before the Tractarian movement, contrasts the newer state of things unfavorably with the older, because the Church in those former days taught us to use religion as a light by which to see our way along the road of duty. Without the sun our eyes would be of no use to us; but if we look at the sun, we are simply dazzled and can see neither it nor anything else. It is precisely the same with theological speculations. If the beacon lamp is shining, a man of healthy mind will not discuss the composition of the flame.

78. Scarlet color prevails among balsamina, euphorbia, pelargonium, poppy, salvia, bouvardia, and verbena, yet none of the scarlets are of sweet perfumes. Some of the light-colored balsams and verbenas are sweet-scented, but none of the scarlets are. The common sage with blue blooms is odoriferous both in flower and foliage; but the scarlet salvias are devoid of smell. None of the sweet-scented-leaved pelargoniums have scarlet blooms, and none of the scarlet bloomers have sweet scent of leaves nor of blooms. Some of the white-margined poppies have pleasant odors; but the British scarlets are not sweet-scented. The British white-blooming hawthorn is of the most delightful fragrance; the scarlet flower has no smell. Some of the honeysuckles are sweetly perfumed, but the scarlet trumpet is scentless.

79. The productive powers of plants, judging from the increased fertility of the parent plants and from the increased powers of growth in the offspring, are favored by some degree of differentiation in the

elements which interact and unite so as to form a new being. Here we have some analogy with chemical affinity or attraction, which comes into play only between atoms or molecules of a different nature. As Professor Miller remarks: "Generally speaking, the greater the difference in the properties of two bodies, the more intense is their tendency to mutual chemical action. But between bodies of a similar character the tendency to unite is feeble."

80. In affirming that the growth of the body is mechanical, and that thought, as exercised by us, has its correlative in the physics of the brain, I think the position of the "materialist" is stated, as far as that position is a tenable one. I think the materialist will be able finally to maintain this position against all attacks; but I do not think, in the present condition of the human mind, that he can pass beyond this position. I do not think he is entitled to say that his molecular groupings and his molecular motions explain everything. In reality, they explain nothing. The utmost he can affirm is the association of the two classes of phenomena, of whose real bond of union he is in absolute ignorance. The problem of the connection of body and soul is as insoluble in its modern form as it was in the pre-scientific ages. Phosphorus is known to enter into the composition of the human brain, and a trenchant German writer has exclaimed, "Ohne Phosphor, kein Gedanke!" That may or may not be the case; but even if we knew it to be the case, the knowledge would not lighten our darkness. — *Tyndall.*

81. Granting that Hegel was more or less successful in constructing, *a priori*, the leading results of the moral sciences, still it was no proof of the correctness of the hypothesis of identity, with which he started. The facts of nature would have been the crucial test. That in the moral sciences traces of the activity of the human intellect and of the several stages of its development should present themselves, was a matter of course; but surely, if nature really reflected the result of the thought of a creative mind, the system ought, without difficulty, to find a place for her comparatively simple phenomena and processes. — *Helmholtz.*

82. When young Galileo was a student at Pisa, he noticed one day, during the service at the great Cathedral, the chandelier swinging backwards and forwards, and convinced himself, by counting his pulse, that the duration of the oscillations was independent of the arc through which it moved.

83. Goethe enunciated the existence of a resemblance between the different parts of one and the same organic being. According to Goethe's own account, the idea first occurred to him while looking at

a fan-palm at Padua. He was struck by the immense variety of changes of form which the successively developed stem-leaves exhibit, by the way in which the first simple root leaflets are replaced by a series of more and more divided leaves, till we come to the most complicated. He afterwards succeeded in discovering the transformation of stem-leaves into sepals and petals, and of sepals and petals into stamens, nectaries, and ovaries, and thus he was led to the doctrine of the metamorphosis of plants which he published in 1790.

84. A fortunate glance at a broken sheep's-skull, which Goethe found by accident on the sand of the Lido at Venice, suggested to him that the skull itself consisted of a series of very much altered vertebræ. At first sight no two things can be more unlike than the broad, uniform, cranial cavity of the mammalia, enclosed by smooth plates, and the narrow cylindrical tube of the spinal marrow, composed of short, massy, jagged bones. — *Helmholtz.*

85. The existence of the so-called blind spot in the eye was first demonstrated by theoretical arguments. While the long controversy whether the perception of light resided in the retina or the choroid was still undecided, Mariotte asked himself what perception there was where the choroid is deficient. He made experiments to discover this point and in the course of them discovered the blind spot.

86. Haüy observed that crystals of "heavy spar" from Sicily and those from Derbyshire (which were considered to be the same substance) differed in their angles of cleavage by three and one-half degrees, and remarked: "I could not suppose that this difference was the effect of any law of decrement; for it would have been necessary to suppose so rapid and complex a law, that such a hypothesis might have been justly regarded as an abuse of the theory." Vauquelin by chemical analysis discovered that the base of the crystals from Sicily was strontia, and that of those from Derbyshire was baryta. These facts, becoming known to Haüy, enabled him by inference to discover that the angles of crystals might be employed as a test for the presence of different substances which very nearly resemble each other in other respects.

87. Graebe, a German chemist, in investigating a class of compounds, called the quinones, determined incidentally the molecular structure of a body closely resembling alizarine, which had been discovered several years before. This body was derived from naphthaline, and, like many similar derivatives, was reduced back to naphthaline when heated with zinc-dust. This circumstance led the chemist to heat also madder alizarine with zinc-dust, when, to his surprise, he obtained anthracene. Of course, the inference was at once drawn that

alizarine must have the same relation to anthracene that the allied coloring matter bore to naphthaline; and, more than this, it was also inferred that the same chemical processes which produced the coloring matter from naphthaline when applied to anthracene would yield alizarine. The result fully answered these expectations, and now alizarine is manufactured on a large scale from anthracene obtained from coaltar. — *Cooke, The New Chemistry.*

88. Sir Charles Lyell, by studying the fact that the river Ganges yearly conveys to the ocean as much earth as would form sixty of the great pyramids of Egypt, was enabled to infer that the ordinary slow causes now in operation upon the earth would account for the immense geological changes that have occurred, without having recourse to the less reasonable theory of sudden catastrophes.

89. Joule's experiments show that when heat is produced by the consumption of work, a definite quantity of work is required to produce that amount of heat which is known to the physicists as the unit of heat; the heat, that is to say, which is necessary to raise one gramme of water through one degree centigrade. The quantity of work necessary for this is, according to Joule's best experiments, equal to the work which a gramme would perform in falling through a height of 425 metres.

In order to show how closely concordant are his numbers, I will adduce the results of a few series of experiments which he obtained after introducing the latest improvements in his methods.

(*a*) A series of experiments in which water was heated by friction in a brass vessel. In the interior of this vessel a vertical axis provided with sixteen paddles was rotated, the eddies thus produced being broken by a series of projecting barriers, in which parts were cut out large enough for the paddles to pass through. The value of the equivalent was 424.9 metres.

(*b*) Two similar experiments, in which mercury in an iron vessel was substituted for water in a brass one, gave 425 and 426.3 metres respectively.

(*c*) Two series of experiments, in which a conical ring rubbed against another, both surrounded by mercury, gave 426.7 and 425.6 metres respectively.

Exactly the same relations between heat and work were also found in the reverse process; that is, when work was produced by heat. — *Helmholtz.*

90. A gas which is allowed to expand with moderate velocity becomes cooled. Joule was the first to show the reason of this cooling. For the gas has, in expanding, to overcome the resistance which the

pressure of the atmosphere and the slowly yielding sides of the vessel opposed to it;' or, if it cannot of itself overcome this resistance, it supports the arm of the observer, which does it. Gas thus performs work, and this work is produced at the cost of its heat. Hence the cooling. If, on the contrary, the gas is suddenly allowed to issue into a perfectly exhausted space where it finds no resistance, it does not become cool, as Joule has shown. — *Helmholtz.*

91. The principal feature in the plan of my attempt to penetrate into the North Polar region, or if possible to cross it, is, in brief, to try to make use of the currents of the sea, instead of fighting against them. My opinion is, as I have already explained on several occasions, that there must somewhere run currents into the Polar region, which carry the floe-ice across the Polar Sea, first northward toward the Pole, and then southward again into the Atlantic Ocean. That these currents really exist all Arctic expeditions prove, as most of them have had to fight against the currents and against the ice drifting southward, because they have tried to get northward from the wrong side. I think a very simple conclusion must be drawn from this fact that currents and drifting ice are constantly coming from the unknown north, viz.: Currents and perhaps also ice must pass into this same region, as the water running out must be replaced by water running in. This conclusion is based upon the simplest of all natural laws; but there seem to be people who will not even admit the necessity of this.

That such currents run across the North Polar region is also proved by many facts. I may mention the great quantities of Siberian driftwood which are annually carried to the shores of Spitzbergen and Greenland; it comes in such abundance and with such regularity that it is quite impossible it should be carried to these shores, so far from the original home, by occasional winds or currents. There must be a regular communication between the coasts of Siberia and those of Spitzbergen and Greenland. By this same communication were several objects from the unfortunate *Jeannette* carried to the Greenland coast. The *Jeannette* sank in June, 1881, to the north of the New Siberian Islands, and three years afterward, in June, 1884, a great many objects belonging to her or her crew were found on an ice-floe on the southwest coast of Greenland. This floe can only have been brought there by the same current which carries the driftwood. By this same current an Esquimau implement, a throwing-stick or harpoon-thrower, was also carried the long way from Alaska to the west coast of Greenland. There can, in my opinion, be no doubt of the existence of such a communication or current across the North Polar region from the Siberian side to the Greenland side. — *Dr. Nansen* in *The Strand Magazine.*

INDEX

Abstract, 20.
Abstraction, 15.
Accent, 160.
Accident, 39 f., 161.
Adams, 272.
A dicto secundum quid ad dictum simpliciter, 161.
A dicto simpliciter ad dictum secundum quid, 161.
Æsthetics and logic, 11.
Agassiz, 72.
Agreement, method of, 222 f.
Algebra and logic, 123.
Ambiguity, fallacies of, 158 ff.
Amphiboly, 159.
Analogy, 151, 187, 314 f., 371, 375.
Analysis, 376.
ἀφαίρεσις, 15.
Aquapendente, 319.
Argumentum ad baculum, 162; *hominem*, 162; *ignorantiam*, 162; *judicum*, 163; *populum*, 162; *rem*, 163; *verecundiam*, 162.
Aristotle, 15, 23, 37, 53, 103, 104, 138, 139, 157, 164, 169, 192, 195, 386 f., 390.

Bacon, 62 f., 169, 192, 212, 213, 230, 310, 326, 363 f., 369, 370, 390 f.
Bain, 169, 327.
Barrett, 204, 360.
Begriff, 5.
Beneke, 185.
Bergmann, 367.
Berkeley, 17.
Beudant, 267.
Bluntschli, 383 f.
Boole, 325.
Bosanquet, 89, 99, 176, 177, 185, 187, 189, 201, 219, 397.
Boyle, 237.

Brahé, Tycho, 215, 390.
Brewster, 187, 233.
Brown, 202.
Bullen, 346.
Bunsen, 345.

Cæsalpinus, 390.
Campanella, 389.
Categorical judgment, 78 f.
Categories, 37.
Causal analysis, 188, 206 ff.
Causation, 41, 195 ff., 330 f.
Chalmers, 210.
Chemistry, method of, 378.
Chenevix, 362.
Circulus in definiendo, 46; *in probando*, 165.
Circumstantial evidence, 346.
Clark, 281.
Classification, 55 f., 316, 372, 374; artificial, 56; as affected by evolution, 59 f.; serial, 58; natural, 56 f.; of the sciences, 62 f.
Clifford, 195, 284 f., 290, 324.
Coexistence, 208.
Coincidence and cause, 345.
Collective use of a term, 160.
Collocation, 209 f., 353.
Composition, 159.
Comte, 62 f.
Concept, 5, 7, 10, 13 f., 25 f.
Conceptual processes, fallacies of, 359.
Concomitant variations, method of, 223, 258 ff.
Concrete, 21.
Concurrence, 207.
Connotation, 42.
Conservation of energy, 196.
Consilience of inductions, 309.
Content, 42.

Contradiction, law of, 98 ff.
Contradictory, 107; opposition, 100 f.; terms, 52.
Contrapositive, 114 f., 116 f.
Contrary, 106; opposition, 100 f., terms, 52.
Converse accident, 161.
Conversion, 110 f., 117 f.
Copernicus, 390.
Copleston, 396.
Copula, 33 f., 73.
Counter-dilemma, 147.
Cuvier, 90 f.

Darwin, Charles, 209, 216, 245, 253, 255 f., 265 f., 277, 283 f., 291, 292, 296 f., 301, 304, 322, 324, 342.
Darwin, Francis, 277, 292.
Darwin, G. H., 244.
Davy, 273, 315.
Deduction, 96 f.; and induction, 169 ff.
Definition, 44 ff.; and determinate reference, 68; by description, 47; for purposes of identification, 48; genetic, 47; nominal, 44; real, 44.
Demonstrative judgment, 68.
De Morgan, 214.
Denotation, 42.
Derivative laws, 352.
Descartes, 325.
Determinate reference, 68.
Determination, process of, 74, 81.
Diagnostic property, 57.
Dialectic method, 53 f., 369.
Dichotomy, 51 f.
Dictum de omni et nullo, 138.
Difference, method of, 222 f., 236 ff.
Differentia, 39 f.
Differentiation, 20; of concepts, 79.
Dilemma, 145 f.
Disjunctive judgment, 78 ff.
Distribution of terms, 124 ff.
Distributive use of a term, 160.
Diversity, 13.
Division, 50 f., 160; as in determinate reference, 68; empirical, 54; logical, 54.
Duhamel, 178.

Elimination by negation, 83, 102; in the syllogism, 123.
Empirical, 16, 30.
Empirical laws, 351 ff.
Enthymeme, 130 f.
Enumeration, 184 f.
Episyllogism, 132.
Equivocation, 158 f.
Ethics and logic, 11.
Eudemus, 139.
Exceptional phenomena, 289.
Experiment, 212 f.
Explanation, a form of inference, 94.
Extension, 42.
Extra-syllogistic reasoning, 149 ff.

Fact and truth, 171.
Fallacies, deductive, 157 ff.; inductive, 359 ff.
Faraday, 204, 213 f., 244, 245, 246, 267, 281, 286, 288, 314, 323, 364.
Fichte, 53.
Figure, 137 f.; of speech, 160.
Fizeau, 280.
Florens, 328.
Forel, 246, 255.
Form and matter, 172.
Foucault, 280.
Froude, 397.
Fundamentum divisionis, 50.

Galenus, 139.
Galileo, 164, 390.
Generalization, 107 f.; hasty, 371.
Genetic concept, 22 f.
Genus, 39 f.
Gide, 269, 342.
Gilbert, 390.
Glauber, 277.
Gore, 216, 274, 292, 315, 319, 360, 362.
Graber, 247.
Graphic representation of method of concomitant variations, 260.
Green, 94, 192, 195, 201.
Grimaldi, 310.
Guyot, 233.

Halley, 276, 281 f.
Hamilton, Sir Rowan, 285.
Harvey, 319, 329.

INDEX

Hatchette, 267, 367.
Hegel, 53, 54.
Heraclitus, 365.
Herschel, 202, 213, 277, 323, 369, 394.
Hildebrand, 382.
Holland, 323.
Hume, 197 f.
Huyghens, 279 f.
Hypothesis, 291, 376 f.
Hypothetical judgment, 78 f.

Identity, 13; in difference, 94; law of, 98 ff.
Idols of Bacon, 364 f.
Ignoratio elenchi, 162.
Ignotum per ignotius, 46.
Illicit process, 129.
Imagination, 299; fallacies of, 359.
Immediate inference, a generalization of, 117 ff.
Impersonal judgment, 67.
Implication, 104; in immediate inference, 103 f.
Indirect prediction, 286 ff.
Individual judgment, 69 f.
Induction, 96 f.; and deduction, 169 ff.; as reverse process, 177; historical sketch of, 385; imperfect and perfect, 185; methods of, 222 ff.; types of, 183 ff.
Inductive hazard, 175.
Inductive methods and the sciences, 374 ff.
Inducto = deductive method, 278 ff., 375, 378.
Inference, 9 f.; a generalization of immediate, 117 f.; immediate, 103 ff.; mediate, 122 ff.; nature of, 85 ff.; relation of, to judgment, 95.
Infima species, 40.
Insurance, 341.
Intension, 42.
Interpretation, process of, 6.
Intuitionalism, 30.
Inverse, 117 f.

James, 93.
Janet, 317, 327.
Jebb, 387.
Jenkin, 212, 284 f.

Jenner, 292, 327.
Jevons, 177, 178, 179, 187, 210, 215, 233, 246, 247, 268 f., 276, 281, 287, 288, 316, 323, 397.
Joint method of agreement and difference, 222 f., 248 ff.
Joule, 285.
Judgment, 7 f., 25 f.; and language, 33; fallacies of, 359 f.; of identification, 8; particular, 40; relation to inference, 95; singular, 67 f.; universal, 36 f.
Judgments of elaboration, 8.
Jurisprudence, method of, 382.

Kant, 53, 197.
κατᾰγορία, 37.
Kepler, 310, 390, 395.
Kirby, 306.
Kircher, 323.
Kirchoff, 345.
Knies, 382.

Ladd, 383 f.
Language and thought, 23 f.
La Place, 276, 295.
Lavater, 170.
Law, 180.
Laws of thought, 98 ff.
Leffingwell, 344.
Leibniz, 102.
Leonardo da Vinci, 181, 388.
Le Verrier, 272.
Linnæus, 323.
Lister, 324.
Lloyd, 285.
Locke, 169, 392, 396.
Lockyer, 316.
Logical squares:— A square, 118; E square, 119; I square, 120; O square, 120.
λόγος, 3, 23.
Lotze, 162, 173, 176, 177, 179, 180, 192, 201, 242, 302, 303, 397.
Loua, 342.
Lubbock, 220 f., 246, 250, 254 f., 307, 312, 319, 320 f.
Lyell, 264.

Mallet, 245.
Malthus, 324, 354.

438 INDEX

Mansel, 200.
Many questions, fallacy of, 165.
Mathematico-experimental method, 290.
Matter and form, 172.
Max Müller, 24.
Mechanical energy, 211.
Mental picture and the concept, 19.
Method, historical, 380 f.
Methods of Mill, 222 ff.
Middle, undistributed, 126 f.
Mill, 148 f., 160, 169, 175, 180, 198, 199, 200, 202, 209, 212, 218, 224, 257, 312, 326, 353, 357, 394, 396.
Minto, 396.
Mnemonic lines of the syllogism, 139.
Modality, 83 f.
Modus ponens, 144.
Modus ponendo tollens, 145.
Modus tollendo ponens, 146.
Modus tollens, 144.
Molar energy, 211.
Mood, 133 ff.

Narrative judgment, 67.
Natural kind, 57 f., 314.
Negation, significant and non-significant, 75, 100, 101; implication of, 76; infinite, 77.
Negative determination, 217.
Negative judgment, 73 ff., 82.
Newman, 396.
Newton, 14, 187, 193, 276, 279 f., 294, 310, 393.
Non causa pro causa, 165, 363.
Non sequitur, 164.

Observation, 212 f.
Obversion, 114 f., 117 f.
Oersted, 286.
Owen, 322.

Particular affirmative, 104.
Particular negative, 104.
Pasteur, 224, 282 f.
Perception and inference, 86; fallacies of, 359 ff.
Perceptive judgment, 68.
Per genus et differentiam, 45, 47.
Petitio Principii, 164.
Plateau, 246, 254.

Plato, 53, 195, 385.
Political economy, method of, 382.
Porphyry, 39; tree of, 51 f.
Post hoc ergo propter hoc, 165, 363.
Potential in inference, 92.
Potential properties in concepts, 17.
Predicables, 38 f.
Predicate, grammatical, 33 f.; logical, 33 f.
Prediction, 278 ff.
Preyer, 199.
Priestley, 242.
Probability, 330 ff.
Proper name as subject of a judgment, 69; connotation of, 70 f.
Property, 39 f.
πρόσθεσις, 15.
Prosyllogism, 132.
Psychology, method of, 379, 383.

Quetelet, 337.

Railroad accidents, 339 f.
Reality, 27 f., 94, 96; as logical subject, 33 f.; metaphysical nature of, 31; in thought, 29.
Reduction, 178.
Reference, indeterminate, 68 f.
Reflection, 4.
Refutation, law of economy of, 108.
Relations, validity of, in reasoning, 152 f.
Residues, method of, 223, 271 ff.
Richter, 367.
Romanes, 311.
Roscher, 382.
Rule, 180.

Saigey, 226, 262, 311.
Saint-Pierre, 328.
Savigny, 382.
Schleiermacher, 169.
Schönbein, 275.
Schopenhauer, 15.
Scientific analysis, 188.
Senses, as source of knowledge, 4.
Sequence, 206 f.
Sidgwick, 363.
Siemens, 281.
Sigwart, 176, 177, 179, 194, 201, 209, 230, 241, 290, 312, 397.

Singular judgment, 27, 67 f., 79.
Smith, Adam, 363.
Social factor in judgment, 31 f.
Socrates, 385.
Socratic method, 74.
Sorites, 132.
Species, 39 f.
Spencer, 62 f., 355, 376 f.
Spinoza, 301.
Sprengel, 320.
Statistical method, 376.
Subaltern, 105.
Subcontrary, 106.
Subject, grammatical, 33 f.; logical, 33 f.
Sufficient reason, 201; law of, 98 ff.
Summum genus, 40.
Syllogism, 122 ff.; hypothetical, 142 ff.; disjunctive, 144 ff.
Synthesis, 15, 376.
System, 5, 79 f., 89 f., 154 f., 170 ff.

Tait, 196, 261, 275, 281, 287, 293, 309.
Teleology, 317 f.
Telesius, 389, 390.
Tennyson, 93.
Term, 35.
Thackeray, 99.
Theophrastus, 139.
Thomson, 261, 275.
Thought, the nature of, 3 ff.

Transformations, 110 ff.
Trichotomy, 53.
Trilemma, 148.
Truth, 11, 171.
Tyndall, 215, 218 f., 235, 237, 262, 263 f., 283, 286, 298 f., 323.

Ueberweg, 89, 169, 181, 185, 190, 201, 368, 387.
Ultimate laws, 352.
Uniformity of nature, 173, 176, 196.
Universal, 4; in inference, 93; affirmative, 104; judgment, 26, 79 f.; negative, 104; of discourse, 101.
Universe of discourse, 101.

Variation, limit of, 19.
Venn, 179, 200, 216, 225, 240, 243, 244, 300, 357, 396, 397.
Verification, 278 ff.
Voltaire, 328.
Von Baer's law, 60.

Waitmann, 314.
Wallace, 304 f.
Warrant of inference, 85 f.
Wedgwood, 367.
Whately, 200, 396.
Whewell, 179, 281, 312, 367, 388, 395.
Williams, 283.
Wollaston, 362.